William Henry Anderdon

# The Catholic Crusoe

Adventures of Owen Evans, navy surgeon's mate, set ashore on a desolate island in the Caribbean Seas, A.D. 1739

William Henry Anderdon

**The Catholic Crusoe**
*Adventures of Owen Evans, navy surgeon's mate, set ashore on a desolate island in the Caribbean Seas, A.D. 1739*

ISBN/EAN: 9783744796040

Printed in Europe, USA, Canada, Australia, Japan

Cover: Foto ©Andreas Hilbeck / pixelio.de

More available books at **www.hansebooks.com**

"Your ruined abbeys, which you visit on pic-nics and parties of pleasure."—Chap. XVIII, p. 76.

THE

# CATHOLIC CRUSOE;

Adventures of

## OWEN EVANS,

NAVY SURGEON'S MATE,

## Set Ashore on a Desolate Island

IN THE CARIBBEAN SEAS,

A.D. 1739.

GIVEN FROM THE ORIGINAL MS.

BY

## W. H. ANDERDON, D.D.

———

Author's American Edition.

———

NEW YORK AND CINCINNATI:
PUBLISHED BY BENZIGER BROTHERS.
PRINTERS TO THE HOLY APOSTOLIC SEE.

Nore.—Some difficulties occur in determining the situation of Evans' island. Newhaven is mentioned as the port whence the *Enterprise* was to sail for her rendezvous in the tropics; or his place of exile might have been among, or not far from, those islands of volcanic and coralline formation which are grouped in the South Pacific. It becomes further probable that he speaks of Newhaven in the State of Connecticut, if we consider that the crew of Hopkins' vessel numbered *Newfoundlanders* among the rest. Against this, however, may be urged, that Malays and Portuguese are mentioned as part of the crew. But seamen from Malacca, whose character as roving pirates was well known, might be found at any frequented port, ready to engage in such an adventure; and might be joined by characters equally unsettled from among the extensive Portuguese colonies.

Moreover, the vessel was "well within the tropics;" and coming from a colder latitude, we are told, the crew had not touched land before. The northern tropic, or tropic of Cancer, is here referred to. But how to suppose that this island should have remained undiscovered till 1739, if it lay within an ocean continually traversed by vessels from such maritime states as England, Holland, Spain, and Portugal? Two considerations will afford a partial answer.

(1) We may overrate the then extent of such discoveries, by regarding them in the light of our own geographical knowledge. In England, and probably in Holland and the Peninsula, the discovery of America rather gave an impulse to the colonization of that continent itself than to enterprises of intermediate research. The date of Evans' narrative is nearly thirty years before Cook's first voyage, the primary object of which was astronomical; and though in the reign of George II., two important voyages had been made, they were for the definite purpose of discovering the north-west passage. The expedition of Anson, the year after that of our author's misadventure, was an enterprise against the Spaniards in the South Seas, though it resulted in important discoveries. In short, new continents, or new ways to old ones, rather than researches among islands and archipelagoes, formed the objects of such expeditions as had preceded the date of this narrative.

(2) The discovery of islands in a wide ocean has been very much the result of circumstance, often of mere accident. Thus, the island of Madeira, notwithstanding the height of its volcanic peak, and its favourable position for discovery, remained unknown (if we except one account which reads like fiction), till a vessel driven, if I remember, out of her course, approached the veil of mist in which it had lain perpetually concealed. If we suppose Evans' island to lie on some less direct route from Europe to the New World; say, at any given point between the Cape de Verd Islands and Guiana or the Brazils, there is no great improbability in its remaining undiscovered till 1739.—Ed.

# INTRODUCTORY LETTER

FROM THE

## Family Solicitors

FOR

## MR. OWEN EVANS'

GREAT GRANDCHILDREN;

GIVING SOME ACCOUNT OF HIS DESCENDANTS, WITH OTHER
MATTERS CONNECTED WITH HIS ADVENTURES.

---

BEING engaged for the representatives of the late Mr.
Morgan Evans, of Great Yarmouth, grandson of the
Owen Evans whose adventures occupy the following
pages, we deem it our duty to carry out the wishes of the
said Morgan Evans by the publication of such writings as
his grandfather left behind him. In the volume itself,
chap. lxiv., will be found a statement of the motives
which induced the author to leave injunctions with his
executors, that the packet containing this account of himself should remain sealed for one hundred years after his
decease. He was apprehensive lest the small colony of
Spaniards whom chance had thrown on his island might
suffer disturbance from the English cruisers, on their
locality becoming known. That injunction has, notwithstanding the curiosity of his relatives, and perhaps to

their pecuniary loss, been strictly complied with. But the time has now arrived when his narrative may safely be given to the world.

Mr. Owen Evans died at Yarmouth on the 16th October, 1763, nine years after committing his "Adventures" to writing. For some time before his decease, an almost total loss of sight had prevented his performing his duties as deputy harbour-master; and he had retired upon a small pension, which was so far increased by the generosity of a friend and staunch patron, the Hon. Captain Byron, as to secure comfort to his latter years. After his demise, some MS. notes were found among his papers, giving an account of such tropical plants as were supposed to have medicinal virtues. These, he used to say, had been compiled partly from his own experience, partly from his conversations with Don Manuel, the Spanish priest, who added some information derived from his missions in South America. A few further botanical facts were obtained from the Indians who were cast away upon the island, as will be related in the following sheets. These additions referred to such specimens as were to be found in their native soil of Toonati-nooka. It was the intention of Mr. Griffith Evans, Owen's only son, to publish these notes in the form in which his father had left them: but the style was so inexact as to preclude this. It was therefore determined to incorporate them as foot notes to an able botanical paper by another hand, which may be found in the second volume of the *Philosophical Transactions.*

The reader may be interested to learn something of Mr. Evans' relations. He left three children, a son and two daughters. His son, Griffith, was articled to a conveyancer in his native town of Great Yarmouth; but, having no inclination to that employment, emigrated to America, and settled for some time in Boston. Here he married a lady of Dutch extraction, named Vanderstegen; and had a son, Morgan, lately deceased, and a daughter, Ann Owen, called so after her grandfather. Griffith Evans brought back his family from Boston, with a small competence, in the year 1811, and died in London about four years after. His son Morgan, whose early education had been interrupted by these removals, contracted unsettled though not vicious habits, married beneath his station, and left a family of five children very scantily provided for. Anne Owen Evans died at an advanced age, unmarried.

The two daughters of Mr. Owen Evans, Martha and Jane, pursued very different paths in life. The elder, following her mother in the strictness of her religious belief, went into France on the death of the latter, which occurred on the 29th May, 1771. This removal was on the invitation of a distant relative of Mr. Evans' widow, who was herself a French lady, as the reader will find, p. 297 of this book. Mrs. Evans' maiden name was Lebrun; she belonged to a family which had for some time settled in Canada. Her third cousin, now referred to, of the same name, was married and living at Nantes, when she offered to adopt Miss Evans as her daughter. But after nearly two years spent under her roof, the young lady preferred to take the veil among the Sisters of Charity in that town; and so lived and died, being carried off by a fever caught in the midst of her charitable ministrations.

Her younger sister, Jane, on the mother's death, was adopted by some relations of her father's in Glamorganshire, where she soon afterwards married Mr. Price Llewellyn, and went to live at Llangevelach, near Swansea. The marriage gave dissatisfaction to the family in general, on account of Mr. Llewellyn being a member of the Methodist persuasion, to which, after some time, he induced his wife to conform. On this event, Mrs. Martha Jane Evans, Owen's aunt (a letter from whom, dated from Glamorganshire, June 10, was prefixed to the first edition of the "Adventures"), altered her will in favour of her great-niece, Jane. This aged gentlewoman, notwithstanding her years, was still in full possession of her faculties. She left to Mrs. Llewellyn the old family mansion of Moat House, near Llandevodiog, which was by that time scarcely habitable through want of repair; together with sundry and divers parcels of land in the said county of Glamorgan, which we need not here enumerate.

We have no additional information for the reader, as to the probable fate of Don Manuel and his infant colony. We have not, indeed, thought it our duty to make any particular enquiries; since the history of Toonati-nooka may be regarded as an episode, or mere adjunct, to the adventures of Mr. Evans. But the intelligent reader will gather, from the tone in which Don Manuel's narrative closes, that he anticipated trouble, or active hostility, from some powerful men in the island. How far they may have been able to influence the king of the place against the strangers so well received at first; whether they succeeded in dethroning him, and thus having the foreigners at their mercy, or what happened after his death, are questions on which we are unable to throw light. It is possible that some notice may exist among the *Lettres Edifiantes*, published (we apprehend) by the Lyons Association for the Propagation of the Faith, affording a clue to such as are interested to follow it up. One thing we cannot help remarking: that Mr. Evans' strict injunctions regarding his MS., while their operation in favour of the colony on his own island is more than questionable, have undoubtedly tended to exclude Don Manuel and his companions from all benefit of finding themselves under the protection of a civilised flag, whether European or American.

For the Executors,

QUILLETT & SONS.

113, Parchment Buildings, Inner Temple,
    April 28, 1864.

# CONTENTS.

# Adventures of Owen Evans;

## THE

# CATHOLIC CRUSOE.

---

## CHAPTER I.

### THE ISLAND DISCOVERED.

FOR a couple of days, or so, we had been going under easy sail, some three or four knots an hour, with a light, fair breeze. We crowded no sail, though the wind was almost abaft; for our skipper would give a last chance to our consort, the *Enterprise* of Newhaven, to whom we had given the *rendezvous* in these latitudes, before we bore away for California. So at least, he said; but I had my suspicions about what he might be intending; and a kind of misgiving had come over me, from the appearance and arrangements of our ship. For no sooner were we fairly out of port, than a couple of long swivel-guns had been hauled up out of the hold, and mounted on spare carriages upon the quarter-deck, so as to sweep fore and aft. Then the men were exercised at these every day, sponging and working them as if in action, and also at the two short carronades we carried; as indeed every trader of our size was used to carry at that period. Our crew had been increased even while the blue-peter was flying at the fore, by ten or twelve as ill-looking, cut-throat fellows as ever you saw; of all nations, Americans, Malays, Portuguese, one or two Newfoundlanders, and so on. They knew none of the rest of the crew of the *Spitfire*, who, on their part, were no better than the general run, nor so good.

But these new-comers fairly outdid them in all cursing and wickedness; and they were the very men who were practised every day in working the guns, handling the shot and powder-lockers, going through the exercise with their cutlasses and handspikes, etc. In short, my mind misgave me, the captain was as much on the look out for some weaker trader to fall in with, as anything else; and I thought there was a wicked look in his eye when he spoke of the *Enterprise*, as if that was the enterprise he was truly after.

I got uneasy enough at these signs of our skipper's intentions; and all this increased the distaste I had conceived against a sea-faring life. It was my first voyage after being certified for surgeon's mate; but the captain (Aram Hopkins was his name: 'tis no breach of charity, I hope, to record it,* for every one that knows the sea, knows he was hanged, three years after, on Staten Island for a pirate); he, I say, asked me to go the voyage in capacity of full surgeon, with my berth and all supplies free, promising to show me something of sea-life. He did, indeed; and something of land-life too, as you shall hear. But my part now was to keep up a good face, and seem as careless as if I observed nothing out of the way. This was no easy matter, as the days went on: and I could see that the captain eyed me with distrust, and more so every day we sailed.

I looked round for some one with whom I might take counsel: but could not tell whom to trust. There was, indeed, an honest fellow named Tom Harvey among us, of whom I shall have enough to say by-and-bye: I could have spoken to him more freely than to any of the ship's company beside. But, then, I did not know how far Tom's discretion might extend: my experience of life having taught me how few people can keep a secret. There was also a Spanish priest on board, Don Manuel he was called; he had taken his passage on board of us till we could land him somewhere near Panama, for San Francisco. More

* Our friend Owen is mistaken here, however. It is always a breach of charity to reveal the faults or sins of others without necessity, or some constraining motive; though the degree of wrong varies according to the nature of the charge and the likelihood of its becoming otherwise known. ED.

than once I resolved to speak to him : but I scarce know what kind of a feeling held me back.   I had been bred up a protestant; and though, at that time, had not much religion of any kind, still I felt awkward about opening my mind to a priest, one of a sort of men I had always looked on askance, and as we say, out of the corners of my eyes.

This priest seemed a quiet man, who had a kind word for every one that came across him, though he did not speak much.   He kept a good deal in the cabin, being a hard reader, when he was not sea-sick.   He would come up, and walk a little on deck, reading his book attentively, and speaking to himself, or counting (it seemed) a string of beads that hung at his girdle.   Methought he was saying his prayers; and I used to wonder how any man, priest or layman, could have patience to say so many prayers in the day.   Once or twice he asked me questions on medical subjects; chiefly on the treatment of wounds and fevers, and the use of herbs in their cure: I could see he had studied those matters.   Well, in spite of our few conversations, the long and short of it was, I had never spoken to a priest before, and would not make up my mind to tell my thoughts to him.

Things were going on in this way, when, about eleven in the forenoon of Monday, August the twenty-third, the man in the top suddenly sang out: "Land on the starboard bow !" and a refreshing cry it was to us all; we having been almost three weeks without seeing anything to break the everlasting sea-line all round us.   Up we were at once in the shrouds, in the rigging, out upon the yards, all eyes straining to starboard.   As for me, who was as eager as the rest, not knowing whether this accident (for we did not expect land) would bring a change to the condition I was in, I made my way up to the mizentop, with my own glass ; a very clear one, that proved a faithful companion to me afterwards, where I did not expect to keep it so long as it and I staid together.

When I got into the top, I could see, plain enough, even without my glass, a haze that stretched away to east-south-east of our course, like a thin bank of fog, and nothing more.   It lay some ten or twelve miles from us, but so faint, I never should have taken it for a sign of land.   The man on the watch was right, however, as it proved. We were sailing, as I said, under a light breeze, three or four points from where the land lay. But the captain now ordered the ship about, and we stood right in for it.

As we drew nearer, I could observe this haze, or heat, gradually melt away from the land, and leave it clear. But the first thing to be seen in the way of land was the peak of a mountain that seemed pretty near the centre of the island (for island we judged it to be), but nearer to its northernmost end. This ran up out of the mist before we could see the coast and lower grounds. It was some-what in the form of a sugar-loaf, like the Peak of Tene-riffe, though so much smaller; only rather flattened at the top. About half-way up, it was clothed with trees, as well as we could judge at our distance, and this was better seen the nearer we sailed. The upper part looked bare, with streaks down the sides of a greyish colour: whence I concluded it to have been a volcano, or burning mountain, and that those were streams of old lava, or melted rock, that had burst from the top of the mountain, and flowed down the sides, hardened by cooling, ages ago. For the rest of the island, as we sailed in, it appeared green and wooded, well enough. We could see some small savan-nahs, or meadow-lands, very fresh and green, opening out among the woods; whence we judged the place must be furnished with fresh running water, or the heat (for we were now well within the tropics) would surely have burned them brown.

So strange a desire now possessed me, that I must needs go and visit this island, if it were possible, and explore some of those green sheltered spots, to see what they con-tained, and whither they led. I wished also for a nearer view of the mountain, having always taken interest in reading of volcanoes, and tracing out the forms of some I had met with in different parts, though they had long ceased to burn, and had become overgrown with wood. In short, it was of no use for me to reason against myself: I was determined that if there should be a landing-party from the ship, go I would, and see what was to be seen.

Turning my glass from it, when I had scanned it over from end to end, from the top of the sugar-loaf to a reef of low rocks that ran out south-west from its base, over which a strong surf was running, I gave a glance down upon deck. There stood the captain holding secret counsel with the first mate, of which I shall have more to say.

## CHAPTER II.

### THE LANDING.

THE long-boat was now being got ready for shore; so, coming down on deck again, I walked straightways to the captain, and asked to be of the party to land.

Here I must needs make a natural reflection on two things which this settled desire of mine may be taken in proof of; firstly, the little foresight we can have of what is to befall us, nay, sometimes the very moment before it will happen; as may be seen in a thousand unexpected turns, for good and ill, in this changeful life. The other is, though I considered it not at the time, to see how the providence of our heavenly Father orders all for the best; overruling, aye, the most untoward events, in the way we had least expected or (sometimes) desired, to work our good in spite of ourselves. Here was I, a youngster by comparison, starting in life with fairer prospects than several of my betters; and now, blind mortal that I was, I came forward to get leave for a few hours, that was not to expire for years, and pronounce against myself, with my own lips, a sentence of banishment on a savage island! Yet, this very thing that I was now about to do against myself, as it seemed, was the means of my preservation, together with that of others. For I make no doubt, had I remained in the ship, both I and five more of us had found a watery, aye, and a bloody grave. She soon after turned pirate, as I have related, with all hands on board; and we, had we been there, would have had the choice of joining

them on their robber's cruise, or paid the forfeit of refusing.

Often since then, have I lifted up hands and eyes to
thank heaven, even with the want of all things, on our
desolate island, for not having been tied, neck and heels,
with a twelve-pound shot to my feet, or sown up in a
hammock and hove overboard, or made to walk the plank,
as the Spanish buccaneers treat the prisoners they sentence to the bottom of the sea.  For, all these things I
afterwards represented to my imagination, adding to it
(though in a secondary degree) the murder of Don Manuel,
Tom Harvey, and the rest who were saved with myself.
And this I used as a sovereign remedy against such fits of
dejection, and almost despair, as came over me in the
course of the years I am about to give some account of;
when things were so bad with us, we were fain to bear up
against them by considering how they might have been
worse.

But to make this short, let me come back to the day
with which our troubles began.  When I asked to go
ashore, I was surprised, knowing our skipper's surly
temper, how readily he granted it.  There was a look in
his eye, and I did not understand it; nor the meaning of
his words.  "We shall not be long before this island," says
he, "but time enough for you to collect some of your
rare plants: for that, I judge is what you are after;
so there need be no hurrying back to the ship till sun-
down."

By this, the long-boat was ready, and all things found
for her.  While the men were lowering two large jars for
fresh water, and stowing our day's rations, together with
some fowling-pieces, two muskets, and ammunition (for
we were to be provided against wild beasts, as well as
have means of killing some luxury in the way of an antelope, or a goat or two; no small treat to men who had
tasted nothing for weeks but salt junk), I ran down the
companion-ladder for Don Manuel, our Spanish priest, to
ask him to come ashore and see what the island furnished.
I found him prepared; he, too, had spoken to the captain,
and got leave every whit as readily.  He had with him a
portfolio of sheets of blank paper, to preserve such plants
as would wither in the hand; a pruning knife to cut them;

and a small case of writing materials, to jot down any-thing worthy of note in his way of remark. This served other ends during our exile; for we each kept a journal on the island after our several fashions, or the reader would not have been troubled with these pages. His prayer-book (his breviary, he called it), that was scarce ever out of his hand; a staff shod with iron, for climbing, or push-ing through the bush; and a large cloak with sleeves, such as the priests of his country wear on their journeys, completed his equipment.

For my part, I hastily laid hands on some things I should want; as, my faithful companion, the spy-glass, which I slung across my shoulders; a rifle of mine, that would carry a good distance, though now somewhat worn; a bag of rifle-balls and large horn of powder, a cutlass or hanger, and a serviceable clasp-knife in my pocket, toge-ther with a ball of twine. I know not by what providence it was, but surely from the whisper of some good angel in mine ear, that I handed down into the boat my fishing-rod and tackle: namely, a leathern pouch, with two or three reels of strong fishing-lines, and a book of artificial flies for casting at salmon and trout. These I had myself carefully tied, to beguile the voyage, having been well used to the fishing of the streams in my native Welsh mountains.

The ship was by this time hove-to, say a mile and a half from the island; they were afraid to venture further in, owing to the many small coral-islets, and jags of rock, dotting the sea all about, as well as the dangerous reefs, which we could see beneath us, the water being very clear. Into the long-boat we got; seven seamen, besides Don Manuel and myself; we pushed off at once, and spread our sail, which was of the kind they call a shoulder-of-mutton sail. The wind became less steady as we neared the shore; there came, now and then, little puffs or flaws of wind from the valleys, that were vastly refreshing; and we could perceive the moist, fresh smell of the trees cast to seaward, so delightful as none can tell who know not the weariness of a long sea voyage.

We had some ado to keep clear of the reefs, which seemed to run out on all sides from this island. The one I had observed from the ship's top appeared the most considerable and dangerous, and the surf beat over it violently, though so little wind stirring. Yet I noticed others too, some above the water and more beneath, whereon we grounded once or twice, and had like to have been stopped altogether.

We were now forced to take down our sail, and trust to our oars, that the boat might answer readily to her helm. As I looked over the gunwale upon the reefs below (the water being, as I said, exceeding clear), they seemed of two sorts, which I could discern one from the other. The one darker, and not coming so near the level of the sea; these stretched away in lines, some very broad, from the island. This kind I took to be streams of lava-rock, once melted, and flowing down, perhaps ages ago, from the top of the sugar-loaf cone: for that, I made sure, was an old burning mountain, though its fires had been quenched, it might be, hundreds of years, or more. The other sort of reefs grew up from the first kind, and these came near to the surface, sometimes quite, but never much above it. I took these to be coral rocks, such as are formed in the Pacific and other seas by the wonderful work of small insects. Some were bright in colour, white and red, or yellow. by which, and their growth, I knew them quite plainly for rocks of coral. In places, they branched out under the sea, like the corals that are brought home to Europe, only larger: others were so decked and grown over with tropical sea-weeds, that there were, I may say, two forests growing under us, plainly to be seen through the water, the forest of rock and the forest of weeds.

But the end of all this was, we had a difficult steerage towards land; and were glad enough to find, after some trials, a winding channel, between two of the reefs of rock that came shelving down from the mountain, and dipped at a sharp angle into the sea. These rocky walls (for they stood pretty high) sheltered us from the surf, which we heard breaking loud on other parts of the shore. Only, a roller, or tide wave, came after us from the open sea, and caught the boat's stern with some force; sending us along the channel swifter than we would. And, had not our steersman been a skilful hand, well up to his business, we had very likely been stove against the rocks before we got further on our adventures. This afforded him ground, with two other of the men, to swear he would not take the boat further than a corner which we turned just after it chanced. Here we found a little natural harbour, worn in the rock by the high tides, when the sea was swollen by the wind from south-by-west. These men now said, plain and rough, they were in trust of the boat, and would not risk staving her, or getting her back to the ship in bad condition. They bade us take out our fowling-pieces, with the jars for fresh water; and explore the island as much as we would, if only we might reach the ship again by the time all hands were piped to hammocks. For themselves, they said, they were content to stay there with the boat, or ramble about the rocks, and try their luck with fishing (for they had brought tackle with them, as well as tinder to strike a light), or to catch fresh crabs and other shell-fish, enough to make a broil of, in the pools below high-water mark.

I make no doubt, in looking back upon this, they parted thus readily with the fire-arms, to take away any suspicions of ours, as to what they intended. Or it might be some touch of mercy in them, such as may be found at times in the hardest and wickedest hearts. Nor were we, on our side (we, I mean, who landed and left the three men and the boat there), so simple as would appear; for their proposal came so reasonable, and was made with such seamanlike frankness, that no ground appeared to harbour a thought against them. But be it that we were wise or foolish (a matter of small use now to determine), sure I am we were heartily glad to find our feet on land. As to the priest, he did not above half understand what they said, so made no great objection. For though he spoke English well, yet it was like one who had learned it passably out of books, as was indeed the case. And there were many of the sea-phrases in use among the crew which, to be sure, were not found in his books: so that he, who of the whole party was like to have made a calm judgment on our proceeding, chanced to be the one who least understood it.

We scrambled up the rocks, as best we might: not without slips and bruises, for the sea-weed was thickly grown hereabout, and slippery as ice. But when we got above high-water mark (and that we did with no small trouble), our travelling was easier, upon one of those streaks or pathways of rock leading up towards the mountain; like a sort of road up-hill, only so rough on the surface, that soon it would have worn our shoes.

Before we left the little harbour where the boat lay, one of the three men came up with our fowling-pieces: as to my rifle, I managed to carry that with me. He also threw us the ends of two ropes worked into a noose, and passed round each of the water-jars, whereby we easily hauled these jars up the rock after us. Then they all bade us not be overtaken by night on the island, and promised (with many oaths) they would stay for us where they were. So we turned away with light hearts for our expedition—and never saw them on shore again.

## CHAPTER III.

### WE START FOR A RAMBLE.

A SHORT stone's cast brought us off this rock; then we found ourselves treading over a thick, soft carpet of mossy meadow, kept fresh by a little runnel of pure and sweet water, that found its way down to the sea through the same shaded valley that led us up into the island. Over our heads, the trees arched and met one another, lacing their branches and thick leaves across, to form a natural bower, which the rays of the sun could not pierce through, or dimly. Many of them were such trees as we had never seen, though I had read of them; with ferns and reeds, from ten to eighteen feet high. For, as we had come from a colder latitude, and had not touched land before, this was our first acquaintance with the rich growths of the tropics.

The change from ship-board, together with the freshness

and perfume of the avenue through which our line of
march lay, which you might have supposed was planted
and kept in order on purpose for us, with the fancy, too,
that we had some hours before us on this delightful island
(so it now seemed) to do what we would and range where
we pleased; all these things did so raise our spirits, that
I, for my part, could scarce keep from racing along the
avenue: and Harvey and another of the seamen broke out
into singing snatches of their rude sea-songs. Even Don
Manuel appeared more elated than was common with him:
and the whole party kept on laughing and talking, some
saying one thing, some another, till on a sudden I stopped,
and bade them remember we were in an unknown land,
and knew not, as yet, what we might have to encounter.
It might, I said, be savages, or it might be wild beasts.
"Please God, it may be neither," said the priest, and
crossed himself. "I hope so too, sir," added I; "but no
one of us can tell; and the part of prudence is, to guard
against whatever may come."

So we agreed to keep close together, and march in
order. I volunteered to lead the vanguard, and told them
the reason; not that I claimed any authority over them
(men being jealous enough about that, where each reckoned himself as good as his fellow), but being better armed
with my rifle, I wished to take a full share of the danger,
whatever it might be. After me, came the three men
with fowling-pieces: the muskets had been left in the
boat, as seemed only reasonable, for defence of those who
stayed in her.

And here is a place, as good as any, for giving a list of
our party, as we stood there, and loaded our arms for our
ramble up the country.

First, I place Tom Harvey at the head of the list; for a
more active, honest, cheerful fellow I believe never sailed.
He became my right-hand man, ready to second me in
whatever was for good order and good fellowship among
our party.

Then comes Edward Hilton; a well-disposed lad enough
in himself, but easily led by others of a firmer nature than
he; one that gave me some little trouble afterwards on
that very score.

These two completed the brighter side of the picture:

as to the other couple of seamen, Richard Prodgers, and Harry Gill, I had not so much trust in them; though indeed they were not quite the black sheep of the vessel's crew, neither.

For Don Manuel, I knew not yet what place to give him in my thoughts. As I have said, he was a Catholic priest, and I no Catholic at all. What I had seen of him was quiet and harmless; but I had my opinion to form; and, on the whole, rather a prejudice against him, except when we talked on the subjects we had in common, as botany, medicine, or the like.

Lastly, as to the three we had left in the boat, they were among the very worst of the crew, though the most in the captain's confidence: and I was glad when I found they were to be none of our party.

Our first care now was to fill the jars with fresh water: it was soon done, by placing them in the channel of the little stream that ran swiftly by us. We scooped out its bed with our hands, to sink them to half their depth in the gravel and stones; then built up the stones we had displaced, into a kind of wall, or dyke, on both sides of the jars, till the water rose towards their brims. So we left them; knowing they would both be filled within a quarter of an hour.

After this, the matter was, to decide upon the plan of our campaign. I summoned a council of war; told them, as our time was not long (it being now past three), we should consider how to explore the island, and the mountain, while our leave of absence lasted. That we had come for a ramble, and a ramble we would have; for I supposed none of them wished to lie down under the trees, and sleep away their time—a thing they might do as well under the shade of a sail on board ship. At this they all declared for an active bout of it till they must go aboard again. Then, said I, let us make a circuit under the base of yonder mountain, following its bend, but keeping in the valley, for plants and game. In this we may spend a couple of hours, or thereabouts: then double back, and return to this spot over a part of the mountain itself, yet not to ascend too high. Our return will take from two hours and a half to three hours, by the rugged travelling we may expect to find on the mountain. Thus, what with our progress through the lowlands, what with the elevation of our homeward journey, we shall explore the island pretty fairly, see what grows on it, have a view of both sides (for to all appearance it cannot reach far beyond the mountain), and may chance to meet with some wild game on the way.

Such was my plan, and no voice was raised against it. Indeed, as is often to be remarked, where there is no point started which touches self-love, or interest, the nine-tenths of mankind are content to have their plans laid down for them, or anything to save them the trouble of thinking for themselves. No one amongst us had anything better to propose, so they agreed, and off we started. I led the way, by general consent: my rifle ready slung for use, and my hanger at my side. Next, very naturally, for we had our plants and what-nots to collect, came the Spanish priest, armed with such a staff as they use in going over the Alps, and other mountainous passes, with his cloak gathered over his shoulders for more easy walking. Then Prodgers, Harvey, Gill, with their fowling-pieces. Lastly, Ned Hilton brought up the rear with a hand-spike he had borrowed out of the boat; for, being an easy fellow, he made no bargain to have a gun; though I afterwards found he could shoot with the best of them, and better than Prodgers, by a good deal. However, in this world things are carried away, not by the most able, but by the most determined, to use them; and the stronger will overcomes the longer head, and the more skilful hand.

----

## CHAPTER IV.

### DESERTED.

FOR near half-a-mile we followed the channel of this stream, which led us inland, up a ground that sloped to the base of the mountain. Here we came again to a kind of mossy lane, over-arched and shaded by groves of various trees, as bananas, plantains, pepul, banians, cocoa-nuts, and palm trees, of several kinds, some tall and fea-thery, others with a broad spreading leaf, such as they use to thatch their houses in the Havannahs and Philippine Islands. It was a sort of natural alley, that any rich owner in those plantations would give a round sum to have near his house; with a swift brook leaping, now to this side, now to that, through all its length; which gathered itself up in little pools of still water, or fell over the stones with a tinkle that sounded refreshing in the great heat of the day.

We determined not to part company with this stream, so long as it did not lead us out of our course; though at times we had to climb over rough ground, and swing our-selves round the roots of such trees as came near the brink, for many times they did quite overhang it, yet this way of travelling was easier than to force ourselves through the close thicket on either side, where we might be torn by the prickly shrubs, and less able for defence against a sudden enemy, beast or man.

For my part, I was on the look-out for an occasion of getting up to the higher ground, that so we might judge of the extent of the island. I believe it was not laid down on any of the ship's charts; and this, I take it, was one reason why Hopkins, the captain, determined with the mate to maroon us on it: that he might escape being tried for our murder, yet have us safe where we had little chance of being picked off again, to give evidence against him.

But now, suspecting no evil, and all in the gayest mood, we judged ourselves to be the first discoverers of the place; and Hilton, taking off his neck-kerchief and tying it to the top of his spike, struck that into the soil, and took possession (he said) of the island in King George's name. We gave a cheer on adding to his Majesty's possessions; then fell into some discussion how to name our new-dis-covered island.

I proposed it should be called Manuel's Island, out of compliment to the priest, whom, as being of another nation, we might consider a sort of guest, claiming hospitality on our ground. But by the men's looks this was a notion they misliked altogether, though none spoke, except Dou

Manuel himself. He at once thanked me with that courtesy which belongs to his nation, wherein they are rivalled by few, I believe, among all the people in the world. "Señor," says he, (that was his Spanish way of expressing Sir,) with a manner between jest and earnest, "you are too good to think of me on such an important occasion. A poor priest has no claim or title to give his name to any spot on this great earth: he is called to spend his strength, or shed his blood, wherever his Master sends him: 't is quite enough," added he, raising his looks, "if his name be written in heaven."

"But," continued he, and his manner as he spoke made us attend; being earnest and natural, and withal so courteous to each, that the rough seamen listened to him as if he had dropped among them from the trees, or the skies :— " whether," says he, " we are really the first who have set foot on this place or no, it must be acknowledged on all hands that we have been led hither by the good providence of God." And here he bowed his head, lifting his hat as he spoke. "So I propose, gentlemen, that in honour of Him who created us all, and has preserved us safe to this moment, we call the island after some of the great truths of that religion He has revealed. And surely," said he, looking round on us with a cheerful smile, " we may find something sacred in which we can all agree, whereby to christen the place ? "

When he had thus expressed himself, the men looked at one another as if they had never heard the like before, and what the priest said was the last thing in their thoughts. I was taken aback, indeed, at what he said; for at that time I must confess myself I was without any serious thought of religion at all; and did not feel to like the priest any the more for having so expressed himself.

"Well, Señores," said he, observing our looks, as we moved onward again, "among my countrymen, as you have known in the course of your voyages, a discovery like this would be marked by some title borrowed from the gospel, and from sacred names.* We should call the

* The reader need not be reminded of such familiar names as *Vera Cruz, Santa Fè, Sacramento, Santiago, San Domingo, Los Angelos,* and others too numerous to mention.—Ed.

island after the Incarnation of the Son of God, that is, the Annunciation; or The True Cross, or in honour of the Conception of His most holy Mother; or after all the Saints; or some special saint, Saint Francis, Saint Dominic, Saint Thomas; these names, with many like them, are familiar to those of you who have touched at the Spanish plantations.  Some of those titles could not be expected in this case, since you, Señores, do not admit the thoughts which they express: but why should we not call the place the Isle of the Resurrection?"

"And I propose," quoth Prodgers, breaking in roughly, "that we call it *No Man's Land;* for it belongs to us all equally, and 't is our property, until the ship fires the evening gun."

"Or Gill's Country," said Harry Gill, "for I first jumped ashore, and set foot on the island."

"And measured it too," remarked Hilton, "for you sprawled at full length among the sea-weed: so let it be *Longlands.*"

Thus, with one discourse or another, but good-humoured withal, we got through our ramble in about the two hours we had allowed ourselves.  We saw game in plenty; chiefly of the hare kind, and a species of peccary or wild hog, with here and there an antelope, rushing through the thicket as we drew near.  But we would not load ourselves with them at that time, trusting to a shot or two on our return to the boat.  Of birds we saw several kinds new to us, together with some flights of macaws and parrots, bright in plumage, and noisy, that flew over our heads.

The wood now grew so thick and pathless, we nearly lost our reckoning; and quite lost our companion the stream, though we had tasted of it several times to slake our thirst on this hot, weary march, for so it now became to us.  Struggling hard, we scrambled by main force out of this wood; and found, by the rise, we were on the slope of the mountain, turning left ways from the side of our first entrance.

At this point we cried a halt; and sitting down, took out what provisions we had brought with us, which we shared equally among our number, and made a meal that was too scanty to be a long one.

This done, "Now," said I, "a short climb will take us

high enough to afford a clear view on both sides ; we shall have a look out to the leeward of this island ; then we must push on smartly for the boat, lest we lose our way in the dark. Remember how suddenly night comes on in these latitudes." I also told them, though we had hitherto reserved our fire, yet (as we had seen no sign of savages, but plenty of game), when once our faces were turned homewards, shipwards rather, we would let fly at anything that came in our way.

This being agreed to, we began the ascent; disentangling ourselves from the last of the brushwood, we soon found we were on the mountain indeed : for it cost us some hard climbing, this side being the steepest. The trees here were well nigh as close as the thicket below, so that we partly lost our way again ; and bending too much back towards the shore, we had, not a view of the further side of the island, but a sight that did not leave our eyes (our *mind's eye*, I mean) for months, and decided our fate for years.

For we came at once on a spot of clearer ground, with an opening left through the trees, that looked straight out to seaward : and see we did too clearly, the long-boat using oars and sail, just within a few strokes of the ship ; then the men we left in her, clambering up the ship's side, and at once all sails set on the *Spitfire* for standing out to sea.

———

# CHAPTER V.

### MIGHT HAVE BEEN WORSE.

WHOSOEVER may have seen one on whom a sudden great misfortune hath fallen, in the first transports of his grief and raging despair, trample the ground, tear his hair wildly, fling his clenched hands abroad, seek for some one on whom to revenge himself, and by a thousand violent actions give vent to the extremity of his passionate sorrow, may have a picture of the conduct of these men and myself, when this most woeful sight burst on us. We first stared, stock-still, as men who are just awoke out of a night-mare; then, venting wild cries, we ran about, up and down the rocks, stamping, yelling like madmen out of Bedlam: we glared at each other like wild beasts; and I hardly know why some of us did not fling ourselves down the sides of the mountain, in bitter grief, to die in the gullies below.

Then, at times again we would pause, and look eagerly towards the ship, as fain to persuade ourselves that all was but a sailor's jest, intended merely to fright us. We said to one another, even fiercely, and trying to believe what we said, we should soon see the long-boat with her sail set, tacking back for us against the breeze, which now blew off shore. We roared out (for it was roaring indeed, as if what was said so loud must be true) Hopkins had played this trick on the priest and me, because we had neither of us been so near the line before. But all this dreadful suspense was ended when we saw the ship fill her sails, and stand away steadily on her former course. When she veered, we saw a puff of smoke; then came the report of one of her guns, fired wantonly, by way of heaping insult on our wretchedness; which gave us to understand, all hope was over for us. At the same moment, the yellow flag (called by seamen the rogue's jack) was hoisted at the fore. At the sight of all this the men broke out anew into such cursings, ravings, and passionate laments, as were more fit for lunatics transported beside themselves, than for reasonable creatures, who should gather spirits and courage to make the best of a bad case.

But reason was, at that time, the last thing to be found among us; and we did but add to each other's grief: for when one, exhausted by his violence, would be silent for a while, another would take it up, as though he had never lamented before; and thus set all off again by the contagion. So that I believe there has seldom been shown a more lively image of the rage and despairing lamentations of those who are lost for ever, than in us five who then found ourselves left on the island without hope.

I say, us five; for we had no thought of the priest all

this while, nor leisure so much as to observe how he bore himself in our common misfortune. We knew what we had lost, and were fully occupied with that: as for him, we knew not, and cared not, either what he had lost, or what he possessed. He had been our companion in our ramble, and pleasant enough we had found him; but when anything more than a mere pastime engaged us, we turned inward on ourselves, or looked on each other only, thinking no more about him than if he inhabited another world, or another island.

At length, wearied with our long march, and exhausted by all this raving, partly too by scant food, we sank into a kind of stupid and settled despair, casting ourselves down on the place were we had stood. There would one seaman lie, burying his face in his hands, weeping even like a child. Another would sit, and clasp his knees, and turn his face towards heaven, but without uttering a prayer. A third man, with his teeth set, and his features awry, more like a savage or a maniac, would watch the sails of the ship as they came between us and the setting sun; then shake his clenched hand at her while she glided away, muttering whatever the old serpent whispered into his ear. Neither can I boast that my angry passions were more under command than theirs, or much more, to signify; yet reason sooner came to the rescue with me, and I saw the need of not giving way, but thinking for the rest. While I sat, thus calming myself down, and rested my head on my hand, I began to cast about what to advise under our unhappy condition. After a while, chancing to turn my eyes aside, I noticed Don Manuel, a stone's cast from us, kneeling on the rock with his hands clasped; and he was plainly deep in prayer.

I watched him for some minutes; but he did not stir, nor did he observe me at all. Then I rose, and went softly to him, touching him on the shoulder. As he looked up, I could perceive the traces of tears on his cheeks; this, I now confess, was what first disposed me more kindly towards him, to see him grieve in our common misfortune, though he had taken it to heart in a way so unlike the rest.

"Sir," said I, with what calmness I could, "it behoves us, in these unhappy affairs, to consult as well for ourselves as for those who are nearly beside their wits with grief, or rage whichever you will: and, as night will soon come upon us, no time is to be lost in preparing (since needs we must) to bivouack upon this island."

He rose at once, looked at me in a friendly way; then, with the manner of a prince, yet quite simple and humble too, he motioned me to a seat beside him on the rock, and taking my hand with much kindness, said:

"Señor, we have all suffered a great misfortune together; or rather let me say," and he crossed himself devoutly, "we have been the objects of a great deliverance. Nothing of this has taken me entirely by surprise, for I have, some while past, observed strange doings among the crew, and guessed they would soon be rid of some they had on board. So we will give thanks to God, and bear our lot with equal mind. We are, indeed, ill provided with things necessary to continue our lives on this place; but, though I much desired to give you a hint before leaving the ship, I could neither do that without being suspected by the captain, nor myself take anything away with me. True, I have little in this world but my cloak, and a few books, for which, I confess, I grieve; yet I grieve more for you. But Providence has shielded us hitherto, and will shield us still.

"Courage," then said he, rising, and still holding my hand; "let us go to these poor men; let us try to console them, and take counsel all together."

So, stepping to the rest, he addressed them in a few simple words. He was sure (he said), as brave seamen, they would bear up against their misfortune: that when a sailor leaves port, he commits himself to wind and weather, and a thousand chances; he is never certain how long he will live, nor how die, nor whether be buried on land, or in the deep. But we had reason, he said, to be thankful to God that our lot was not a worse one. We might have been boarded by pirates, massacred, or sold as slaves, pressed into harder service, or kidnapped for the plantations; the ship might have been burnt at sea, and we swamped in the boats, or perishing of hunger. We might all have foundered together in deep water, or suffered shipwreck, and been cast by the fury of the waves on some inhospitable coast with nothing in our hands, a defenceless prey to cannibal savages. It was the part of brave men, therefore, not to be cast down so long as a hope remained of repairing their fortunes; that the preservation of our lives was an instinct implanted in us by the Author of our being; finally, that our business for the moment was, to establish ourselves in safety for the night upon this island, and leave all further care for the morrow.

In short, though I do not pretend he expressed himself in these terms with great readiness, seeing he was forced to translate his thoughts into our language; yet he made us so moving a little discourse, and so persuasive, partly from the argument, partly from his manner, that it was plain the poor men were strengthened and encouraged by it to a great degree. Having so far succeeded, he directed them to search in the thickets for the driest and fittest brushwood to kindle a fire. With the help of my hanger and the seamen's clasp-knives, it was done as he advised; and a space found on the rock, like a natural hearth, hollowed by no hand of man into a kind of shallow basin. This we cleared of its earth and moss, and disposed our brushwood there for our bonfire. We laid aside another heap of brush, and a quantity of dry turf, which we pulled up in large clods from the soil, enough to feed our fire through the few hours of dark. Then, by Don Manuel's advice, each one looked carefully to the priming of his piece, and freshened it, lest the powder might take damp from the night dews, and so render us defenceless against any attack. For the same reason, they were to keep the locks of their fowling-pieces carefully covered while they lay down to sleep. But Tom Harvey volunteered to keep watch over us all, and not to lie down through the night. I offered to share this duty with him, turn and turn about, in the manner of dog-watches on board ship: but he said cheerfully, it should be my turn the next night, if I would; that he had rather stay awake one night and have full rest another, than have broken rest for two; which indeed is the hardest part of all sea-service.

For beds we were at no loss: there was moss all about, and dry leaves in plenty, very sweet-smelling, as was also the wood we burned on the fire. Don Manuel stepped a little aside to finish his prayers, as I could well perceive by the fire-light : for now, the sun being down, the darkness of the tropics. was upon us at once.   But we, without any prayers at all, like ungrateful heathen wretches that we were, cast ourselves on these couches of leaves, with our feet to the fire, and so all was still.

---

## CHAPTER VI.

### NIGHT AND MORNING.

I HARDLY know whether the rest slept that first night of our exile ; only that all was quiet, and Harvey with his gun going to and fro, near to our fire, feeding the blaze from time to time with fresh armfuls of the dry brushwood.   This, I felt sure, would keep off any wild animals that might be prowling in our neighbourhood ; it being well known by hunters, and such as camp in the woods, that even the fiercest tigers of the Indian jungles, unless pressed by great hunger, will not so much as approach a fire by night.

Being made easy on that point, and on that only, I fell to considering our unhappy deserted lot, which did little improve for being thought upon.   True, no one of us was cast ashore alone and solitary, as Selkirk* and some others have been, yet the benefit of mutual society could not outweigh the destitute state we were in, unprovided with anything but our fire-arms only.   "How," I reflected, "shall

* Alexander Selkirk, a Scottish seaman, owing to some disagreement with his captain, was left ashore in 1704, on the island of Juan Fernandez, off the coast of Chili.   He had nothing with him but his clothes, bedding, a gun, and a small quantity of powder and ball ; a hatchet, knife, and kettle ; his books, and mathematical and nautical instruments.   In this solitude he remained four years and four months ; employing his time in chasing and taming the wild goats of the island.   He constantly kept a guard of tame cats about him, to defend him from the rats, with which the place was infested.   He was at length taken off by a vessel from Bristol and arrived in England

we build, or plant here? how so much as burrow dwellings
for ourselves in the earth or the rocks, like some savage
tribes? How shall we cut down a tree, or smooth a plank,
or snare the birds and animals of the island, or tame them?
By what means can we supply ourselves with the rudest
clothing, or defend our lives against the monsoons and
rainy seasons of the tropics? And, when our small stock
of powder is spent in coming at our daily necessary food,
with what contrivances are we to purvey to ourselves a
means of living from that time onward?"

To these questions I found no cheering answer in my
thoughts; and, as if I had turned Job's comforter against
myself, I went on to consider thus: "You are," said I,
addressing myself, "surrounded indeed by companions in
misfortune, who have all one common interest with your
own; to wit, mutual assistance and kindliness in bettering
their sad condition But who shall warrant that they
will view it thus? For men, in the very blindness of a
selfish desire to have their way, are prone to run counter
to their true interest, and that of others with them. Or,
if things begin well, yet with such rude materials as are to
hand, how long will they last so? And what authority
can you establish among them, for the benefit of each and
all?

In a word, after tormenting my thoughts, as many
another has done, with the prospect of future ills, and in-
venting a multitude of possible and imaginary ones, as,
attacks from cannibal savages and wild beasts, poison from
venomous reptiles or unknown noxious herbs, and I know
not what other forebodings of harm, I yielded to weariness
like the rest, and fell asleep till morning. One thing I
did not forget; that was, to wind up my watch, as I knew
mine to be the only time-piece in our whole colony. "Yet

by a circuitous route in 1711. The enemies of Defoe, the author of
Robinson Crusoe, accused that writer of having pirated many of the
details of Selkirk's life from papers left by the latter in his hands.
It is undeniable that Defoe, like Shakespeare, founded his wonderful fiction upon facts, which already stood recorded. Yet a perusal
of the narrative of Captain Rogers, who took Selkirk off the island,
brief and comparatively meagre as it is, forms the best proof how
little Defoe was indebted to any actual occurrence for the charm, or
more than the first idea, of his story.—ED.

what matters time to us," I asked myself, my gloomy thoughts coming back again, " now that we are commencing the life of savages here? It will be enough for us to see the sun rise and set, to know another day is added to our misery. And for the seasons we shall feel when it is warm and cold, and when it is wet or dry until we feel nothing further." Thinking in this way, I did indeed know nothing further, till I was awoke by the sun through the trees, and the screaming of the parrots over my head.

'T was a wonder I had not awoke before this; for two guns had been fired, and with some success, to procure us our first breakfast on the island. One of these was Harvey's piece, and the other Gill's. When I shook off my sleep, and came to where they were seated round the fire, I found they had brought in some game: for Tom had shot (at least wounded, and then secured by some hard running) a young peccary, such as we had seen the day before; and Harry Gill had brought down a bird like a bustard, that he had sprung in a piece of marshy ground, some quarter of a mile from our encampment.

Though I considered it imprudent to let off fire-arms when we knew so little of the island, still, the thing being done, and so much remaining to be settled when breakfast was over, I said nothing to it, but bade them good morning as cheerfully as I could, and set to work to help in cooking our meat. Here was indeed a difficulty for us; for though several of our number (like most practised seamen) were tolerable cooks, as far as a plain boil or stew on board ship, yet what will the best cook do when he has nothing but his meat and his fire? Here were we, with no sign of a kettle, or pan, not so much as a dripping ladle to prevent our meat burning; plenty of material but no way to make it useful to us. And though the proverb says, too many cooks spoil the broth, I believe there have been seldom collected so many cooks together, with so little chance of having any broth among them.

There was abundant proof of the difference in men's characters as we all stood around the fire, and looked at the game we could find no means to dress. Some grumbled and swore, some laughed at their own perplexity, some set about devising first one thing, then another.

Prodgers was chief among the surly ones, as Tom Harvey among the jokers. As to Hilton, being (as I said) one of those who take their cue from others, he now swore with Prodgers, and then laughed with honest Tom. However, for want of better, we cut us some sharp straight reeds from a thicket, of a kind of bamboo, to serve for spits; we skinned the animal and plucked our bustard, then spitted them, and prepared to roast.

But who should come to our help, and show us a better way? The last person, except a wild Indian, we could have guessed at. Don Manuel had been, up to this, walking slowly to and fro, at a little distance from us, reading his book, as usual. He now drew near; and in his cheerful, courteous way: "A fair morning to you," says he, "Señores and brothers in misfortune: let me try and contribute my small efforts for our common good." Then he explained, that he had heard of some natives of such islands as abound in hogs and goats, who had an ingenious way of cooking, or baking their meat. They make, says he, a hole in the earth, line it with stones red-hot from the fire, to serve as a rude oven; then put in the meat, covering it with layers of broad leaves, and overlay the whole with earth and stones. "So now, if you will," continued he, "we will take a hint from the savages, until we find out some better method for ourselves."

We thanked him heartily, and with some surprise, at discovering that he knew anything about such matters. But he said, with a smile, a priest who left his own country upon foreign missions was obliged to be

> Soldier or sailor,
> Joiner or tailor,
> Gentleman, apothecary,
> Ploughboy, and all!

Where he had picked up those odd lines I know not; but I know his cheerful, friendly manner did more to comfort us under our hard lot, and put us in good humour with ourselves and each other, than anything at that moment could have done. Every one began to feel a sort of trust in following his advice; and the prospect of a good meal quickened our motions. So, having understood his plan, we bustled about to follow it. Some went in search of stones of the size and shape to heat in the fire; and these were put into the hottest of the flame. Others got a heap of dry brushwood to freshen the fire itself, which soon blazed out more fiercely than we could well stand to. One went in search of leaves to lay upon the meat when the hot stones were ready to put round it; a fourth cut a sharp stake or two from the thicket, to make shift for spades. With these we turned up enough of earth to bank over our oven. All being now ready, we waited a short time till Don Manuel, who directed the whole, told us that the fire had heated the earth and stones to the right pitch, and that we might clear away the embers to build our oven on the rock.

----

# CHAPTER VII.

### THE FIRST MEAL, AND THE FIRST PARLIAMENT.

"MOREOVER, gentlemen," said the priest, pointing with his hand to a high tree that grew perhaps two hundred and fifty yards from our fire; "see if a merciful Providence hath not sent us bread as well as meat for our food! Truly, we should be doubly ungrateful not to thank Him with all our hearts." The men looked at him, doubting what he spoke of. Only, sure were they, from his manner, that he was not jesting now. "I am much mistaken," added Don Manuel, turning to me, "if yonder be not one of the bread-fruit trees we have read of; and the first," added he in his cheerful way, "who brings us some of the fruit, will be a herald of good news to our colony."

No sooner said than done: Harvey started off, and Hilton with him, after this new bread; while we stood cheering them with our voices, and clapping of hands. They reached the tree nearly together, and began shaking it, one on either side, to make the fruit fall into their hands. But the trunk was too stout for that, so they did but lose their labour; and the fruit itself, which grew in a kind of large apple, or gourd, the size of a good penny loaf, was so high out of reach that, do what they would, there was no getting at it, no, not by jumping their best. "I see," said Don Manuel, "I must be baker's man as well as cook;" and he moved towards them with his long staff. But Harry Gill was now beforehand with him; for, seizing the hand-spike, he made off at the top of his speed, and before the other two could pick off a single apple with stones, he had brought half a dozen of them to the ground.

Don Manuel met them half way. "It is indeed the bread fruit tree!" exclaimed he, when he had examined the fruit. "Give thanks, my friends, for a great boon from heaven; as I doubt not you have given thanks for your deliverance out of the ship. If this be not a solitary tree, which is very unlikely, and if it be the kind that will grow from slips or cuttings, we shall have enough of excellent bread, and to spare. So, let us first pay our tribute to the great Giver."

Seeing that none of us stirred or assented (I am ashamed to record it against ourselves), he then solemnly took off his hat, laid it at his feet, and raising up one of the fruits in either hand, uttered, with a loud, clear voice, something in Latin, which, though I was not used to his mode of pronouncing that tongue, I took to be a short form of praise. Having spoken this with his eyes raised to heaven, he kissed the fruit, as though he had received it straight from thence: then, turning to us, he said: "And now, Señores, it is time to look after our breakfasts."

I know not by what magic this man seemed to have gained such an ascendant over our minds. Every one went hither and thither, and just did this or that, because he so recommended it; yet there was nothing of authority in his words, which would at that time have revolted our wills against him: for all was quiet and gentle, in the extreme. But I greatly believe, this influence he had over us arose from our perceiving him to have no ends of his own to serve in what he proposed to be done; also because he was willing cheerfully to bear his part in every fatigue and inconvenience that affected us : in which disposition none came up to him, except only Tom Harvey ; this we felt the more, as time went on and we were better acquainted.

But to return to our breakfast, or preparing for it : Don Manuel, to our great satisfaction, promised us some excellent toasted bread with our pork : and though the men scarce knew how this was to be purveyed, having never seen or heard of the bread-fruit before, they believed it would, somehow, be as he said.  So, by his directions, the hollow slab of rock where we had kindled our fire over-night, was now swept clear of the burning wood ; and the stones, which by this were red-hot, ranged around by the help of our gun barrels and sticks, so that an open space was left, large enough to hold the game we had killed. When we had placed our peccary and bustard on this heated rock, and surrounded them with the stones, whereon we likewise placed our bread-fruits in slices to bake, by and bye such a savoury smell arose, as tempted us to fall-to without waiting further cookery.

Prodgers, in particular, who was the most self-willed, or the hungriest, began to insist on having his share at once.  But he was out-voted by the rest ; and we covered the meat with the palms and plantain leaves we had gathered : over these we laid other stones, and made all tight by strewing on the top a layer of earth and rocky sand.

" A short half-hour, gentlemen," then said Don Manuel, " will complete our arrangements : and I propose that in the meantime, we make an expedition to the rocks on shore, to see after a few dishes and spoons."

We looked again at one another, doubtful what he could mean ; he explained, that as we came along the rocks the day before, at that part of our island where we first landed, he had noticed a bed of largish oysters that lay within reach of any active cliffs-man among us.  The shells of these, he said, at least the larger ones, would supply our table with a kind of crockery-ware, till we had learned to furnish ourselves better in some other way.  " So, my friends," added he, " the fish and the dish, you see, are sent to us together ; and both from One Hand : " then he looked upward and smiled cheerfully. This man seemed to have his thoughts continually on God; on whom our thoughts were, I may say, never. But it was out of the abundance of his heart that he was speaking in this way; for nothing was further from him than any attempt to preach to us, though he seemed to look to us for some correspondence with his grateful feelings; and not finding it, he went on all the same, to himself, as it were, in his expressions of thankfulness and trust.

We were cheered about the oyster beds he spoke of; to find, on our first settlement, these new possessions of ours were likely to be so well stocked with wholesome fish as to place us beyond present want. But before we started that way, or sent any of our party on the errand, we reckoned that, take what short cut we might to the place, we should only get back to find our meat and bread-fruits burned to a cinder. So giving up that enterprise for the present, we prepared to take our meat with sticks, as the Chinaman will pick up a grain of rice with two chopsticks instead of a fork or spoon. We took the lid off our oven, and found everything done passably well, for a party of famished sailors who were not over-nice. But Don Manuel, after saying grace, which he never omitted at any meal we partook of with him, told us pleasantly, had we been less hungry or more patient, our feast on taking possession of the country would have been worthier the occasion.

This whole time, I was turning in my thoughts how I should address our party on some things needful to be said. If order and rules were not established amongst us from the first, then, I saw clearly, we should lie exposed to the unrestrained violence of several wills here present, that boded us no good. I had seen enough of Don Manuel to feel a confidence in consulting him; but I lacked opportunity, for the thing had to be done at once, and before our first joint act was undertaken, whatever that might be. Hastily gathering my thoughts into the best shape I could, while we were employed in cutting up our game with hanger and knives, and helping ourselves to the slices with bamboo-sticks and fingers, I ran over in my mind the characters I had to deal with, and what I would have them lend a hearing to. When our meal was ended, feeling that if ever they would be disposed to listen, it was likely to be now, I begged their attention for a few minutes.

So, getting upon a little ledge of rock which offered a natural platform to speak from, I delivered myself as follows: "Friends," said I, "as we are so strangely cast into society with each other, and that for such a time as we cannot foresee its end, you have to consider, in the first place, whether you will remain in community, or separate in different quarters of the place where we are, and live alone and independent. For my part, I am ready to follow whichever plan may seem good to the greater number of us; and I call upon you to decide."

Here they broke in at once, and cried out each for himself, that to disperse over the island was a thing not to be thought on. We shall be devoured, said they, by wild beasts, if any are here: we shall fall singly and defence-less into the hands of savages who may inhabit the place, or visit it in their canoes. Then, to live alone, was a savage, unnatural state of existence; they would become barbarians, little better than the wild animals themselves, who still, for the most part, go in herd. In short, never was anything so concluded as that, come what would, we must still consort together.

"Well, friends," I continued, "that is my own wish, too. I would put both before you, and I think you have decided right. But then, see what follows upon this. If we live together, we must have some kind of government established among us."

When I announced that, which I did with a resolute manner and voice, I observed some change in the counte-nances of a few among our small number. They had no idea, it seems, of living by any law but their own wills; they imagined, to talk of government was to introduce tyranny into our little society, even in its infant days. Richard Prodgers at once showed himself displeased, by a surly look; swaying to and fro with a dissatisfied air, he was going to break in, when I went on:

"Nay," said I, giving the thing a jesting turn to per-suade them the more heartily, "do not suppose any one is going to set up for a king here. We will have no standing army to drain our pockets; for we are all, indeed, the militia volunteers of the place, ready to turn out at a moment's notice, and fight our enemies without pay. We will have no taxes levied throughout the whole island and if the tax-gatherer do but dare show his face, we 'll warn him off the premises in a twinkling. Our friend, Don Manuel here," and I made the priest a little side bow as I spoke, "will collect no tithes but with our own free will. And I hope we shall do without police, or summonses, or quarter-sessions; no lawyers, no big-wigs, no gallows, stocks, nor pillories; no juries, no prisoners at the bar, no treadmill; not a yellow-jacket amongst us, nor a bridewell, nor anything in that way."

At this, they could not but laugh, do what they would: even Prodgers was forced to it with the rest. And having secured their good-will, I explained that the government I spoke of, was that each should bind himself to conform to some plain, simple regulations for his own good and that of all: and that one of us should be appointed by general vote to see them carried out. At this, they were well content; and after some discussing among themselves, they voted that I should tell them how such rules ought to be framed.

"First," I continued, "we may look upon ourselves as the lords and masters of this whole place, for aught that appears. If it prove so, we can portion out to each man a measure of land, to be chosen by lot; and every one must then engage to help his neighbours to build something of a hut, and afterwards dwell at peace with them, in mutual service and good-will. But, before all things else, we must needs set about to discover whether there be any other inhabitants in this little kingdom of ours: wherefore let us bind ourselves to stand by one another to the last, and join in an exploring party to search the island."

This proposal was much to their mind, and they would have set about the thing at once. But I was desirous, while they were in so favourable humour, to impress on them some points needful to us all; so begging them to wait a moment, I laid before them the necessity of attending to the following particulars:

1. That we had no real government as yet; and hoped to do without so much as naming the word *punishment*, which would be the ruin of our small society, and set

every man's hand against his brother: it was therefore of exceeding need that each should keep guard over himself, his temper and words, to avoid all occasion of offence.

2. That whatever we possessed, which was little enough, should be looked on from the first as common property; to be used by each for the good of society as well as his own: namely, the three fowling-pieces we had brought with us from the ship, and the ammunition; our clasp-knives, the jars for water, and our small store of rope-twine. To give an example, I threw my rifle and hanger into the common stock. Later, I said, when we had seen what turn things would take, we could portion out different offices according to each one's turn. Meanwhile, as every man was to be moderate in his demands, so no one was to be refused a reasonable use of this our common property.

At any other time, I could have smiled at making so much of a common seaman's clasp-knife, and an earthern pitcher. But the circumstances we are placed in, quite alter our value of things: we were now in a state of life like that of the savages, who will barter away their gold dust, their ostrich-feathers, and pearls, or whatever has most price in the European markets, for a knife, an old hoop of iron, or a few nails.

They all agreed readily to these proposals: indeed the thing was reasonable, and to the advantage of all; let them be as self-willed as they might, they could scarce do otherwise. I was content with this beginning; but I foresaw what difficulties would arise if I set about to control and keep together such rude spirits, who were only in order under the captain's eye, with the fear of the lash before them. "Well," said I in my own mind, though with not much spirit of religion about me, "the morrow shall take care for the things of itself; and we will live for the day."

# CHAPTER VIII.

## A DISAPPOINTMENT AND A DANGER.

WE now set forth again, much in the order we had observed before; and began to round the shoulder of the mountain by degrees, still getting higher as we went: so our course took the shape of a spiral curve, bending up to the north-east of the island. This we did, to gain a bird's-eye view of the other side, both over land and sea; to remark the nature of the place itself, for soil and produce, and whether inhabited, as I partly feared, or desert. Also, we meant to certify ourselves what hopes we might entertain of deliverance from that easterly quarter of our prison, by a chain of communication with some land further off. I nourished within me a lurking hope, perchance this same growth of coral rock that made our difficulty in landing, would serve to help us off again on the further side. Could we but make shift to put together a raft of branches, no matter how rude, if not too hazardous in calm weather, then we might, I considered, provision ourselves for a short voyage, and drift from island to island, or from reef to reef, the currents being supposed favourable, or some contrivance made to stand in place of a sail. And here I stayed in my thoughts, not finding a way to conclude this plan with any satisfaction. Nor would I breathe it to my companions, fearing I might raise hopes only to have them dashed by the event.

As for the side of the island we were leaving, we had suffered so much misery there as made us mislike the very look of it. For outward things take their colour from the hue and disposition of our minds, so as to appear bright or gloomy according to the mood in which we view them. And now, this part of the island, which in truth was fair enough in itself, for its variety of landscape, appeared odious to us, so that we seemed to breathe freer as we quitted it. Every step we took led us away to a new scene; and as the life of a seaman is a changeful one, and little secure from disaster day by day, so these men now seemed almost to forget their past misfortunes, being as much taken up with our exploring as though it had, indeed, been the party of pleasure on which we came from the ship the day before.

When we got higher on the mountain, a beautiful sight did truly unfold itself to us; for then the extent of the island appeared by degrees, until we could see it spread out before us plainly, as a coloured chart might be on canvas. So far as could be measured by the eye, we judged it to be some two leagues in length, reckoning from the mountain southward; and in breadth, where that was greatest, something over a full league. The sides ran pretty even one with the other, only tapering towards a point as they drew near to the southern end. But I must not omit, that the shore on either side was much broken by reefs of the coral rocks, whereof we had already gained some experience on the western side, and which now, we saw, prevailed yet more to the east; so that the whole of that coast was broken up into shoals, surrounding that east part of the island with fringes of rock, over which the surf beat with so great violence, that I was sure no boat that man ever built could live through it.

Here, then, I saw the downfall of my cherished hope of deliverance, unless the north-east part of our mountain should give a more encouraging prospect when we got thither. But at the same time, these walls of rocks were the best safeguard we could have against the landing of savages on our island; for they formed such a natural rampart, and so formidable, that not the boldest, though they might be skilful in managing their canoes, would attempt it. And thus, as often is to be found in this che-quered life, disappointment and comfort met us hand in hand.

We had now travelled round three sides of the mountain, or thereabout; yet no sign appeared of any other island or continent neighbouring our own. And this view was made complete when we rounded so far as to see to the east-north-east; further we needed not to go, for the rest we had already viewed from the ship. All appeared open sea, with here and there a table-land of rocks, some not twenty yards across, lying outside the fringe of our protecting reefs: at least, this was as much as the haze or sea-vapour drawn up by the heat (the sun being now very powerful), allowed us to discover.

The heat, indeed, was by this time become so intolerable over head and under feet, by reason of the sun striking on the bare rock, for we were now got above the region of trees, quite to the upper portion of our mountain; the heat, I say, now forced us to seek a shelter; so with one accord we plunged down the slope into the woods, not following the course we came up by, but in a straight line, making for the length of the island, as though we were bent on reaching that point to the south which we had viewed from the height above.

Added to this inconvenience of the heat, was another we had not foreseen; for we found these parched rocks swarming with reptiles, as horned beetles, scorpions, and a large kind of centipede, or what they call in the West Indies the *forty legs;* some of these last we saw, grown to be seven or eight inches long, running about the loose stones; so that we feared to sit anywhere to rest ourselves, knowing these creatures to be well-nigh as venemous as the scorpions. Some serpents also we heard, hissing at us as we approached, and saw several, and pretty large ones, glancing swiftly through the thickets. We hastened to get out of so unwelcome a neighbourhood; though in truth we knew not what might meet us of that kind where we were going to.

As we went down, an accident befel us that had near taken off one of our number by a sudden death. It chanced as follows:—When we had left the upper part of that mountain of ours, and came once more among the trees, we noticed the leaves and stems of some of them tinged with a dust of a whitish yellow, having the smell and taste of brimstone. Any one in his senses surely would have been made cautious by this unwholesome appearance: but I know not how it was, Don Manuel and I, who had most knowledge on such matters, were occupied, I suppose, each with his own sad thoughts: and mine (I well remember) were running on the disappointment I had received from our look-out, at finding no way of escape, nor opening to devise any. So when Harry Gill, who had got ahead of us, called out that he had found a cave in the woods, we thought not of bidding him beware how he ventured his head into the lion's den, as (in one way) it proved to be.

This cave of his was no great things for size; but rather a kind of crack or fissure in the rocks, and overhung by several sorts of wild plants, all powdered with this brimstone dust. These hung down so low over its mouth, he was obliged to creep on all fours to get even a little way in : and it was well for him he did not go in further.

When I caught sight of what he was about, and that Hilton was ready to follow him so soon as he should be fairly within the cavern, I shouted to them to beware of some wild beast that might be lurking in this den; "and be sure," added I, "you keep your guns before you, ready for action." But almost before I had said it, and while Gill was half crept in, we noticed him drop on his face, like one taken on a sudden with the falling sickness. We rushed forward, and pulled him out with main force by the heels, not without scraping his face and hands somewhat roughly against the rocky bed of his new-discovered cave.

No sooner had we got him fairly out, than I at once perceived he had been poisoned by some noisome vapour exhaling from the earth : for his face was of a leaden colour, his eyes stark staring open, and he foaming at the mouth, but quite insensible. There being no water at hand to dash into his face, and so bring him round, we did the best by waving our hats before him, to give him air ; and I took out my lancets (from which I parted no more than our priest from his Breviary) to breathe a vein. But this he soon needed not : for as we were busied about him, some unloosing his neck-kerchief, some fanning him, some clapping the palms of his cold hands, or striking the soles of his feet as if he were undergoing the bastinado, we had the satisfaction to see him slowly recover his senses.

Soon he was able to sit up: and Prodgers, having (as we then found for the first time) smuggled a small bottle of rum from the ship, now relaxed so far from the selfishness of his nature as to offer poor Gill a dram of it. But when the rest saw this unlooked-for bottle, they all cried out, "A prize ! a prize !" and began to insist it should be equally divided among them, agreeably to the understanding we came to before starting on our expedition. Prodgers, on his part, was not the man to yield up anything that belonged to him because others wished it; and, between half jest on their part, and whole earnest on his, words soon ran high amongst them.

I saw the danger in our society of any quarrel on what had afforded the pretext for many such since the flood; I mean drink. So, stepping at once between them, and parting them by force, wherein I was helped, though with more moderation, by Don Manuel, I cried out with some heat:

"Madmen! will you wrangle for a vile pint of liquor over the half dead body of your comrade?"

This brought them a little to themselves; and Harry Gill being now pretty well recovered from his fit, or swoon, they were eager to ask him how it had taken him, and what he thought it was owing to. I saw at once that the low cave he had thrust his head into, had oppressed him with some heavy, creeping vapour, that from its weight could not rise high; like that grotto in the kingdom of Naples, which suffocates a dog when it goes into the cavern, while a man standing at his natural height escapes the choke of the foul air. And this was confirmed by the account which Harry himself gave us of his misadventure.

"I wanted to discover," said he, "where this hole in the ground led to; partly for a mere freak; also, methought I might be the first to invent something of a fortress or habitation for ourselves. So without more ado, I began to creep in; though there came such a whiff of brimstone smoke into my nose and mouth as well-nigh stifled me on the instant. I went on, thinking I should soon be past the crack from which it was coming up; but I had not crawled three paces when I found my head swim round on a sudden; then I remember nothing more, till I found myself lying thus with all of you round me, and Richard here (hearty thanks to him), washing down the brimstone with a mouthful of grog."

We thought ourselves well rid of the business as it turned out; and, forasmuch as we poor mortals (a reflection I borrowed from Don Manuel, who made it in his quiet way when the danger was over) never know what value to put on our advantages, until they are like to be taken from us, so was it now. For if Gill had died there in that sulphurous hole, as he surely would by running on before us further, and our not missing him till too late, our party had been weakened both for mutual assistance and defence. I had a thought in my mind, but checked it, that another of our number might have been better spared. And yet poor Richard had shown signs of something better than usual: and I reflected, there are few persons who possess not a better side to their character as well as a worse, if only we will cultivate them as we would stubborn ground, and bring out those qualities to ripeness.

## CHAPTER IX.

### DINNER, AND A BATTLE AFTER IT.

HARRY GILL'S mischance put me on considering the nature of the island we were upon: and I concluded with Don Manuel, as after-experience fully showed, that the entire island had been thrown up out of the sea by fires from beneath; except what might have been added by the industrious coral insects in the course of ages. Not the mountain alone, I felt sure, but the plain country, was composed of lava rock, only covered by the depth of its rich soil. 'T was not in the way of speculation that I followed out this; but for a practical end, and one that touched on our security. For, as all countries that were first formed by volcanoes, are ever liable to eruptions of fire, earthquakes, devastations of hot springs, effluvia of fatal gases, and other such evils, it was well we should prepare ourselves what to expect in that way, and what to avoid.

So this accident to poor Harry, when the effects of it were over (and he soon plucked up spirits again to join us as if nothing had chanced), might be looked on as a wholesome warning, we were in a place where nothing was to be ventured hap-hazard, or beyond what we understood.

As we continued our march, "See, my dear friends," said the priest, "how near we are to peril, and sometimes to death, when we least think of it. Here was our friend Geile (so he pronounced it, and made us all smile at his way of talking English), was a strong sailor a quarter of an hour ago; and now, see—"

"He's as weak as a cat," replied poor Harry, and indeed, so he looked.

At this, we "shortened sail for him," as Ned Hilton expressed it: and, what with one thing and another, we all concluded that we had earned a halt under the shade of the trees which now branched thick over our heads. The heat was indeed extreme, and we were glad of a breathing time. For though on board ship the thermometer had stood at nearly the same point (and I believe we were at least 95° in the shade), yet the breeze that played over the sea, on and off, hindered the actual heat from oppressing the spirits as it did in the thickness of these island coverts.

For, putting all things together, the priest and I reckoned, though we had not an instrument for taking an observation, nor could clearly determine the points of the compass; yet, by what had dropped from the captain and mate before they so barbarously left us here, we concluded that the place of our captivity lay somewhere between ten and twelve degrees north of the line, and in the same latitude with the South Carribbean Sea. This taught us we might expect to meet with both the goods and ills of such a latitude, so long as we remained here; or till our deaths, if we were at last to find our graves on this lonely place.

We then began to ask, for what aim we were hurrying in our exploring party through the island? We should but reach the end of our tether the sooner; and there was a bitterness (I well knew) awaiting us, when we should arrive at the southern end of our prison-yard, as we were already acquainted with the northern. No sign of inhabitants had been seen by any of us; for aught that appeared, we were the lords and possessors of all we surveyed;

which was poor comfort enough.    So, this being considered, we sat down under the shade of a large tree of the pimento kind: and the men, in spite of the hearty breakfast they had made in the morning, now voted it to be dinner-time.    We had packed up the remainder of our meat and bread-fruit, which Harvey volunteered to carry on his shoulders, wrapped in palm-leaves.    This was now spread for us on the grass, and we fell to, some more, some less, according to the character and appetite of each.

Sailors mostly live for the day; so used are they to chances and changes, it little matters to them where they make their shake-down when the day is over.    I could not discover, by what fell from these men, they had any plan of life settled in their minds in these strange circumstances of ours.    They seemed to leave everything to Don Manuel and me; though they would have shown themselves jealous, and rebellious too, had we dictated to them.    It was all one in the end; we had to consult, and suggest, for the whole party, at every turn.    Don Manuel, on his part, seldom gave his opinion, except when there was a question of right and wrong; or when he could guide our minds to the better things whereon his own was fixed. On those occasions he spoke; and always with the same cheerful temper which had gained our hearts, or some part of them, from the first.

As we sat or lay down, to rest and dinner, I took that occasion to speak again.

"Let us think," said I, "what sort of habitations we shall fix on, and how we shall best seek to support our lives.    No more caves for us, if you please, unless we can find one that has no sulphur fumes coming from it.    Tell us, Harry, how say you?"

"No, indeed," answered he, making a wry face, and with an oath that did not add anything, but profaneness, to his discourse.    And this Don Manuel gently reminded him of.    "Well, I was wrong," added Gill, taking the reproof better than I expected from him: "but I have n't got the taste of the brimstone out of my mouth yet, and that, I suppose, made me to swear.    Give us another slice of cold pork, Harvey: and a crumb of our outlandish loaf, there, and no more about it."

"Now," said I, continuing, "the first thing, as seems to

me, is to devise some method for supplying ourselves with food, not for to-day nor to-morrow, but for as long as we may have to stay here. This cannot be by shooting down our game from day to day: for we have not powder and shot among us for more than forty or fifty rounds; and what becomes of us when these are expended? So I vote that we choose first some spot for a preserve, in which to keep such animals as we may snare, or wound by shooting; and so husband our ammunition as much as we may, for future need."

No one raised a voice against my proposal; so I regarded it as passed, and went on.

"Next," I said, "let each of us name some of the things we are most in want of: and let us see how we are to procure or make them; and what we must needs do without."

At this, all fell to considering what they should name as most important to us in our distress.

"Come, Prodgers," I went on, with a motion aside to Don Manuel, to let him see I gave the surly old fellow this precedence to make him more favourable: "what, think you, should we make for ourselves first?"

This set Richard Prodgers a-thinking; he began to search his wits as most sailors do: that is, fumbled in his pockets, twirled his hat round once or twice, turned a quid of tobacco in his cheek, and finished by refreshing his memory from his bottle of rum. At that the rest fell to laughing at him, and insisted he should say what was uppermost in his mind.

"I think," said Prodgers slowly, with a very thoughtful look, "the first thing we should provide is, a supply of hog for our dinner to-morrow."

"And grog, I suppose," added Harvey, pointing to the bottle that peeped from Richard's pocket.

Prodgers looked angrily; but I took up the discourse, and said, none could doubt that our food must be looked to without delay, as I had already expressed. "And what say you, Ned Hilton?"

But Hilton had strolled away while we were speaking; and was eyeing one of the trees overhead, which was a cocoa-nut tree.

"It is!" cried he, with great glee. "Hallo! messmates:

4

a real live monkey!   Look, there is another; and a third
again!"
Up they all were at once, and not another thought about
our plans, so eagerly did they enter into this monkey-
chase.   I must own it was a diverting thing to see the
monkeys, great troops of which we now discovered in the
trees, where they had been watching our movements,
scamper off in all directions with much swiftness, until
they seemed to think the distance among the higher
branches made them secure; then they looked down at
us with such grimaces and chatterings as I believe would
have made an owl laugh.   There was no chance of
catching any of them by climbing the trees, though our
men could climb like monkeys themselves: for the trees
grew so thick together that their branches interlaced, and
the nimble creatures could easily have fled from one end
of the wood to the other without once touching the ground.
It seemed also to be no matter to them whether they used
hands, or feet, or tails; for their tails, as we afterwards
found, measured nearly two feet in length, and were
longer indeed than themselves; they being of a smaller
kind of monkey, though exceeding active and mischievous.

It is scarce to be believed how they would hang themselves by the very end of these strong flexible tails of
theirs, clasping a small branch with them, as we might
hook up a rasher of bacon on a nail by a small hook; then,
suspended in this way, they would swing in any direction,
till they swung themselves near enough to another branch
to catch it, or leap on to it, and so be as much at home as
before.   They would fling themselves about with such
astonishing certainty of lighting in safety, as almost
equalled a bird upon the wing.   In short, they being
among the trees in their own natural element, as I may
say, and we beneath them on the earth, which was ours,
they had us at a disadvantage in this game: and this
they seemed to know; for leaping and shaking the
branches till all the trees above us were in a commotion,
by their strange grimaces and chattering noises they appeared to be laughing at us, and bidding us come up and
do our best to catch them.

Such a conduct irritated the men to that degree, that
they ran for their fire-arms to shoot and bring some of the

monkeys down: but I entreated them to be still for a while longer, promising them some cocoa-nuts for their forbearance; for an idea had come into my head, and methought I had hit upon a means of getting some of these nuts without the pains of climbing for them. So I bade my comrades to pick up some stones and clods of earth, with which we sent a volley into the trees, that we might provoke the monkeys to return our compliment. And so, indeed, they did; for after sending down upon us all they could readily lay hands on, as leaves, and a few dead boughs, or the like, this not satisfying their vengeance, they leaped with one accord into the cocoa-nut trees, of which a good number grew hereabout, and began plucking and tugging with all their might (or some of the oldest and strongest among them) at the nuts, to get them off to cast at us; and held fast to the stem of the tree with their tails, to keep from falling. So great was the rage of these creatures, that they put forth all their strength upon it; and if one could not pull off a cocoa-nut, then another would come and help him, till they managed it with much effort between them.

It was well for our heads that these monkeys were more expert in getting off the nuts than in taking good aim with them, or some of us might have come off the field of battle with cracked crowns for our pains. But the nuts were so large, in their outer cases, as well nigh overbalanced the monkeys that threw them, so that they could not send them at us very exactly. Only, some few of the more cunning of their number (for it seems, among monkeys as among men, there are those who take the lead, by reason of their superior intelligence, or greater watchfulness and cunning), first taking a firm hold of the tree with their tails, swung themselves towards us, and delivered the cocoa-nuts straight at us, as a cricketer would deliver the ball at a wicket; by which it happened that, though we kept our eyes about us, as indeed we had need, and jumped aside nimbly to avoid these cannon-balls, we were hit once or twice, and that smartly; for I must tell you, a full ripe cocoa-nut, thrown by an angry monkey from a high tree, is no joke upon your head or arm.

# CHAPTER X.

### WE DISCOVER WHAT A PRIEST IS.

HAVING now secured a plentiful supply of cocoa-nuts, I thought it time to put an end to the fight by the superior force of our fire-arms: the more so, that the cries of those of our assailants, already engaged against us, had drawn others of their tribe to the spot, so that their numbers increased continually, and the wood seemed alive with them. For this reason, I gave the word for the three fowling-pieces, which formed the main stock of our artillery, to be discharged into the trees; which the men did with a hearty good will. As the pieces were loaded with a kind of swan-shot, equally fit to bring down small animals and the larger sort of birds, we should have done great execution among the monkeys; but that, by a kind of sagacity or instinct, such as I cannot account for (seeing they had never been fired at before in all their lives), no sooner did they mark our preparations, than, slipping behind the stems of their native trees, they placed themselves in shelter, so that we could scarce touch them. Then they would look out cautiously, and grin again at us, as if daring us to do our worst. The end was, that besides wounding a few, which increased the noise, we did but kill one outright, and that was a poor monkey with her two cubs; one of them she carried under her arm, while the other clasped its hands round her neck. She was so encumbered with these, as not to get nimbly enough out of the way. I say, we killed this one; but it could not be said, we brought it down; for the poor creature took firm hold of the tree with her long tail, and hung there, like a malefactor in chains, only head downwards, and the cubs still clinging, and crying, like little infants, with the fright, and strain of hanging on. I called out to Harvey that they would soon drop, one after the other; and so they did, while he held his hat to receive them.

This was the result of our battle; one killed, and two prisoners, or adopted subjects, which you will. For the rest, they scampered away at the report of the fire-arms as though they could not get far enough from the scene of action, and we saw them no more that day. As to the dead monkey, we left it in the tree, as not worth climbing for; and thinking the sight of it hanging there would drive away the rest from the spot, if we made our plans to return thither.

As we went along, we took up our debate again, as to the kind of dwellings we should furnish ourselves with. Of natives, we had not seen a trace; yet we did not on that account feel secure: the nature of savages being, to lie hid so close in the bush as scarce to be discovered till (I had almost said) you may walk over them, like a hare in her form; then, rising up, to take you unawares, or wait for a night attack, when they may burn and massacre all before them. And, if any were on the island, they had certainly had notice enough of our coming, what with firing of guns from the ship, and our own fowling-pieces, together with our heedless shoutings; and so had been enabled to put out their fires, and hide their canoes in some of the creeks on this eastern side.

Yet, on the other hand, the island being so small as we had now made it out to be, it could not support more than a few of such people as lived altogether by chase, and knew little of tilling the ground: and the game we had already seen was so plentiful, we found it had not been thinned out by hunting. Also, if our enemies should appear, and not in great force, we had a vast advantage in our fire-arms; which, beside the deadly execution they do among defenceless savages, are always known to astonish more than they kill: being looked on as dreadful thunder and lightning from heaven, by such as know only bows and arrows, or spears armed with fishes' teeth, for weapons of offence.

By this time, we were within three quarters of a league of that southern point whereto we tended; when, seeing to our left hand a little eminence rising up clearer of trees than the thick woodland, we made for that, to take an observation. It rose, as far as we judged, seventy feet or more, above the sea-level; when we gained the top, we could see pretty well around us, though some lofty groves of cocoa-nut and other tropical growths here and there shut out the view. But the open sea was clearly enough to be distinguished on both sides, and to the south also; more particularly we noticed that the eastern coast was clearer of the lava rock, but more occupied by reefs of coral. These ran out into some such fantastic promontories, with capes and headlands, creeks and bays, all in miniature, as I have seen japanned on a Chinese screen. And not only did it make up a beautiful prospect, with dwarf cocoa and palms growing thickly upon them, dipping their broad leaves down to the very edge; but promised us some quiet nooks of deep water where we might get good fishing for our support.

We stayed some time on this spot, which everything made delightful, but for the heat of the sun and want of water; and finding the situation so favourable, we gazed on all sides, each taking my spy-glass in turn, and looking out sharp enough (you may be sure) for any sign of an inhabitant. But we became assured by degrees, to our satisfaction in one way, that we were indeed the only human beings on the island. Don Manuel gave a little sigh when he heard us express this to one another.

"Why, sir," said I, turning to him with some surprise, "you would not wish to find savages on this place? and should we not be thankful to have a clear field before us, and no enemies to drive out of it, or shoot down in self-defence?"

"True, Señor," answered he, "I am not saying anything against that; we ought surely to be thankful for every mercy and deliverance, and resigned under every trial."

"But why, then," I began again; but stopped myself, for there was a something, I know not what, about the priest, that made it difficult at times to question him, all meek and cheerful as he was.

The men listened with attention; I saw they wished, like myself, to get at the priest's mind about this. So I tried again.

"You expressed a hope, sir," said I, "yesterday, when we first landed, that we might meet with none, man or beast, to eat us up."

"Indeed, I did, my dear friend," answered he, with his open smile, "and I do so still; for I should not like to be devoured just yet: unless," he added, "it were His most

"These ran out into some such fantastic promontories, with capes and headlands creeks and bays, all in miniature, as I have seen japanned on a Chinese
screen."—CHAP. X, p. 46.

holy will." And he lifted his hat, as was usual with him, when he spoke in that way.

There was that about his manner (I could not tell why, nor wherein it lay) which stopped me as if I had intruded into his thoughts; I was going to let the subject drop, half inclined even to beg his pardon for what I had seemed to ask. But after a few moments, seeing us silent and still looking at him, he laughed in his quiet way, and said to us:

"Well, comrades, don't let me be making mysteries out of a very simple thing. As you take my little sigh so much to heart, I will explain it in a few words, and then have done about myself. Or, you shall help me to do it. Tell me, then, what is a priest?"

This was, I must own, a hard question for us to answer out of hand; and I felt that, in a courteous way, our friend had turned the tables upon us. As he stood there, leaning on his staff, with his cloak dropped about him, his broad hat, and he looking at us with his friendly smile, expecting our answer, I thought within myself, whatever other priests might be (and I had heard, from my boyhood upward, talk enough against them) there was one whom I could respect as a being superior to any one I had yet fallen in with.

"Well," repeated Don Manuel after a while, still looking round at us, and I know we felt awkward as we stood before him; "well, my good friends, what is a priest?"

Ned Hilton seemed to think it concerned the honour of our party that the Spaniard should get some answer. So, clearing his throat, and making the best of himself, he began:

"A priest, sir, I take it, is a man who——." Here he stopped, and twitched the collar of his jacket, shuffling with his feet, as not knowing how to go on.

"Who what?" asked the Don, quietly.

"Why, of course, you know, is,—without any doubt— why, he is a priest, I suppose."

At this explanation, no one could help laughing: Don Manuel, having enjoyed it a little, then said, more gravely:

"A priest, my dear friends, is, or ought to be, one devoted

to the service of his Master, who has called him.  He ought never to be so happy as when speaking to Him, or working for Him.  Every labour or suffering for His sake ought to be welcome.  Each one to whom the priest may do good, he should consider as a brother, a friend, a spiritual child of his.  I confess I have been nursing a hope within me, that as I am disabled by this misfortune of ours from going to those among whom my superiors sent me to labour, I might at least find some poor heathens in this place and win them to God.  It is not to be so : and now you know the meaning of that sigh which escaped from my heart.  May His holy will be ever done, and by us all. I remain at least *your* servant.  And now, shall we not be moving onward ? "

There came over each one of us, I believe, such a feeling while he spoke, as we had never known before.  On we moved, as if he had ordered it so, and none spoke, for each was wondering at what he had just heard.  But I forgot to mention, we had agreed, before this, to give to the place the name of Prospect Hill; and it was the first spot on our island that we had named at all.

---

## CHAPTER XI.

### THE BEST AND WORST SHOT.

A SOUTHERLY bearing down from this hill, brought us to a spring of water gushing from the hill-side, as clear and fresh as that we had met on landing.  We were glad enough to discover it ; being all now athirst with our long march : so, sitting down by the spring, we fell into talk about the mode of life that was before us.

First came the question, how to build us some huts to dwell in.  Here we were, without any tools, or prospect of making any.  I considered, too, we were drawing near the rainy season, which was like to set in fairly ere a month or six weeks were gone, it being now the last week in August. We knew by report the violence of these rains when they set in; and Harvey and Prodgers had cruised in these latitudes before, and had got many a wet jacket in the autumn equinox, and after. So we had need to do something in the way of house-building out of hand, if only to last over till next spring.

A thought came upon me, as I looked at the guns that lay by our sides. "We must sacrifice," said I, "one or more of these to make us some tools." They looked at me; and, plainly, their first thought was to refuse. But I went on to show that it was needful to the good of all; that unless we had a way to cut down trees we could neither build, no, not the rudest hut, nor clear any plot of ground for plantations; that our ammunition, with the greatest saving and care, would soon be spent, and then what was the use of the fowling-pieces to us? To all this, Prodgers, who took on him the office of objector-general, said, in his surly way, what could I make out of a gun? But I had my answer ready, and told him smartly I could make a gun into a gouge. What moved the others to come into my plan was, in part, they enjoyed seeing old Prodgers put down so readily: also, it was plain that, in our unhappy case, nothing better could be devised.

"And which gun is to go, then?" asked Richard, jealous about his own. Now, it so happened, he was the worst shot in the whole party; so that, if any one had to surrender his piece, it should be this man: this every one felt, except Prodgers himself; and he (it was just like him) would not hear of it.

But I had ere now been going to propose a shooting match among them, to decide which should carry the fowling-pieces on our expeditions; and this seemed a fitting occasion for doing so. No sooner did I mention it than the three men, Harvey, Gill, and Hilton, agreed at once; so Prodgers was outvoted, and took it in no good part. I was appointed umpire for this trial of skill; and I bade them take notice of a fruit of the orange kind, which by reason of its bright colour was a good mark for the eye; it grew on a low sized tree, within fair range for a fowling-piece from where we stood. "Now," said I, "he who plants most shot in the rind of this fruit shall be first marksman among us, and wear a feather in his cap; and so of the next." Saying this, I went towards the tree, and called to Prodgers, as the eldest, to fire.

So indeed he did; but hit neither orange nor orange-tree, as I could plainly know by the shot pattering into another bush that grew near. However, I own that poor Dick made us bound to thank him; for he brought us our supper when he least thought of it. For in the very bush he fired into so clumsily, there sat a largish monkey of the same kind that we had put to flight before; he had sat there, I suppose, watching our motions from a distance till he knew too much of us, poor fellow, as some of his companions had. But of this, by and bye: at the present, we discovered not the execution Prodgers had done; for the monkey was killed stone dead, and we found him afterwards, by accident, as I shall relate.

It was now Hilton's turn to fire: and, to make this short, he and Gill went so near one another in their shots, as each to plant some grains of swan-shot in the orange; and both of them distanced Tom Harvey, who only peppered into the branches. I adjudged the fowling-pieces to these two men, and gave preference to Gill for first choice. It was easy to discover which of the three guns was oldest and worst; this we condemned at once to be broken up, stock, lock, and barrel, to make such instruments as we needed for our carpenter's work. So we took it with us, till we could break it up at leisure.

Moving onwards, we came to the bush into which Prodgers had scattered the contents of his blunderbuss; and here we found the dead monkey lying at the roots. We took him up, and looked at as ugly a caricature of our poor human nature as ever was drawn by a malicious pen. We decided upon taking the monkey with us, and cooking him for supper when we should halt for the night. Only, we could not bear either to take him or cook him as he was; for the creature looked so human as well as hideous, that our men, though no way squeamish, declared they would not touch a bit of him unless he was cut up and baked or broiled piecemeal. So Prodgers, as he had the best right to him, undertook the office of purveyor preparing for the cook; indeed, he was helped by most of the rest. I contented myself with cutting off the monkey's

long tail and putting it into the hat of Harry Gill, instead
of the feather I had promised him, as best man in the
shooting-match. Don Manuel turned for awhile to his
prayer-book, as he generally did when there was a leisure
moment.

I may as well here finish the history of the two little
monkeys that fell into our hands out of the cocoa-nut
tree. Harvey did his best to keep them alive, putting one
into each of his pockets to huddle them up warm, and tried
to feed them with cocoa-nut milk: for, I forgot to say, we
brought the cocoa-nuts also with us, and very refreshing
we found both milk and pulp in these great heats. But,
for the monkeys, both of them died before the second day
was out; Tom Harvey, who was much concerned at this,
buried them under two tall palm trees, not far from Prospect Hill. Going that way some time after, I found he
had placed a large stone over them, and had scratched on
it this epitaph with his knife:—

> " Here lyes ye bodys of two little apes,
> Short was their lives, ugly their shapes;
> One would 'a been Pug, and t' other Joko,
> But, alas, I couldn't rear 'em on cocoa.
> " T. H. 1739."

----

# CHAPTER XII.

### HOW MUCH GOODNESS GOES TO FORGIV'NESS.

GETTING under weigh again, after our trial of skill
we soon reached the shore on the S.S.E. of our prison.
As to the point due south, it ran up into rather a high
cliff, and would have cost us a climb to gain it. We now
found ourselves in a little cove, wherein the water lay
very still, under this cliff: the bottom being of a fine
white sand, shelving out by degrees; not getting to a
great depth till it was some twelve or fifteen yards from

the shore.  After that, indeed, it went sheer down into deep sea.  Also we noticed, that in a part of the cliff beyond this deep water line, was the mouth of a very low cave, scarcely showing two feet above the sea level: so that at first we took it for some dent in the rock, which, at that part, overhung it as steep as the wall of a house. But shortly we made it out to be indeed an inlet into the cliff, from the hollow sound of the water inside as it came and went, though the cove was so still.

"Come, boys!" cried I; "here is an adventure for us: who will be first to swim into yonder cave's mouth?" Hilton and Tom Harvey were forward at once: as for Harry Gill, he shook his head, and declared he had known enough of caves for one day.  But second thoughts reminded me it was best one should go alone, if indeed it were worth the while to do it at all: and let the rest stand on the watch to see no harm happened to him.  I did not say what had come into my mind: but I felt uneasy, after I had proposed the swim, lest there should be any sharks, with which these seas are known to abound, cruising thereabouts.  For so great is the swiftness and voracious hunger of this dreadful fish, as no swimmer, be he never so active, can escape him: and the number and sharpness of his two rows of teeth, or more, is such, it needs but one bite from him to take off a limb as clean as any surgeon could do it.  There was some safety, 't is true, in the coral reefs which seemed, by the surf dashing over them, to surround this part of the island at fifty or a hundred yards off shore.  Nevertheless, I feared some inlet between them into our cove, through which these gentlemen, the sharks (sea-lawyers, so the men called them), might find their way, though a boat would be stove without remedy in the passage, by the violence of the outer sea.

In short, it was a relief to me when Don Manuel took up the discourse, saying in his quiet way: "I thought, my friends" (he had left off calling us Señores, at least mostly, since we had known each other better); "I thought," says he, "we agreed to look without delay for something of a dwelling to house in.  Now this cave," he added, smiling, "whatever wonders it may contain, could hardly afford this to us; and "—

"Begging your pardon," says old rough Prodgers, "I

don't see that at all: for I've some thoughts of living in it myself."

At this, the three men set up a shout of laughter, and began to banter him, as if he were never to hear the end of it. One called him the hermit of the cave, another, the old man of the sea. Harvey said, he would grow into Neptune, or become finned, or at least web-footed, or a Triton; Hilton declared the fishes would come and ask him to reign over them : "and then," says Gill, " we shall see his majesty drive out for an airing in a turtle's shell for a coach, drawn by six sword-fish." " With a body-guard of monkeys," added Hilton again. "Armed with fowling-pieces that kill only by chance," concluded Gill.

This last stroke was too much for old Richard, who started to his feet, and challenged Harry to fight him on the spot. The other was no way backwards; so they began in earnest, before Don Manuel and I could interfere. "Good humour, ahoy!" shouted Tom Harvey, holding back Prodgers, while the priest and I tried to reason with Gill. In short, we restored them to peace with some difficulty; and only by Harvey and myself, with Hilton (who joined the better side this time) telling them in a determined way, if they offered to strike another blow, we would knock them down and tie their hands behind them.

When they were calmed down, though there was some grumbling yet on either side, we made them shake hands, and no more ado about it. Don Manuel whispered to me, it were prudent to look after their knives, lest they might bear one another a grudge, and take worse revenge. But I answered him in a whisper, that 't was the nature of a jack tar to knock his man down in the first brush of a quarrel, and then help him up again; that when once they had shaken hands after a fight, where they might have gone within an inch of murthering one another, they would be the best of friends and messmates the next moment, each ready to risk his life to save the other's; that, as to grudge borne for a fair blow, 't was a thing unknown among them, as little thought on as to fire into an enemy's ship after she had struck her flag and you had taken her in tow.

All this seemed to surprise him at the time; and he

plainly thought it over; but there was no leisure then to pursue it. Only, next afternoon, as we walked together at a little distance from the rest, he took up the discourse again, as I will here relate.

He said then to me : " Señor Owen, a strange thing was that you told me yesterday about anger and fighting. In my country, it gives the priests no small work to try and persuade people to forgive injuries, as these two men now seem to have forgiven, and forgotten too. In Spain, I am sorry to say, owing to our hot Spanish blood, when a man thinks he has received an affront from another, his first impulse sometimes is to vow revenge, and too often he begins planning how to compass it. If he abandons himself to this evil passion, and neglects the warnings of conscience, he will keep this settled purpose in his heart, aye, sometimes for years, till he meets or makes the opportunity; and then will wreak his vengeance to the full. Now, how different is the conduct of these seamen ! They seem as good friends again as ever, after the hard knocks they gave each other."

" That they are," I answered, "and believe me, if either Prodgers or Gill were to fall into any danger, the other would pull him out of it, if he could, at the risk of life or limb."

" God forgive me, then, for a harsh judgment," said the priest, striking his breast; " I find they are much better Christians than I took them to be."

I could scarce help smiling at the notion of these men being good Christians; but I answered him with respect (indeed I respected him as much for his humbly accusing himself, as for the other qualities I had marked in him), and said, shaking my head :

" I fear, sir, most of the Christianity among us is wrapped within your reverence's cloak. Sure I am, in many ways we have practised the clean contrary to all that is meant by that word."

" But how do you tell me," answers he quickly, " how do you tell me, Señor Owen, that they are not good Christians, since they have performed one of the most bounden duties of a Christian, and one of the hardest; forgiving injuries, as they did but yesterday ? "

" Well, sir," said I, "I am no great divine. But you

asked us yesterday what a priest is: now, let me ask, what do you mean by a Christian?"

"A brief question, friend," replied the priest, "and a long answer. I want to know, for my part, why these men are not to be reckoned good Christians, inasmuch as they forgive?"

"Because," answered I, readily, "it costs them nothing."

"Ah," says he, drawing a long breath; "costs them nothing, you say?"

"Nothing, sir. 'T is part of their rough-and-tumble life to knock down and be knocked down in turn; when they jump up again, all is forgotten, in the tuning of a fiddle."

He seemed not quite to understand; so I explained my meaning in other words, and went on:

"Now, virtue, I believe, sir, is doing good, or keeping from evil, in spite of the difficulty we feel in acting thus. Am I right?"

"To be sure," answered Don Manuel.

"So, if I do a thing that is good in itself, without finding it difficult, but do it just in an off-hand way, as I would hand my neighbour a portion at dinner, when I had enough and to spare; there would not be much goodness in that?"

"There may be a natural goodness," says he, slowly, "that cannot be called supernatural."

"What do you mean, sir," said I, surprised in my turn, "by supernatural goodness? Miracles have ceased, and a miracle is something supernatural."

"I will tell you another time," says he, smiling again.

---

## CHAPTER XIII.

### A LESSON OUT OF A SHARK'S MOUTH.

TO go by strict order of time, this conversation is out of place by a day. But now, taking up the thread of our adventures, as we ranged about our cove, Harvey, who had got out on a ledge of rock, that divided it from another inlet to N.E., called to us, he had found a skeleton lying in shallow water. We started at this sudden news; our minds running back on the old apprehensions of some savage inhabitants of our island; we thought, here might be one of their dead, drowned by accident or killed in war. However, when we got to where Tom stood, looking down into the water beneath, which was about four feet in depth, we saw the skeleton of a large fish, partly fallen in pieces, and the tail part disjointed, lying here and there in the white sand. The flesh (or fish, rather) was completely gone, as though it had been picked clean. But the head-bones and jaws were entire, pointing inland; and as the body of the fish was turned on its side, I judged it had pushed so far into the cove in pursuit of some prey, and stuck fast on the sand while seizing it, or been left by the ebb of a high tide after gorging it: for the mouth of the shark (and a shark this plainly had been) is so formed, and so far under the snout, that it cannot seize nor swallow its prey but by turning on its side.

Don Manuel, when I made him observe this, remarked how the providence of God, by so ordering it, prevented that tremendous fish from thinning out all other inhabitants of the ocean; setting bounds to his power of devouring, when there were no bounds to his appetite and cruelty. But I, meantime, full of other thoughts, saw only a valuable prize. "Here boys!" cried I, here is what will turn to account when powder and shot are gone."

"How so?" asked they all; looking down into the water.

"See those teeth," continued I; "and tell me if they will not make the best of arrow points for arrows of such bamboo as we ate our dinners with to-day."

"Hurrah for the bows and arrows!" cried Hilton; with that he jumped into the water, only throwing off his jacket, and was followed by Harvey and Gill. They were determined, it seems, to have the shark piecemeal on land. And no light job they had of it; as well from the depth in which it lay, full four feet of water, as by reason of the size of the fish itself: the parts that hung together being no less than ten feet in length; and the tail that was broken up would have made the monster from fifteen to eighteen feet in the whole. Having to dip their heads under water each time they pulled at him, and not being used to such diving, though all of them good swimmers, they were exhausted to that degree, they were forced to give over, without getting more than two or three joints of the back-bone, which they threw up to us on the rock. The reason was, the greater part of this sea monster, that is, his ribs and spine, were firmly bedded in the sand, whereby we concluded he had lain there some time, and had settled down into the sand by degrees. Seeing they could not do better for this turn, I called to them to leave the body of the fish, and try for his head: after much effort, pushing with the hand-spike, and hacking with their knives, they got the head free from the neck joint, with no little trouble, and dragged it out to land.

It might have made any one's hair stand on end to view the monstrous jaws of this fish's skull, armed each of them with three rows of teeth, sharp as knives, and whiter than the polished knife-handle, aye, at a nobleman's table. When we felt the edges of these teeth, it was easy to credit the accounts of what a shark can do; which I had put down among other sailor's tales. We closed the jaws and opened them again, marking how the rows of teeth shut upon one another, the outer on the outer, and the inner on the inner, so that what was not clean cut asunder in these cruel jaws would be mangled and torn, as by a two-fold and threefold set of pointed knives.

"A pretty fellow," at length, said Hilton; "a nice customer this, to meet with on our swim into the sea-cave. We should soon be past praying for, if he got a snap at us."

"Past praying for?" asked Don Manuel, not under-standing his words. "How, friend, can any one be that, who is not certainly in heaven, nor certainly in hell?"

"I mean," says Hilton, a little surly at being taken up, though it was so gently; "I mean we should surely go down at once to Davy Jones's locker."*

"Whither?" asks the priest again; and it was plain he wanted to understand what the man meant.

---

* An expression among sailors for the bottom of the sea.—ED.

"Why, of course," broke in Prodgers in his rough way, "any of us who got into such a brute's jaws as that, would be soon dead, and something worse : that's what he means, I take it."

Don Manuel looked graver than was common with him ; and turning upon old Prodgers, mildly and quite calm, he says :—

"Comrade, there is indeed one thing worse after an unprepared death : and there *are* jaws more cruel to fall into than those of a shark.  If you meant those solemn wholesome truths, we thank you for putting us in mind of them."

Every one felt what he intended by this, and there was a silence amongst us.  Prodgers had no answer ; even he was subdued, this time, by the priest's manner of speaking his few words.  But it was Don Manuel's way to make us grave and gay by turns.  After a little pause (for he seemed to wish us to think on what he had just said), he added, more cheerfully :

"Well, my friends, acknowledge that the Catholic Church is a gentle and compassionate mother : for she never reckons any to be *past praying for*, as long as she can hope they have died in grace."

---

## CHAPTER XIV.

### WE DO SOMETHING UNCOMMON.

"MEANWHILE," continued he, "what we have never settled is : where shall we pitch our tents?  For, like the patriarchs, we have the land all before us to choose. You, friend Owen, opened the parliament this morning with a neat little speech ; but we did not finish the debate.  'T is a great question for us, how and where to lodge ; so I vote we continue it now.  And who will give us any ideas on this?"

"Eldest go first," says Ned Hilton, nodding at Prodgers.

"Well," answered old Richard, gruffly, "I mean to take to a sea-faring life, and build myself a boat to fish in, and steer round the island."

"So you 'll make the cave your boat-house?" asked Tom Harvey: "the difficulty is, how to get in, or out again."

"That's my plan," Prodgers went on, not minding him; "and while I'm building my boat, I shall lodge somewhere about the rocks in this cove."

"Now, Harry," said I, "we listen to you."

"Well," answers he, "why not strike across the island, where you have shade, and clear water, as well as our water jars, and all with a westerly aspect?  Besides," added Gill, "that might be our best chance of seeing a ship, and making signals to be taken off this place."

I confess this idea had more than once occurred to me; in my mind I had debated which side of our island had the better prospect of some stray vessel touching there, or sighting it from a distance.  It was plain that what Gill now said had an effect on the men, who harkened eagerly.

"And you, Hilton," said I, at length.

Ned Hilton was one who seldom thought for himself; so he answered, that he would go for the present with Gill and look about him.

"Now, friends," said the priest, "will you hear a word of counsel?"

We listened to him; so he went on.

"Let us keep together, then," says he, "as we first decided, yet not perhaps to dwell under the same roof. Tastes differ, and dispositions too: we may best avoid little rubs and jars by having each our own hut, meeting every day for dinner, and for another thing, which we have not thought of much, as yet."

"And what's that?" enquired Gill.

"Prayer," says Don Manuel, laying a stress on the word; "prayer, my companions, which we owe to that bountiful Lord, who created us, and has now kept us from so many dangers.  I do not think we have said one prayer together since we have been on this island—each of us a monument of the Divine mercies.  Shall we not begin?

Shall we not even thank Him, nor ask Him to preserve us still? " and he looked round on us, waiting.

Any one of those he spoke to, I believe, would not have refused to kneel down with the good priest, had it not been for the others. But there is a kind of shame, of which the devil is the author, that holds men back from manfully professing that they feel the presence of God. And we were all so hardened in wickedness, and knew each other to be so, as made none of us willing to be the first in this new occupation. Prayer was what we had not practised, I may say, for a length of time; we were as awkward at beginning as a schoolboy who is called up to repeat a task he does not know. In a word, the enemy, as he often does, held us back from the first right step, by representing it as an insurmountable difficulty.

Thus we were all ashamed of each other as regards prayer, when we had not been so in our cursing and sin. But I resolved to shake this off, and set something of an example. So placing myself on my knees, and joining my hands (and I verily think the last time that had been done was by my mother on her death-bed, five years before), I bowed to the priest, and said:

"Well, sir; let us pray."

Tom Harvey, as I looked at him, shuffled a little; stood first on one leg, next on the other; then, as if he were doing a strange thing, he blushed liked a child that is caught stealing sugar, and went down on his knees.

As I guessed, so it turned out. Ned Hilton made the third, though with some hesitation. But Gill and Prodgers stood as they were, with their hands in their pockets, looking straight before them, and whistling, as sailors are used to whistle for a wind; but Prodgers was the more dogged in this, and Harry somewhat less so.

"O my God!" exclaimed the priest on his knees, looking up to heaven, "let there be none of us resisting a good inspiration: no spectators in this our first united prayer!"

Still, the two men did not budge.

"Señor Gill," pleaded he, in such a manner as I think few could withstand, "do you remember how lately you were all but gone into the other world, if that kind Providence, to whom you now refuse to bend the knee, had not guided our steps after you in time to find you lying sense-less in the cave?"

This shook Harry Gill, I could see; but his pride was not yet broken.

Just then, Tom Harvey, on his knees beside me, caught hold on my arm, pointing towards the cove. I followed his hand with my eyes, and plainly saw the back-fin of a large shark steering about over the water. He was right between that point of rock whence Harvey and the rest had jumped in, and the low-mouthed cave in the opposite cliff, to which they had well-nigh set out to swim.

"God ha' mercy!" cried Harvey, the tears in his eyes; "and we might have been by this time in his jaws. Lord be praised for His goodness to us poor fellows."

"Amen," said Hilton. Gill too, and even Prodgers felt moved at this sight; which did indeed seem like a re-prieve to a criminal when the rope is round his neck, and he just going to be turned off the ladder.

"Now, O Lord!" cried out Don Manuel from the depth of his heart: "let Thy grace at length triumph!"

So indeed it was. Gill fairly gave way now, and dropped on his knees, his face to the cove, keeping the shark before his eyes, to animate his thankfulness. The fish was steer-ing about, up and down, partly to seek his food, partly to play and bask in the sun; now he would break the water into ripples with slight strokes of his powerful tail, then he would float lazily again, but kept so near the surface of the water that the high back-fin was seen above. He was plainly of the white shark kind, like his elder brother whose skull was in our keeping: and this kind is the fiercest and most devouring of all the tribe.

He seemed to me in the water, what a savage bull is in a field, when he paces up and down, tearing up the earth and sods with his hoofs, lashing his sides with his tail, and seeking some one on whom to vent his rage. As I looked at that cruel fish (and he gave us opportunity to observe him at leisure), I felt more gratitude in my heart, than for many a long year, to our Father who is in heaven, and rules all things above and below, for having preserved us from the monster when we were about to rush into his very jaws.

We now waited only for Prodgers: as to the rest of us,

we were anxious, some more and some less, the priest should teach us how to pray. I had well-nigh said the shark taught us with as great effect; for he kept moving about full in view, as though he were a living witness, before our very eyes, of the good providence of God to us sinners. And this worked in Richard's mind till he, too, could resist no longer. He rubbed his eyes with the back of his hard hand, and slowly went down on one knee, as though he would have gainsayed it if he could, but was pressed down by some angel's hand upon his shoulder. Only I must remark, as the priest's prayer continued, Richard went down on both knees, like the rest.

## CHAPTER XV.

### PRAYER HINDERS NO WORK.

OUR good friend knew human nature too well to make this first prayer of ours a long one. But he poured out such fervent gratitude for the mercies we had received, and so humbly begged pardon for our want of thankfulness; he made such protests of amendment, he put our good resolutions into such glowing language, that our hearts at length went along with every word: there was no mistaking the men, that they were subdued and softened to a degree. These rough sea-faring men wept like very children before the priest concluded; and I believe every one of us now felt a pure pleasure in acknowledging our sins and the divine mercies, that we had been strangers to for years, if we had ever felt it before. I was in a manner transported out of myself: a new world was opening to me; from my inmost heart there rose the desire, "Oh; that this may continue!" Then I turned it into a prayer; "Good Lord, let not this pass away again!"

But the voice of the priest ceased; and there was silence

among us: so that we could hear (though we heeded it not) the ripple of the water that flowed into the cave where some of us had so nigh found a cruel death. Every one staid on his knees, as though he were afraid to break that newly-found holy calm. And as I stole a glance round on them, surprised at this, I saw most of our number with their eyes closed, as men who pray to themselves, or pondered on what they have heard.

It may be as surprising to others as (I own) it was to me, to find a change like this wrought upon such rude hearts, in so brief a space. But they that will put all things together; our double escape, first from the ship, then from this monster of the deep, together with the plenty and comfortable prospects (by comparison) we had found on this island, our security from savages, as also the influence Don Manuel had gained over us all, and our solitude itself, the nurse of devotion and good thoughts :—I say, let any one sum up the total of this, and he will, in some measure, cease to wonder at what I here record.

Be it as it may, before we wearied of our new employment, the priest stood up from his knees; and, turning to Prodgers, who chanced to be next him; "My dear brother," says he, "we have given thanks, and confessed our sins, to our common Creator and Lord: and now let me beg *your* pardon also, and through you to the rest, for any want of good example I have given you since we have known each other. You have heard," added he, with a little smile, "and heard often, I dare say, of people confessing to the priest; well, as you do not do this, here is the priest confessing to the people." So saying, he laid his hands on Prodgers' shoulders, and embraced him in the Spanish fashion.

"Oh, sir," faltered out Prodgers, and was scarce able to speak; his voice betrayed his emotion, whether he would or no: "we've never seen nothing in you, I'm sure, but what was good." And a murmur went round the rest, echoing the same.

"Nay," says Don Manuel, in his cheerful way, "we will not carry this on, friends, any further. But at least shake hands all round; and as you promised to stand by one another as companions in misfortune, do so now all the more as companions in consolation and prayer."

Never, I believe, or seldom, was there such a shaking of hands in Europe, or out of it.  The men all joined in a ring, and grasped each other's hands hard, while the tears stood in their eyes, and they looked upward.

"Now," cried Don Manuel in a sprightly tone, "having done this, for which I humbly thank God from my heart, let us think of our good friend, the shark yonder.  'T is time to look after him, for he has been patient to wait for us all this while."

We caught up our guns, eager for the sport : and were marching down to the shore, when all at once I bethought me.  "Halt!" cried I; "though I do not take this gentleman to be one of your timorous kind among fishes, like a shy trout in a pool, that hides himself among weeds and stones, yet there may be such a thing as frightening away a shark, after all.  So let us observe some generalship, lest we lose him.  Our best chance of killing is, to hit him in the head ; otherwise, the monster has as many lives as a cat, and will swim off easily with all our bullets in him, and laugh at us as he goes."  "I think, though," said Harvey, "it were well if one of us aimed at the heart or so, to have a double chance with him."  "But how will you get at his heart?" asked Harry Gill; "for he's a sturdy sort of fellow, mind ; and I don't think," he added, his recklessness getting the better of him again, "you'll be likely to soften him, as we were, by asking him"—Don Manuel laid his hand, quite friendly, on his shoulder, and Gill stopped, grew red, and looked down.

"The only way," said the priest, saving Harry from this confusion being noticed, "the only way to hit him in the body, while he keeps under water, is to fire *into* the water, on this side of him."  "Why so?" asks Prodgers, questioning everything, though not quite in his old rough way.  "Because," answered the Don, "you make the water convey your bullet at an angle to the mark you would hit, which it does almost as free and forcibly as the air."

"Like the Irishman's gun that could shoot round a corner," says Hilton, laughing.  "And so it could," replied the priest, good humouredly, " if there was a wall, or tree, at the corner, for the ball to glance from.  Did you never hear how one of your English kings, William Rufus, met his death ? "

" Never heard of him at all," says Hilton.

## CHAPTER XVI.

### FIRE INTO THE ENEMY'S CAMP, AND RETREAT TO OUR OWN.

ALL this time, the shark, our enemy, showed himself no ways disposed to get out of reach.  I think he had caught sight of us, and was waiting to see what chance he had of making a supper off some of our number : this I judged from his lifting his head ever and again over the water, turning his eye our way ; for the shark can turn his eye every way, like a human creature, which gives him that cruel look he has, as though he meant mischief. We thanked him for his good intentions, but resolved to be even with him, if we could any how compass it.  So we formed our plan of attack, thus :

Harry Gill was to get out on the ledge of the rock, from which Harvey had seen the skeleton in the shallow ; to be ready to cut off the enemy's retreat, should we only wound him ; and to give his worship a parting salute, to finish him off.  This being agreed on, Harry started, to take up his post, and be in readiness : but we called to him to beware of his footing, and keep away from the edge (the sea-weed being as slippery hereabouts as on the other side of the island) ; lest a false step should bring him more than a ducking, and cast him into the jaws of this monster, who kept his eye on him all the while as he drew nearer, and swam nearer also, edging towards the low reef of rocks on which Gill was picking his way.  However, we needed not to caution Harry ; for the danger was full in view, and he went on steadily, till he judged he had got far enough. Then he stood still, and looked back to us, waving his hand.

As for the rest, we drew up in a line, ready to give our shark a volley on the first sign of his sheering off. But Don Manuel came in with a word of counsel.

"Throw him," says he, " a piece of the monkey ; then fire at his heart, as he turns to seize it."

So said, so done : Prodgers took up a leg, and pitched it into the water with a good splash, and the bait fell in, about half-way between the fish and the strand. No sooner had it touched the water, than the shark darted at it like a cat after a mouse, lashing the sea into foam as he swam to it. "Now, be ready!" cries Don Manuel; and we levelled our pieces at once. We had not to wait an instant ; for the shark, after trying to gorge the bait as he darted at it, turned on his side to take it into his jaws ; then the under side of this huge fish was a fair mark for our bullets.

"Fire!" shouted I, and pulled my trigger. So did the rest, with steadiness ; thus the two fowling pieces and my rifle (for we had loaded the old condemned piece for this turn) were all discharged, and took effect, as we found afterwards.

It was getting so dark, we could just see the whiteness of the creature's side as he turned to gorge his prey, and the flash of the water as we hit him. But we heard, plain enough, the snort he gave, from pain and rage, as he shot off towards the open sea on receiving our charge. It was plain, also, from the motion of the back-fin above the water, that he swam more feebly ; indeed, spite of the great strength and power of life possessed by this monster, he must have been badly wounded with all he had got.

"Now, Gill! now, Harry!" cried out every one, as the enemy sheared off from us ; "don't let him go, man ! Why don't you fire ?" "Like a land-lubber, as you are," added Prodgers, in a heat.

But Gill took steady aim, kneeling on one knee, and propped his gun surely : then, as the fish went by him, he delivered his fire like a true marksman, aiming at his head. Then we heard another bubbling snort, louder than the first; and the shark dived, or sank, under water.

" 'T is all over for to-night," observed Hilton: for we could now scarce see the length of the muzzle as we pointed our guns; and there being no moon at this time, the sooner we prepared to encamp the better. So we followed our plan of last night; gathering our brushwood, though we found it not in such plenty on this part of the island. When this was kindled, we unpacked our supper, and spread it on the ground: then, what with the monkey, which we munched, with our eyes shut, and wry faces, what with the remains of our peccary and bread-fruit, eked out by the cocoa nuts, we made out a meal pretty fairly. But all our talk was of the sea-monster, and what chance we had of him in the morning. Gill made sure of having hit him in the head; indeed I hoped so too, from the noise he made, and his going down at once on getting the shot. "That," said Hilton, "with what he had got before, would settle him quietly." Tom Harvey thought he had managed to get out to sea: and so, though he might be dead as a door-nail, we should be none the better of him. "Well," said I, "if we get him after all, he will be no small prize in many ways." "What will he serve for," asked Prodgers, "more than to rid us of one enemy, while there may be more of his squadron cruising on the same tack?"

On this I told them, if we could capture our fish to-morrow, he would serve many useful ends. First, his teeth would furnish us with more arrow-heads; and with the stock we had, would fill our quivers, had we been so many Tartar bowmen. Then, the liver is known to yield an abundance of oil; sometimes to many gallons. "If we were Russians, instead of Tartars," says Gill, "that would be a prize." "Besides," continued I, "can we anyhow contrive to skin him, his rough hide will make shagreen for us, that will come in useful for more things than I can now tell. And his bones will turn into tools we can hardly do without: as, gimlets, files, pincers, and I know not what."

In a word, like housewives, more eager than sage, reckoning their chickens before they are hatched, we disposed of our shark, all to his bones, while as yet we

knew not if we should see him again.  And, having thus
cut him up and finished him, we finished our supper likewise.

"Now, my dear friends," says Don Manuel, "we have
proclaimed ourselves this day to be Christians, with a
sense of gratitude in our hearts : and we shall go to rest
as Christians, I am sure of it."

This time, it was no new idea to us to fall to our
prayers.  Our good priest knelt down, making the sign of
the cross on his forehead and breast ; wherein, I observed,
Hilton tried to do like him, awkwardly enough.  Then
Don Manuel, adoring the presence of God, and thanking
Him anew for His protection, proceeded to examine his
conscience aloud, while we listened on our knees, all wondering ; this being a thing stranger to us even than
prayer.  He asked himself how he had spent that day ;
did he give his first thoughts to God ?—how often had he
recalled the divine presence?—what had been his thoughts,
his words, his actions?—had he carefully kept himself
from sin, whether of anger or any other kind ? (here old
Prodgers gave a gruff sort of "hum!" that nearly set
Hilton off laughing :) had he considered others with
charity, or provoked them to offend God? (and at this,
Harry Gill got rather red) : and so on through a few
other questions, which were almost as strange to us as
though he had spoken a foreign tongue.  Lastly, the
priest asked himself, what were his resolutions for the
time to come, if his life was spared through the night ?—
did he detest his sins because they were displeasing to
the Good God? and, breaking forth with fervour, he then
said :

"O my God!  I am heartily sorry for having offended
Thee ; and I detest my sins most sincerely, because they
are displeasing to Thee, my God ! who art so deserving of
all my love for Thy infinite goodness and most amiable
perfections : and I firmly purpose, by the help of Thy
grace, never more to offend Thee, and carefully to avoid
all occasions of sin."

Our souls being thus refreshed by prayer, we settled
down to refresh our bodies with sleep ; and stirred our
fire, though we now felt more secure against wild beasts ;
yet, on these few first nights in this strange place, we

used it as a precaution, that we might go to rest without
an anxious thought. Then, gathering round it as we had
the night before, we lay down in full trust, and most of us
were sound asleep in a short space; only, Don Manuel
stepped aside to finish his prayers by himself.

---

## CHAPTER XVII.

### FIRE-SIDE TALK.

NO one will expect (should this record of the misery of
six poor men ever fall into any reader's hands) I am
to go on recording the after part of our exile as fully as
these first two days. One of my chief cares, which I imparted to the priest (for our two heads, I must say, had to
think for the rest), was, how to employ the men, and keep
them amused. 'T is true, we had enough to occupy our
time; for we had to build, to plant, to snare and tame
animals for our support; to fish, whether angling, or with
such rude nets as we might make shift to contrive; to
learn shooting, with arrows and javelins when our powder
was out; lastly, by some rude weaving, or the skins of
wild animals, we should have to supply us with clothes.
By these employments the time would not hang heavy,
could we persuade the men to keep to their work, and in
peace with one another. This last thought was the one
most on my mind, how to preserve harmony amongst us.
A short time had shown how ready the men were each to
indulge his humours at the expense of his fellows; and
how soon, with their uncurbed passions, provided, too,
with fire arms, some deadly feud might spring up to
plunge our small society into war, and give our island its
first taste of blood.

As I sat by the watch-fire, I mused in this fashion till I
was weary of thinking alone; and was glad when Don

Manuel stepped again into the circle of the firelight, and spread his cloak for his night's rest.  I asked him if he was too inclined for sleep to talk with me a while; then stated to him all that was in my thoughts.

"Well, friend," says he cheerfully, as was his wont; for of all men I ever knew, he was, I think. the cheerfulest: seldom laughing loud, like the rest, when the fit took them, but as seldom looking any ways downcast, and never sour or stern; "well," says he, "for quarrels, you see we have been able to build up something of a wall against them."

I could not make out what he meant by a wall; and looking at him to explain himself: "why, to be sure," says he, "by beginning to pray, and pray together."

"I must confess, sir," answered I, "these two turns that we have knelt down all in a body took me by surprise, like a new thing, and gave me another notion altogether of what praying means."

"Why so," asks he, turning his face upon me quickly: "you have prayed of course, my friend, ever since you were a child?"

I felt overcome with shame to be thought so much better than I deserved; and to have it taken for granted I had done what I knew myself to have been far enough from doing.  But Don Manuel went on, without taking notice of my silence; and, as if he spoke part to himself, part to me:

"Prayer," he said, "is the elevation or lifting of the soul to God.  Now, the higher the soul is lifted, the nearer it draws to Him; and the nearer it draws, the more like Him does it grow: then, you see, as God is the eternal tranquility and peace, so man, when he begins to pray, begins to know peace; and knowing peace in himself, loves to be at peace with others.  He gets one degree, say, of this blessed love of peace when he prays once; and is likely to get another degree of it the next time he prays, and so on:  just as a mason or bricklayer lays one course of stones or bricks for his wall, then another again, resting on that.  At last, the soul gains a confirmed habit of peace, and feels a great pain at being out of peace with anyone, or witnessing any breach of peace or charity: and this is like topping the whole with a coping stone. So, that is what I call building the wall. Is it not good masonry, my dear friend; and is it not worth while to raise such a wall against hatred, violence, misery?"

I could not answer him, I fairly own; for my heart filled, and well nigh overflowed. I sat looking into the fire; I felt the truth of all this good man had been saying. Yet his talk was as simple as a child's, as to the manner of it: only he seemed to speak with knowledge, and a sort of quiet authority, from having practised his doctrine, which I make no doubt he had done for years. After a while, I turned to him, and pursued our discourse:

"And there are some people, sir," said I, "who are not content to be at peace, but strive to make all others be so too."

He seemed a little put out, as if I had said what he did not know how to answer, and did not like to hear addressed to him.

"Yesterday," continued he, as if to turn it off, "when we were going up that mountain, we got into clearer air the higher we went, and could see further on every side of us. If any one asked you why, you would answer: of course, because we were higher up. So it is with our souls. When we struggle against the power of things present that would draw us from God, be they in the way of pleasure, or anger, or what you will, we are climbing up the mountain; sometimes with difficulty and pain, and in spite of many weights that would drag us down again. When we pray, we are climbing. When we give up to others for peace—when we must needs stand against others for principle—when we do good to others for charity—we are climbing. The oftener we do these things the higher we climb, and the stronger. The higher we climb, the more pleasant is the exertion, and the more delightful the prospect. I will give you some lines written by a poor heathen as much as two thousand five hundred years ago; and then reflect, if even *he* could see all this so clearly, what ought we Christians to think about it?"

Then he repeated with his strong foreign accent:

> " Baseness is easy, chosen by the throng,
> Nor rough the way, nor far to seek, nor long:

> Severer toil th' immortal gods have given
> To fence the narrow track that leads to heaven,
> All strait and steep, until the height be won;
> Then with a gentler toil it leads the traveller on."

"You see," continued Don Manuel, "a poor man who had so little idea of the One true God that he calls his idols 'the immortal gods,' still knew something of the truth we speak of.  Reason carried him a certain way: though by *virtue* he only meant a proud conformity of the life to the natural conscience; and knew nothing of that charity which is the true fulfilling of the law."

" Nothing of charity? " asked I.

" Certainly not," answered the priest, "for charity is a Christian virtue, and follows upon faith."

" Faith? " pursued I, as if I were determined to make objections: "but you, sir, as a Catholic, would say that we, who are not so, cannot even have faith? "

" You cannot, indeed, my dear friend," answered he, looking at me with much concern in his face; " and the greater pity for you.  But you may have several things like it, or paving the way to it, or producing some of its effects."

I looked at him, as if he were talking riddles.

" We are both too tired now." said he, giving a little yawn, " to follow this much further.  But you may have the beginnings of faith, or what prepares the way for it, or what is borrowed from its teachings to its own disciples; so you may do the same things (to some extent) as if you had faith, by a kind of imitation."

---

# CHAPTER XVIII.

### A FEW LITTLE DEBTS.

HE saw I was not satisfied; indeed, my looks easily showed it.

" If, now," pursued he, looking upward, " we had a moon at this time, which we have not, and if it were shining over our heads: it would be very bright, would it not, and very beautiful, and would sway the tides, and light the traveller on his road, and serve to read by, to some degree?"

I nodded, but could not see his drift.

"Well, after all: would it be the sun?"

I waited to hear further.

"No," pursued Don Manuel, speaking now with so much energy that he half roused some of the sleepers; and Prodgers began to mutter an oath in his sleep: "No! take that bright moon at her full, when she is most cloudless and most powerful; all her light is borrowed: it is a mere reflection from the sun. She is herself a dark, dull body: only capable of giving back and (as I may say) *reporting* the light she receives from the sun, the fountain of our light. Take away the sun, and the moon would be absolutely dark, as she is in a total eclipse. Do I weary you with this?"

"By no means," said I: "I do not see whither you are going; but I wish to follow to the end."

"I am only going to this point," replied he, smiling; "that the Catholic Church, to whom alone the mission of teaching the nations is given, fully enlightens her children, and also enlightens partly those who reject her. So that they still hold, as religious opinions, some portions of her teaching, though not by faith, nor in the right way. They get light from her, as the moon from the sun, by reflection. The faintest glimmer of twilight, or a meteor that shoots and expires, is better than total gloom: and a reflected light, though imperfect, is light as far as it goes. The Church has lower and lesser benefits for those who will not accept her best gifts; and at every turn makes many her debtors who least acknowledge the debt. But come; it is time to snatch a few hours' sleep."

"Stay one moment, sir, I beg you," cried I again, as he was settling himself to rest "What you say moves me, I can tell you. I do not half understand it, though.. Will you give me an instance of what you mean? What have we borrowed from your Church?"

Don Manuel reckoned up on his fingers.

"First," says he, "the sacred Scriptures themselves;

for without the authority of the Church you would not know which of the writings in the volume were inspired, even of those you acknowledge.   The Bible never tells us what *is* Bible and not Bible."

"Do not interrupt me now," added he, good-humouredly, "if you wish me to go through my list; 't is getting too late to do more than just read it over.   Let me go on. Secondly, you owe to us the change from the seventh day to the first day of the week, as a day to be kept holy; and if it were not for that, you would be grievously breaking one of the commandments every Saturday, and practising a vain observance every Sunday."

This staggered me, I confess; for, little as I had observed the Sunday for many years, except to idle it away, I did not forget the words of the commandment: "Remember thou keep holy the Sabbath day . . . the seventh day thou shalt do no manner of work."

"Thirdly," he went on, "but indeed, I should have put it first, you owe to us, as far as you really hold them, the true doctrines of the most Holy Trinity, and the Incarnation."

"Nay, now sir," cried I, with some heat, and felt angry with him, for the first time since our acquaintance; "how can you say we owe *this* to you?   Why, 't is part of our teaching too, I 've always heard—"

"Remind me as early to-morrow as you like," answered the priest, gently, "of the names, Sabellius and Nestorius; and I will explain my meaning.   Would you like me to finish my list?"

I made a sign, and not a gracious one; for I was put out by what he had said.

"Fourthly, then," continued he, "though I fear to vex you again by mentioning it, you owe to us the rest of all that is found in the Creeds, the Apostles' and the Nicene, as well as the Athanasian."

"Fifthly, 't is only by authority of the Catholic Church that you ventured to-day to taste of the peccary and the bustard, or the monkey without fear of sin."

By this, I thought he was laughing at me: no sooner did he see it in my countenance, than he laid his hand on my shoulder as I sat, saying:

"You do not suppose I would jest in that way?   I was

never more serious. It would take some time to explain what I mean : only remember, there was a divine command against eating flesh with the blood in it, issued before the law of Moses, and continued after it, by the Apostles.* Now, unless the Church can pronounce that the command was not always to bind, you are bound by it, at this moment. The Council of Jerusalem, which was assembled under the guidance of the Holy Spirit, bound it on the disciples, even when they were freed from the Mosaic law. But if you are bound by it, you have been guilty of a grievous sin this day, and most days of your life, as I have stated. That is what I mean ; and thus, your release from that law of not eating blood with the meat makes your fifth obligation to the Catholic Church."

I could not have kept anger in my heart against him, so simple and frank was he ; even had he meant a jest upon me ; but I now felt sure he did not. So I begged him to go on, and my old trust in him revived.

"I've done with the little finger of my left hand," says he, smiling, "and give you notice, friend, I'll not go beyond the middle finger of the other. Three more points, and then I go to sleep."

"In the sixth place : do you not owe to the Catholic Church whatever benefit you reckon to belong to confirmation, if you think you have been confirmed? for she has always taught and used it as a sacrament, and they who say no, have kept it as at least a form."

"Seventhly ; as you (or your teachers) think you have among you a Christian ministry, handed down from the Apostles : though I could not honestly say you have, yet if you had, you could only have it from us, as your learned writers acknowledge, nay, maintain tooth and nail, as their only chance."

"Eighthly—and last : if not from the Catholics, whence do you get your solemn cathedrals, that you make so little use of ; your beautiful parish churches, each with the title of a Catholic saint, each with the altar-steps from which the altar has been broken away ; your stately colleges and halls of learning, whose very names, as Corpus Christi, St. Mary's, All Souls', Peterhouse, prove they

* See *Gen.*, iv. 4 ; *Acts*, xv. 20, 29.—ED.

come from us; your ancient alms-houses, where even now, a dole is given daily (I am told*) to the wayfarer and the mendicant, as was once done at every convent gate; your fasts and festivals, which you keep, or not, just as you please, eating your salt-fish with egg sauce before your roast beef, on Ash Wednesday and Good Friday; your ruined abbeys, which you visit on pic-nics and parties of pleasure; your healing springs, that cure even those who take them to be only chalybeate or medicinal waters :—and so on, down to the market crosses in your provincial towns, which afford a pedestal for the town clock, and a shelter for the town crier with his bell on rainy days."

"Enough for to-night," added he, yawning a little again: "so I omit Magna Charta, Habeas Corpus, and other bulwarks of the British Constitution, together with the whole banking system, that would keep us up till midnight.  Now, wholesome slumbers with the blessing of God."

The priest wrapped himself in his cloak; and making again the sign of the cross, nodded to me with a kind look, and was soon quietly asleep.

## CHAPTER XIX.

### WE GAIN OUR PRIZE.

I SAT there by the fire, thinking on what he had said; and found much in it very new to me, and some things I would fain answer, but could not: till I dropped off to sleep in my turn.

We were woke in the morning by a shouting that caused

---

* This is at least the case at the hospital of Holy Cross, near Winchester, at the gate of which (by antient charter) a piece of bread and cup of small beer may be daily claimed by every wayfarer.—ED.

us all to spring on our feet; we caught up our guns, to be ready against surprise. Our first thought was of savages having landed in the night: but seeing Hilton was not among us, we listened again, and presently knew it was his voice that shouted to us from the cove. We ran down to him, eager to get some news of the shark: for that, we judged, was the meaning of the noise he made.

So soon as we got clear of the trees, we saw the shark indeed, floating quite dead (as it seemed), about a quarter of a mile off shore, and Ned Hilton almost beside himself with joy; he danced on the sand with extravagant gestures; he sang snatches of a sea-song; then he shouted, now to us to come quick, now to the shark, inviting him to land: in short, I thought he had taken leave of his wits, so like a senseless creature did he behave. Indeed, I believe he was as over-joyed at this discovery as ever a needy man who found in his garden a pot full of guineas to pay his debts with.

Such conduct in a rough jack-tar might at first appear extravagant, even to madness: and my putting it down thus simply, just as it happened, is like to expose me in the eyes of some critics to a charge of romancing:—inasmuch as romances, I suppose, are made up of overstrained feelings and unlikely adventures, which make real life, and common events and duties, appear dull and flat enough after them. And in this (said Don Manuel to me, later) lies their chief harm: not that they be always vicious—though too often even so—but that they excite and keep a strain on the attention and spirits, even as a dram does the nerves; and so weaken the strings that ought to link the emotions of our minds to the acts of our will.

However, to return to Hilton and his extravagant joy; it is to be considered, the interest we take in the objects round us is measured by the degree of employment we have for our thoughts. And I have read of a poor prisoner, chained for many years in a dungeon, who by great patience had tamed a spider in his cell, so that the creature would come to him, when he whistled to it, out of a crack in the wall; and how fond he grew of it, and made it his companion: how the brutal gaolor, finding what delight the poor man took in this reptile, shook it on the ground one day when he came in, and crushed it with his foot;

also how the man took it to heart, and was like to pine for
the loss of his friend the spider.   So that poor Ned might
be excused for the excess of spirits he showed when the
shark came back to us, after we had so nearly lost him.

Our concern was now, to possess ourselves of this monster, and bring him to land.   First, we could not be sure
he was truly dead: for these creatures keep their life in
them so long, I judged it fool-hardy for any one to swim
out to him and fasten a noose of twine round him, which
was what Hilton proposed.   After a while, we had the
satisfaction to see the tide was setting in for the cove;
we had but to wait till the carcass should drift in nearer.
But I proposed to try with the rifle (the only piece among
us that would touch him at that distance), if he were dead
beyond a doubt: and I complimented Harry Gill by giving
him first shot at our enemy.   So Gill began by marking
the bullet, to know it again; then, taking good aim, fired
and hit him (as we judged) under the side-fin; but he
stirred not, nor gave sign of life; whereby we knew him
for dead, and cheered for Harry Gill, whose shot had killed
him yesternight.

After this, I raised no objection to any one swimming
off to take the shark in tow.   But all were content to wait
till the tide should bring him in, which it did nearer at
every beat of the waves; a little wind blowing at the
time up the cove.   As he lay broadside on, he came drifting in heavily, till we could measure him with our eyes:
then we saw he was indeed a monstrous fish, bigger than
the skeleton that lay in the shallow.   We judged him
nigh thirty feet in length, as it afterwards proved, when
he came to land.   To be short, the tide brought him so
near, the four men waded into the water with the hand-
spike, and Don Manuel's walking staff.   By help of these,
they managed to turn the shark's head in shore, and so
waited till the tide should ground him, which it did about
half an hour after our shot.

# CHAPTER XX.

### BLOWN INTO HARBOUR.

THE wind kept still blowing up the cove, and freshened as the morning advanced: for had it not, I believe we had never got our prize high enough on shore to be of use to us. This wind increased so much upon us within half an hour after the shark touched land, as made us look out for a squall: but when it came, 't was no squall, but a hurricane. The sky grew blacker in the offing than ever I saw it in my country on a dark day in November; on every side the sea-birds flew screaming in, and swept close by us, so that, had we nothing else to do, we could have knocked them over with our staves: and the power of the wind was such as bent some palm-trees near the shore, as though they had been saplings, or whips of osier.

Our only safety was to throw ourselves flat on our faces; which we all did at once, not before the wind had twirled away Prodgers' hat, and sent it high in the air, so that we found it not for near a se'ennight after, in a banana tree some half mile (I am sure) from the place we were in. But now was no moment for grumbling, or thinking on hats: for the storm waxed to an awful pitch, as it does in the tropics when it bursts in earnest.

What with the rending of the branches of trees, and roar of the waves, that came driving up our cove, as fleet as a race-horse, and raging like a tiger, tossing their foam high as the very trees, and drenching us with the spray; and what with the thunder of the surf that broke on the coral reef outside our harbour, the scene was beyond anything I can put down on paper. The tide washed up so near the place where we had anchored ourselves at full length, we were no longer safe in staying there: I began to think a third wave (as they say the third wave is ever the highest) would go over us, and suck us back into the wild sea. So, choosing a moment when there seemed a lull, or at least the wind not being so raging as before, we

were up and scudding before the storm ; till we reached
some underwood that lay perhaps two hundred yards in-
shore : yet not under the higher trees, for that we dreaded,
lest they should be torn up, or their branches rent off, and
crush us out of life.

As to our prize, that we had been so anxious to secure
one short hour before this tempest broke upon our heads,
we thought of it so little, that all the sharks that ever
swam might have floated out to seaward, without our
bestowing a thought on their loss to us.   So important do
things appear to us mortals, till something more weighty
comes in, to wipe them clean out of our minds !

But this was not all : for the rain, or water-spout rather,
began now to pour down upon us in a deluge ; so that we
were forced from our brushwood, would we or no, and
driven to seek some shelter, though already we had not a
dry stitch on us : a thing woeful enough, seeing we had
no change of garments awaiting us in this wide world.
We dragged our way, so well as we could, the force of the
wind not abating, into the wood ; holding on by the bushes,
till we were sheltered by the trees, cocoa and banana,
with others, that grew pretty thick hereabouts, and plenty.
We ran which way soever the wind would take us, not
thinking of aught, but to get free of this deluge of rain :
however, we guessed at the time, we were making for the
ridge, or back-bone of rock that formed the south end of
this island.

"T was not long before we saw the upper parts of the
cliff towering above our heads ; and the trees that crowned
it, bending and swaying every way under the tornado of
wind : then, working our way further, we got under this
wall of rock, which rose sheer up, like to the side of a
house.   But what comforted us most, was to see, about
twenty steps as you turned to the left, a mass or crag of
rock, that had fallen (I suppose) from the height, or been
split off from the main cliff by some earthquake.   This
bent over to the cliff it had been torn from, at an angle, so
that the upper part I guessed to be within eight feet of it,
while the base was at least as many yards distant from
the cliff : it looked dangerous, as though it would fall upon
us if we got under it : till we considered, it had hung in
that way for many ages, forasmuch as trees of a large

growth had sprung up between the two portions of rock. Besides, the fallen mass was covered with shrubs that grew upright on it, feathering to its very top.

"Here," says Don Manuel, looking about him, "is our shelter till the hurricane be past: and I see not but it may be so for many a day to come: for where will you find," continued he, as we wrung out our jackets, "a better shelter than this rock over head? see, no drop of the pelting rain hath reached us here: then, the trees round about will be both shade and defence, and we could plant ourselves out from the world, so that neither savage nor wild beast could find our hiding-place."

"Aye, but," persisted Gill, going back to his first idea, "we have no view here of the sea: a ship might touch at the island, and send her boat ashore, and we be none the wiser, and so lose our chance to get out of this prison."

"I see a way out of that," says Tom Harvey; "for 't is easy to climb this rock, and so to the cliff overhead; then we shall have a clear look-out both ways."

"You 've hit it, messmate," cries Hilton, clapping him on the shoulder, "so here goes for a scramble;" with that, he sprang up the rock, by help of the roots of the brushwood that grew on it, as he would up the shrouds of a ship. Harvey was after him; and we all followed; for by this time the worst of the hurricane was over, though the wind moaned and the waves were lashing in fury, as high as ever. But we were now soaked through, and feared neither rain or spray, nor wet branches neither.

From the top of our rock on to the main cliff was an easy leap; for, as I said, the distance at top was not more than seven or eight feet; and there was a little dent, or landing-place in the cliff opposite, worn by rain, or sawn out by the branches; it gave us sure footing, so we sprang across. Then a smart climb brought us to the look-out, from which we could sweep the horizon round, stopped only by our volcano (so I called it always) to the north of the island. We gave a glance out to westward of our little kingdom; but all was quiet there, at least by comparison: for this gale had come upon us from east-by-south, or from that to due east. Harvey begged for the loan of my glass; then laid himself down flat, pulled his hat over his brows, and looked out in the wind's eye.

# CHAPTER XXI.

### A NEW ARRIVAL.

AS he looked, I heard him say softly, to himself: " Some-thing 's out there in the offing I cannot make out. Is it another big shark, or what ? " Then, after looking, long and steady, he jumped up, and shouted out: " Boat, ahoy ! "

I do believe, had a dead man spoken, we could scarce have been more taken aback than by this cry of Tom Harvey's. All were on the alert, and Prodgers and Gill scuffled for the glass between them; but Tom gave it back to me, while I lay down flat to take an observation of the unlooked-for stranger. It was indeed a boat, I saw, but of what kind I could not so well distinguish; only, from the prow of it running up (so far as I could judge while it sported like a feather on the angry waves) into a high peak, like the Indian canoes of the South seas, I set it down for no boat built in Europe or the colonies. It came driving in; and first through the glass, then with the naked eye, we could see men in it : they seemed to be three or four, but could not manage the boat, as was plain from the way she tossed and drove before the wind. So they came on for the coral reef, and we expected every moment to see her go to pieces. " Lord, have mercy on their poor souls ! " cried the priest, dropping on his knees. We all answered, Amen ; for the danger was so great, we gave them up for lost, and kept looking on, and wondered to see the boat hold out still. Only Don Manuel kept kneeling, and prayed on without moving. By this the boat was within a wave or two of the reef; in a few moments more, a huge roller lifted her up, stern foremost, right over into our cove, with all on board: she was capsized as she came, and the crew flung into the boiling sea.

At this, with one impulse, we ran down at our best speed towards the shore ; making for that ledge of rock on which Harvey had stood, as I said, when he found the dead shark that had nearly decoyed us into the jaws of the live one. For this point we made straight; judging, as we ran, 't would be our best chance to deliver this ill-fated crew, who must else perish before our very eyes in the water. The boat had been flung clean over the coral reef, as you might cast a stone or weed over a garden wall; as we came nearer, we could observe she floated, only keel upwards; for she had a rude kind of jury-keel fastened on her, though partly torn away. Nor did she fill, nor go down, as she would if the wave that sent her into the cove had been less full-bodied or powerful; for then she must have knocked about, on and off the reef, till she had either sunk, or fairly gone to pieces.

But the condition of the poor souls that had manned her was scarce less desperate than if they had been left outside the reef. The surf was still boiling so high and wild, we could not well see how matters stood with these poor fellows: but soon we saw, to our sorrow, one of them was dead already; for he was rolled over and over again by the furious waves, and made no motion to swim. For the rest, they made a struggle indeed, but a weak one, against the fury of the rollers that drove over them: two of these savages struck out for land, swimming manfully, though every other moment they were under water again. One (he seemed but a lad) clung fast to the canoe; this one, we thought, had the best chance, if only he could hold out a while longer: for he had managed to scramble on to the keel, and held on with the grip of despair, while the boat came higher up the cove with each stroke of the waves. Yet he was not the first to reach shore, neither: for by this time we had made shift to reeve our twine (the best cable we had) into a noose, and Harvey had found a log of a tree, of a biggish thickness, to answer the purpose of a rude kind of life-buoy.

Having secured this log or billet in the noose of our twine, we all stood as near as we dared to the margin of the cove; with one heave we hove it into the sea, to the nearest of the men that were struggling to reach us. The Indian, as we had already seen them all to be, swam for it with his remaining strength, and after catching it once and losing it, he caught it again, and held it fast. Indeed it held him fast, too: for in the confusion of the waves that boiled around him, twisting him about like a straw in a mill-dam, he got the twine round his arm, and it cut him till the blood came. But this he regarded not: for what will not a man disregard when life itself is at stake? besides, he was by this time so spent, I question if at the moment he much felt it. After all, he ran a chance of being strangled in the water for very weakness: had not Hilton and Tom Harvey now waded in, and pulled him by main force to land.

Dead enough this Indian seemed to be, as the priest and I carried him from the surf, and laid him on the sand: but by chafing him both together, with holding his head so as to disgorge the sea-water he had swallowed, we had the comfort to bring him round, after a while. Then I left him, to see to the other two, that were still struggling in the waves; but Don Manuel stayed with the first one, lest he should faint again. His fellow-swimmer, as we watched him, had a harder escape; we judged him older than the first, he swam so feebly; and while he still had some little way to make, we saw him cease to strike out altogether, and then he sank slowly.

At this, the poor lad who still clung to the canoe, set up the most dismal howl you ever heard: more like the cry of a wild beast at night, than any sound from human lips. We knew not then, this old man was the lad's own father; but his cry, and the sight of the sinking Indian, put us to our wits' ends to save him; yet all without success, had it not been for Tom Harvey again.

"Life is sweet, boys!" cried he; "though it be but the life of a savage Indian. Join hands all in a line, and I'm foremost man at him!" Don Manuel came running down to take his share in this action, and dashed into the water, next to Harvey. Then came Gill, forward for anything, and so the others, holding hands firm: so Harvey, part swimming, part wading, though he was beaten back once or twice, and the chain of hands all but broken by the waves (which yet were subsiding apace), came up to the savage, whose head was now above water again, driving on for shore, though at the last gasp; and seizing him by his long hair, Tom called to the rest to haul them ashore.

We soon found, our brave Tom had risked his life in more than one way to save this fellow-creature's; for the sinking man, feeling something to grapple with, clung round Harvey with such a grasp as was more than he could do to shake off.  In another minute, they had both surely sunk together : when Harry Gill without more ado, caught Don Manuel's staff out of his hand before he was aware, and dealt the Indian such a blow with it on the head as sent him under water again.  There came another wild cry from the lad, who was drifting in upon his canoe ; and he sprung off it into the waves, to try and save his father.

It seemed a cruel act at the time ; and doubtless admitted no defence, were it not a balance between losing two lives without remedy, and risking one only.  Add to this, Harvey was a Christian born, and so a life nearer to us than the savage's ; he our comrade, and the other a stranger cast upon our shore ; he had risked a life, too, that was in no danger, and that was his own to keep, for a life that was all but gone ; and that life we had a chance of saving, after we had rescued Tom's.  I know not what our priest would have said in the case ; for after the thing was over, it never chanced that we discussed it among ourselves.  But putting all together, though my first impulse was of anger against Gill, yet, thinking on it after, I knew not how to blame him much for what he had done on the spur of the moment.  Be that as it will, our first concern was to fish up the poor old Indian ; which we managed at length, with no small pains : and brought him to the surface, and so to land, as dead as a door-nail, so far as we could see.

We all were in sad case enough, when this was over : wet and wearied, and chilled to the bone ; Tom Harvey half choked with his struggle, and the sea-water he had swallowed ; Don Manuel not much better : and, for our captives, or guests, call them which you will, one seemingly dead, with all our chafing of his limbs, for it failed to bring him to ; the other scarce able to sit up and moan ; and the young savage howling and tearing his hair like a mad thing over the body of his father.  To look at us there on the shore, one would have thought a slave-ship had been wrecked in that hurricane, and we, part of the crew, with a few of the slaves, escaped with our lives from the raging sea.

## CHAPTER XXII.

### DOCTORING AND PURVEYING.

THE second Indian, with all our skill and care bestowed, came round but slowly: we were busied around him, Don Manuel and I, in the mode of regular practice, and the young savage in a ruder way, for he crumpled up his father's fingers, and pulled his ears, enough (one would think) to make a very statue cry out. But it was done out of love, to bring him to: for I never saw more concern expressed than in this poor young creature at what he supposed his father's death. Now, he would kneel beside him on the sand, using those cruel remedies: now he would fling himself on the body, weeping and howling: then he sprang up, stretching his clenched hands towards the sky, as pleading to the gods he was taught to worship, to give him back the life of his father. At last, espying a sharp shell on the sand, he seized it in an access of fury, and began to give such wounds to his own head and cheeks, that he soon ran down with blood.

The men had looked on, up to now, with much concern, to see the wild grief of this untaught nature; but when he thus began to scarify himself, Harvey and Prodgers seized each a hand, and stayed him. The young savage struggled from them with all his might; when they took the shell out of his clenched fist, he turned upon them with threatening gestures, still pointing upward. This action we did not understand at the time, until we had learned to communicate with these savages in a mixed language, part English and part Indian: then, indeed, we made out from the lad that he had offered his blood as a sacrifice for the life of his father.

But Richard Prodgers, having begun to practise charity, seemed inspired with another happy idea; and pulling his flask of brandy out of his pocket, handed it to me, saying: "Try the poor old fellow with a drop of this; and 't is a wonder I had n't thought on 't before." Indeed, it was dull of myself, too, not to have thought of the brandy as a remedy for drowning. However, now we applied it in right earnest, and gave the dead man (as he seemed) his first taste of that "fire water" which has been so fatal to many another, savage and civilized alike.

Whether the brandy took more effect on one who had never tasted it, or that all we had done for him began to revive him; certain it is, when we had poured some of this down his throat, he began to choke violently, then sneezed once or twice, and opened his eyes. We now lifted him up; though he could not stand, we propped him up for some time, then began to walk him about slowly, till he gained some use of his limbs.

But you should have seen the joy of the son when he saw his father revive again. Nothing was too extravagant for him to make known his feelings by: he gambolled and capered on before him, shouting, patting him on the head and cheeks, talking to him in his own language, which had the strangest discordant sound, formed, as it seemed, down in the throat: so he went on, till the old man, growing faint, pointed with his finger to his mouth, to make known to us he wanted food.

Want of food seemed now the prevailing disease amongst us : every man felt by this time he had earned his breakfast, but when we set about preparing for it, we found little enough left in the larder. The shark had devoured the last of our monkey; and of the remaining provender, all but a few scraps was gone, so wasteful had we been. So, setting Don Manuel, with Prodgers and Harvey, to have an eye to our Indian friends, lest they might give us the slip, and get into the woods, to be a trouble to us after (though the creatures were too weak and dispirited to have any thoughts of it at that time), I took my rifle, and ranged with Hilton and Gill into the thicket, to cater for the party. We took the young savage with us, motioning him by signs to keep close at our heels, and not get before us ; as well that he might be out of danger from our shot, as to prevent him from escaping. But he, for his part, had nothing of the kind in his head : being occupied with observing us, which he did with all astonishment ; he regarded us (so we judged from his looks) as beings of some superior order in human shape, and much, I suppose, as we should regard an angel that were to appear to us ; though anything less like angels, in appearance or spirit, seldom has been seen on this earth.  However, the Indian had followed us obediently; and, seeing from our actions what we were about, he took up a smooth stone or two that lay in his path, making signs to us that he would knock down any animal that came in his way, and kill it, and bring it to us to eat.  All this we made out readily from his dumb show, which was so expressive, we could not mistake it, and so ridiculous, we could not choose but laugh at it heartily.  We answered him likewise by signs, bidding him come along, and drop the stones again; which he did with submission, and followed us like a very slave, crossing his hands on his breast.

We had not gone very far, till we roused an animal out of the thicket, such as we had not seen before: neither did we often meet with such in our residence on the island; nor could I well account for our meeting this one at the present.  Something it was of the hog kind, though not in all things like our peccary, neither: but anything in shape of food was acceptable to our hunger, so I knocked it over with my rifle, and Harvey picked it up stone dead, or drew it along, rather.

But we, that were used to the sound and effect of fire-arms, did not reckon on what they would produce upon the spirits of one that never yet had heard them.  We were surprised to see our young savage fall to the earth on the sound of my piece's discharge: he lay like a dead thing, on his face; and when we came to him and stirred him, bidding him get on his feet again, he only rose to his knees, supplicating us with the most moving gestures, and pointing to the rifle I held in my hand: then speaking to it, as though it were a live thing, and beseeching it not to kill him.

This made us merry again; till the distress of the savage moved us to some compassion.  I came to him, and took him by the hand, holding my gun behind me, to assure him I meant him no harm, and so raised him to his feet. When he had gained some courage, he looked anxiously about for the piece that had been fired: but when I brought it forward, all his fears revived, and I believe he would have fled away, only by my voice I half commanded and half encouraged him to stand still.  Then I presented to him the stock of my rifle, and moved it towards him:

he trembled from head to foot as he eyed it; at length,
falling on his knees again, he placed the butt of the piece
on his head, and clasped his hands over it, by which I saw
he meant to worship it.

## CHAPTER XXIII.

### WE ARE TAKEN TO BE GODS.

AMONGST us, there were not many scruples, or grains,
of religion, except what our priest had taught us
lately: notwithstanding, we were struck with horror to behold this ignorant savage bowing himself down thus to the
stock of a tree.  I took the rifle from him angrily, pointing upwards to the sky; to make him understand that life
and death came from thence alone.  He seemed partly to
understand me; nodding his head and smiling, he pointed
upwards too, and then to the gun; by which I made out
that the god whom he had worshipped (in his blind way)
had sent down this piece upon earth, or had come to dwell
in it, and so had worked the wonderful effects he had seen
it produce.  But when I handled the rifle again, and began to sponge it with my ramrod, and load it with powder
and ball, then he changed his opinion, and began to think,
as I was master of this terrible engine, and could do with
it as I would, I must needs myself be a god.

He crept to me with all possible signs of reverence and
fear; touching the ground several times with his forehead as he came; then, drawing nearer, he took my foot
with a trembling hand, and placed it on his head as he lay
in the dust.  This I refused with a frowning countenance;
and raised my hand again to heaven, forbidding him to
worship a creature such as I: but all was of no use.  The
poor Indian could not get it out of his thoughts that we
were masters of the thunder and lightning, and could do
what we would with life or death.  So I gave it over
for the time; resolving to speak to Don Manuel, and see

7

what could be done to enlighten this dark soul, and teach him to know something of God. Meanwhile, I motioned to him to take this animal (the one, I mean, that we had killed) on his shoulders, and run before us to the rest; which he did willingly, and arrived before us in spite of the weight.

At sight of this food, the savages were hardly to be re-strained: indeed, taking into account their long fast (for we made out from them later, they had not tasted bit nor sup for the best part of two days), we thought it well to let them have their way; so, cutting off a leg and shoulder for our own use, we abandoned the rest to their heathenish gluttony. And short work, truly, did they make of it, without so much as a thought about cookery of any kind. But I must record here, on the other hand, the tender filial attentions paid by the poor lad to his father: for, seeing the old man still so weak as scarce to be able to raise hand to mouth, this young savage (less a savage than many a son more civilised) occupied his whole care about feeding his father with the choicest morsels he could tear off with his fingers; putting them lovingly into his mouth, and talking to him all the while with that strange kind of jab-bering he had used at first. This talk, or some part of it I made out to be about the firing of the rifle, and wonderful killing of the animal, without arrow, javelin, club, or even stone: for first he pointed to it (or as much as was left after their meal), then ran along swiftly on his hands and feet, to imitate the creature's running, which he did in the most laughable way you ever saw. Then he stood up-right to take me off, too: but that he did not, till he had first inclined towards me with great reverence, crossing his hands on his breast again, and uttering some words or sounds, that were meant to show respect for the person he spoke of. Then, stretching out his left arm straight, at full length, pointing his finger by way of muzzle to a gun, he snapped his other fingers smartly for the click of the lock, and made a booming sound or kind of rude bellowing, to express the report of the piece. Then again, he turned himself into the animal I had shot, and went tumbling and rolling over and over; then lay still, as though he were dead, and so got up again, and came back to the rest.

All this pantomime amused our men well enough: as for Ned Hilton, he turned to Harvey, and bade him cheer up, and not take on for the loss of his monkeys, if they should not live (the two young monkeys, as I said before, were sickening at this time, and died soon after): "For here messmate," says he, "you have a young monkey in this nigger, as full of tricks as any; and you may teach him to fetch and carry: see, he's not afraid of speaking and being put to work." *

As for the Indians, they seemed to think there was nothing laughable in what the young savage told them: no sooner had he finished his story, than they rose up, and coming towards us with the same gestures of submission he had used before, bent down before our feet; then touched our feet gently, and were for placing them on their heads, in sign of servitude or adoration. I noticed that the only one of our number who seemed proud of this being done was Prodgers: as for the rest, Hilton and careless Harry laughed at it; Tom Harvey, too. was amused at the odd gestures of these poor savage men. Don Manuel did what I had done before, only in a better way, for it came more natural to him. He took the hand of the Indian who had offered him this homage; this was the old man whom we had so hardly fetched back from death, who seemed to single out Don Manuel as the one who had best title to reverence. This old Indian came creeping to him as though he were more than human: the priest put that by, with marks of displeasure though kindly; then, taking his hand, raised it with his own towards heaven, to make him understand it was God had saved him, and that he must adore God alone.

Thus, our first communication with these savages was, so far, on the side of Christianity; a thing I am glad to think on now. "Too often," said Don Manuel to me when we talked it over, "they who ought to have carried to the heathen the light of the Gospel, have only stirred for them the fire of hell."

---

* The negroes in the West Indies had a notion that the monkey was human, and could speak if he would; but that he held his tongue to avoid being employed as a slave.—ED.

# CHAPTER XXIV.

### A LESSON IN INDIAN.

NEXT, we had to devise means to establish some language to converse with these new and strange friends of ours.  After consulting by ourselves a little apart, the men asked me to make the savages a speech in dumb show, to gain their confidence, but their submission too.  Don Manuel joined this request; though I asked him to try it himself, he still motioned me forward.  So I drew near to them, where they sate huddled together with much anxiety, their chins resting on their hands, and eyeing every movement of ours with their great rolling eyes.  But when they saw me go towards them with my rifle, they all sprang up in terror again, and prostrated their faces in the dust, making no doubt I had determined to kill them. Nay, it seems they thought we were going to eat them too, or at least one among them : for the men were even now preparing a fire to cook some portions of the hog for our meal, and they supposed I was come to fetch one of themselves to add to our good cheer.

Finding this, I laid aside my rifle, placing it on the sand; then still advanced a few steps, and held out my open hand to them, to show them I had no such intention as they feared.  I could see they watched my movements closely; and with much joy, you may be sure : so, seating themselves in a row, and with gestures of submission, they listened without interrupting me.  I say, listened; for I found I could not get on with my dumb show only, but must accompany it with words : though it may appear strange to any who reads this, yet I believe he will find, by placing himself in my circumstances, he would help out his actions by words even as one who speaks on what interests him much, helps out his words by action.

My address ran somewhat as follows :—

"Friends," said I, in a mild voice, smiling on them all the while, "we have rescued you from those waves;" here I pointed with my hand over to the sea, which was now growing calm.  This action they understood very well; and bowed their heads to say, 't was true, and they were very grateful to us for saving them. "We are glad of it," continued I ; " and thankful, as you ought to be, to that great God who has preserved you from death " (raising my hand, and pointing upwards, though my heart rebuked me for preaching gratitude when I had put it so little in practice. But if we measured our instruction by our own deeds, which of us would say a word to his neighbour for his good?). Well, this second action of mine was plain enough to them too : only, while I pointed straight up to heaven, they all pointed with both arms stretched out to the sun, to make me know that was the god they thought had saved them from the sea. This made me feel angry again; yet not so much as I determined to make show of, that I might wean them of that horrid idolatry of theirs. So, putting on a frowning countenance, I closed my fist, and shook it at them, to threaten them : at which they dropped their hands again, and bowed their heads, as saying, it should be just as I would. I supposed at the time, and made out from them after, what was their notion about us ; viz., that my God must needs be much greater than their god, since I was myself so superior to them ; also, that it was my God who had saved them, and not their own, inasmuch as the tempest had obscured the sun. However, I now went on, part by words which they understood not, part by signs, which they did; I made them sensible we would be good masters to them if they would behave themselves orderly and well : that we would not beat or ill use them (this I explained by taking one of the handspikes, and making as though I was beating some one severely, together with kicking, shaking, and beating with my fists : then threw the pike from me with every mark of abhorence, as though all this were what I detested, and should be sorry to be forced to).

Strange it was to see how quickly these poor savages took up my meaning. They nodded at me with many outlandish grimaces, crossed their hands on their breasts, then placed them on their heads, in token of their devoting their very lives to our service. Then I, on my part, made them great promises, pointing to some cocoa-nuts that grew at a little distance, pretending to fetch them the fruit to eat : then to some portions of the hog that lay about, as though, I offered to them all good things they needed.   At this, they clapped their hands, and broke out into a kind of song, rocking themselves too and fro as they sat, with gestures of great contentment.

What they sang sounded much as I here set it down:

> 'Ooama atahai, oora, oora,
> Tangata makoee, kaoo, toroo;
> Eree-hina wariû!'

It was not till some time later that I chanced to ask the middle-aged Indian, one day when he was hoeing in our plantation, what was the meaning of this song: and in particular, of the last words, which they repeated again and again, drawing out the notes to a great length, and raising their voices to a high pitch.   He told me, in the broken English we had by that time taught him to speak, 't was a song of gratitude for the promises I made them: and this is how he put it into English; *Brown man happy, very good, very good: he work, he laugh, morning, evening: kind to him white lords!*

After all, I thought it best to show them, as there was a smooth side, there might be a rough one in our dealings with each other.   So, in the best way I could, I began acting another pantomime, expressing first a disobedient, froward servant, dishonest to his master; this I did by catching up a cocoa-nut, and running a little distance with it as though I had stolen it: then came back and pointed to them, to make them see I meant themselves by this; so, pointing to myself, I moved towards my rifle, catching it up and presenting it at them, as though I would fire.   But this renewed all the poor savages' mortal fright, as I meant it to do, for a wholesome lesson to them: they cast themselves once more down before me, stretching forth their hands; and all at once cried out with the utmost vehemence, *Udan, udan!* which means in their language, *No, no!*  Whether they meant to beseech me this most dreadful thing might not happen to them, or to assure me they would not deserve it, I cannot say; but 't is like enough they meant both.

# CHAPTER XXV.

### FREEDOM OR SLAVERY.

IT perplexed me to know how to secure these new subjects of our little kingdom, or employ them: and
after our meal, which we cooked and ate in our accus-
tomed fashion, I walked a little apart with Don Manuel to
consult on the point, placing the savages in charge of
Tom Harvey. This I did, both for their safe custody, also
to prevent any of the other men playing off their sailor's
tricks on them, or ill-treating them with any tyrant usage;
a thing I apprehended, not without reason. For, though
our men were improved by our common misfortune and
Don Manuel's influence, yet 't was plain they regarded
these Indians as beings of a lower grade, who might be
employed as their slaves, or treated according to the humour of the moment. Indeed, this was the question I
proposed to the priest, how far our savages were to be
looked on as slaves whom we had bought with our money,
or prisoners taken in war.

He answered me very gravely, and with an earnest
countenance, saying, we had no right at all to regard
them so: for, putting aside, says he, the whole question
of slavery, which you and I need not now enter on, these
poor men are cast by misfortune on our coast; and we owe
to them a share of those rights which man has with his
brother man. "If we should deprive them," he went on,
speaking more strongly, "of their liberty, in what are we
better than those inhuman wreckers who come down from
their cliffs like so many sea-robbers, or vultures, to seize
the property of the luckless mariners that are cast on their
inhospitable shore?"

To this I saw no ready answer; yet, thinking awhile;
"These creatures," said I, "are savages, who have no
law of property, nor understand any right between man
and man, except what the strong arm gives over the weak."

"But every man," answers the priest, "by the law of
nature, has the right to possess himself."

"I doubt not," pursued I, for I wanted to look at this

from all sides, "had we been cast away on their coast, instead of they on ours, they had robbed and killed us by this time, aye, and eaten us besides."

"Even so," Don Manuel replied; "that would have been because they are savages and heathens. Shall we measure our conduct by their standard?"

"Has then the heathen savage," I objected, "the same rights with the Christian and civilized white man?" But as I spoke, I felt a twinge of conscience, to think what sort of civilized men we were, above all, what sort of Christians we had proved ourselves to be; though Don Manuel let it pass without notice.

"We must not confound two things together," says he, smiling. "By the law of nature, the white man and his darker brother have the same title to life and liberty: though by the law of society they may not have the same privileges in other ways."

"After all," said I, "the one is savage, the other civilized."

"That is what I mean," insisted he, though quite mildly, as was his way. "The difference between them and us makes it impossible to put equal power into their hands; because the savage knows not how to use it rightly. You cannot trust him, just as you cannot trust a mere child. When the child is grown in years, in knowledge, in experience, he passes out of the state of a pupil, and becomes a citizen. You must educate him for his future position; then give it to him. So, you must train the savage, who in many ways is a child; and, when he has served his apprenticeship to liberty, he must be free, absolutely free!" He spoke this with some warmth, raising his voice as we walked on.

"Then you think 't is our duty to educate these Indians, and treat them as equals?" asked I.

"*Think*, my dear friend?" answered the priest, turning short upon me; "I do not think about it, for I am sure. Educate them first, and you thereby make them equals. Let us take care," he added, "we do not find them some day our superiors."

"Just what I apprehended," said I, taking him up wrongly: "what if some day they should find the means to overmaster us?"

"Build my wall round about them," said he, in his cheerful way: "for to be encompassed with that wall is the truest freedom."

I knew well what the priest meant: and, after I had thought for a few minutes; "Yes, sir," said I, "that wall has stood us in good stead, and I see not but it might do much for these poor fellows, to teach them to pray, too."

"And not to bow to the sun," added he, sighing deeply, as he thought on it. "We must clear away all that, and a great deal more, before we can lay the foundations of our wall."

"Then it is our duty to make them Christians, too?"

"Who can doubt it?" answered he. "Duty! is it not a privilege? Are they not sent to us for that very thing?"

He looked at me, in wonder that I did not answer; which I was indeed slow to do, for the idea which filled his mind was new to mine. Except for what he had said when he asked us, the day before, what a priest was, I must own the thought had never crossed me, of converting such savages as we might fall in with.

"Yes," said the priest, speaking to himself; "therefore are they come: even therefore are they come!"

He had scarce uttered the words, when our thoughts were diverted by a cry that rose among the men we had left: soon we saw Hilton coming towards us in haste, beckoning us to come back. My mind misgave me, something was going amiss with the Indians; I ran back at once, up a little slope of ground that had hidden us from view, and Don Manuel followed me close. We had fetched a compass in our walk of perhaps two hundred yards: but now, taking a short cut through the trees, I was soon upon them, and saw at once what I was sorry enough, and angry enough too, to see going on.

## CHAPTER XXVI.

### THE WHITE MAN NO HERO.

FOR some of the men, being left to their own devices, forgot all they had gone through, in the pleasure of tormenting the unhappy Indian savages: seeming to regard them as their absolute property, or so many head of mere cattle without souls. No sooner were our backs turned (this we made out later from Harvey, and from the Indians later still), than Prodgers and Gill, always our most untoward members of society, began such pranks as a school-boy might have felt himself above practising; as, plucking the hair of these poor ignorant creatures, blackening their dark faces with a burnt stick, making pretence to shave them with their clasp-knives; in short, whatever tricks are played off on passengers in a ship at first crossing the line, were devised, and executed too, by those scapegraces, spite of all Tom Harvey's efforts. He reasoned with them, and defended the Indians to the utmost of his power; he ended by threatening them outright, he would knock them down, did they attempt it further. And 't was just at this stage of proceedings we came upon them.

I ran up at once, and spoke out my mind; laying hands, roughly enough, on Prodgers' collar: bidding him desist, or we would come to blows. The rest joined in this; reasoning now with him, now with Harry, to persuade them how absurd as well as cruel they had been: above all (for that thought came chiefly into my mind), how we should destroy our influence with these savages by showing them, they whom they had so lately taken for gods were subject to all the caprices and fooleries of mere men.

This had some little effect, for both of them now became somewhat ashamed of the part they had played. But pride next came in, to bolster up what could not be maintained by reason: and Richard Prodgers, turning sulky again, seemed resolute to have his own way, or leave us altogether; for so he declared himself.

"Hark ye," says he, "I give you all notice, I, for one,

do n't understand this submitting here and submitting there, nor do n't mean to practise the same. I mean to do as I please, for one : so, good bye t' ye all, if that 's all, and no more about it."

With that, he catches up his gun, and was for making off. But I saw at once, to let him go with his weapon in that style would never do; for Prodgers armed, and in dudgeon, might prove an awkward customer to the rest of us, if he meant mischief. So, thinking to coax him back to good humour, I was beginning in a hail-fellow-well-met sort of way; but Don Manuel laid his hand on my arm, as though to say, such would be of no use for the present. Nor indeed, knowing the man concerned, do I think it would.

"At least," said I, "you do not carry away the gun ; for we have already voted that into the common stock : and he who withdraws from our commonwealth has no claim to private property."

The men closed in here, and cried out I was in the right of it : but Richard Prodgers was not the man to yield that point, you may be sure : and a struggle followed for the piece, in the midst of which, I know not by what means, it became cocked, just as Don Manuel, who stepped in on one side (while I, on my part, pulled Richard away), struck up the muzzle with his hand. And, so doing, he saved the life of Ned Hilton; for, the next moment, the piece went off, and some of the shot grazed Hilton on his cheek : had not the priest done so with a calm presence of mind, it had without all doubt shot Hilton through the body. But Ned, chafed at this, angry and bleeding as he was, with one blow of his fist felled Prodgers to the ground.

This put an end to the contest; each one being too much concerned in preventing further mischief; so Richard was held down, till he promised good behaviour if we let him rise. But good behaviour meant, thrusting his hands in his pockets, and turning away from us, while we consulted apart what was best to be done with him.

He saved us much further trouble on that head; for turning to us again with a determined air, " I wish all here a good morning," says he, "and shall take myself off."

So take himself off he did, till we lost sight of him among the trees that bounded our cove to northward : but afterwards it appeared, from what followed, he struck down again towards the rocks on the shore beyond.

I believe, none of us felt sorry to be rid of Prodgers so easily ; only we knew well he must soon come back to us and beg for food : for except his knife, that would not serve him to kill wild game, he was unprovided with anything whereby to support life for a day.

"He may comfort himself with the rest of the brandy bottle," said Gill, and then we thought no more of him, being occupied with our savages, to see what use we could make of them.

But first, Don Manuel took up that discourse, representing to the men, as strongly as he had to me (but not in a like way of discussing the question), that we must not think of making slaves of these Indians. We might call them apprentices, he said, and hold them as such, if they chose to stay with us. Only, we must give them their choice, whether they would stay at all, or take chance of the sea again in their canoe. They were free to go or remain ; and, remaining, had a right to good treatment, as man should treat his fellow-man.

I could plainly see, this discourse was not well relished by all that heard it ; and there was silence among us for a little while, the men looking first on each other, then on the ground. For to oppose the priest, who had become our benefactor in many ways, was a thing no one was forward to do : yet, on the other hand, Gill, and Hilton too, had settled in their minds they might lord it over these savages, and so lead easy lives on the island while the slaves worked for them. They now saw their property, as it were, snatched from their grasp.

"Come, friends," said the priest, after a pause : "do justice to your better thoughts, and let me be spokesman for you to these poor souls, who are created, like yourselves, to the image of God."

With that, he stepped to them ; speaking in his native Spanish to give effect to his signs, he asked them (for I had some acquaintance with that tongue), whether they would stay on the island with us : and here he struck down his staff on the earth, then pointed to us with his hand. Or, says he, will you get into that canoe again (for the canoe had by this come near the shore, but had not righted,

and was floating keel upwards), and go back again over
the wide sea? All which he made clear to them by the
signs accompanying his words.

Our Indians did not debate which to choose; but all
falling on their knees, they took up handfuls of the earth,
and first kissed it, then put it on their heads, after swallow-
ing a little of it, and throwing some into the air : devoting
themselves, as we understood, to live and die on the place.
Then they pointed to the boat, and made signs of disgust,
turning away their heads, and shaking their hands at it :
to make us know, they had no wish to embark again, but
the clean contrary. At this, Don Manuel gave tokens of
satisfaction, and renewed the promises of good treatment
I had made them before.

While we were occupied in this way, we heard the
voice of Richard Prodgers cry out, as if in terror or pain,
from the rocks beyond, out of sight. An instant after, he
shouted for help : we caught up our guns and dashed after
him, motioning to the savages to follow us. So indeed
they did, and outran us too, having armed themselves
with some stones that they caught up dexterously as they
ran. As to their running, they distanced us fairly; for
such fleet creatures I never saw in human shape; all except the old man, who could very hardly keep up with us.
I thought it dangerous to let the other two go on, lest
they should escape us altogether; so I called out to them
to come back, which they did with great submissiveness;
thus it chanced we all came upon the scene of action together.

## CHAPTER XXVII.

### PRODGERS LEARNS HIS LESSON.

WE plainly saw, when once clear of the trees, poor old
Richard was not crying for help without a cause :
we found him kneeling on the rocks, holding them with all
his might, in a deadly struggle against somewhat that

pulled him to itself, with a force greater than his own, while he cried out in the extremity of his terror. We ran up to him at full speed, and horrible it was to see him in the grasp of a large cuttle fish, that almost had gotten him within its jaws. This monster had a body of the bigness of a biggish gourd, and each one of its eight arms (or legs, call them as you will) was no less than four feet, I am sure, in the length, with suckers at the end, such as I have seen boys make in leather, and pull up stones by them at the end of a string. It had fixed one of these suckers on Richard's face, leaving him scarce mouth enough to roar with; and by this, and three or four of its other arms, it was pulling him towards its beak, hooked like a parrot or hawk's beak, that was open to devour him; whilst its large fishy eyes were fixed upon him, and the rest of the legs clasped the rocks with the grasp of a blacksmith's vice.

We were afraid to fire, lest we should miss the monster, and hit our comrade instead; besides, a bullet or two might have gone through the cuttle fish, without doing it much hurt, and would not lessen the dreadful power of its arms, that were still drawing, and drawing, till Prodgers' face was within half a foot of the cruel beak that would have gored it in a moment more.

Let me live as long as I may, I never can forget the look of agony Richard cast, nor his shrieks, as the monster closed on him. But just then I ran up, and laying the edge of my drawn hanger on the arm of the fish, drew it swiftly across, and severed the limb at a stroke. Then the rest of the men fell-to with their knives, and we made short work of him: for we could find no bones but the back-bone, and all the fish's strength lay in the contracting power of his muscles, which pull with a strain like a ship's cable.

Our attention for the moment was all on our poor old messmate; he had fallen into a deadly swoon from the fear of what we were just in the nick of time to save him from. We had some ado to recover him, which we did by the aid of a few drops from his own flask, with dashing some salt water in his face. At last he opened his eyes, . and nodded thanks to us for our care, sitting on the knee of Harry Gill, who thus repaid him for his good offices of two days ago, when he got the brimstone choke in the cave. But in another minute or so we saw Richard Prodgers slide down on his knees, still holding by Harry's shoulder: I thought at first he was going off again into a swoon, but soon I heard him say, only faint and low: " My God, I thank Thee, for saving me ; I am sorry for all my sins against Thee ! Help me : I will do better for the time to come ! "

On this, Don Manuel wept aloud for joy ; and he that had been so calm up to now, and calming the passions of other men, surprised us no less by his passionate emotion than Richard by his prayer. However, the priest took no notice of us or our wondering ; he cast himself down on his knees beside Prodgers, and throwing his arm over the old sinner's shoulder, he looked up to heaven and cried :

" It is fit that we should make merry and be glad, for this our brother was dead, and is come to life again ; he was lost, and his found ! "

I know not by what blessed contagion, we all cast our-selves on our knees together, and could not help it; then, for the third time since our banishment in this place, Don Manuel prayed for our whole company, and guided our prayer. He thanked the divine mercies for Richard's deliverance ; he invoked a blessing on his head for his good resolutions, and prayed that he might persevere in them ; pleading for this by what I shuddered to think we had seldom heard mentioned on board ship but in cursing and blasphemy—the Blood and Wounds of Him who hung on the cross to save us all.

This time, too, he ended before we had wearied of our prayer; then stood up, and we followed his example. All of us, I think, guessed by a sort of instinct what was coming next, as he took Richard by the hand, and led him towards Ned Hilton. Ned was still stanching his wounded cheek with his neck-kerchief. Prodgers put out his hand, and did not hesitate. "Forgive and forget," said he, " mess-mate ; 't was a mischance, after all." Ned seemed to debate with himself for a moment, then grasped his hand in return, and all was well between them from that time.

" Into hospital, gentlemen ! " cried the priest gaily ;

"these little accidents have laid us up, and we must recover before we think of ought else, if you please."

No sooner said than done: we placed the wounded men sitting on the rocks, and I began to examine Hilton's face, that was grazed by the shot. Now was the first time the savages proved of use to us; for no sooner did they remark what was going on, than the middle-aged Indian (so I still call him, but we made out afterwards his name was Rermimebolamba, which means "*Pounder of the enemies' heads*"), coming towards us with signs of great reverence, pointed first to Hilton's wounds, then stretched his hand towards the woods in the interior of the island: making as though he would gather something there, and apply it to the cheek.

I was inclined to let him have his way, knowing how skilful savages are in healing wounds by herbs and simples, though unpractised in other branches of the healing art; and, surgeon as I was, I did not disdain to take a lesson from the savage: the more so, as I had with me no instruments or any other remedies, these having been left behind in the ship. So I bade Harvey take one of the guns, and go with the Indian into the wood. giving him strict charge to prevent his escaping, and rather to shoot him down than lose him in that way.

"Stay," said Don Manuel, with much concern when he heard me say that; "did not we agree, a while ago, these men had a right to life and liberty? So no shooting, Señor Tomaso, for that would be downright murder."

"But if he escape," says I: "he will be dangerous to us all: he may lie in wait for us in the woods, and we shall never be secure of our lives for a moment: then, he may signal to any canoe he chances to espy, and bring other savages on us."

"You have no right to his life," replied the priest, "unless it be absolutely needed to preserve your own." And he spoke this with more authority than was his wont: for he had at times the air of a prince; and when he showed this, I felt awkward and shy before him, do what I would.

"Put him in leading strings, if you think it necessary to your safety," said he, after a pause, and smiling: "provided he consent, for he has a free choice. You have some string about you: well, let me ask him to become our prisoner, as well as our 'prentice."

I handed him the ball of twine; he took it, and came to the Indian, making signs to him to tie his own hand, and pointed to the woods, to make him know, he might go thither on his errand when he had done this. John Pounder (so we called this savage after a while, when we came to know the meaning of his Indian name) nodded and laughed at what the priest signalled to him; then took the end of the twine: with his right hand and his teeth he tied a knot round his left wrist as cleverly as ever I saw a sailor knot a rope; then gave back the ball into the hands of the priest, and pointed to the woods, as impatient to set off.

"See, friends," said Don Manuel, turning to us, "he has done for himself, by dint of a little gentleness, what no one had a right to compel him to."

"Give a man rope enough and he'll hang himself," says Gill.

"Not in this case," answered the Don: "but I will cap your proverb with another we have in Spain; it may be put into English thus:

> ' Up the Sierra Morena
> A green bough 'tices a restive mule.' *

Have you any like that, among the sayings of your country?"

"I take it," said I, "'t is much what I have heard said, that you may draw folks with a skein of silk, all round the world, when you can't drive them a yard."

"Ay, just so, just so," said he, again and again, looking much pleased: "kindness is the real load-stone that draws everything. But now, off with you to the woods, or our friend Hilton's wounds will grow cold."

The Indian did not seem so content to go with Tom Harvey; for Harvey had the formidable gun in his hand,

---

* Whatever may be the original of this Spanish proverb, its meaning is obvious enough. The Sierra Morena is a rugged chain of mountains running between Cordova and Estremadura; the ascent of which was, in earlier days at least, toilsome and difficult, demanding some enticement to the sumpter mules and other beasts of burden employed in transporting merchandize across the height. ED.

to him so supernatural and dreadful a thing: the poor savage looked beseechingly to the priest, and stretched out his hands, as begging him to take him rather. But Don Manuel smiled upon him again, stroking his head; then laid his hand upon his own heart, to make him see he pledged himself for his safety. This seemed to content the other; so he crossed his arms on his breast, and they set out at a round trot, and soon were in the woods out of sight.

Now I turned to Prodgers, who by this had got back some of his strength: only *his* face too had need of doctoring, what with the violent drawing of the monster's paws, or suckers that had grasped it; what with a kind of poison that must have exuded from them: for his face was becoming bloated, and covered with a redness, or a purple colour in spots, that looked serious. He seemed to feel some fears himself: for he said to me, in a subdued way, quite unlike his former:

"Do you think, sir, I am in danger of dying?"

"Oh! I hope not, old fellow," answered I, wishing to cheer him up; "why should you entertain such dark thoughts?"

"Why, death," says he again, slowly, "is an awful thing, when you come to think on it; I never felt so much about it before. I fell overboard once, 't is now a good eleven years ago; while I was struggling in the water, I had not so much fear of death as now that I am sitting on this rock. To pass out of life—what is that? 'T is to have one's soul taken out of one's body, I know: well that must be a shrewd wrench; where does the soul go to then?"

God forgive me, but I gave some light turn to this, to keep up his spirits, as I thought: when Don Manuel, who had taken his prayer-book, overheard us, and shut it again as he drew near.

"Whither," said he, "do you ask? Why, you know, my friend, as well as I, the soul is no sooner sundered from the body, but it stands before its Creator to be judged."

At this, I pressed the priest's arm, to make him sensible I desired to keep such thoughts from the mind of my patient: but he went on more earnestly, and said a few simple things about death and judgment that seemed to go straight into Prodgers' very soul, so awe-struck and humble did he look : and Gill too, with Hilton, listened in silence to every word he spoke. But we now saw our Indian running to us at full speed from the wood; for Harvey had released him when he got clear of the thicket on his way back. His hands were full of herbs, which he brandished aloft, laughing and gibbering, as he flew to us with the speed of a mad thing. When he came up, we let him have his way, which was, to chew those herbs into a pulp, and lay them as a plaster on the men's faces, making signs to us to tie them up with their kerchiefs. There being no other remedy at hand, Hilton submitted to this with a tolerable grace : as to Prodgers, he was tamed to that degree, he submitted like a child. And, such was the healing virtue of these herbs, they soothed the wounds and inflamed faces of our patients so as no apothecary's drugs could excel them : and soon the two men laid them down under the shadow of the rocks, to snatch a bit of sleep; and Harry Gill followed their example.

---

## CHAPTER XXVIII.

### WE DESIGN A SAFE RETREAT.

MORE anxious than ever did I now feel, how to secure ourselves against attacks from without. For 't was plain, though we had found no trace of savages inhabiting our island, we were somewhere within reach of their canoes from a distance. And if a small boat (I reasoned) setting forth, maybe, on a mere fishing expedition, or to cross from one island or one shore of a creek to another, could be driven upon us in this way, what might we not expect from a larger war-canoe, or an entire fleet of them, fitted out for discovery, or missing their course, and so espying our mountain, as we had done from the ship? For, did they once land, I felt sure their Indian cunning would light on some token of the island being inhabited;

and then they would never give over their search till they had found us out; and we should beyond all doubt fall a sacrifice to their cruelty.

This gloomy apprehension having taken hold on my spirits, I could not well shake it off, do what I would: but must impart it to the priest, for I would not at that time give a hint of it to any of the rest. Don Manuel, I found, was prepared for what I said.

"The same thought," says he, "is present with me ever since we pulled these poor creatures out of the water: but I delayed to speak to you of it, till I could propose some plan for safety." Then he went on to say, that in his country was an old deserted palace, belonging once to the Spanish king; and in the pleasure-grounds of it a labyrinth, or maze, formed of close-cut hedges laid out in suchwise, and with so much art, that among a number of turns to right and left, there was only one, and that one hard to hit, that would lead to a summer-house in the centre. "The king," says he, "in former days, when kings had little else to do, would amuse himself at his palace-window, watching his servants, or visitors, not masters of the secret of the place, how they would turn and wind, and run this way or that: for the most part wrong, and forced to double back again, or sit down wearied till one who knew the secret came to show them out. Now I think, with the help of our apprentices," and he smiled as he used the word, "we might plant such a maze as this: for I have seen some of the prickly pear, and other close-growing shrubs, fit to form the hedges of it, in several parts of our island, as we came along. It will take time, indeed; for we shall not be secure till our hedges have taken root and grown thick: but we will pray that we may not be attacked before then. God helps those who help themselves."

"Or what think you, sir," said I, "of going back to the cliff where we took shelter, and looking out for some cleft or natural cave that we might enlarge, and so burrow deeper till we had made us a house in the rock?"

"That is good, too," observed he, thinking, "but why may we not do both? An archer has two strings for his bow; a rabbit makes two entrances to his burrow; and many birds and animals provide both summer and winter

# OWEN EVANS' MAZE.

*" I set to work to devise a maze, that should be difficult for those who had not the clue, but easy to those who had," etc.—*CHAPTER XXVIII.

quarters, by the wonderful instinct that is theirs. At all events, I will try and draw the plan of my maze: come, here is a scrap of paper for you; do you the like, and we will compare notes over our fire to-night."

I liked the idea well enough, and I set to work to devise a maze that should be difficult for those who had not the clue, but easy to those who had. I tried to draw it out on the paper with one of Don Manuel's pens, but a blotted work I made of it after all: what with correcting here and there, and opening passages where I had first closed them, the thing was so smeared that I was half ashamed to show it when it was done. The priest got on better with his; whether he was more used to drawing, or more patient in trying to do each thing well that he undertook, certain it is, a neater performance he made when he finished it.

"And now for your other plan," said he, rising and putting by the paper, with mine too, in his portfolio: "for, having got on the track of a habitation, we must lose no time. Remember, the rainy season will soon be on us."

By this, we had come back to our company, from whom we strayed in our talk: Don Manuel, seeing the three savages eyed the monstrous cuttle-fish with longing eyes, as though they would have fallen to, and devoured it outright, proposed to give them leave; "for none of us," says he, "will have much taste for him, I suppose; and, to be sure, not our poor Ricardo, that hath suffered so much from him already." But first, he desired to secure a bag of inky fluid, or *sepia*, as painters name it, which this strange fish is furnished with; whereby he can darken the water around him, and thus escape from his enemies, be they fishermen or brother-fishes. Borrowing Tom Harvey's knife, Don Manuel cut out this ink-bag dexterously from the dead fish, and filled his ink-bottle from it; then took one of the cocoa-nut shells, and poured the rest into it, stopping the hole with clay; to be able, he said, to record the rest of our adventures in this place of exile.

But we made up our minds to secure some portion of our big fish for our own supper, too; for I had read, 't was a delicacy in former times as well as our own: so, slicing off as much as we thought to make a broil of (there being enough of the monster for us all, and to spare), we wrapped this in some cocoa nut leaves, and let the savages have the rest; after I had secured the back-bone to make some polishing powder, and his formidable parrot-beak, for a trophy.

We left the two sick men asleep where they were, but not without devising a live telegraph* between us and them. We made signs to the old Indian to climb up a tree, one of the highest in the wood between the rocks and that cove of ours, which we henceforth called Shark Bay. This tree overlooked both sides, and we too could see the Indian watching in it as he sat among the branches.

As we went along, taking the other two savages with us, I told Harvey and Gill, as we had practised various trades in this our strange life, we were now to turn masons and stone-cutters also, to make us a cave wherein we might lie snug during the rainy season. They agreed to this readily, expressing themselves willing to labour, as indeed they proved to be. So, going as straight through the second wood as the trees would let us, we tried to hit that same cliff we had climbed up in the morning. We judged it to be a convenient spot, by reason of the separated rock that leaned towards it; for that piece of leaning crag hid the place where we meant to burrow into the cliff, and gave us an easy ascent to it: some of us afterwards called it our hall·door, and some, our grand staircase, or companion ladder.

'T was no little time, indeed, before we found our cliff again; in part, from the thickness of the wood, which gave security to our hiding-place; also, because we now came upon it from a different side. But by keeping our right shoulders as near the ridge of rock as the thick trees would let us, we knew we should surely come on it at last; and soon we did.

Placing ourselves between this rock and the cliff it had fallen from, we discovered 't was just the place that suited our needs; for about the part where these leaned nighest together, there was a kind of hole in the native

---

* The reference here is, of course, to that antient system of telegraphs which, by certain combinations of the position of their wooden arms, symbolised the letters of the alphabet. The most noted of these telegraphs, in England, was that which communicated from the roof of the Admiralty in London, to Portsmouth. ED.

cliff, not much bigger than I have seen a mountain fox's burrow in Wales; it gave us hope, we should find the rock not too hard or stubborn to work. This hole lay perhaps ten feet below the brow of the cliff, and 't was difficult to come at it: which fitted it the more for our design, if only we could contrive to enter it from above, or from the leaning rock over against it. We determined on the first way, as less dangerous; so we set about contriving a rope to lower one of us after another, in turn, to work at this hole, and enlarge it into a cavern.

But where in this wide world should we provide us a rope? Nothing in that shape had we, but the twine, and my fishing-lines, much too slight to bear even a quarter our weight, put them all together. Think as much as I could, I could devise nothing to the purpose; when Don Manuel said, laughing:

"Now you shall see Æsop's fable put in practice in an island he never dreamed of! so true is it, wisdom is the property of the human family everywhere."

"Look at those strong creepers," said he again, "how they climb about the trees, and lace in and out; well, no one of them would bear us by itself; but put a dozen or so together, and bind them round with our twine, and you shall see, we shall soon have rope enough"—

"To hang us all," broke in Harry Gill, who never could keep back a joke that came into his head.

"Or to hang the captain and first mate, not to say those gentlemen who landed us here so civilly the day before yesterday," added Tom Harvey.

Don Manuel smiled at Gill's remark, but did not look pleased at the other; however, he went on about his rope.

"Union is strength," said he; "and what is beyond the power of one, can be done with ease when more are combined. You all remember the fable of the old man and his sons, and the bundle of sticks, I dare say?"

"No, indeed," answered I: "pray tell us, sir."

## CHAPTER XXIX.

### WHAT IS TRUTH?

AT that moment, the old Indian, our watchman, shouted from the tree where we had left him on the look-out: we caught up our arms again on the instant, but there was no occasion, for we found he was calling to the men we had left asleep, to show them where we were. Prodgers and Harry soon came to us through the wood; the Indian clambered down from his perch, and joined us too.

Now we began to benefit by having more pairs of hands than we had landed with: for we no sooner showed our Indians what we were after, and that we would have them collect these creepers for us to make a rope, but they sprang up the trees (at least the two younger) with the nimbleness of cats, and soon tore down enough for us to begin with. I scarce think our trade of rope making would have come to much, but for these savages; who showed themselves ingenious to a degree, in binding together the green withs by others of a like kind, round and round, at every three feet or so: till, after a good two hours' work, we saw ourselves possessed of a passably strong and pliable rope, fit to bear a good weight, and eighteen or twenty feet long at the least. We were proud of our new cable, and began bending and straining it every way, to try it: but it did not part nor untwist, so well had our poor 'prentices worked it.

Our next concern was, to find something of a cross-bar to reeve into our rope, for our mason to sit on, while we let him down to work at the entrance door. Harvey and Ned Hilton went searching through the woods for some fallen branch; but I drew Don Manuel aside, to impart to him what had come into my mind: for, as we had to break up the condemned gun to make chisels and other tools, I thought it best this should be done apart from the savages, lest they might lose their great dread of those guns whereby they were kept in such awe. So we agreed to take it deeper into the wood; and beckoned Harry Gill to come along with us, leaving Prodgers to look after the

Indians, who were still hard at work, finishing the rope. This we could now do, with no apprehension of their being hardly dealt with : so changed a man was Richard Prodgers become, and from a lion, or a bear, had grown more like to a lamb.

By dint of hammering with stones, and bending the barrel back and forward, till it broke at last, we got two long chisels, or augers, out of our old gun : they were rude enough, to be sure, but proved serviceable. One of them, the shorter, we kept still fastened to the stock, to have more purchase in working. Don Manuel carried these, wrapped in his cloak, till we could conceal them better from the savages. But Gill went on before, and left us together.

I had gained that confidence in the priest, 't would have made me uneasy to hide from him my thoughts when they chanced to turn on the right or wrong of a case : and just then a thought came into my mind as we returned together out of the wood.

"I know, sir," said I, "what some people in my country would say to what we are doing."

"What would they say, friend?" answered he, and looked me straight in the face, walking on quietly.

"Why, to be plain, that 't is deceiving these savages, to break up the gun by stealth, to make them still think the guns to be something more than they are."

"Eh, Señor," returned he, "how long is it ago, that you thought we might perhaps even enslave them?"

"Well, sir, what I say is because it came into my head, and I wanted to discuss it."

"True, my dear friend," quoth he, in his own mild way; "and 't is my duty and pleasure alike to answer such questions to the utmost. Let us see ; you think we ought to tell them outright, a gun is a gun?"

"I would not like them to think," answered I, "a gun was an idol, or a god."

"Nor I neither," replied he, grave enough ; "but are we making them think so, by any act of ours?"

"We break up the gun in the wood, out of sight," persisted I ; "lest they should lose their fear of our other guns."

"I will answer you in this way." Don Manuel said, after

a moment, smiling. "When I was a boy, I went to a school in my native town, kept by one Lopez Tuero d' Alava; he was a stern man, and very stately in his ways. We boys looked up to him as the greatest man alive: and he took care to keep us impressed with that belief. One day, the governor of the province, his Excellency Don Pedro Guzman da Cuença, came suddenly to pay a visit to the school, and entered at the head of all his train. The school-room was filled with guards, chamberlains, attendants of all kinds, in waiting on the great man. When our first surprise was over, we all looked anxiously to see what Lopez Tuero would do. Had he taken off his hat, or made any sign of submission to the governor, his authority in his school might never again have been what it had been; for we should have learned, there was a greater layman in existence than he. This he knew quite as well as we did. So, rising from his desk in his most stately manner, he moved down the school with the air of a king receiving an ambassador, or any other great man treating with his equal; wearing his hat as if it had been nailed to his head. High courtesies passed between the two, till the governor took his leave: and it was not till after I had entered the University of Salamanca, that I learned, Lopez went the next day to the governor's palace, cast himself on his knees before him, and humbly begged pardon for having acted in a way he had felt best for those he had under his charge.

"Now," pursued Don Manuel, "was that a wrong deceit?"

'T was more than I could answer out of hand; yet, thinking a moment, "I suppose," said I, "he felt it necessary."

"But was it *wrong?*" insisted he; "because what is wrong never can be necessary."

"May not a lie sometimes be necessary?" asked I.

"Never!" exclaimed the priest, and seemed to put his whole soul into the word as he spoke it.

"And is a lie always wrong; under all circumstances?"

"Always! always!" repeated he, still in the same way.

Now, indeed, I felt puzzled; for 't was the point I had in my mind as to the breaking up of our gun in secret. Don Manuel saw this; for he had, I am sure, a great readiness in reading men's thoughts : he smiled, and saved my putting it in words, which I was loth to do.

"I know what you are thinking," said he, "as though you said it; and I will say it for you. Catholics, you have always heard, think little of truth ; are careless about it : and a priest is likely to teach it to be a matter of small importance. Is that it ?"

I was startled, I own, at the way he put his finger on it; for that was just what ran in my thoughts.

"Well, listen then," he went on. "The teaching of the Church is, that a lie is in its own nature evil; that it is a sin; that, being a sin, 't is a greater evil than anything imaginable, which is not an equal or a greater sin : 't is a greater evil than any mere misfortune, or series of misfortunes ; greater than pain, sickness, poverty, bereavement, death : greater than famines, pestilences, earthquakes, or the destruction of the globe itself. For these calamities, dreadful though they be, affect the creature : but a lie, as being a sin, is aimed against the Creator. So, if by telling a lie I could save your life, my dear friend, and the lives of all our companions ; if I could by one little lie work out the conversion of our poor savages, and secure the salvation of us all ; nay, of all England, all Spain, all other nations and countries together : if by telling a lie that would harm nobody, that would only be a little venial sin, I could empty Purgatory (which you do n't believe in) of all the suffering souls it contains ; and block up the mouth of Hell (which I suppose you *do* believe in) that no soul should ever be cast into it more : I should be doing the greater evil to obtain the lesser good. And after this, what do you think of a lie ?"

I remember these words, as I here set them down, because they were so impressed on me at the time by his manner as he spoke them. Then he went on to say, 't was one thing to deceive a person by word or deed, by stating falsehood to him, or acting falsehood before him ; and quite another, to allow him to draw his own conclusions from what he observed, when you did nothing to lead him that way, and when you had a just cause for letting him have his opinion, at least for a time.

"If," pursued he, "we showed them, a gun might be broken by working at it with a stone, they might try the experiment while we slept ; and then what becomes of our lives ?  Another boat-load of savages might land on the island ; or these very men, with the craft and cunning they have learned at their mother's knee, might take a fancy to sacrifice us to the sun or moon, to secure a good voyage home again.  Then we are murdered, and they remain heathens.  Is it not for their good, as well as ours, that we should not disarm ourselves by taking away their wholesome fear of our fire-arms ? "

After a little while, the priest added :

" I gave you a sort of parable just now ; well, let me give you another.  Suppose a furious murderer, with a drawn sword, rushed suddenly upon a child, and threatened to kill it unless the child told him by what road its father had left the house, that he might go after him, and take his life.  What would you advise the child in that case ? "

" I think there is no doubt at all," said I, readily.

" But what ? " insisted he.

" Of course, the child might tell the murderer the wrong road ; nay, ought to do so, to save its father's life, or indeed any other person's life."

" Then the child might tell a lie ? "

" Could it not point down the wrong road ? " I asked.

" That would be a lie in *act*," insisted he ; " and as truly a lie as one in words."

" Well, then, the child might tell the lie, or act the lie, either way, for such an object as to save a life."

" You are quite wrong, my friend," returned he, laughing : " for no one ought to do any such thing."

At this, I looked at him in some surprise.

" Did I not say," he went on, " that a lie is always a sin ; and that a sin is a greater evil than any mere misfortune ?  Now, 't would be a great misfortune, doubtless, for the father to lose his life, and the child to lose its father : but no child, no any one, has a right to make even a venial sin avert even a great misfortune."

What he said turned out so against my expectation, and he proved so much more severe about truth than I had supposed him likely to be, I had nothing to say.

" You remind me, now," pursued he, gaily, " of a bad horseman, who, when you put him up on the horse at one side, falls over on t' other.  A while ago, you stumbled at what was lawful ; and now, nothing will content you, but that falsehood must be lawful in an urgent case.  Extremes ! my dear friend, extremes !  And you see, extremes meet sometimes."

"Aye," he added, thinking, and slowly, "we must always go from side to side of the road, like an unsteady driver, unless we have a sure guide and a sure track."

"And who or what is that guide ?" asked I, for I felt anxious for his answer.

"Ah ! who indeed," said he, very slowly, looking me in the face ; and said nothing more.

## CHAPTER XXX.

### THE SERPENTS' HOLE.

SOON after, we set about our operations of mining into the rock : but first we had to decide which of us should take the lead in being lowered to explore that hole.  I thought of casting lots for it, as 't was a post of honour and of danger alike ; for we knew not what we might encounter down there, whether some wild cat-o'-the-mountain, or, more likely, a brood of serpents in their nest. But Don Manuel insisted on being first to explore, in a way I knew not well how to answer.  "If anything befall me, friends," said he, "you will be little the worse of it ; but you could ill spare the help of one another in your exile."  I would still persuade him not to venture ; but he finished all by saying, cheerfully :

"On the banks of the Ganges, I have heard, children are used to leave their parents when they become old and useless, as a prey to the alligators : and you may as well let the wild animals have a chance with me for the same reason."

"You have quoted a heathenish example for us, sir," answered I : "but I suppose it must be as you will : and we will stand watching you above, be sure, to help to our utmost in case of need."

So, having knelt down to make a brief prayer apart, and made the sign of the cross over himself, he threw off his cassock; and bidding the men knot our new rope fast round the roots of a cocoa-palm that grew near the edge, and keep a good hold, as he said smiling, "for the honour of the British flag," he slid from the cliff, and swarmed (as our sea-phrase is) down the rope, till he soon had his feet resting on the edge of the hole: he carefully bent himself down, and looked in.

Before we could count ten, we heard him cry out, "Pull up, pull up quick!" We did it with a will, yet so as not to scrape his hands and face against the cliff; and soon we caught him in our hands, and had him safe again on the top. Then he told us, we were right in our conjecture, for that the place was swarming with serpents.

On that news, we determined to smoke them out of their hole, or smother them in it; and making my wish known to the savages by signs, they soon collected for us some brushwood and other branches, pretty dry. But we would not as yet trust them out of sight, and made them know it by our threatening gestures; though I believe the poor simple creatures had now become so attached to us, looking on us, also, to be some superior beings whom they could not oppose, we might have trusted them all over the island. However, they soon gathered us a good heap, enough to have smothered whole families of serpents; and did more than that, too; for John Pounder, crying out, "*Kukui, kukui!*" pointed to a kind of dwarf-tree with grayish leaves, that looked like an olive at a distance, though we had not noticed it before: making signs, 't was good for our purpose.

I let him have his way; so off he darts to the tree, and comes back with some biggish nuts in his hand, motioning to me to cut a slender stick sharp at one end. I did this, to humour him; so he plants the stick upright in the earth, the sharp end uppermost; and sticks three or four of the nuts on it, one over the other. His next performance was to get a light after his country fashion, which I had heard of, but never seen done before. For he begged so beseechingly for the use of my knife, I could not deny him; but threatened him again to make no bad use of it. He searched about a while, till he found a short thickish branch, of the bigness of my wrist; he quickly brought the end of this to a point with the knife; then, coming to a stump of a tree that had been broken off, quite dry, and half touch-wood, he held the point of the stick on it, and began twirling it about with the palms of his two hands as swiftly as ever you saw a carpenter bore a hole into a board with an auger. He had not done this for five or six minutes, when first there rose a little smoke, then the tree smoked pretty thick, and all at once there burst forth a flame of fire under his hands.

Our men expected this so little, for they had laughed at Master Pounder's contrivances, that now they greeted his success with a hearty cheer: and the other savages showed, in their fashion, they were glad he had pleased us, though noways surprised at what he had done; for it seems, this method of kindling a fire is their common way. But now, gathering up a handful of dry leaves, he lights them, and comes to the nuts strung upon the stick; and they took flame readily, by reason of an oil they are filled with. Then Pounder, while the nuts burned slowly down, like a candle, prostrated himself before us again, till we bade him rise.

To find candles thus ready made, and growing on a tree, pleased us greatly, and more afterwards, when we came to use them in the winter evenings. But for the time, we had, as the saying is, other fish to fry; for we were to dislodge the serpents in the hole by fire and smoke; and take possession of their lodging. The way we set about it was this:

We tied our dry brushwood, the leaves inside, into bundles, or faggots, seven or eight of them, ranging these in order on the top of the cliff: but first, we sent Pounder for some more candle-nuts, and thrust a few of them into each bundle, as I have seen housewives in Wales bind up a pitched stick in a faggot, to light their fire the better. When all was ready, and nothing wanted but to descend to the hole, and so set fire to the first bundle, and push it in, to give our gentlemen there a warm entertainment, we questioned, which of our number to send on this adventure. For now we knew the fulness of the danger; we felt sure, unless the man who went down was quick and steady, to stop the mouth of the hole with the very first bundle, the serpents would spring out on him; and we guessed that to be certain death.   All of us stood looking, one on the other; at length, we well-nigh thought to give up the enterprise, and seek some other place.   But then, again, this place was so commodious, or might be made so, for its dryness and security, we took up our resolution to make the venture.

This was put an end to by the old Indian; I may as well call him Mark, for that was the name we gave to him when he was afterwards baptized.   He now drew near to us, with as much reverence as before, holding John Pounder by the hand. He made us a long speech in his own tongue, of which we understood not one word; but he went on, part speaking, and part by signs, to offer Pounder for this venturesome feat; who, for his part, offered himself too, with great eagerness; expressing, by many odd gestures, his contempt for the serpents: (for the savages had made out from our signs, 't was serpents that inhabited the hole).

The men had gained that degree of good feeling, that none of them were willing to risk our 'prentices in this service of danger.   But, to our surprise, Don Manuel now urged that Pounder should be allowed to go down.

" 'T is not here," said he, " a question of life against life, nor of equal danger to one or to another; in that case I would say, let none of us go.   But I believe these savages are so used to deal with serpents, and to disarm them of their fangs, or can so easily find a simple remedy in the woods if they receive a bite, that 't is little risk to them by comparison.   I could tell you a story (only it would take too long now) to show this; but I have heard many such, from trustworthy persons."

Pounder seemed to understand his meaning, in some part; he nodded his head with many grimaces, then, catching up one of the green withs we had bound about our rope, he twisted it every way, to represent a serpent; wound it on his arm, shook it about, laughing all the time, and finished by stripping off the end of it with his teeth, to show us how he would bite off the snake's head for him. Then he pointed to my knife, and the hanger by my side, as begging me to grant him the use of them: so armed with these, he went to the rope, as though he would slip down it at once.

# CHAPTER XXXI.

### NOTICE TO QUIT.

"HOLD on, a bit," cried Tom Harvey; "were it not best we should load a brace of the guns with small shot, and fire into the hole, to bid them look out for us?"

We all agreed to this; only, we thought one of the guns enough, not to waste powder and shot; we put in a full charge, and gave the piece to Gill; for since his victory over the shark, he was voted our captain of marksmen. But this proceeding was very much against the grain for our savage friends; who, I think, would sooner have faced a wood full of serpents than one discharge of our terrible guns. They cast themselves on their faces, and remained there, trembling, while Harry Gill leaped back across the gulf with his gun, and clambered leisurely down the hanging rock; and this was a work of danger, too, for he had to go down the under face of it, as it leaned over him. But he kept his footing, with the gun slung over his shoulder; and went down with hands and feet two or three yards, till he came nearly opposite the hole. Then he leaned against some twisted roots springing out of the rock; unslung his piece, with a good aim, and so fired into the hole. The piece made a terrible report, being discharged in so close a place; the echo went back and again from cliff to crag, and from crag to cliff; and the Indians were half dead with fear. Out of the hole there came sounds of hissing, by which we knew, however much execution the shot had done, yet Gill had not killed all the brood. But, what was worse, at that moment, whether from the shock or his weight, or both, the roots that poor Harry had leaned against. now gave way under him. He had just time to catch at some saplings as he fell; but he managed so to do, like a nimble seaman as he was: and there he hung by his hands, three fathom above his mother earth.

We, who watched all this from the cliff, were so distracted at the sight, that what to do we knew not: for, did we pursue our advantage over the serpents, we must leave our comrade hanging there, and then drop he must soon, to the peril of his neck or bones : or, did we go over to help him, we feared our enemies might escape from their hole, and glide down, and so get at him if he should fall before we came to the rescue.

Amid the confusion of our thoughts, as we looked this way and that, the priest called out, with all the decision of a general leading his men to the charge, and a voice like a trumpet :

"You, Owen, take my cloak; away with you, and Tom, and Hilton !  Hold it under him !  Break his fall !  Ricardo and I will do the rest here !"

Quick as thought, we obeyed the words : I seized on the cloak, and cleared the gulf at a bound.  The other two were after me ; how we found ourselves on firm ground below with our necks unbroken, we never stayed to inquire. We spread out the cloak under our messmate, and held on hard,. keeping it taut, perhaps five feet off the ground. Then we hailed him, and bid him drop himself soft and steady.  So indeed he did; but withal his weight broke away the cloak out of our hands, pulling us all down together in a heap.  Though his fall was greatly broken by the cloak, he did not altogether escape, neither ; and coming down lengthways, bruised and stunned his head a little, but hurt his shoulder more.

Don Manuel, seeing him safe (though the worse of his fall) beckoned Pounder to go down the rope ; at the same time, he slung down a bundle of our combustibles to the hole's mouth, having kindled it from our stickful of nuts, that was burning still.  The Indian went down quick, as readily as if there were no serpents within a mile of the place ; and with Don Manuel's staff, pushed the burning faggot right into the hole, which it stopped up ; then with my knife he cut the twine, and the priest hauled up the end to tie another faggot, and let it down to him.  So they went on, faggot after faggot, Pounder doing his work well ; though I believe he would sooner have shown his skill in wringing the serpents' necks than smothering them thus by blockade.

We made out by the loud angry hissings that came from the hole, our enemies had no other way of escape ; a thing we had rather feared, for in that case our fire would have

driven them out and dispersed them in the woods, to make
the whole place unsafe for us.   One of them, and 't was a
small one, found means to glide out through some unper-
ceived cranny, and wriggled himself with great speed
down the face of the cliff: but we had an eye to him, and
just as he alighted, I scotched him with a stone.

When the last faggot had blazed out, John Pounder,
swinging by the rope, made no difficulty of thrusting his
head and one arm into the hole, though the smoke was
like to blind or choke him: then, in a few moments, drawing back again, he shouts out " *Oora, oora!* " which in
their language means *Very good;* laughing now to us, now
to Don Manuel above; and in his hand was a serpent, dead
and half roasted, that he kept swinging about, and then
flung it down to us.   So, by degrees, with the end of the
staff and his hands, he rakes out nine more of them, great
and small, and flings them down.   When he had finished
this, " Well," cried I up to him, " John, are there any yet
to come out? "   He understood what I would ask, and
shook his head, laughing, and cried out again: " *Oora,
oora,*" with a war-whoop, that made the rocks ring about
our ears.   Then, shutting his hand tight (for he held on
to the rope by the other, together with his feet), he
stretched forth, first one finger, then another, counting all
the time, till he came to five; then shut his hand again,
and so did the same over a second time: then one finger
alone, and so pointed to the ground, where the serpents
were lying all about: to make us know, there were but
eleven in all, and they dead or dying there below.

This was joyful news, you may be sure ; we now looked
on the place as our own, and were impatient to take possession and begin our mason's work at it.   But by this,
the light warned us, no more was to be done at present;
and we must think of supper, and our night quarters. We
told Pounder by signs (for, what with fire-lighting, and
his other services, we now looked on him as our special
footman) we would have our fire kindled : this he soon did,
with the help of the other two, who gathered the brushwood fast enough, while we sat at our ease, and talked
over the day's adventures.   Then we supped, as we could,
on cuttle-fish ; though we found it coarse and strong-
tasted, not the delicacy 't was said to be: but this fish

was a largish one, which might be the cause; though not so large, by far (if all tales be true) as they are found in the Indian seas.*  Only, Richard could not be prevailed on to taste a bit: so we gave him all the cocoa-nut we could spare, which was not much; and he eked it out with a sup from his bottle. As to the Indians, they made a horrid meal on the roasted serpents; in which we cared not to disturb them.  But when we had done, and Don Manuel had said grace for us, we called the savages to us again, not to lose sight of them in the dark.

---

# CHAPTER XXXII.

### THE MOTHER TONGUE.

AT our bivouack round the fire, we whiled away the time in teaching our savages a little English.  They surprised us by their quickness in learning our words, with some short sentences we taught them by degrees;

---

* " Mr. Pennant, in the fourth volume of his British Zoology, speaking of the eight-armed cuttle, tells us, he has been assured from persons worthy of credit, that in the Indian seas this species has been found of such a size as to measure two fathoms in breadth across the central part, while each arm has measured nine fathoms in length; and that the natives of the Indian isles, when sailing in their canoes, always take care to be provided with hatchets, in order to cut off immediately the arms of such of those animals as happen to fling them over the sides of the canoe, lest they should pull it under water and sink it.  This has been considered as a piece of credulity in Mr. Pennant, unworthy of a sober naturalist.  It is certain, however, that a great variety of apparently authentic evidences seem to confirm the reality of this account.  The ancients, it is evident, acknowledged the existence of animals of the cuttle-fish tribe of a most enormous size; witness the account given by Pliny and others of the large polypus, as he terms it, which used to rob the repositories of salt fish on the coasts of Carteria; and which, according to his description, had a head the size of a cask that would hold fifteen amphoræ; arms measuring thirty feet in length, of such a diameter, that a man could hardly clasp one of them, and beset with suckers or fasteners of the size of large basins, that would hold four or five

and I may here say, that in four or five days or so (for Don Manuel and I worked at it with them a little every day) we contrived to hold talk with them pretty well about common things. Only, we got out of our depth, for want of expressions, when we would come at their notions of religion, or the nature of the earth, the sky, the seas, and so on; all which the priest laboured at with great patience and zeal. We were curious to know their names for some things, as well as impart to them ours; and we went about it thus:

I would point to the fire, then look at them, nod to them, opening my mouth, moving my lips as though I would speak, but not speaking at all; then I would put my hand to my ear as though I listened for somewhat they were to say: thus I made them understand, I desired to hear their name for the thing I pointed to. This went on well enough; for when they once made out my dumb show, they answered very readily. Then, listening to what they said, I would shake my head, and look a little displeased, as though that were not the true name, and I

gallons apiece. The existence, in short, of some enormously large species of the cuttle-fish tribe, in the Indian and northern seas, can hardly be doubted; and though some accounts have been exaggerated, yet there is sufficient cause for believing that such species very far surpass all that are generally observable about the European seas. A modern naturalist chooses to distinguish this tremendous species by the title of the colossal cuttle-fish, and seems amply disposed to believe all that has been related of its ravages. A northern navigator of the name of Dens, is said some years ago to have lost three of his men in the African seas, by a monster of this kind, which unexpectedly made its appearance while these men were employed, during a calm, in raking the sides of the vessel. The colossal cuttle-fish seized these men in its arms, and drew them under water, in spite of every effort to preserve them; the thickness of one of the arms, which was cut off in the contest, was that of a mizen-mast, and the acetabula, or suckers, of the size of large pot-lids.

"But what shall we say to the idea of a modern French naturalist, who is inclined to suppose that the destruction of the great French ship, the *Ville de Paris*, taken by the English during the American war, together with nine other ships, which came to her assistance on seeing her fire signals of distress, was owing, not to the storm which accompanied the disaster, but to a group of colossal cuttle-fishes which happened at that very time to be prowling about the ocean beneath these unfortunate vessels?"—Polehampton's *Gallery of Nature and Art*, vol. 5, pp. 361-2.—ED.

misliked the sound of it; then I would give the English, and repeat it three or four times, till they caught the sound; and I would do so louder and louder, as insisting they should repeat it after me, which they did willingly, and seemed delighted with the new name; for they kept on repeating it till they had it perfect.

In this way we learned some of their Indian, too. I suppose the language will die out, if white men come to penetrate into those native countries of the savages; or, at least, 't will become mixed and changed. So I here set down some of the words they gave us, till they had got our English so well, we ceased to ask them further.

First, I will set down the name of their country, which we made out after some pains; for 't was a hard question for them to comprehend: at last they did, and gave the name of it, *Toonati-nooka*. They described it by signs to be an island, with another island lying near it, smaller, and either not fruitful, or disagreeable from some cause, or, maybe, at war with the inhabitants of the first: for when they named it John Pounder shook his head, with a look of disgust, and pushed out his hands, as though he would push the island from him: this second island they called *Hai-vavaoo*.

The young savage, whom I will call by the name he gave himself, *Poula-faihe* (but later we christened him Francis), drew a plan of these two islands very neatly with the end of a stick in the sand, as we sat: and while we let him work on, he finished such an excellent raised map of the two islands, as I never saw in a museum. He hollowed out the sand, and smoothed it to represent the sea-level; then got some sharp stones and shells to stand for the cliffs and headlands of their island; he also stuck-in a few leaves and sprigs for the groves of trees; then he raised up some little mountains in miniature (as the saying is, "making a mountain out of a mole-hill"); in a word, he worked at his map with such diligence, that soon he had it completed in the rough. So, standing up, he looked on it with much satisfaction; clapping his hands together, he danced round it, he leaped across it back and forward, pointing now to one island, now to the other, singing out all the time: "*Toonati-nooka!*" then "*Hai-vavaoo!*" But Pounder, stopping in his talk with us to

examine this map, misliked some parts of it, and began to
alter them: he pulled up one of the groves, knocked down
a cliff or two, or changed them to other places: carried
away a mountain here, set it down there, and made such
changes as pleased him, but displeased Francis in turn;
in the end they appealed to the old man as umpire in their
dispute.   And the old Indian's decision had every respect
from the other two; for no sooner had he spoken, and
made some alterations of his own, than all questions were
set at rest.

I must not forget to note down their names for such
common things as we pointed to: some of them we learned
that evening, and others later on.

| English. | Toonati-nookish. | English. | Toonati-nookish. |
|---|---|---|---|
| Fire. | *Teta-hai.* | To shout. | *Eraboa.* |
| Wood (*plural*). | *Oopanee.* | To dance. | *Oomarra.* |
| A branch. | *Maneea.* | To fight. | *Eharoo.* |
| Green wood. | *Oopa-poore.* | To kill. | *Ewhaee.* |
| Dry wood. | *Oopa-taata.* | To heal. | *Oowhya-da.* |
| Wet. | *Há-warre.* | A wound. | *Eeree.* |
| Rain. | *Taina.* | A scar. | *Eraeea.* |
| Thunder. | *Pateere.* | One. | *Oteo.* |
| The sea. | *Anonohao.* | Two. | *Enara.* |
| A rock. | *Epoote.* | Three. | *Paape.* |
| A cocoa-nut. | *Efarre.* | Four. | *Eheeo.* |
| A monkey. | *Tohyto.* | Five. | *Honoo.* |
| A shark. | *Kerekaia.* | Six. | *Paya.* |
| A canoe. | *Looamao.* | Seven. | *Teire.* |
| The head. | *Emaa.* | Eight. | *Myde.* |
| The eyes. | *Ete-rahai.* | Nine. | *Paeena.* |
| The nose. | *Páraou.* | Ten. | *Tarooa.* |
| The mouth. | *Taeea.* | Twenty. | *Taroo 'nara.* |
| The tongue. | *Ry-poaeo.* | Thirty. | *Taroo-paa.* |
| The teeth. | *Eneeheeo.* | Forty. | *Taroo-ehî.* |
| The hands. | *Tootahai.* | An hundred. | *Taroo-ta-roone.* |
| The feet. | *Amarehaa.* | | |
| To walk. | *Otooetee.* | A great many. | *Eaha-noue.* |
| To run. | *Horoee.* | A few. | *Poheea..* |
| To work. | *Tangatya* | None. | *Te-moönea.* |
| To laugh. | *Makoia.* | All. | *Moönaee.* |
| To weep. | *Hánoaa.* | | |

They who may chance to read these adventures, will by this have had enough of the language of Toonati-nooka. If the words seem not so harsh, written down on paper, as I described them to be in the sound, this is because it is hard to express, by any writing or accents, the strange way they had of forming them down in their throats, with a kind of gurgling noise. And on their part, they told us after awhile, our English sounded to them the most chirruping thing; and when they came to know us better, they called it *a language of birds*.

## CHAPTER XXXIII.

### VARIOUS DISCOVERIES.

BY the same kind of pantomime, John Pounder told us this larger island took two months to go round it in a canoe; pointing to the moon (for a young moon had begun to appear), then holding up two fingers, and sweeping his hand round Poula-faihe's map of the island; then motioning with his hands as though he were paddling one of their canoes. It was very fertile, he said, and well wooded (so he expressed by pointing to the trees round us, then to the leaves and sprigs the other had stuck in the map, making signs of pleasure and admiration): and that it had a great many inhabitants; so he told us by pointing to himself and the other two Indians, opening and shutting his hands several times, and calling out *Eaha-noue* (" a great many ") each time he did it. And this was all we learned from him that night; for Don Manuel called us to prayers: and soon after, we were all asleep, having wrapped our guns carefully in our jackets, and laid them under our heads, together with the broken one. But we had agreed Ned Hilton should watch for us to-night, till he saw the savages asleep: indeed he had not long to watch for it.

Our hard day (so it had been to us all) made us sleep so

sound, we woke later next morning than our wont; when we found a clear sky and the wind quite gone down, as if no hurricane had blown at all; for by this time, it had blown itself out.  A flight of parrots came screaming and whistling over our heads, with troops of monkeys, too, chattering after their way, in the trees ; so there was noise enough, as Gill said, to pipe all hands from hammocks. Up we rose, and shook ourselves free from sleep ; then, by a common feeling, all looked for Don Manuel, as our chaplain.  He was a few paces off, reading his prayer-book to himself; so soon as he saw us risen, he put it by, and came to us.

"You have stopped your own prayers for ours, this morning, Señor," said I, coming to meet him; and I pointed to the men, who were waiting ready.

"I am happy to do so, my dear friend," answered he ; " and 't will give me another reason to say a *Gloria Patri* when I begin them again."

So, without more delay, he shook hands heartily with the men, all round ; then we all knelt down together, and the three Indians, seeing this, followed our example, out of submission, I suppose.  The priest led our devotions praying with us, and for us ; and he put in some little petitions, suited to the change in our state from the arrival of the savages: as that we might be kept from the sins of tyranny, oppression, and injustice to our inferiors ; that they, too, might remain submissive and peaceable, and at length have grace to become Christians.  This, with beseeching the Divine majesty we might be kept from sin through the day, and from all evil accidents or sudden death, and might advance His glory and our salvation, made up the priest's short and fervent prayer.  Nor need I mention after this, he had got us all so into the way of praying that we fell to it regularly thenceforward : and soon the men would as little have thought of going without morning or evening prayer as losing their breakfast or supper.

Breakfast, indeed, now engaged us all ; though we had but some scanty slices of our enemy, the cuttle-fish, with a little pulp and milk that remained of our cocoa-nuts. We broiled the fish and pulp together, to make out a meal; for I was in haste, and they too, to get down to the shore

and see after our shark: our sharks, I should say, for we
hoped to find the hurricane had lifted the skeleton too,
handier to us.  Prodgers could not be got to taste of the
cuttle fish; being persuaded, say all we could against it,
there was some poisonous quality in the meat of the fish
as well as in the suckers of its limbs, that made his face
all of a smart even now.  As we had dressed our whole
larder already, poor Richard had a chance of going without his breakfast; when Samuel, our young Indian, seeing
this, stood up, and bowing down before us, made a little
speech, pointing to an open space beyond the wood.

We could only make out that he promised Prodgers
something to eat, out of the earth: for he made as though
he were digging, or tearing up some vegetable with his
hands.  We had gained confidence now in our savages,
that they would not desert us nor do us harm: so I waved
my hand to him to be off on his errand, and he darted
away like a wild stag, striking up for the middle of the
island, as though he would make for Prospect Hill.  When
he had been gone a few minutes, I doubted my wisdom in
letting him go at all; and hallooed after him to come
back to us: but presently he came back through the
woods at another point, and appeared laden with some
large vegetables on his shoulders, though he ran very fast
under the weight.  When he came panting up to us, and
threw them on the ground, those of us who had been in
the West Indies knew them to be yams.

This was a precious discovery to us; more so, by far,
than if we had found a mine of rubies or diamonds on our
walk.  We might now look on our kitchen-garden as in-
differently well stocked (what with bread-fruits, cocoa-
nuts, and now yams beside), let us remain on the island as
long as we might.  Don Manuel did again what he had
done when we had discovered the bread-fruit: he held a
yam in each hand, having first laid his hat on the ground;
he raised the yams as a thank-offering to heaven, and said
his *Gloria Patri*.  But the difference now was, he was
joined by us all in this, as a matter of course: so much
can misfortune and good example soften the hearts of the
rudest.

Then, raking together the ashes of our fire, we peeled
one or two of the yams, and sliced them; these, with

some oil from our candle-nuts, make out Richard's breakfast well enough. But the water hereabouts was brackish;
for I suppose the sea-water somehow filtered in through
the soil. And this, we saw, might prevail against our
making our abode hereabouts except we could discover
some other spring, or find means to convey pure water
hither from a distance.

The badness of the water was Richard's excuse for
taking a little pull at his bottle: after that, he surrendered
it to me with a good grace, saying he would have it reckoned into the common stock, and kept for a case of sickness, or other need  So we all took our way down to
Shark Cove.

We were sorry enough to discover, as soon as we got
clear of the trees, not the shark only (though he was there,
too) but the dead body of that fourth Indian, whom we had
seen drowned as their canoe capsized over the reef; the
body had been flung by the force of the tempest, high and
dry, and lay stretched on the sand. The savages set up
a loud wail on seeing it; they ran to the dead man, and
began to lament over him, after their fashion. But I believe 't was more out of custom than much regard: for we
made out from them, he was not of their kinsmen, though
of the same tribe; and had gone a-fishing with them when
the hurricane caught them all, and drove them on the island. However the first thing we had to do was, to give
the poor savage decent, if not Christian burial: we set to
work to dig his grave on a rising ground, safe from the
reach of any tempest; nothing but another deluge (we
thought) could touch it: though we lived to find our mistake.

----

## CHAPTER XXXIV.

### A FUNERAL, AND A LESSON FOR THE LIVING.

WE were some time in digging the Indian's grave, to
make it deep enough: having nothing to dig with
but a kind of flat sharp stones, like slates, that we found  .

near the spot.  Yet as we had leisure for the work, we thought to do it thoroughly; and putting our hands together we made the grave, I am sure, near five feet in depth.  Then the old Indian, who had asked by signs to go into the wood, came back with a load of leaves of the cocoa, palm, banana, and other broad leaved trees, together with a quantity of the same creepers we had made our rope of.  In these they lapped the body of the dead Indian from head to foot, and bound it about: then, at our bidding, they lowered him carefully into the grave.  When we came to know them and their ways better, we found they did this out of submission to our will, thinking the white man's way must be best in all things.  For their own custom in disposing of their dead is, to place them on a ledge constructed of poles, in some place apart, till with the sun, and weather, and process of time, they are wholly consumed.

But now Don Manuel, standing bare-headed over the grave, lifted his voice, and said aloud: "May the Lord be merciful to all whom He knoweth to be His!"  With that, we shovelled-in the earth, and made the grave secure with such large stones as we could find; some of them so large, we were forced to roll them, two and three of us together, to the spot.  This we did, to secure it against being disturbed by any wild animals of prey that might haunt the island; though as yet we had seen none.  Then we named the place *Indian's Rest*, and so left it.

Our next concern was the shark, which had been thrown further up the shore; for he was the sport of the hurricane at its first burst, but the Indian only came to land when it began to abate.  A big, ugly monster did this fish look, truly, as he lay along there; and called forth from us again some natural expressions of thankfulness for having been kept out of his cruel jaws.  After consulting, we resolved to skin him first, and then cut him up: neither of them were pleasant things to do, but useful to us in our need.  "He is a mine of wealth to us," said I, "as I told you.  We shall get shagreen from his rough skin, then oil from the liver, knives and arrow heads from the teeth, and all kinds of instruments out of the bones."  "And pickled pork," added Hilton, "from the flesh, could we but salt it well, for many a long day to come."

"From his jaws, too," said the priest, "which we will set on a pole, we shall have a memento to calm us into content again, if we are tempted to repine at our present lot."

"Aye, indeed," chimed in Prodgers and Harvey together.

"I warrant," says Harry Gill, "our 'prentices"—he looked at the priest, and laughed a little, but 't was now in a civil sort of way, "have skinned a shark for their own use before now. What if we bid 'em do it, and leave the job so?"

This seemed reasonable; so putting our knives into the Indians' hands, we made them know, we would have the monster skinned, and that his skin should be carefully dealt with, to preserve it. They set to work cheerfully, and with skill: when I saw from their first slices, they would do justice to our wish, I proposed to the rest to go back and work at our habitation in the rock. We left Richard, with his gun, for a captain over the savages, being secure of his behaviour now: and Don Manuel said he would take his turn at watching from the tree, as the old Indian had watched before. "I have some of my prayer-book to read," says he, "and can do that as well in the tree as on *terra firma*."

"I believe, sir," answered I, as we went along, "you could pray anywhere."

"My dear," he answered with affection, and his hand on my shoulder, "in all parts of our lives, and everything we do, 't is not so much *where* we are, as *what* we are."

"That's true, indeed," says Hilton: "I little thought, when an old uncle of mine took me, I may say dragged me, by the ears, to church in our village, the Sunday before I ran away to sea, the next time I prayed (except once when I prayed in a storm) would be on a savage island in some unknown latitude, no one knows where."

"In *No Man's Land*, eh, Señor?" asked Don Manuel, looking on him archly.

"Ah," says Tom Harvey, laughing, "that was what old Dick said when we first landed, and grumbled at having the place called Manuel's Island."

"I don't think," said I, "Dick would make that kind of

speech now. From the rough old tar he once was, 't is wonderful to see him 'fined down into another being."

"Many people," the priest said, taking up his former vein, "think they would be better Christians, and more able to save their souls, were they in different circumstances, surrounded by other people, engaged in other duties. Now, 't is true, each man has a vocation to be this or that, would he take pains to discover it. But 't is likewise true, all depends on the *will*, whether a man shall be good or bad; whether, too, he shall be slothful or fervent in good. He may be good in a camp of soldiers, or bad in a choir of monks: for God gives him liberty, and sufficient grace, which he may use, or sin away, at will."

"And could he be good in a ship like the old *Spitfire ?*" asked Ned Hilton, more grave than he was wont.

"If any one," answered Don Manuel, "should find himself where he could *not* be good, from the flood of wickedness all around him, he would be bounden to depart out of that place as soon as he might. For he has to save his soul in the first place, and to fulfil other duties of life in the second. That is what we Catholics are used to call, avoiding the occasions of sin. But come, here is my tree; which gives me the occasion of serving you. So we will each fulfil what is expected of us; you to work beyond, and I to watch up here."

"Watch and pray, sir," broke in Harry Gill, "as the parson used to say in North Budenham, where I was brought up."

"And if the parson had never said anything worse than that," answered the priest, rather gravely, "I should have had some respect for him. Let us not make a jest, friend, of sacred words."

So saying, he clambered into the high tree, and left us on our way to the cave.

# CHAPTER XXXV.

### OUTWITTED.

CLAMBERING up the rock, we sprang across the cleft, eager to begin working at our hole. It appeared, yesterday's attack on the serpents was a triumph; for we saw nothing, nor heard either, of any more of that family. We were glad, too, that the fire having burnt so freely showed the place to be free from noxious vapours within: for these would have quenched any fire as well as put out human life. So we now cast lots among us, which should begin our mason's work; each man wishing to be first: but no two could work together till the opening was made bigger. The lot fell on Ned Hilton: so down the rope he went, merrily; and lashing himself fast to it by aid of the twine, twisted with four or five strands together, he made all snug, and began chiselling away.

He found, to our satisfaction, the rock was very proper for our purpose; being composed of a dark sand, or sandstone, such as I have read is found in plenty about the city of Rome, made up (as is thought) of sand once thrown out of burning mountains, hardened and compacted by time. It worked freely under the stroke of Ned Hilton's chisel, though a rude mason's tool enough: but we, who watched from above, thought he was making the entrance too wide; we called to him, to leave that as small as that a man could creep in on hands and knees (lest the place should be discovered easily), and work more to the inside. In forty minutes, or so, of hard hewing, he fairly made his way within; then, unlashing himself, he called for another to come down.

Harvey now begged for his share of the work; so I sent him down, while I stood watching; and, to be short, between them they worked a passage of nine feet, or so, into the living rock, wide enough for the two to work abreast, though not high enough to stand upright: for they crept along and chiselled on their knees. It seems, they wanted to discover if the whole cliff were made up of the same rock; which they found it to be, with this in their favour, that it grew softer the further they got in: at length they worked it easy enough, and threw out the loose sand with their feet. But crack or hollow they found none, as they hoped, to make their labour easier; so 't was plain, we must make good every inch of the way, by sheer labour. For my part, I was glad of this news; I thought any chasm in the rock would be filled (more than likely) with such poisonous vapours as had nearly been the end of Harry Gill on our way down from the volcano.

When I found, by their voices, they were well into the heart of the rock, I must needs go down too, and take my part in the business. So, without bestowing a thought on securing the rope, I slid down to the hole and crept in as best I could, for the rubbish hindered me greatly. But the rope had now got so loosened from the roots of the tree we bound it to, by the weight of three men straining upon it, one after the other, 't was a mercy I had not broke my neck with my want of heed: and it gave occasion for some enemies of ours to play a trick on us that might have cost us dear.

No sooner was I got within the hole, than I heard a noise of chattering above, and swinging of branches, such as I could not well account for. It made me anxious, as I well knew, by report, the cunning of savages, who might have laid concealed in ambush all this while, waiting for their moment to take us unawares. And, truly, a more favourable moment for them scarce could have been; for with their arrows and javelins they might have killed us all three defenceless in the cave there, before we had brought our arms to bear on them; or have overwhelmed us by numbers, in spite of our shot. I looked up, and un-slung my rifle, ready to do what I could; but before I had time to fire, my vexation was to see a dozen monkeys' faces that peered and grinned at me from the cliff; and the shaking of the rope plainly proved they were tugging at it to loosen it from the tree. In short, whether from mere imitation of what they had seen us do in tying it, as they watched us unnoticed from the trees; or whether some instinct of mischief more than common is possessed by these strange caricatures of ourselves, I know not: but within a minute, as I had got ready my rifle, to discharge it upward, with no hope of killing, but every hope of frighting them from their mischief: at that very moment, I say, the rope came tumbling about my ears; and, but that I caught one end, would have fallen to the ground below.

Let me be as vexed as I would at this mishap, I could not forbear laughing at the cunning of our enemies, and their success. There was nothing for it, but only to go on with our work, and wait till the rest came to us, and so with their help make fast the rope again. I would not throw it down out of my hand, lest some unforeseen chance might cause us to need it to let ourselves down; though nothing less than a mere necessity could persuade us to that; for the rope did not reach the ground, I am sure, by fourteen feet or more, and he might have likely met a shrewd fall who should attempt it, besides leaving his comrade (if not two) imprisoned still in the hole.

So we worked on, in quietness if not content, for three hours more, or thereabout, one resting always, and two working, by turns; by which time we had got a good way into the living rock, considering our number of hands. I say, one resting; but I mean, one was not handling an instrument; but he had work, all the same, though of a lighter kind, in shovelling the loose sand with his feet towards the entrance, then shovelling it over the edge, to get rid of it.

We meant to work straight inwards, to discover what we might; but, having with us no level, nor instrument to gage our work by, and keep us straight, we found on looking back, it was bad irregular work, indeed: for here it rose, and there it fell again, here the height was greater, and there it was less. Only, we had not turned much to the right or left; at least, nothing to speak of: for in that matter we had guided ourselves by the light behind us.

10

# CHAPTER XXXVI.

### WE AIM AT A PROVISION STORE.

PRETTY tired we were now, with our morning's work, and thought it high time we were released out of this hole: the air, too, had become hot and stifling, and our limbs felt cramped to a degree by the straitness of the place. 'T was no good wishing to be out, however; so, as a first effort, we joined our voices in as loud a halloo as we could raise all together; then waited and listened. But whether the depths we had reached stifled our voices (for we could not be at the mouth all at once, and were much in each other's way), or whether the sound was beaten back by the rock opposite, we got no answer to our hail. Again we tried it, and a third time; but heard nothing from Don Manuel: we then began to think we should have to stay there till the others had finished their work with the shark, and came to look after us for dinner, or supper, rather.

"Once more, comrades," said I; "with a long pull, and a strong pull; as if we were cast adrift on the open sea, and were hailing a ship as our last chance!"

So, putting our hands to our mouths, and our whole hearts into it, we gave such a hail as (I think) three men had seldom given before: so that Hilton fell back exhausted. We had now the satisfaction to hear Don Manuel shouting to us in return, from his tree: though the sounds came to us very faint. Nor could we hear him at all when he turned the other way (as he afterwards told us), and shouted to Prodgers and the Indians to come to us quick, not knowing what might have mischanced.

The savages were quick enough in coming; for they were the swiftest creatures I ever beheld a-foot: all but old Mark; and he, too, distanced Prodgers in the race, by a good deal. No sooner did they see our plight, than catching the rope's end, as I threw it down to him, Samuel (who ran in first) was up the rock in a twinkling, and over the gulf in another, with Pounder after him; and knotting the rope firmly again to the tree, he slipped down, and darted into the hole, to give us help. By coming on us thus of a sudden, it is true, he perceived our broken gun plain enough: but 't was all one to him; he thought (I suppose) we could do as we would with those terrible engines, so great was the power of white men. Nay, when we bade him take up the piece of gun, and go on with our work, he did so with great obedience, handling it with some fear, indeed, but more curiosity: and Pounder creeping in just after (for by this time old Mark was on guard at the rope above) we fairly set them both to work, and gladly swarmed up the rope, to get a breathing.

We then went down, as before, by the hanging rock, and met Don Manuel, and next Prodgers, who arrived soon, somewhat the worse for his race. Yet he found breath to tell us how the Indians had not only skinned, but cut up the shark too, in good style; so that, had we but tubs and brine, all was ready for pickling the monster, or some quantities of him. Brine, truly, was there in plenty, in the great salt sea on all sides of us; but where should we get pickling-tubs, for love or money? However, talking it over, we were so possessed with this notion of pickled shark, as put us on contriving some way, if even rude and imperfect. Could we make shift to dig salt-pans in the earth, and line or smear them inside with somewhat that might serve us for mortar, to keep the pickle from soaking away into the ground, and so slice up our shark, and lay him in the brine, and cover him over air-tight; could we, I say, have contrived all this, our task had been done. But that was, to my thinking, as reasonable as if I should exhort my companions to build us a ship out of the trees of the island, and so sail away from our place of exile; or to do anything else that was out of our power.

I gave them my thoughts, however, as we went along; and finding them to catch at this: "Well, sirs," said I, "let any one propose a method to make a lining for our salt-pan."

"Caulk it," says Harry Gill, who was ready always with the first word, "as you would caulk the sides of a ship."

"And where's your oakum, then, and your caulking-irons, and your rosin, and your boiling pitch?" asked Prodgers, grumbling a bit, in his ancient fashion.

"Boiling pitch!" says Don Manuel, thinking; "ah, that gives me an idea: I should not wonder if on this island of ours, which was plainly once a burning mountain, we found such a pitch-spring as is met with in other like places, where the pitch comes hot out of the ground, at boiling point."

"Or, could we find some such clay," Tom Harvey said, "as might be proper for the purpose."

"Nay," answered I, "if we light on any clay, we have found pots and stew-pans in plenty, with a little care and labour; and we must needs come to something of that, if we are not to live like savages to the end."

Meanwhile, we agreed to cook some slices of our shark for dinner, in the way we had taken for our first meal on the island; this we did with our own hands, for we could not, as yet, trust the savages, who might (we thought) find means to poison our food.

We dug an oven in the ground, we gathered wood, or our servants did it for us; for having them at hand, we now grew lazy at that kind of work: then Pounder kindled our fire, as he had done before, and we heated our oven with stones, then filled it with slices of the shark, with the remainder of our yams. So, banking it over with earth, we left it in charge of Prodgers, who was the least active among us on a march; and Don Manuel stayed with him too.

We took the savages with us, all but old Mark; for he, with the priest and Prodgers, was to do something in the way of digging holes in the sand, to stow the rest of our shark in, for the chance of preserving him. The six of us started on a party to explore the island for a league or so northward, along the east shore; and particularly to look out for any potter's clay, or such natural pitch as Don Manuel had spoken of. But, for this time, we found nothing of the kind, nor came to aught particular in other ways; only that in a piece of marshy ground we lit on a self-sown plantation of bamboo canes. We hailed these with joy, foreseeing they would prove useful articles to us, as they afterwards did, for several uses. Some of the middle-sized we tore up by the roots; 't was a hard task (so deep were they bedded in the mud), yet easier than to cut them with our knives.

Having loaded ourselves and Samuel (for I sent back Pounder to help in the great larder business, before we had reached half a mile); having, I say, got our load of bamboos, perhaps three or four dozen in all, greater and smaller, we found ourselves knocked up with our wading, knee deep, through the slush and mud that had lain in our way. For several streams, running down from the neighbourhood of Prospect Hill, discharged themselves into the sea on this side the island; and some, being blocked up with coral reefs and banks of sand when they came to the shore, rose on their channels, and formed marshes and quagmires that made our travelling difficult along the shore.

So we turned our faces homewards (if we could call it *home)* slow and weary; glad enough we were to cast down our burdens of bamboos at length where the skeleton of our shark was lying; for the rest of our number had so disposed of him, I might call him a skeleton almost as much as the one we dragged out of the water. They had buried portions (as much as would last us for months, if only pickled) in six or seven small pits they had contrived to dig; and the two Indians were cleaning the bones with great diligence. To be brief, we lit our evening fire under a spreading tree, a little distance from the shore; our supper of shark we found palatable enough to men who had hunger for their sauce; then we spent the dark hours talking over our day's adventures, till 't was time for prayer, and so to bed.

---

# CHAPTER XXXVII.

### THE FIRST CATECHISM.

A BETTER writer than I am might fill a book, and a large one, with all the talk that went on between Don Manuel and the Indians, by our watch-fire o' nights.

I will give one of these discourses, so well as I can recall it; only, as I do not undertake to put the savages' broken English into fitter language (as I cannot pretend, neither, to very choice English myself*), it must be by jotting down just what they said, as far as memory serves.

"John," said the priest to Pounder, who was busy fixing some shark's teeth into a handle, to serve for a saw; "let me see if you remember what I said to you yesterday. Attend, now, for our talk must be serious. How many Gods are there?"

"White Sa," answered Pounder (so they called us, trying to say, Sir), "White Sa he say, none but one."

*Don M.* "But do you not see, yourself, there *can* only be One?"

*Pounder.* "White Sa he say yes. Me s'pose; me no know. Rer-mimebolamba know small." He meant to say, he was ignorant, and understood but little.

*Don M.* "But Rer-mimebolamba can think. If there were two Gods, or many, would they be equal, one as great as the rest, one as powerful as the rest? or would one be greater, more powerful?"

On this, poor Pounder mused for some time; then he said, meekly: "Me no know; me say what White Sa he say. Eberyting all right."

*Don M. (smiling).* "Yes, but that will not do. You must know and believe for yourself, my dear. Listen to me again: What is God?"

With much reverence he said this, and raised his hat as he spoke, bowing his head. Pounder bowed his too, but said nothing. Mark, the old man (his Indian name was Toefaoloo), took it up here.

---

* The state of education in Wales during Owen's younger days must be taken into account in criticising his entire production. Supposing him to write fifteen years, or so, after the events he records, and to have spent a part of that time in civilized society, we have still to account for the total want of polish, and even accuracy of expression, which marks his narrative. It has been thought, however, that it would prove more satisfactory to the general reader to have Evans' plain unvarnished tale presented to him, in the dress in which the author clothed it. And it must be remembered, that the "Welsh schoolmaster" of that day stood as the very type of much that was rude and uncultured; as the very reverse of the "schoolmaster abroad."—ED.

*Mark.* " White Sa, Paowanga, he our god.  Erronana-toona, he our god.  Tamaete-solloo, he our god. Havaeo-eeke, he our god.  Eaha-noue, eaha-noué (great many, great many), he all our god " (he could not express the plural, *they*, in his English).

At this, Pounder and Samuel nodded, and kept on say-ing, " *Oora, oora.*"

*Samuel.*   " And Kongadoowaia " (pointing to the moon), " he our god."

*Mark.*   " Oora, oora, Poula-faihe ": as much as to tell the young Indian, he had well spoken.

*Don M.*   " But which of all these gods, think you, is the greatest ? "

*Samuel.*   " Me s'pose, Kongadoowaia, he most most."

*Pounder.*   " Udan, Udan (no, no) :  Erronanatoona, he most most."

*Mark.*   " Udan, Rer-mimebolamba : me s'pose, Paowan-ga, he most most : me s'pose Havaeoeekee, he most most." (He meant by this, he could not decide in his mind, which of the two he named, was the greatest.)

*Don M.*   " So, it seems you are not able to balance among them all.   But *I* say to you, now, there cannot be more than One God.   To say, many gods, is to say, no God.   None of those you tell me of, is God at all."

*Mark.*   " Me s'pose, none of 'em god at all."

*Don M.*   " Well, then, is there no God ? "

*Mark.*   " Me s'pose, no god. Eberyting all right, White Sa he say."

*Don M.*   " Ah, poor creature ! hast thou lived all these long years, and grown old, in this dark state ?  Good Lord, assist me to do somewhat, and enlighten this soul which Thou hast created !  Now, Toefa-oloo, tell me : where does God live ? "

*Mark.*   " Me s'pose, Erronanatoona, he live here (point-ing to one quarter of the heavens): Tamaete-solloo, he live here (pointing to another quarter): Paowanga, he live Toonatinooka (the name of the island they came from): Havaeoeekee, he live in oloeeo : Eaha-noue, eaha-noué (he meant, all the rest of his many gods) he all live here, here, here, here, here " (pointing about on all sides, up and down).

*Don M.*   " And what is *oloeeo* ? "

Old Mark seemed not well able to explain what he meant

by this : he sat for awhile, and looked into the fire, shaking his head.  Presently, Don Manuel tried Pounder, to make him explain it better.

*Don M.*   " Well, Rer-mimebolamba, do you tell us, what is oloeeo ? "

*Pounder.*   " White Sa, oloeeo all same as place where Havaeoeekee he live, he sleep, he stay."

*Don M.*  ' " Is  it  up  there,  then ? "  (pointing  to  the heavens).

*Pounder*, shaking his head.   " Udan, udan."

*Don M.*   " Where is it, then ? "

*Pounder.*   " Rer-mime (so he called himself for short-ness), leave it Rer-mime's house, six suns back." He would have said, six days before.

*Don M.*   " Left it in your house? is it so small ? "

*Pounder*   " Rer-mime hold it so, so " (doubling up his hand).

This caused a silence again : we could none of us make out what he meant by this oloeeo.   At length Don Manuel began to question him once more :

" What is it like ? " says he, " what is it made of ? "

Pounder held up the shark's teeth he was working at, and the handle he was fitting them into; and said :

" Oloeeo this way." *

*Don M.*   " And do you think, one of your gods lives in a thing like that ? "

Mark interrupted here, but with great respect : " White Sa, Havaeoeekee he live in oloeeo this day, he no live in oloeeo that day," meaning, not always.   " He live in oloee, if no Paowanga he drive him out some time."

In short, the deeper we went into their miserable dark

---

* In an account of the island of Madagascar, of about the same date as this narrative, mention is made of an *owley* (the English version of some native word), as being an amulet in frequent use in that country.  It is supposed to be the residence of one of the local demons, and, like the *Fetish* of the African tribes, appears to be regarded at once as a charm, or talisman, and an object of quasi-adoration.  These owleys are described as small and portable, "made of a peculiar wood, in small pieces, neatly joined, and making almost the form of an half-moon, with the horns downwards, between which are placed two alligators' teeth ; this is adorned with various kinds of beads," etc.  It is not difficult to suppose the narrative referred to, and this passage of Owen's adventures, to present us with something in common.—ED.

misbelief, the fuller did we find it of absurdities, each gain-saying the other. Nor did they seem to have so much as the first rude notions of the true God, nor capable of receiving them as yet: though they submitted to all the *White Sirs* chose to say on that, or any other matter. But such discourses had a good effect on our men, though seeming lost on the savages: for after a while, Harry Gill broke out with saying:

" 'Tis a great treasure, Sir (as I find), we have had all along; though, I fear me, I have little thought on it. We have always known there was One true God; and that is something these poor niggers, it seems, do not."

"Indeed, 't is something," answered the priest, "and much, as the foundation of all beside. Then, also, you have known, that the true God has spoken to you."

*Harry Gill.* "Spoken to me, Sir? As how? I don't understand that."

*Don M.* "Has He never spoken, my friend, to your understanding, or to your conscience, or to your heart? And did He never speak to those that went before you, from whom you have derived, at least, a part of His message?"

Gill seemed puzzled how to interpret this: he remained for a little while thinking; then said, in a low tone:

" I never heard God's voice, Sir."

*Don M.* "Well, we have talked enough for to-night: but, if you desire to know what I mean, I will tell you to-morrow night, *if we live.* May God give us rest now, and eternal rest in heaven."

---

## CHAPTER XXXVIII.

### WORTH THINKING ON.

THREE words that had dropped from the priest gave me a sleepless night, I well remember: *If we live.* I had somehow taken it as a thing of course, in spite of dangers and chances that had befallen me, that I should live to a ripe old age, after all.  True it was, I had heard of others dying on a sudden, when they and their friends least thought on it: I had seen younger men die, who were shortly before in the vigour of youth: also, in my studies and practice of surgeon, I had stood by many a death-bed, unable to stay that cold hand of death from grasping the heart-strings of others: all this had not taught me, my own time was coming too.  If I ever figured to myself my own death, 't was as an old man, dying many years after: the real truth is, I never thought of it at all.

But now, whether 't was something had shocked me in the horrid heathenism of our new acquaintances, who were living "without God in this world," or that those few words spoken by Don Manuel in his simple way, as of a thought familiar to him, impressed me so as the same thing never had hitherto done: I lay before the fire turning them over in my mind; they now possessed a strange power with me, such as I could not shake off.  It was in vain to compose myself to sleep: still there came, as if it were a small voice, that whispered in mine ear; *If you should live;* then, *If you should die!*  Those two came, one after another, ringing through my brain, as it were, in turn; like the solemn ding-dong of the two old bells I have heard, times out of number, chiming to church in my native hamlet of Llanddwy-Cwmyoy.*  *If you should live! If you should die!  If you should live!  If you should die!*

* Probably some obscure village in Glamorganshire, which seems to have been Owen's native county, from his mention of Cardiff and Llantrisant, both situated within its confines.  I am unable to assign an exact meaning to the addition, *Cwmyoy;* but the former part of the name signifies the Church of St. David.  This is a name of frequent occurrence in Wales; many churches having been dedicated there in honour of the great Archbishop of Minevia, the patron of the entire principality, whose name was given, after his death. to the present Cathedral and diocese of St. David's.  Thus, we have Llanddewibrevy (the Church of David on or near the river Brevy), in Cardiganshire, the spot where the great British Synod was held early in the sixth century against Pelagius, at which St. David assisted. There is also Llan-ddewi-Abergwesin, in Brecknockshire, Llanddewi-Skirrid and Llanddwy-Rytherch, in Monmouthshire, and doubtless many others in Wales proper; to which may perhaps be added Llandewednack at the Lizard Point, in the kindred Celtic district of Cornwall.  ED.

I almost thought I was dreaming, at one time. But no; there I was, broad awake; and I did not so much think as listen to the words which some one else seemed to repeat and repeat again.

I felt my pulse, and found it somewhat heated and feverish: this, I began to think, might explain it: yet, on the other hand, the voice (as I must call it) sounded so quiet and gentle, like the voice of a friend anxious for my good; and there were no disturbed visions before my sight, as would appear if a fever were setting in.

I now gave up all thoughts of sleep; I rested my head on my two hands, my hands on my knees, and set to work thinking in right earnest. *If I should die!* What then? I began to ponder. After all, I was not so ill taught in some truths of religion, but I knew "after death comes judgment." But then, Judgment, I had been used to think, would bear hard upon such villains as thieves, murderers, traitors, pirates, spoilers of widows and orphans, robbers of churches, highwaymen, utterers of base coin, forgers, and such like; of which I was none, nor ever had been.

That was a comfort, so far as it might go; but it somehow grew lesser, by a good deal, as I thought it over. For then I began to consider how many good gifts I had had given me, and that I must be judged for them all; what illuminations in my spirit, what a knowledge of the better path I had still not pursued; how many examples from others, warnings and encouragements in books, and in actual life; lessons at every turn: and I, like a perverse, ungrateful creature, had closed my eyes and ears and heart, against all! Now, as I thought on them, they seemed to multiply before me; as groups of stars come forth at night when the man at the helm, or on the watch, keeps gazing into the sky; now here one, now there another, and another again, till the heavens appear filled with their number, or without number.

So then, I began to see, every rational creature is accountable for his gifts to God, who gave them, if even he never hath offended against the laws of his fellow-creatures: and a man may be respectable and upright (though I was unwilling to acknowledge it), and yet be condemned, too, for offences against the divine law.

What (said I to myself), if the great Judgment shall take a like course with that providence which bestows talents and powers unequally on mankind?   I have heard men say, human justice is a copy and image of the divine: and what is the known rule in all human courts?   Criminals are recommended to mercy, or get a lighter sentence, if ignorance can be pleaded for them : on the other hand, they are heavily punished in the degree of their knowledge or advantages.   I remembered what happened in my boyhood, when once being taken to Cardiff assizes, I heard the trial of two men, one William Lloyd, and one Jones Pen Rice, for forgery; who were tried before Sir Peregrine Tullock, and Baron Brainerd, when they went the Welsh circuit that year.   Lloyd was a poor simple man, who could write but ill, and from journey-man baker had become master baker in a small way, and from that rose to be an exciseman; but Pen Rice was a practised schoolmaster all his days, and for smartness of scholarship worth two of the other.   It came out on the trial, the schoolmaster had overpersuaded his poor neighbour, Lloyd, to counterfeit the sign-manual of the junior partner in a linen-draper's firm, while he himself had forged the name of the senior, to some quittance or other.   But the upshot was, the exciseman being no such adept as the schoolmaster, his clumsiness betrayed them both : so that every one that heard the trial wondered how so shrewd a man should employ so poor an agent when his neck was the forfeit.   Nevertheless, all things taken into the account, Lloyd got off with seven years in the hulks : but Pen Rice was cast to be hanged, and hanged he was.   To make a long story short, I well remembered the sentence of Justice Brainerd in addressing the prisoners (his brother judge, Sir Peregrine, being taken with a touch of gout, and not able to sit that day, for the trial lasted two days and a-half, so subtle a defence did Pen Rice make for himself and his accomplice).

"For you, Jones Pen Rice," says the judge, putting on his black cap, "I can hold out no prospect of mercy from the Crown.   Your education, your intelligence, the sacred duty entrusted to you, of guarding the morals and forming the character of youth, the influence which, by superior endowments, you acquired over your unhappy accomplice, and which you employed to so base an end, all combine to stamp your crime as one unpardonable in the eyes of man. That you may find mercy at a higher tribunal is my hope and prayer for you: to that end I exhort you to spend the short time remaining to you on earth, in fervent supplications to obtain forgiveness of your crimes from your offended Maker. The sentence of the court is, that you be taken hence to the place from whence you came, and that on the fifth morning after the present day you be drawn on a hurdle from thence to the gallows erected on the place called Piper's Heath, and there hanged by the neck till you be dead, dead, dead! and may the Lord have mercy upon your soul!"

On which, I also remembered (for by this I was all but nodding off to sleep; and our snatches of dreams bring strange fragments of memory, with oddly assorted words and things, little thought on during the interval), I remember, plainly, I say, that when the judge had solemnly pronounced those words with a deep voice and shake of his head, and the crowded court was hushed, except the poor wife and daughter of the condemned man in the gallery, shrieking, and in hysterics, the head-waiter of the King's Arms elbowing in near the judge, leaned forward, and said in a loud whisper; "So please your lordship, my lord, my master bid me say, the haunch of venison will be ruinated and burnt to a cinder." On which the court breaking up in haste, adjourned to its further duty of dining at the King's Arms, to drink his majesty's health, and the rest of the royal family.

Just before I dropped to sleep, I heard Don Manuel speaking to himself: "Toonati-nooka!" Methought he was practising the name of the savages' island; but, looking at him, I perceived he was sound asleep: then I guessed, his dreams were taking him to that heathen place, and he was bent on something for their good. Presently, he became more restless, and began to murmur things that I could not catch so well: all at once, he started, broad awake, crying: "Save them! Save them, or they perish!" then, seeing me, gave a little quiet laugh, as though at himself, and turned from the light of the fire; so I heard no more.

# CHAPTER XXXIX.

### A POSITIVE PRECEPT.

A TRUANT pen, I find, is like a runaway horse. When I began this record of our misfortunes, I meant no more than to note the heads of what befell us; to guide my memory more than for any other's sake beside: and already I have blotted many sheets with the history of a few days of our exile in that place. Yet our situation on the island was so strange as few, I think, could match by their experience; and, had I but the fresh remembrance, as I have now the leisure in my latter days, such things as befell us there demand as full an account, day by day, as I have given of them up to this.

I know not whether to record the bare heads of the journal I began to keep (after our first week or so) on some of Don Manuel's folio paper, and with the cuttle-fish ink; or to go on drawing out at full what I then put down in brief: for as I read those notes over, the whole time and place, and almost every word then spoken, seem to start up before me, though now some years agone, as fresh as anything I did a month since. As I write now, in my little parlour-room, looking over Yarmouth harbour, with the pier-head and shipping right in view, my wife beside me, and my children round me, I seem almost to hear with mine ears, and to see with mine eyes, that past and half-savage life come round again. But there is a portrait that hangs against my wall, the portrait of my good and dear Don Manuel—God rest his soul, if he need such a prayer—that looks down on me, seeming to bid me go on, and record all and each, to the best of my memory. How mild he shows there, and how humble: how grave, yet how gay, both strangely mingled! My Yarmouth painter, that I tried to describe him to, has done his best to produce him on the canvas; but the man has not caught that look, neither, and small blame to him. For that portrait's sake, I will go on as before: leastways, till I have completed the history of a week, then we will see.

Above all, could l but read, in turn, the thoughts of my readers (if any there should be), to discover the interest they take in what interests *me* in the remembrance, I should know better how to guide my pen. For a man may be the hero of his own adventures, and to his own satisfaction only: as our old schoolmaster at Llantrisant was used to describe some conceited persons as *sui amantes, sine rivali.* But, rather than be counted among those self-satisfied prosers, who satisfy no one beside, I would cast what I have here written behind the fire, and turn to use my spare time somehow else.

Well, we woke the next morning, and our first thought (after our prayers) was that pickling trade we had re-solved to engage in: it seems we had all been thinking, or dreaming of it, for each one had his plan. Some were for digging a pit, or salt-pan, lining it as best we might, with such earth or clay as came to hand; baking it hard with heated stones and burning wood, as we were now used to bake our daily meal. Some were for hanging up slices of shark's meat to dry in the sun, rubbing them with handfuls of salt, which we might find in holes of the rocks; so to pickle or salt them dry. At last Hilton cried out:

"What about the jars we left in the stream, that day we were betrayed, on 't other side the island? We have not bestowed a thought on them; yet they would serve us to admiration!"

We all answered with one voice, that 't was the best plan we had hit on: though a second thought told us, how unlikely it was, the villains who had betrayed us would leave us anything so good or useful as the jars; yet we determined to make an expedition, and hark back to that side of the island without delay.

"Besides," said Harvey, "we shall have some chance of knocking over another peccary, or so, among the woods on our way."

"Or, what will be better," added Don Manuel, "of getting some of those oysters I saw on the rocks there-abouts."

"Under favour, though, Sir," returned Harvey, "I see not how oysters are better than peccary for us."

"Better for us to-day," said the priest.

"To-day?" asked I, taking it up here, and looking at him, surprised.

"Yes," replied he, smiling, "for the week is running round, friends, and this is Friday morning, you remember."

"Ah," said I, thinking a little, "Catholics are used to take no meat on a Friday, I remember."

"Catholics, my good friend?" asked he: "certainly. But I have been told by those who know your prayer-book (for a fellow-student of mine at Salamanca was preparing to be sent as chaplain to our ambassador at St. James', and he had studied the point;) it seems, I say, your own book enjoins you to abstain from meat on all Fridays in the year."

"I fear me," said I, "the Spanish chaplain knew more of our prayer-book than I: all I know is, I never heard of this custom being enjoined, nor knew of it practised, by any protestant, in my life."

"Now I think on 't," says Tom Harvey, "there was an old aunt of my cousin's wife, that never would touch meat on a Friday, nor through the Lent, till she fell sick; but she had been brought up half a Catholic, by her grandmother; and she, again, had this handed down to her by a priest, who came to that side of the country from foreign parts, and was hanged soon after at Worcester."

"And why was he hanged?" asked Don Manuel, and Hilton, both in a breath.

"Indeed," said Harvey, "I cannot say; but he was looked on as a kind of rebel, or foreign spy, as I 've heard tell; and would not take some oaths or other, I never rightly knew what."

So that discourse dropped for the present.

I cannot pretend, what the Don had said on the point in hand came home with that force to us, that we readily conformed. For (as I now see) the precepts of natural religion, planted in man's heart as man, apart from Christianity, can appeal even to the half-awakened conscience, telling us to assist one another in need, to deal just and fair, forgive, ask forgiveness, and come before our Maker in prayer, and so on. Whereas, here was a precept of positive law declared to us, beyond anything laid down in the law of reason written in my mind; and the authority whereof I was not prepared to bow to. For my reason (if

that were all) would teach me, the animals I had a dominion over were as much given for my use on Fridays, as
on Thursdays, Mondays, or any day whatsoever. From
this arose my doubts, whether I, or the rest, could be held
bound by such a law; to which we had never subscribed,
either formally or by any other act, I thought, that implied
it; in which none, whether minister or layman, had instructed us by word or writing; which our elders and
betters had not observed; which we had not heard of,
read of, dreamed of, till Don Manuel brought it up on a
sudden.

'T was, indeed, a small matter enough in itself; nor any
denial, to speak of, for men who were used to fare hard,
and reckoned a piece of salt junk, with a biscuit half full
of weevils, and a horn of weak grog, little better than
bilge-water, to be feast for an admiral. But then, again,
it came with an air of authority: though I would have
done the thing ten times over, and heartily, to oblige a
mess-mate, or relieve a poor disabled seaman; my will (I
own) kicked against it, when it claimed to bind us by an
obligation.

I turned the question over for a while: but for breakfast, was no controversy, for nothing but shark was to be
had; and shark was fish, all the world over: so to it we
set, and broiled some pieces, with yams and bread-fruit,
having freshened our stock of these from the neighbouring
woods, by help of the savages. But savages I must call
them no longer; for, if they began by submissiveness,
they were now devoted to our service: indeed, they told
us after (when they had gained language enough) nothing
could equal their joy to find by degrees, we were neither
going to eat them, nor sacrifice them to our gods: this
being their custom, it seems, with all who are wrecked or
cast on their shores, or taken in war.

After our fish-breakfast, we bore away north-north-east,
at a smartish pace; we all desired to see whether these
jars remained to us or no: yet each, I believe, felt unwilling (some more, some less) to revisit that part of the
island where our great misfortune first had burst on us.
But after all, during the five days, or so, we had spent in
this strange unlooked for way, our minds had been so
raised to better things, our hearts, too, so calmed and

11

softened, by the society and example (more even than his words) of our companion, that we were prepared, if not willing, to look again on a spot where we had cursed, and raved, and ground our teeth, so shortly before.

---

## CHAPTER XL.

### RAMBLING IN WALK AND TALK.

WHEN we had stood, three days ago, near the top of the mountain, viewing the extent of the island, we had made out its length to be some three British leagues : that is, two full leagues south from the mountain top (as the crow flies), and about half as much to the northward, on a guess.  Coming, as we did now, from the extreme south-east, or nearly so, meaning to leave the slopes of the mountain well on our right, we reckoned there lay before us a march of a couple of leagues, or thereabout. But the greater part of our way took us through the thick woods, with high trees arching over; so we did not fear the heat.

We felt, though, our want of a compass on this march ; the more so when we left the shore, plunging into the thick growth of trees, that might entangle and mislead us, to the loss of our time.  If any one should smile to think of our reckoning the value of time, seeing we had nought in this wide world to do with it, but to keep from sin and save our souls, as best we might ; let him consider again (as we did) the rainy season was at hand, and we must needs house ourselves in the cave before it came on us.  We were so anxious about this (I mean, the priest and I, for 't was our two heads alone that seemed to forecast anything, if I make some exception for Harvey), I felt regret we should lose a day upon our expedition ; I think, had I not been ashamed to abandon it now, I had more than likely proposed to turn back to our mason's work.

Our present business was, to note the position of the

sun, and so guide ourselves by guess-work towards that channel, or inlet, of our first unhappy landing. Could we have used the sagacity of our Indians here, I doubt not they had struck out the path for us; but they knew not whither we were going, and trudged at our heels, like so many faithful hounds. We kept all together, to guard against surprise; and marched in this order: first came I, with my rifle ready for action; next, Don Manuel with his piked staff; then the three Indians, each with a bamboo, which he had pointed at the end, and burnt the end hard with fire, so making it into a formidable kind of javelin, enough; then Ned Hilton and Gill, whose office 't was to keep a sharp eye to the savages, with their guns ready against the least sign of treachery; next Prodgers, last, Tom Harvey, brought up the rear, each armed with a bamboo-pike too.

Before we had got on very far, we were stopped by a marsh, that spread out so wide as made it impassable: for we knew not how deep it might be in the middle. All we could do was to strike up to the right, keeping to firm ground; we could see this quagmire was narrower to that side than towards the left, and so we judged it to be formed by some stream that came down from northward. We found ourselves right in this; for the soft ground grew less and less, until we traced the opening of a small stream that ran into it.

Here we came upon a discovery; and 't was due to Hilton, whose foot, slipping on a sudden, nearly brought Ned down upon his nose. As he looked to see what he had slipped on, he cried out: "Clay, as I'm alive!" We crowded round the place, for this was joyful news to us all; we found indeed, he was not mistaken: for the east bank of this small stream was made up of a greyish marl, or clay, very fit for moulding into pots and dishes, if only we had had skill as well as material. We traced the clay (some of us searching up the stream, and some down) for sixty or seventy yards; then we gave over, finding we were rich enough to employ many score of hands in the pottery work, had we been so numerous; and to drive a thriving trade with Toonatinooka.

We rejoiced at this, and rendered thanks to God; but would not delay on it for the present. Our only concern was, to mark the place, that we might come hither again when our house was built (I mean, our cave hollowed wide enough), and so employ our new-found treasure.

"And let that be soon, friends," said Don Manuel: "for next to a lodging, a good householder looks to his furniture. In Holland, where I once was, the houses of the better sort, indeed of all, from the burgo-master down to below the middle rank, are ornamented chiefly with such glazed delf-ware and tiles as they have a great art in making; and they have such a wealth of this pottery-ware as descends from father to son, and is valued even beyond its worth. Though we cannot rival their native manufacture, on our first essay, we may contrive, with pains, some vessel that will stand the fire, and cook a hash."

"Or make a fish-soup on Fridays," says Harry Gill; and with that he made a little wry face, which the priest did not see. But, though Harry had taken the place of being scape-grace amongst us, which Prodgers had left vacant, there was no great malice in him, neither; only he did some harm to Ned Hilton. For Hilton (as Don Manuel once said of him) was like the animal they call a chameleon, that takes the colour of everything 't is next to, and is green among the leaves, but gray on the bare ground.

To mark this spot, and find our clay-quarry again, we bade Samuel climb a high tree of the fir kind, over against it, and take with him the saw that Pounder had made of the shark's teeth, to notch the rind with such a mark as could be seen from below. When the young Indian made out our wish, up he went, as spruce as any monkey: and before five minutes he had cut a cross deep into the bark of the tree, on the side looking towards Shark's Cove. Then he came down again as nimbly, and we went on our way.

I could not but remark to the priest, 't was strange how the young savage, who had not so much as heard of Christianity, should choose the sign of the cross to cut into the tree. But he smiled when I said it, and answered me:

"Nature, friend Owen, and Grace, both come from the same Lord: is it any wonder, then, that even nature sometimes witnesses to the things of Grace? The Arabs, as I have heard,* in the sandy desert, mark their camels with the same precious sign, either to know them among others, or as a sort of charm. Not that they believe in the Cross (poor souls!) or in Him who died on it: but, I suppose, because 't is the most natural sign, and comes first to hand, as you may see yourself, if you try. Children in their games, when one has to make a sign against the other, choose a cross and a round *O*, because these are the easiest made. Some of the most beautiful flowers are cruciform: and they say, no plant whose flower takes this shape is poisonous. So it is, our loving Lord speaks to those who will listen to Him, and prepares (in some degree) the minds of those He has never spoken to. But this would lead us too far, to follow it up."

"Not too far for me, Sir," said I; for this man's lightest sayings seemed to wake up unusual thoughts in my mind: "pray go on, if it doth not weary you. You are so used, and I so little used, to ponder these things, it must seem to you like teaching a school-boy his A, B, C."

"Well," pursued he, "many of our early Church writers, or Fathers, while she was persecuted in her infancy, as well as after, remark as follows: that in the natural forms of things, you often may see the sign of the Cross where there is struggle, contention, motion, *et cætera;* not so much in things that denote peace. In the square-yard of a ship placed cross-ways against the mast, that is to endure all the buffetings of the storm; in the outspread wings of a bird beating against the air; in the arms of one who is violently running or struggling; in the cross-hilt of a sword; a cross-bow, and the like. I do not affirm how much there may be in this remark, but 't is, at least, a beautiful idea; and it would come home to them, who were called on to bear the Cross from day to day, and sometimes were crucified, to the very letter, even as their Lord."

So he went on, with more than I can recall, about virtue lying in carrying the cross, in continual strife and resistance against enemies, within and without; that we all profess to be soldiers of the cross, and must not desert from our standard; that if the cross were thus impressed

---

* So says a Protestant traveller to the Holy Land. ED.

on mere nature (as Poula-faihe had just shown in the tree, when he least thought on it) 't was, far more, the very foundation of all things in Grace; the sign of that redemption without which we had all of us remained hopeless slaves of the devil, and the heirs of hell: again, how reasonably the Catholic Church taught her children often to make the sign of the cross, to keep these things ever before their eyes and hearts.  Then, as I asked him to do, he showed me the way Catholics had of making this sign, and repeated to me, in Latin, the words wherewith they sometimes accompanied it: in nothing of which I could perceive the least departure from what was lawful or reasonable.

Such discourse was broken by our discovering, when we had traced the stream a little way up, this was the very same that flowed from the southern declivity of Prospect Hill.  For there was the hill itself leaning (as I may say) on our right shoulders; but we chose to give it the name of River-head instead, and drank of the fresh water again, to the success of our expedition.  "And who knows," quoth Hilton, "but River-head may one day become a famous place in history?"  "I warrant," says Don Manuel, "'t will have more harmless fame than many a celebrated spot, where men have cut their brothers' throats by wholesale, betrayed a town, or proved themselves villains on a large scale."

Going still forward, we had scarce got two miles on, when Pounder called out, pointing to something that grew in another swampy piece of ground to our left. From the look of the plant, though the pods were not yet burst, I knew it for the cotton-plant, and bade the Indian go and gather us some.  He brought us a good handful, which Don Manuel and I examined; but we were not so greatly rejoiced at this as at our former pieces of good-luck, seeing the difficulty of weaving this cotton into any cloth for ourselves.  At last I said: "'T is true, we cannot weave, for we have no means to come by a loom, nor skill to make one: but we can learn to knit, I suppose, and that will answer us as well."

At this, the men all burst into laughter; they asked, when were we to begin this old-wife's trade, and sit at our doors knitting, with spectacles on our noses?  Then

Gill, like a luckless Harry as he was, turns round on old Prodgers, and tells him, he would make a famous grandmother at that sort of work. I know not what Richard might have said or done; nor how far his new-found gentleness had stood proof against this sudden thrust of the reckless fellow: but Don Manuel laid his arm gently over Prodgers' shoulder, and called out good-humouredly: "I mean to begin at it! see, if I don't take out a patent for the first pair of stockings!"

Many a true word is spoken in jest, says the proverb: so, thinking it over, I resolved to see if we could turn our spare time to account in this way of cotton-knitting: in truth, our clothes even now were not of the best; and if our exile was prolonged (as there looked every prospect of it) that trade might become, not a comfort, but sheer necessity.

But now we journeyed on; though, partly mistaking our way, we bore up somewhat too much to northward; when we felt ourselves getting on the slope of the volcano, we struck west again, and after a while came upon the head of that glen through which the stream came down that we had placed our jars in. We were alive with eagerness to see whether these were left to us, among our small possessions; so we made a headlong rush for it, and one or two of us fell into the brook over the slippery roots of trees: till we got into that mossy lane we had travelled up before; and found (as indeed I more than suspected) the fellows who landed us had no more charity than we gave them credit for: for one of the jars was clean gone, and the other lying beside the bed of the stream, broken into pieces; whether out of sheer malice, or by some accident, is more than I can say.

We uttered something of disappointment, 't is not to be doubted; but I heard not a single curse among all our number. Should this appear to any as a small matter, or not one to lay stress on, to me, on the other hand, who knew the way of seamen, and how glibly an oath slips from the lips of men that have given themselves to uttering them, it seemed next door to a miracle, to find how much had been done in the line of good within five short days.

"True," said the priest, when I remarked on this to

him aside; "it only shows that every one *can* keep from
sin, with the help of God, where he is resolute to watch
over himself.  I will tell you what chanced once in Spain,
on this subject of swearing, to prove what I say."

————

## CHAPTER XLI.

### THE SWEARER'S BUTTON.

"IN the town of Espinosa," says he, "in the province of
Toledo, was an officer, quartered with his regiment;
he was a good sort of man, possessed with some fear of
God. But, from living in camps, with bad example around
him, having also to deal with men under his command on
whom soft words seemed wasted, he had contracted a vile
habit of profane swearing; and this came out whenever
he was roused to impatience, or anger.  That much, with
the remainder of the story, I heard him relate afterwards
at the table of the bishop of Cuidad Real.  It seems he
made some efforts to overcome this evil habit of his; but
all to no purpose.  At length, the beginning of one Lent,
he applied to a Jeronymite monk, of the convent in Espinosa, to explain his case.  The father asked him, was he
in earnest? did he truly wish to unlearn his swearing
habits?  The captain professed himself, that he did indeed
desire it.  Then, says the other, will you punctually
follow the advice I am about to give you?  The captain
says, again, there was nothing he would not do to correct
himself; and so gave his promise as a soldier and a man
of honour.  'Well, then,' says the good monk, 'I will
hold you to it, *hijo mio:* and what you shall do is this:
The very next time an oath slips from your lips (remember, you have promised me) draw your sword, and cut off
the top button from your uniform coat: and so on, a
button for every oath after that.'

"A bargain is a bargain, among men of honour: as this
officer had promised, he held himself bound to perform.

But he felt much confused at the bare thought of appearing in his uniform with a button less; and determined by all means to avoid the disgrace. Well, he left the monastery, and went back to his quarters, full of good intentions; scarcely had he set foot within the barrack-gates, when something went wrong, and one of his men gave him cause of offence. Out came a thundering oath, according to custom; and, when he bethought himself, there was the old evil done again. How should he act now? Being a man of his word, cost him what it might, he draws his sword, and cuts off the top button, just under his chin. Though perhaps none of his fellow-officers noticed it, yet he thought every eye was on the place where the button should have been; and he went about all day in a sheepish kind of way, feeling something was amiss with him altogether."

"Now," continued the priest, turning to me, "how many buttons, think you, did he lose, owing to that promise?"

"Truly," said I, "'t is to be feared, he was soon left without so many as would hold his coat together."

"On the contrary," says he, smiling, "he never had to cut off a second; and the careful guard he kept on himself, lest he should lose the next button, grew into a habit, that cured him of his swearing."

I was much struck with that story, I own; and needed not that the priest should enforce its moral: he, for his part, did not add another word.

Nor do I find any particular thing to record in the after part of this day. Don Manuel led us to the place where he had observed the oysters; which we found in abundance, and of a prodigious size: whether I am to call them oysters, or cockles rather, they furnished us with more food than we needed.* As if, too, we were to be rewarded

---

* For the size to which shell-fish grow in the tropics, see Cook's Voyage round the World: "At four o'clock in the afternoon the boats returned with two hundred and forty pounds of the meat of shell-fish, chiefly of cockles, some of which were as much as two men could move, and contained twenty pounds of good meat." Friday, 17th August, 1770.

As to the "sea cra-fish," or lobsters, Anson (or his biographer) assures us that on the island of Juan Fernandez, "they generally

for our obedience to the precept, now first announced to us, of eating no meat on this day, I must note that, even as the people of Israel, turning from the flesh-pots of Egypt, were sustained in the wilderness by manna from Heaven, so now, besides our oysters, that were (as our priest had said before) both " fish and dish," we discovered, in another creek somewhat to the south of these rocks, such a colony of fine cray-fish, as made us have nothing more to say to shark on Fridays.

Indeed, as far as fish went, I concluded we had settled on the worser side of this island. But we had taken a fancy, or whim (whichever I may call it), in favour of our cave, and determined to stick to it: as men have stuck to things less reasonable, before now, just because they willed. Stewing our cockles and cray-fish in their own shells, and dining excellently well, we then loaded the Indians with some of each sort, to establish a fish-pond, or preserve, in Shark Cove; and set our faces homewards. Having but ill secured the claws of the cray-fish, one of the larger of them got loose, and gave Samuel a shrewd nip on the shoulder, as he was carrying him. The poor fellow started off like a fury, yelling louder than any mad-man with the pain: he rushed through the wood, with the rest after him ; shaking himself in vain, to be free of his tormentor, then rolled on the ground, and roared till the echoes rung again. Pounder now proved his title to the name he bore, and finished the enemy by hammering at him with stones. But Samuel was under my hands for three days after, for the creature's nip was no joking matter, believe me.

Saturday was a day of hard work at our cave, with nothing more to chronicle. We took turn-and-turn about, and made progress; working on a regular plan : and for dinner we had a young peccary that we had met (to his grief) in the woods the day before ; for we killed him, though we ate him not, on Friday, without remorse or scruple.

weighed eight or nine pounds apiece, were of a most excellent taste, and lay in such abundance near the water's edge, that the boat-hooks often struck into them, in putting the boat to and from the shore."— Anson's *Voyage Round the World*, p. 177, ed. 1748. ED.

# CHAPTER XLII.

## A GERM OF THE FUTURE.

SUNDAY, the thirtieth of August, 1739, was the first Sunday we had spent in this exile; and so Don Manuel reminded us, while we sat to breakfast under a spreading tree.

"And we may see, friends," says he, "how wise, how loving, is the commandment to keep one day in seven as a day of holy rest: not only to refresh our wearied bodies from toil, but to raise our minds to that heaven where we hope to be one day, and for ever; remembering, we are on earth but for a short while, at most."

"'T will seem a long while, though," says Gill, rather down-cast, "if this kind of life goes on, upon a desolate island. I don't know, but, for my part, I'd as lief be in a tight, well-trimmed craft, with a smart crew, and sixty guns, or so, upon a cruise after some of them Spanish galleons, under favour, and no offence, Sir," says he, touching his hat to Don Manuel, "with a sharp look-out after my share of prize-money, than "—

"Than in heaven, do you mean?" asked the Don, quietly.

"Well," pursued Harry, shaking his head, "I suppose I ought to say no such a thing; but I can't help feeling, all the same, that heaven, d' ye see, is a place I 've no acquaintance with; whereas, a sea-faring life, with its ways of going on, in ship's companies, calms and breezes, dog-watches and idle times, leave to go ashore, and ups and downs, like, is what I have used, and understand 'em."

At this, the priest smiled a little, not much, seeming as if he only would not look too grave at what Gill said. Ned Hilton chimed in with much the same: he declared, for his part, sometimes he had as soon be in the Old Bailey, or the hulks, as on this island."

"Nay, mess-mate," cried Harvey, breaking in here, "'t is not for me, of all men, to turn preacher: but we should be unthankful dogs, not to compare our state with what it might have been: had we been clapped under hatches by old Hopkins, now, how had that suited us, I wonder?"

"Or left to the tender mercies of the chief mate?" Prodgers added.

"And," said the priest, "when you speak of prisons, never forget, there are prisons more dreadful, more hopeless, than mortal eye hath ever seen.  You tell me, dear friends (or some of you) you had rather be on earth than in heaven: what think ye, then, of hell?"

With that, he settled the question; leastways, no one seemed disposed to answer: and now, having an idle day before us, we began to straggle about under the trees; and the men, from sheer want of something to do, were for throwing stones at a mark, or jumping height and distance, getting up a wrestling match, or anything else, to kill time.  I foresaw, some untoward thing might come of this idleness, for our quarrelsome passions were, as yet, only like the candle that is newly blown out, smoking still, and easy to be kindled again.  I whispered this to Don Manuel, who whispered back to me, he had his own fears about it, and something must be invented to occupy them.  At the same time, he asked to borrow my claspknife, to show them, he said, a game played by the country folks in Spain, with four sticks laid across.

When he took the knife, I saw him look curiously at it, as being in make and fashion different from what are used in Spain: suddenly, he cries out with joy and wonder, so that we were startled, in a literal sense, and came crowding round him.  He remained, without noticing us, looking earnestly on the knife, which he had not opened; he spoke a little to himself, then grew silent, as if he pondered something deeply, but never takes his eyes off the knife, the whole time.  All of us were amazed; as we looked at him, we grew afraid: for I believe, the rest thought as I did, he might be losing his head.  Perhaps, said I to myself, with much alarm for him, these wrongs we have all suffered together, that roused *our* angry passions for a time, have gone deeper into this man's soul, being of a graver and a more reflective turn; the sense of them hath lain working there unseen, till it comes out at last in this strange, unheard-of way.

Soon he recovered himself; shook his head once or

twice, then fetched a deep sigh, and thinking aloud, he says, "I fear me, 't is not possible." With that he opens, the clasp-knife carefully, and shakes something out of it into the palm of his hand : then reaching his hand to me, showed me what lay on it, and said, with gravity and a touch of sorrow : "Look, here is a grain of wheat."

I found it was so, on examining it : one single grain, that had stuck in the knife, between the hasp and the blade : and now I remembered I had thrust a handful of it into my pocket from the corn-bin on board ship, like an idler as I was ; and thought I had ate it all. This one grain had worked into the hasp of the knife ; and so, by a strange providence, this one grain, that might lay the foundation of a harvest, and feed our whole population, turned up at this odd moment, and was the best discovery we had made hitherto, if we had to stay our lives-long on the island.

But I could not account for the sadness which Don Manuel showed, after being the instrument of this discovery to us. Indeed, putting all together, there was something so out of the way in his conduct, we were not yet assured he was right in his mind. He had before told us what made him sorry to find no savages on our arrival whom he might convert : but we feared to ask him anything about the present case, dreading to confirm our fearful thought of his understanding being gone. For by this time, though not of his religion, we had learned to think and feel about him as a guide and a friend.

He soon relieved us, however ; for, fetching another sigh from the very depth of his bosom : "Friends," says he, with a sad smile, shaking his head ; "I have been dreaming of other times and employments ; this little grain of wheat has made me do it."

We looked at him, and looked at one another ; still the same idea running in our minds. Then I ventured to say, watching his countenance narrowly :

"Dreaming of what, sir, may I ask ? "

"Of Mass," answered he, and looked up again to heaven.

"Yes," he went on, after a little, "I was thinking whether it would be possible to celebrate that august sacrifice which we have in the Catholic religion, even here, on this desolate island. Most of the essential things, I have felt, were lacking and could not be had; when suddenly I come upon one of them, and that is wheaten corn. Still, where are the others?" and again he shook his head, and became silent.

"And what are they, sir," asked Tom Harvey.

"Several," answered he, "but chiefly, the fruit of the vine, and a consecrated altar-stone. Come, come," he added more cheerfully again, like himself, "if we cannot have the reality of that great blessing, why not unite ourselves in spirit with those who have? Listen to what I am going to say."

---

## CHAPTER XLIII.

### "NIMBLE THOUGHT CAN LEAP BOTH SEA AND LAND."

"THIS very day," continued Don Manuel, "many millions of Christians, spread over the face of the globe, of every clime, colour, language, race, are kneeling before such an altar as I vainly wish for, hearing Mass said by one of God's anointed priests. They come, because the Church, inviting them at other times, *commands* them to come on Sundays and some days beside. But the more earnest of them come also because they love that thrice-holy Sacrifice, and feel they need its benefits, and have special intentions to bring to it. I say, this *day;* but I say not, at this hour alone: for all day long, from early dawn to night, Mass is somewhere being said: when, 't is early in one part of the Church, 't is late in another; she is truly that world-wide empire on which the sun never sets. That voice of prayer, and still more, that act of Sacrifice, girdles the earth round; since the habitable globe itself is but the appointed dwelling of the universal family, ' the household of faith : ' and the dawn, as it runs swiftly westward, wakens anew that consent of hearts, that union of intentions, and that one great Catholic act of obedience and love. So is fulfilled, Sunday by Sunday,

day by day, hour by hour, a prophecy of Malachias, the last of the prophets, in which holy Mass was foretold, as clearly as if the seer had beheld the priest at the altar with his bodily eyes; yet four hundred years before our Lord instituted the same in Jerusalem, the night He was betrayed. I will try to put the words into my poor English, and they would run: 'From the sunrise to the sunset, My name is great among the nations: and sacrifice is made in every place, and a pure oblation is offered in My name: for great is My name among the nations, saith the Lord of hosts.'"*

"Now, dear friends," added he, after a while, "shall we not join them? shall we refuse to unite our intentions to theirs?"

"How can we join them," asks Prodgers, objecting still, but not like the Prodgers of a week since; rather puzzled than objecting; "how can we do that, sir, when we don't see 'em, and perchance are a thousand miles away from 'em?"

"We can join them in *intention*," says the priest, "though not seeing them."

"Does not your perspective," and he turned to me, "bring close to you, as it were, things that are clean out of sight of your unaided eye? Or the captain's speaking trumpet, does n't it make the sailors in the main-top hear him above the howl of a tempest, quite beyond his natural pitch? And will not *faith* carry our souls one degree further than the perspective carries the sight, or the trumpet carries the sound? 'We walk by faith,' the Gospel teaches us, 'not by sight.' If a dear friend of mine were in the next room to me, and a thin partition between us; while I heard his voice, would my regard for him be cooled or lessened because I did not actually see him? Or, if I ceased to hear his voice, while I knew he was there, should I regard him the less for neither seeing or hearing him? If I heard him praying in his room, would not my heart unite itself with his prayer? If I could not *hear* him pray, but knew he prayed at that moment, might I not join my prayers, my *intention*, with his? If I were blind, and in

* *Malach.*, i. 11. Don Manuel quotes the prophet with tolerable accuracy from the Vulgate, and even renders *sacrificatur*, perhaps, more literally than the Douay version.—ED.

the same room with him, could I not pray with him just as well?  What is there in the mere want of sight to hinder all this?"

He stopped, looking round on us: I am sure, he read in our faces, we listened with attention, and some wonder; yet no one spoke.

"If, now," he went on, "from our Cape-Look-Out" (so we had named the promontory over our cave), "or from your volcano, Señor Owen, we saw a vessel in distress, though leagues away on the wild sea; would not you, with your seaman's eyes, know at a glance what was doing, and what was amiss; would not you, with your hearts of men used to danger, have a fellow-feeling with the sufferings of the crew?  Say that the vessel, amid all that peril, sheers out of sight: you would not cease to think of them, nor cease (now that you have learned to pray) to pray with them, because you saw them not?  Well, then, we may assist at Mass, with intelligence, and offer a 'reasonable service,' in some vast cathedral, too far from the priest to catch an accent of his voice: and we may join, with true devotion, in the *intentions* of a Mass that is celebrated a thousand leagues from the spot where we kneel."

As he paused again, there was something so new to me in all this, I found neither words to answer, nor objections to propose to him.  But I said:

"Once, sir, in Buenos Ayres, as I strolled about the town on some holiday or other, I turned in idly to see the cathedral, following a whole posse of people who were flocking in from every side.  Mass was going on, I believe; at least something at the altar, which I could not see nor understand, being such a distance off.  At first, I own I thought it all mummery; the priests (there were three of them, and some attendants), none of them took any notice of the people; and there was bowing and burning incense, with movements from side to side.  I never saw anything half so strange; there was nothing of common prayer about it, like a minister getting into a desk to say, 'Dearly beloved, the Scripture moveth us,' or whatever 't is they say.  But I must own, as it went on, a something came over me, like nothing else I ever felt: whether the behaviour of the people (at least some of them, for others were careless, looking about them, almost as we did in Wales), whether 't was their devotion impressed me, or what, I cannot say : but when a little bell rang, and there was a hush all through the place, so that you might hear a pin drop, and the most careless and fidgetty went down on their knees, bowing their heads, and beat their breasts,—at that moment, I knew not why, nor know to this day—the words came rushing into my mind (and where *they* came from, I know not well), 'Put off thy shoes from thy feet; for the place whereon thou standest is holy ground :' and I found myself on my knees with the rest, calling on God earnestly, as they did. Yet there was no moving music, nor fine discourse at the moment : nothing but silence, dead silence, broken only by a little bell. What was it spoke to me thus, I wonder ?"

" 'T was the presence of God," said the priest, with reverence : " God was really present on that altar, yet you saw Him not ; as truly as He was, even then, enthroned in the heaven of heavens; and from that altar He addressed you, yet you heard not His voice. He who created you, spoke to your understanding. He bade you reason and think. He told you, a Christian assembly, some of them with much education and intelligence, representing a greater multitude then alive all over the globe, and more again, extended through seventeen hundred years, were not likely to have met, Sunday by Sunday, to witness a mere act of mummery, and listen to a little bell. He bade you suppose, there must be something beyond all this; something you could not see, nor that multitude neither; but which they knew and believed, while you did not. More than this : He who redeemed you with His precious Blood appealed to you from that altar ; He whispered to your heart, that He was there Himself. And you responded; not by faith, for that had been a miracle, and your conversion sudden, like Saul's on the road to Damascus—but by an emotion of the soul that prepared the way for faith, and signified its first dim awakening. And when was all this Señor Owen ?"

" Nay, sir," said I, " 't is three years since, at the least."

The priest lifted up his eyes, and said words (in Latin) which I now know to mean:

"As yet, the vision is far off; and it shall appear at the end, and shall not lie: if it make any delay, wait for it: for it shall surely come, and it shall not be slack."*

"But what," I pursued, and the others seemed to ask the same by their looks and manner, "what, after all, *is* Mass, that I was present at then?"

"I promise you all, friends," says he, looking round on us kindly, "to answer that question in full, the next time you ask it. For the present we have spoken enough, and I fear to weary you. 'T is now almost time to think of preparing a dinner for our oven: then we can leave it baking, and talk again; and I propose a quiet walk, after. But, as 't is Sunday, and our minds are turned on such great things as we spoke of a while ago, are you disposed to listen, if I can scrape together enough English to give you a little Sunday sermon?"

The men all voted 't would be a treat for them; so much had they began to respect and regard him already, that every word he spoke went deeper into their hearts by what they saw his conduct to be. So, after some quiet amusement, followed by dinner, he took us aside to where there was a shady bank of turf to sit on, and a little platform of rock: and getting on it, he said a few prayers with us, wherein we joined heartily; then delivered himself much as follows:

———

# CHAPTER XLIV.

### DON MANUEL'S SERMON.

"MY dear friends and brothers," he began, "I know not how the words of my text run in any English version; so I must give them to you from our Latin Bible: and they are thus:—*Quæ videntur, temporalia sunt: quæ autem non videntur, æterna sunt.*† That means, in plain

---

* *Habacuc*, ii. 3. ED.

† ["The things which are seen, are temporal: but the things are not seen, are eternal."—II. *Cor.*, iv. 18.—ED.]

words, that all we now see round us, above us, below us, all our eyes rest on, near or far off, will only last for a time: these things have their day, though it be a long one. Then they will have their end; they will pass away. But there are other things, that we do not see yet: we shall see them soon; we shall find ourselves amidst them; and they will never pass away; never! they have no day, but the endless day of eternity. So, ' the things that are seen, are for a time: but those which are not seen, are for ever.'

"Yes," he went on, " time is to-day, and the things of time; the trials, and the griefs, the temptations, duties, opportunities, and graces, of time. They are all with us to-day. To-morrow comes eternity, and the things of eternity; the rewards, aye, or the punishments, of eternity. Time! Eternity! the Now, and the Then! the passing, the enduring! the shadow, the substance! the labour, the reward! or the sin, and the punishment!

"There are only three points, dear brothers, I would have you fix your thoughts on; and I will be as short upon them as I can. Listen; they are these:

" We are placed in time, to prepare for eternity:

" We are only placed in time *once*, once for all:

" Our eternity depends on our use of time.

" First: We are placed here, to gain a happy eternity by our conduct here. Here, I mean in life; and also here in this island: for why, think you, friends, do we find ourselves here in solitude and quiet, removed from dangerous temptations, with abundant leisure to cultivate our souls? Why, but because our loving Father, who knows our weakness, hath placed us here, that He may the sooner and the surer take us to Himself? But, whether here or elsewhere, we, and all other men, even our poor savage friends that have been sent to us, are all in life, that we may thereby inherit life eternal. How, do you ask? By prayer to be strengthened to obey the commands of God, by keeping from sin, corresponding with grace, increasing it, and so growing like to Himself. And by what power? Surely, by no strength of our own, but by His grace. And what grace? Ah! that is a subject for another time; one on which I should have much to say, and you have something to learn.

" Well, then, if life is the time given us to prepare for eternity, is it an important time ?  Nay ; who shall tell how important, how valuable ?  Ask a man of covetous soul, whose affections are centred on scraping money together, what he would do, if one hour, just one hour, were given him to spend in a rich gold mine.  If he is honest in his answer, he will tell you plainly, he would spend that hour with diligence, anxiously, to the very last minute, husbanding every scrap of time, to get as much gold out of the mine as he could.  He would work while his time lasted ; he would do the utmost he was able ; and he would be sorry when the last moment was come.

"But all this very feebly sets forth the value of our time ; very, very feebly indeed.  No gold or precious metals, nor anything that bears the highest price on earth, can be weighed in the same balance with time :—time, that can gain for us a brighter crown, a nearer place to God's throne, and so a fuller measure of bliss, for ever and ever.

" No, I assert it, my friends, you must be able to measure the distance from earth to heaven, you must weigh that which comes to an end against what endures for ever, ' the things that are  seen, and temporal,' against 'the things that are not seen, and eternal,' before you can prize at its true worth, any hour of any day of that time in which we are placed, to prepare for eternity.

" Eternity ! but eternity has no measure, except only itself.  Eternity is not a number of hundreds of thousands of years, nor any possible number of them multiplied into itself ; nor the ages of millions of worlds multiplied into themselves.  In this way of calculation, you may get to conceive a sum so vast, that your mind cannot really grasp it ; no, not for a moment.  But that is not eternity. That is time, though a vast sum of time ; only time, after all.  If an insect crept one inch in fifty thousand years, till it travelled from here to the sun ; that is not eternity ; 't is only time.  Eternity is like nothing but only itself. For ever ! that has nothing to do with time. Yes : but time has one thing to do with *it* ; 't is given us to prepare for it.

" Secondly : all this would be true, had we several lives to live, one after another ; could we come back again from

death, to repair the error of a mis-spent life.  Even then,
how valuable would each life be, as it was given in turn !
For it would be an opportunity of making up lost time
and lost ground; it might save the soul in one life, that
had not been saved in a former life.  But no such opportunity is given.  Once, and once only, and once for all, we
are placed in time.  Once, only once, once for all, we can
prepare for eternity.  Once, only once, once for all, I say
again, we are able to save our souls.  When this one life
is once over, no second time of trial, no day of grace,
comes after.  As we die, so we are judged; when we die,
then we are judged.  If we die in grace, in the favour of
God, we are safe, and safe for ever : if we die out of His
grace, we are lost, and lost for ever.  In the one case, we
are safe, without fear of being lost; in the other we are
lost, without hope of being saved.  The sacred Scriptures
express this truth in striking words : ' *If the tree fall to the
south, or to the north, in what place soever it shall fall, there
shall it be.*' *

" Thus, dear brothers, had we been murdered on board
ship, we had been taken away by the hand of death:
rather, conducted by the hands of our guardian angels,
placed at once before our Judge.  No more time for us
then : none of those prayers, good thoughts, lessons of
God's love and providence, acts of repentance, we have
experienced since.  We should then have known the
worth of our souls, and of the time we had to save them
in; but we might have known all this too late.  Had we
died then, what state were our souls in ? how far prepared to meet our God, and be judged ?  But why do I
say *then* only?  No; look back over your whole lives ;
view them at a glance, as you will view them when the
last moment is indeed come.  At any moment of any day,
you might have died a sudden death, as others have died
before you, as others will die after you.  That very moment, you would have been judged ; sentenced for eternity:
for there is a particular judgment awaiting each man at
his death, as well as a general judgment for all mankind
together.  Once sentenced, there is no reversing, no miti-
gating, no recommendation to mercy, no appeal to another

* *Eccl.*, xi. 3.  ED.

court, or to a fresh trial.  As we die, so we remain ; for ever ! for ever and ever ! for evermore, without end !  We are placed in time once ; and once for all.  Are these things true, my dear brothers?  Am I making them out too strong, or drawing from fancy ?  Nay, you know I am not.  If they are true, what conclusion must we come to from them?  How ought they to affect us?  What rules shall we lay down for ourselves *because* they are true ?

"In the third place, our eternity depends on our use of time; that is, we have the power (by divine grace) to determine whether the eternal state we are hastening into, shall be happy or miserable ; an eternity of pleasure, or an eternity of pain.  But what happiness and pleasure?  Or what misery and pain ?  The greatest, either way, we can imagine or conceive.  Is that all?  No ! far greater than we can imagine ; far greater than we can conceive : such as ' eye hath not seen, nor ear heard, nor hath it entered into the heart of man to conceive.'  And the choice lies with us : with *ourselves !* we are bidden to choose ; we cannot help choosing ; we choose every day, every hour we live : for every day, every hour, we take a step one way or the other.  We step towards heaven, or we step towards hell ; one degree nearer to one or the other, every action we perform, every word we say, every thought we deliberately think.  O my brothers ! 't is an awful thing to step towards hell ; to take one step, by one foot-breadth, by one hair-breadth, away from God, towards the edge of the pit !  Can you dare to do it ?

"Even if you were sure how many steps, exactly, you could take that way, without falling down the sides of the pit ; yet what rebellion, what ingratitude, to take one step, one little step !  But you *cannot* measure this ; you cannot tell which step will be the last, the irrevocable one ; nor how many steps off it is from you now, nor how sudden the slip may be.  ' He who despiseth little things, shall fall by little and little.'  He who places himself, by his own act and deed, on the downward slope that leads to the pit of hell, has only himself to thank, if he slip on a sudden, and never regain his footing : if he goes down, and down for ever.

"But there is not only a hell to be avoided ; there is a

heaven to be gained! Hell! Heaven! Eternity in hell! Or eternity in heaven! O my brothers! 't would be impossible for any soul to sin against God, that had once looked down into hell, once looked up into heaven. Souls fall into hell, and lose heaven, because they know nothing really of hell or of heaven; nothing of eternity. Strictly speaking, they do not disbelieve those things; they only live as if they had never heard of them. They live on, day by day, as if time were all, eternity nothing: then they come to die, some one day or other, and find (find too late!) time is nothing, eternity is all!

"Ah, bring me back, if you can, one soul that has fallen down into the pit of hell; the soul that died yesterday; the bad Catholic who died in Spain, the poor misbeliever who died in England! Bring back the soul that was condemned yesterday to an eternity of torment—to everlasting fire! condemned by a God, all-merciful, all-loving, but all-just, to that lake burning with sulphur, to that prison-house of pain, to that gnawing worm, to those chains of darkness, to that company of devils, to their merciless torments and insults; above all, to that banishment from God, that shame and everlasting reproach, that despair, that self-accusation, that hatred of God, of goodness, of self, of all! Bring back that soul, that we may question it: ask it what it thinks now of time, of eternity. What would it give *now*—now, when too late, too late for ever—only to find itself on this upper earth again? though in prison, poverty, slavery: banished to an island like ours, with the means of being saved? How much would it give? At what price would it redeem, one little month, one week, one day, one hour, only to repent? What for a chance, what for a loop-hole, aye, but one ray of faintest hope? How would it despise wealth, honour, pleasure! how would it make nothing of pains, mortifications, penances! Anything, anything! if only it could set one foot out of hell! All the wealth of the Indies, all the crowns and diadems of earth, all the priceless gems, mountains of gold heaped one on the other, any price you may name or think of, would be absolute nothing, for one little drop of water to cool that hell-parched tongue, that fire-pierced tongue!—that God-blaspheming tongue!

"Or, could I call down but one of those happy souls

who have entered into the eternal bliss, who bask already in the countenance of God : the very least, the lowest, in the kingdom of heaven ; that one just withinside the golden gate !  Ask that soul now, what is the value it places on time past ?  Does it regret one good action, done with denial of its own will, done with difficulty, toil, and pain ? is it sorry for time spent in fervent prayers ? does it regret having overcome temptations, and been watchful over itself, and against the demons, its cruel foes ?  Ah, it now blesses Almighty God continually for having placed it amid so many opportunities to gain merit for eternity.  Each of those pains endured, those temptations overcome, is now a jewel in its bright unfading crown.

"But, ask it again : What would you do, were you decreed to return for awhile to earth ? if you still had five, ten, twenty years to spend in this state of trial ?  Oh ! I seem to hear the answer quite plain.  'If I were sent back to earth,' says that blessed soul ; 'if I were still on my trial, and could still gain merit, I would labour, without pause, to reap-in the largest harvest, to go before my God at the end of my time with my hands fullest.  I would reckon myself to have done nothing, while I could yet do more.  Even if I knew my salvation secure, I would labour, I would delight in it, to let each moment and each act have its merit.  I would be as the bee in the garden when 't was near sunset, laborious on one thing alone, to be able to fly home, laden with honey, back to the hive !'

"And you, *filii hominum*, O sons of men, whose salvation is *not* secure, and who know it : *usqueqo gravi corde?* how long mean you to be so dull, so heavy and slow, so indolent, so heedless, in the great affair of salvation ?  *Ut quid diligitis vanitatem?*  Why are ye so in love with all that is empty, and leaves your souls empty too, while you miss the true, the solid good ?  *Et quæritis mendacium?* And wherefore make you as though ye sought to persuade yourselves to a falsehood ?

"For time, my friends, is a mere show and falsehood, under any view but as a preparation, a training, for eternity.  'What is your life ?' asks the holy Apostle.  'It is a vapour which appeareth for a little while, and afterwards shall vanish away.'  What is your life ? asks again St.

Bernard : '*Momentum, unde pendet æternitas.*' A moment, he answers ; but a moment on which eternity depends. Yes, I say again ; time, eternity ! time is nothing : eternity is all. *Quod æternum non est, nihil est.* That which is not eternal, and has no influence on our eternity, is nothing. But our eternity depends on our use of this moment of time. *Depends !* do we understand that ? According to our use of minutes, which make up days, which make up years, you and I will be in heaven or in hell, when days and years and ages are no more ; when there is nothing but one long, changeless eternity, without division of time, or end, or death ; only eternity, and yet again eternity, and eternity, and eternity ; in the fulness of bliss or the extremity of torture and despair, as long as truth is truth, and goodness is goodness, and evil is evil, and the soul is the soul, and God is God !

" *Usqueqo gravi corde ?* Let us awake, dear brothers ; let us begin to use our knowledge of these great and tremendous truths ; let us live, and not dream life away. We are here on a desolate island ; but we have duties even here : duties to God, to one another, and to ourselves. Let us work, watch, pray, repent, cultivate all the virtues within our reach, and ask for more ! Live as those who may die any moment ; who *must* die some moment ; who know not when. Live as they who are daily preparing to be judged for the whole of their time. Then I promise you (all other things supposed, of which I will speak hereafter), I promise in the name of my Master, a holy life and a happy one, a blessed death, a favourable judgment, and heavenly joys for ever."

----

## CHAPTER XLV.

### THE ARCHERY CLUB.

SO (within a little) I have concluded the history of our first week on the island ; and, because 't were tedious to my readers to go through with like details, I shall be content with a summary of what befell us thenceforward. We began to portion out our time like a company of philosophers, or statesmen; so much to work, so much to amusement, so much, again, to ranging the island, which partook of both: 't was work in the way of providing us food, and brought us acquainted with every lurking nook of our domain; but 't was recreation, too, for the variety of things and places we came across, with a number of adventures, and dangers now and then, some of which I will set down.

A serious thought, however, began to engage us; I mean, the wasting of our powder and shot, of which we had no more than perhaps twenty rounds left in all. 'T was a dismal prospect for us, who had only been a week on the island: and what to do when that small stock was spent, or how to hinder the spending of it, I knew not; unless we found means to snare the wild creatures for our food, or betook ourselves to bows and arrows, wherein we had no skill.

In this, another consideration perplexed me; for what, said I to myself, if you teach the Indians the use of this archery? or, if they know such weapons already (as 't is likely), what if you put them into their hands? how can you be secure they will not turn them against yourselves? Now came back the old fears of these savages escaping into the woods, to run wild there, and lie in ambush for us, to harass us, and so hunt us down at last.

When I stated these thoughts to my companions, 't was agreed not to allow the Indians any use of bows or arrows for the time; and to keep a close watch on them, to hinder their contriving that or any other weapon of offence. Not, I must say, that we had seen in them so much as a sign of independence, far less of conspiracy, since they were thrown among us; but he that is on the safe side is secure, as Prodgers remarked, when we debated it.

However, not to deprive them of all means to knock over some food for our common use, I made trial of what they could do with mere stone-throwing. Calling them to me on the shore, at a place where the reef was parted by an inlet, and so the breach of the sea had freer access to wear the pebbles smooth, I set up a bread-fruit by way of mark, on the point of a rock, perhaps seventy yards from where they stood : telling them by signs and words alike (for they now understood us better), I desired to see who could knock it over first.  To it they went, with a good will; and proved themselves skilful marksmen, too, considering the distance.  The old man was least expert of the three, his hand not being so steady nor vigorous, nor his eye as true, as I warrant it had been in his best days.  So Pounder and Samuel had the match between them : after making the rock ring again with their pebbles, so close to the fruit, 't was a wonder the stone did not hit it outright, going within such a hair's breadth; at last, I say, on the sixth shot, John Pounder voted with a plumper, and sent the bread-fruit skimming into the water beyond.

This was enough for me, and the rest who looked on; for we found the savages would be a full match for us at that work, should they grow ill-disposed : and 't would be little odds to a dying man to be sent out of the world by an arrow, or a dart, or by the blow of a stone.  So we bade them desist, somewhat sternly, and this trial made us a little jealous of them again.

For ourselves, we set about to purvey us some archery weapons; first, the bamboo canes we had pulled out of the marsh proved quite serviceable for bows, being more springy than English yew, and as much to the purpose as the hiccory wood of the American forests, which the natives make use of for their bows.  As regards bow-strings, too, we found means to dress some sinews we had met in cutting up our shark; which proved tough and springy to a degree, sending off the arrow with a twang like the sound of a Welsh harp on my ear.  Only, our stock of arrows was scanty; we found nothing fitter for the purpose than the younger and slenderer of the bamboos we had brought home; and out of the whole bundle we contrived no more than seven arrows in all, cutting them to the proper lengths : measuring that from the clenched fist of our left hand, stretched at full length, to the tip of our right ear.

It cost us some labour to smooth these canes for arrows, each of them being encumbered with three or four knots at the least : but in this work the Indians were our journeymen, with help of the shark's teeth and our knives; and in two or three hours we managed to have them as smooth as a tobacco-pipe, or a gun-barrel turned out complete by a Bromwicham gun-smith.

Thus, we formed ourselves into an archery club; I mean, Gill, Harvey, myself, and Ned Hilton, who were like to be most expert at the practice ; as for Prodgers, he volunteered, to our surprise, to stand near the butt (which was the stump of a tree) and fling back our arrows that missed the mark : also to keep our score.  Nor did I see in anything more than in this, the change that had come over our old comrade : for he that a while ago had struggled for the gun with so obstinate a temper as had like to end in manslaughter, now stood in the best of humour while we shot, and gave us back our arrows without a thought of rivalry or discontent.

We were careful to send the Indians out of the way during our first practisings, lest they might see we were inferior to them in anything.  Don Manuel engaged to lead them, the first practising day, to the bamboo-marsh, to fetch us a fresh supply of canes.  Telling Samuel of this, he made him guide of the party, and they went off at a pace.  They were away about three hours in all ; when they came to us again, 't was with a good load of bamboos, mostly of the smaller sort : but three or four, too, of the oldest and biggest they could meet with ; and these were Don Manuel's choice, he told us, to make trial of a plan that came into his head while they were cutting them.

For he wanted to see if he could make these large hollow canes any how serve as a conduit to convey to our cave some of the fresh water from River-head, or elsewhere. This was a first necessity, indeed ; the water near our Castle (so we called that hole in the rock) being saltish in taste, and unwholesome, which was the chief drawback, we began to see, in our choice of the place.  We now applied ourselves to this work ; we lit a strong fire, and thrust the longest piece of gun-barrel into it, having fitted a smaller bamboo to this, by way of handle.  When 't was red hot, drawing it forth, we thrust it into the end of the large cane, till we burnt quite through the knot that stopped the passage : or, part burning and part boring, we got through it somehow.  Then we did the same again and again (there being no fewer than fourteen knots within a length of three yards or so) till, burning through them, now at this end, now at the other, at last the hot barrel bored the length of pipe clear through.

But then, we reckoned how much time it might take, and how many bamboos employ, to lay a conduit from point to point; that is, from the fountain to our cave, which we now found to be farther off than it seemed before. This, with cutting the bamboos, and dragging them to the spot, we reckoned would be a work of months, and hard work too. To save needless labour, we made some expeditions into the woods, in parties of two or three at a time, and all our aim was to search every way for water. But finding none to compare to the spring at River-head, and being determined, on the other hand, not to abandon our castle, we e'en made up our minds to go on with the conduit: and appointed gangs, or working parties, to carry on that trade, together with the mason's work we had in hand.

It is time I should now inform the reader how we distributed ourselves to these employments. It must be noted that we had three great trades to carry on; house-building, or mining; making our conduit; and purveying food: and nine workmen to employ in them. I say, nine workmen, for the priest would not hold himself released from the burden, neither; and when I told him we were well content if he would but pray for us, or take such light employments as might turn up, he reminded me, Saint Paul was a tent-maker, and Saint Peter and the other apostles, fishermen: "as though," says he, "to teach us, 't is not alone eyes and brain, heart and tongue, but hands and feet, thews and sinews, that are to be used in the service of our Master."

Thus we divided our working gangs:—Harry Gill and I were charged to provide our daily meal from the woods, turn and turn about; we charged ourselves, too, above all things, to be very sparing of the ammunition, and never waste a shot. But in no long time we learned to spare our guns altogether, and brought down everything by archery. Prodgers and old Mark were set to bore the bamboos with a hot gun-barrel, and keep up the fire; Pounder had to make some mason's tools out of shark's teeth, and flints hammered to an edge (he fitted them into handles of a hard wood, which we called iron-wood, and bound them tight with the shark's sinews); Samuel, who was supposed to be more or less under the eye of the priest, went back and forward to the marsh to fetch bamboos; which he did very actively, and by little and little brought in a middling-sized heap. The other men, Tom Harvey and Hilton (with Gill or myself, whichever had not the shooting turn that day), worked steadily at our cave, of which more hereafter.

Among these employments came our archery practice, which we persevered in daily, always having the Indians at a distance, employed on some hand-labour, with Prodgers or Don Manuel to watch them. As a prince has his standing army under constant discipline, with field days, and manœuvering, no less than his finance, victualling department, and board of works, so we, in our small kingdom, reckoned our archery among such military operations as are always, I hope, the profession of a gentleman.

----

## CHAPTER XLVI.

### ARCHERY AND POTTERY.

AND now we laid aside our guns altogether, to husband our powder to the utmost: so, depending on our archery, as though we had no guns, 't is incredible what a skill we attained within a few weeks of practice (for we practised at the least an hour and a half daily), till at length we made nothing of hitting a bread-fruit without fail at eighty or ninety yards. I said, the priest and Dick Prodgers made none of our party at this; but 't is only true to say so at the first: for, hearing of our skill, they begged for their share in the practice too. They came, at a disadvantage, being late in the field; yet, by extra diligence they made up for lost time: at length, I scarce could tell which bore away the palm. I am sure, the worst of us would have been hailed a first-class shot at any archery in England, and I question if Robin Hood had many to beat us in his Sherwood band. Yet on a comparison, though some days one and some another, again, would shoot surprisingly well, and then fall back, we ranged much in the order I here set down :—

Harry Gill, captain, by consent of all;

Myself, fairish, and pretty equal;

Ned Hilton, unsteady, now better, now worse;

Tom Harvey, diligent, never making a great miss;

Don Manuel, the same, only with want of practice;

Richard Prodgers, worst, but good humoured about it.

We could now show ourselves as archers before the Indians, without fear of being looked down on; so one day, taking them with us on an expedition, our guns slung over our shoulders, our bows in our hands, in the course of our ramble we knocked over, each of us, and quite with a natural ease, a something to prove our skill: one a bird, another a fruit, a third fixed his arrow in the knot of a tree: in a word, we shot so well that now we gave each of the Indians a bow and arrow like our own, and elected them members of the club: having provided a plenty of bamboos, great and small, in two or three journeys we made to the swamp.

Let any one explain it as he may, but these savages, by some natural instinct, gained ground quickly upon us in the use of their weapons; so that soon we ceased to have trials of skill, lest we might be worsted, and confined ourselves to what archers call *ranging*, aiming at any chance thing that met us on our walks, instead of a butt or target.

So, to enlarge my list, I put down the Indians in the order wherein we reckoned them, though we did not let them know it. Thus we stood :

John Pounder, captain (without knowing it).

Harry Gill, as before, but, stirred up to rivalry by Pounder's shooting, improved daily;

Samuel, came very nigh to Harry, and beat him soon;

Myself (though I say it) not much behind Samuel;

Ned Hilton, mended his shooting as he mended his character for steadiness;

Tom Harvey, got on by degrees;

Don Manuel, ditto, but with a better eye than Harvey, though his hand not so strong;

Old Mark, rather past his shooting, but managed to hit fairly well;

R. Prodgers still brought up the rear.

While this went on, we made some attempts to mould the clay we had found by that stream I spoke of, into pottery ware; but our attempts were awkward, and the things we produced were clumsy enough. Our Indians brought us five or six heavy loads of the clay, and did what they could to help us in the work; but here they were novices, like ourselves. For (it seems) they had never hit on any of the like manufacture among those savage tribes; but were content with such calabashes and other vessels to hold water as they could fashion from gourds and suchlike rinds, dried and baked in the sun: as to boiling or stewing, they had not a notion of it, further than to put some pieces of flesh into a calabash with water, and throw in hot stones as a make-believe to boil, and nothing more. All this we made out from old Mark, who wondered, with the others, what we were after. The truth is, we were tired of seeing nothing before us but baked meat at table (getting fanciful, as is human nature to do, amid our abundance), so, resolved to persevere at this making of pots and pans, till we had produced a kettle, and a boil or stew of some sort.

They say, man can compass, by perseverance, whatever is possible in itself; and succeed we did, at last, enough for our needs: though it were a curious catalogue to present the reader with, did I number up all the larger boiling kettles and stew-pans, some deeper, some shallower (for we tried all ways, and all shapes and sizes), together with such smaller attempts, as butter-boats, drinking mugs, oil-flasks, and what not, that we cracked in the oven, trying to bake them hard. We made a vast collection of dry wood for this purpose; and spent many hours experimenting, now with a fierce fire, now with a slack one; now we made the clay so wet it was mere mud, and would scarce stand upright; then we worked it so dry, 't was hard to work at all. Each time we moulded one, and heaped wood round it, setting it on fire, we stood by to watch, and hoped it was going to be the first success. Never, I believe, did a chemist in his laboratory so eagerly watch some great experiment going on under his eyes, as we did, when we raked away the ashes with great care from round our clay-vessels, and drew them forth with bamboos; but all cracked and useless, like the former.

At last—it was on a Saturday, the eleventh of September, just before the rains set in, and a great day in the history of our colony—whether we had tempered the clay better, or got it from a finer vein, or whether the fire had been kindled more evenly round the clay, or kept up steadier to the right pitch (for these we discovered to be material points in the business), at length, I say, to our inexpressible joy, having slackened our fire for the third time that very day, preparing our minds for a fresh disappointment—to which we had become used, as the eels are to being skinned—this one blessed time we drew forth, with shouting, a large, ugly, mis-shapen thing, but sound as a bell, and burnt red as a brick-bat, that would hold, I am sure, from four to five gallons of water. I say, shouting, but I might add, dancing too: for we began to caper, like so many madmen, round the work of our hands, as the men of Israel danced round their golden calf. You might have supposed us all (I mean all but Don Manuel, who stood by and shared our joy) to be a party of wild Indians, performing a war-dance round some captive they had taken, before they fell to eating him. When our extravagance had subsided, we returned to the fire, and found with fresh joy one large flat dish, three mugs, and a plate, all good enough, besides a few that were part spoiled, but could be made to do till better offered. And from that time we burned some every day, with much success, till the rain drove us into covert in our cave.

------

# CHAPTER XLVII.

### THE CASTLE WITH ITS OUTWORKS.

MY readers may wonder, that all this time we had not looked after the canoe that was thrown ashore; seeing how anxious we were to devise some means of escape from this prison of ours.   But the truth was, Prodgers in an idle moment had strolled down to that part of the beach, and found the thing lying keel upwards, half buried in the sand, and so broken-backed as to be no longer sea-worthy for the calmest sea.   When he reported this to us, we gave up all thoughts of refitting her, having no tools proper for the purpose ; for knives and gun-barrels never yet built a ship, nor repaired one : though, to be sure, our Indians might have done something in that way, had we so employed them.   But we hasted to house ourselves before we were caught by the rains, which we expected to come upon us almost daily : so working at our cave, together with purveying our food, became our chief employments.   Nor can I write the annals of our little colony, even briefly, and not give a word to each of these works.

First, *Our Cave.* By dint of steady mining in gangs or relays, we had now got some way in, without finding crack or vein in the rock, nor aught to give us help nor hindrance : all seemed of one material, only it got softer, the deeper we went.   At last we worked nearly as much with a large bamboo sharpened, about three feet long, and pointed with a large flint, as with our gun-chisels, which we spared as much as we could.   We had gone in, I am sure, twenty feet before we began to enlarge our cave in height or breadth : but we were soon forced to set about that work too, from the heat and closeness of the air, which scarce permitted us to breathe freely, and hindered our working long at a spell.   Beginning with height, we now worked and chipped away over our heads, till we could stand upright at the inner end, which was a relief to us : for up to that, we had gone on nearly bent double, or upon our knees.   So now, having some inches to spare overhead, we set our faces (I mean the two that worked together, one hewing to his right, the other to his left), towards the entrance, and worked steadily back on our steps : till, nearing the entrance, we left that pretty much as we found it, small and rude, like the cave of a jackal, or mountain-bear, for our safer hiding.   As to the rest of our cave, it grew more spacious every day : and little over a fortnight from our beginning to work, we found ourselves possessed of a comfortable house (though very dark), thirty feet long, with a height ranging from six to seven feet, and about the same in breadth. Besides its roominess, our house or castle was much drier than many old houses I have known in civilised parts; there being but one place where we discovered the least drip of water. As we found this water, on tasting it, very cold and pure, free from taint of sulphur, or any other, we reckoned it no small advantage to our cave, and later we enlarged it into a well or reservoir, that supplied us fairly.

So far, we were prepared for the rains, come when they would. Only, the easier we worked, and the further we went in, the larger grew the heap of rubbish we were forced to throw out of our cave; at last it reached much more than half way up from the ground outside, to the mouth itself, like a pyramid of loose sand, leaning against the cliff. We feared to leave it where it was, knowing 't would easily betray our whereabouts to the cunning of any savages who might visit the island; and the first thing to do now was to clear it away, or (better still) make it a part of our defences. So, quitting our inside work altogether for a time, we considered how to dispose of this great heap of sand. For let any one reckon a mining work of the measurements I have stated, and add to it this also, that the rock which was compact in its native quarry, made up a larger bulk when 't was thrown out as loose sand; and he will have some guess of the mountain of work that now lay before us.

But the worst was, we had no tools whatever, such as shovels, to set to work with; nor the prospect of any but the clumsiest make-believes to stand in their place. All we could devise was this: to fit some such slaty stones as we had dug the Indian's grave with, into bamboo handles: this we managed passably well, but spent upon it the remainder of our twine; yet, after all this contrivance, the slates were for ever breaking in the work, or coming unbound from the handles. However, for want of better, to it we went; supplying for the badness of our tools by the number of workmen (for we now called all hands to this, and Don Manuel, too, took his day's work like any journeyman), and by an extra stock of good will and good humour.

Our plan was, to block up with this sand the whole pas-

sage between the cliff and leaning rock, on the side by
which we first entered our hiding-place; for on that side
the trees were scantier. and 't would be more easy to find
us out.   Then, when the rainy season should be over, and
the earth left moist and easy to be worked, we resolved to
plant all outside of this bank of soil, and the bank itself,
with young trees, or shoots, such as we might discover to
grow quickest, and bear transplanting; so as both to
bank and plant ourselves out from the world altogether.
But this was a mighty labour indeed, for nine pairs of
hands and nine awkward spades; and I question if they
who built the pyramids of Egypt had more work before
them, considering the number of workmen, than we with
our bank of sand.   We did the best we could; though
't was a bungling bit of business, after all; and bonded
our work together with such large stones as lay in the
neighbourhood, heaving them to the spot with levers of
bamboo: then using them as masons use the larger stones
to bond a wall.

Upon the whole, this was harder work than mining
into the cliff, and without the interest of discovery to animate us: for our Royal Sappers and Miners (so we called
the two workmen) were always expecting, every stroke
they made, to break into some cave already formed in the
heart of the rock, and so end their labours at once.   In
short, our sand-banking became so irksome and laborious,
we had no small ado to keep the men at it, during the
time (which was four full hours) we had agreed to devote
to it every day.   The weather, too, was sultry, which
added to our labour, and increased the discontent of those
who were disposed to grumble: so that every now and
again, one would throw down his tool, and protest, for his
part, he was no galley-slave, nor any slave, black or
white, to keep on at this work any longer.

I had to behave like the captain of a ship when signs
of mutiny appear on board; now I humoured them, now
reasoned, now joked with them: sometimes I went the
length of a threat, if they would not make common cause
in our labour, they should be banished from our commonwealth, and sent to the further side of the island: though
matters seldom went that length.   But what persuaded
them to endure, more than all words, was the example of

our patient, cheerful Spanish friend; who worked harder, in proportion, than any of the rest, with a smile and a word for all; nor ever rested, but to take up his breviary awhile: though you could see, he felt this hard labour more, by far, than the rough tars working side by side with him; and his hands bore witness he had been used as little to handle a spade, as a rope or an oar.

As to the further entrance, I mean that other side of the passage between the cliff and our grand stair-case, opposite to that one we were banking up; we had less care for that, seeing 't was more thickly set with trees, and turned away more from any practicable landing-place: therefore we would not bank up that, but kept it for our own approach to our castle below. Only, we contrived a winding path through the trees, narrow, and difficult to hit; clearing away some bushes here, and matting them together there: besides getting rid of a tree or two that stood right in the path, by burning it all round, a little above the roots, with our gun-barrels heated red-hot, and sawing it through afterwards with Master Pounder's shark's teeth saws. In this winding path we also contrived several traps and blind alleys, to mislead an enemy who had not the secret of the place; though not with so much art as Don Manuel and I had drawn our mazes with, yet enough to puzzle a stranger, or several of them, till we should get ready, and give them a warmer reception. Moreover, we dug two or three narrow pitfalls here and there, as deep as the height of a man, and as narrow as saw-pits; covering them with small weak branches laced across, and a thin layer of earth over all. Cunning places they were, and into one of them old Prodgers fell, not long after, by taking a wrong turn in a hurry; and proved (against his will) the excellence of the trap, not being able to free himself till we pulled him out with a rope. All this happened some time after: but I set it down here to show how we made our defences complete to the utmost we were able.

## CHAPTER XLVIII.

### OUR LARDER AND FARM-YARD.

IN the next place, *Our Food*.  Harry Gill and myself (I have said), being better shots than the rest, were mostly purveyors to our society; and after, when we laid aside our guns, taking to the bows and arrows, and went ranging through the island for practice, still 't was to us they chiefly looked for securing the daily meal.  Our island furnished game in plenty, as we were thankful to find, more and more, so we had no lack.  We went on adding, too, to our stock of arrows; and, with our growing skill in archery, became lords and masters of all the live stock in the place, four-footed or winged: I might say, web-footed too; for as time went on, we found numbers of sea-fowl that harboured in the rocks on the s.w. of the island, at least during several months in the year.

But these we rather looked on as distant allies, or wandering tribes on the frontier, than regular subjects of our kingdom; and spared them all the more, fearing to lose our arrows by aiming at them: nor did we ever attempt it but when the tide was setting strongly in-shore.  'T was no loss to us to let them alone; for one or two that we pierced from time to time, when they floated in, proved to have an indifferent, fishy taste, not fit for the table of gentlemen who had the stock of an island to pick from.  All things, indeed, are by comparison; for I have heard of some poor fellows turned adrift in a boat on the open sea, to whom a booby or a penguin, when they could knock them over, have been delicious fare in their hunger; and we should have been ungrateful wretches not to acknowledge our better plight.

One of our great endeavours in the article of food was to take some wild animals alive, so to preserve or tame them, and make a farm-yard around us by degrees.  'T was some time before we succeeded in this; at last, one day, Harry Gill and I being out together, we came on a sudden upon a herd of peccaries, old and young.  Rather, I should say, they came upon us, for we were in their way in the middle of a path they had worn for themselves by constant traffic through the woods, to get at fresh water that flowed between the volcano and the w.s.w. of the island. Now the peccary, like many human creatures, is a much bolder and fiercer gentleman when he has numbers to back him, than when you take him alone; yet even alone he is apt to be savage, and turn short on you with his tusks, if you slightly wound him, and despatch him not outright. This we knew well; having at times been forced to dodge among the trees, to get away from a wounded one, till we could settle him by a second shot. So now, finding ourselves face to face with so many together, we gave them the wall (as I might say) with great respect: slipping quietly aside into the jungle or bush, Harry Gill on one side, and I on the other, to leave their path clear.

On they came, at a kind of shuffling trot, grunting and squealing like a herd of wild pigs, as they were: first came some of the older and stronger of the herd, with formidable tusks, like pioneers to clear the way; and, 't is my belief, had they charged against a regiment in a line, they had put many a veteran soldier to the rout. Next cantered on several scores of others, led by these brave captains, and the little young pigs enclosed among them for protection. But 't was just one or two of these youngsters we had fixed our minds on: so making a sign to Harry Gill to get into a tree on his side the path, I did the same on mine; when, being both well settled in our perches, "Now!" cried I, "aim at the young pigs, Harry; and try to disable them, not to kill!"

At the sound of my voice, the leaders of the herd stopped short; for by this, they had all but come up to our ambush, and began snuffing the air, grunting with rage to know an enemy was nigh, yet not able to see him. After a little, when they had poked about among the bushes, they seemed not to like the chances, and determined on a retreat; so, giving a deep grunt or two, as word of command, they all wheeled about, and were for trotting back the way they came.

That was not the welcome we meant to give them by a great deal; so, bidding Gill take good aim, and have a second arrow in readiness, we both let fly, and winged each our pig; then, fitting at once another arrow to the string, we gave it them again, before they had recovered the first surprise: on which, there rose such a grunting and squealing of the herd as would have sent a musician cut of his wits: however, the end was, they all scampered, leaving their wounded to fare as they might. When we saw the coast was clear, and heard them hurry pell-mell through the woods, we came down from our trees to secure our booty: and I must take credit for our archery, seeing but one out of the four we had shot was dead, the rest only wounded, as we designed, and one so slightly, it cost us no little trouble to secure him.

On this, we blew our horns; which calls for a word of explanation here. I should have related before, we had found a kind of conch, or large winding shell, among the rocks, on our first Friday's expedition to the further side of the island, we soon found means to fashion these into a kind of trumpet; and they served us, as if we had been so many Tritons, giving forth a deep sound, like the bellowing of a bull, that might be heard a good way off. These horns soon brought to us two of the Indians, Pounder and Samuel, who, from their swiftness, were the light skirmishers of our party. Amongst us all, we managed not only to secure the three piglings, but to bring them home, together with the dead one. But these young peccaries were fiercer than their size or age warated: and we had some ado to escape being torn by their tusks, though small; indeed, we did not come off unscratched from the fight.

When we got them home, we were at a loss how to bestow them; first, we had to heal their wounds, next, to keep them safe: we feared they would die and be useless to us, or live and run away to the woods again. By degrees they grew tamer; and we cultivated their friendship on the same terms as the slave who, fleeing from his master, took refuge in the lion's cave, became friends with the lion he found there with a thorn that festered in his paw: that is, we extracted our arrows with more tenderness than we had shot them; then, by aid of the Indians, found some of those same leaves they had plastered Prodgers' face withal, and applied them to the wounded peccaries. At length, the poor little beasts began to look on us as their benefactors; and we, on our side, grew more liberal in giving them such food as they liked: for at first we kept them on short commons, to tame them by hunger.

All this while, we had them tied by the leg to three trees, just outside our encampment, where we could see them from the cave's mouth: resolving, if ever we observed a sign of savages visiting the island, to turn them loose into the woods, lest their squealing might betray us. To make a long story short, after a time they grew so tame, I believe we might safely have cut the ropes, and they had stayed with us: but, having come by them hardly, we would run no risk of parting with them lightly: so, fetching a compass with them till we found means to mount them up on a part of Cape Look-Out, we wattled off a small piece of table-land there for a farm-yard, weaving branches of trees in and out, till we made a ring-fence large enough for them to range in. We strengthened this here and there on the outside, driving in some live stakes of a tree of the nature of a willow: but it took root faster and firmer, and sent out strong shoots the very next spring; so that we lived to see our stakes form a circle of flourishing young trees. This is the history of our farm-yard in its infancy; and this was the last out-door work we engaged in before the rains came to shut us in.

---

## CHAPTER XLIX.

### WE CARVE OUT A KITCHEN.

SOON after this, the rainy season came, and came in earnest; those of us who had not yet known the tropics during the autumn equinox, had to learn (as they now did) what rain can do. 'T was not a shower, nor a tempest, and then over; but it rather came down in sheets of water than in the way of rain; and that too, day and night continually, as though it were poured out of some mighty reservoir in the heavens above. Don Manuel, on our remarking this, spoke to us of the great deluge that was once sent upon the earth for the wickedness of man : when "the flood-gates of heaven were opened, and the rain fell upon the earth forty days and forty nights," till all the human race was destroyed but eight persons alone. This, he said, might stand as one testimony of the extreme provocation of sin against the Lord who commanded His creatures' obedience ; so going on, from one discourse to another, while we were busied at work in our cave, and turning all into good, like the old king in the fable, whose touch turned all into gold.

Being now close prisoners (for we could not stir out without being drenched), we set to work on completing our cave architecture ; we determined to make it a regular habitation, and commodious enough to hold ourselves and our stores together. Our first care was to provide a kitchen ; which I hope the reader will not take amiss, as though we were grown too fond of the good cheer the island afforded, but will remember (as the saying of some wise man is reported), though we did not live to eat, we must eat to live. Well, this kitchen of ours was the part of our mansion that gave us most trouble, by far ; and that, because of the chimney it needed, which at first was beyond all our engineering. We tried, once or twice, to cook our meals in the great vestibule, or cave itself, that we had hollowed ; but we were fairly put to flight, and driven out into the rain, by the stifling smoke that rose from our wood fire. So, making a virtue of necessity, we set about smoking what meat we had provided (as several flitches and hams of peccary, together with some large wild-fowl we had brought down with our arrows), and so laying it up in store to consume by degrees. Here we employed our Indians, who were not so much afraid of a wetting ; making them understand what we would have done, we had the satisfaction to see them, under our own eyes (for one of us always stood to mount guard at the cave's mouth), set up a small booth, or curing-house, of four trees thatched with leaves, to smoke the bacon in. They built this booth within the embankment I have spoken of, which we always called our fortification, or outworks, leaning one side of the booth up against the cliff.

The benefit of this plan was, we needed not to gather dry wood for the business; but on the contrary, green wood smoked the meat more thoroughly, and we saved our dry fuel to warm us by, or for a little slow fire of very dry sticks, almost like charcoal, whenever we would boil our vegetables, or make soup of a piece of flesh, with yams and bread-fruit, in one of our clumsy pots and pans. Yet, after all, a kitchen and a chimney we must needs have, and that for three purposes at once; namely, first, to warm ourselves by, and dispel the damp of our cave, if we found the rain to penetrate; but that it never did, except in the one place, where it formed our well, so our fears were groundless on that score: then, secondly, to cook our daily meal, for we could not endure the smoke that arose even from our little fire for boiling; and, thirdly, for our oven; inasmuch as we were now grown too dainty to be content with bread-fruit, but must have real bread beside. So we set about our kitchen as follows:

We resolved, as the smoke from our chimney must find some vent to the upper air, this should be turned as far as possible from that part of the island our Indians had been driven upon: fearing it might invite a visit from some others of the fraternity, not so easily tamed as these. Little did I think, indeed, at the time, what benefit a smoke from the island was to bring to us hereafter. But I must not outrun my narrative.

For this purpose, we went to the furthest end of our cave, being, as I said, full thirty feet from the entrance: then turning left ways (for we would not have our fire in a line with the cave's mouth, lest its light should betray us), we cut a passage nearly five feet wide into the living rock, working two at a time, in gangs, or relays, as before. When we had got fifteen or eighteen feet in, the two workmen then parted, each his own way, facing away from one another, and began hewing round again in a half circle; that is, the right hand man bore over towards his right shoulder, and the left hand man towards his left; till at length, after incredible labour (I am describing in a few lines what took several weeks to accomplish), each man completing his half round, they came out again, nearly opposite one another, into the passage they began by cutting, as I said, and which led out of the ... in cave.

To be sure, this did not look much like a kitchen; for 't was nothing but a circular burrow, about the height of a man, with a straight passage, broader, running through it, to divide it into two halves: as my reader will see, if he hath attended to my rude account of it. Nevertheless, this was our kitchen in outline: and now, setting about to complete it, we resolved in the first place, we would leave enough of the rock on either side (I mean, of the solid rock round which we had mined this burrow of ours) to stand as a natural pillar, and prop up the roof. For we feared to leave so large a stretch of roof without support; lest our cave might, some day, on a sudden, prove our sepulchre too. Thus we went on, making the passages wider, and reducing the two masses of standing rock: now the whole of our party could work at it at once, and it went on much quicker. Only, our tools were so imperfect, for ever breaking and getting out of use, it made the work slower, and tried our patience more; the gun-barrels were now much worn down with constant hewing, and we began to debate on sacrificing one of the other pieces to break up into mining tools. Indeed, our bows and arrows had taken the place of these weapons, nor had we burnt a grain of powder since we perfected our archery. On second thoughts, prudence bade us keep all our fire-arms in readiness, in case of any attack from savages; for we reckoned, one discharge of our guns would be of more service in terrifying them, than whole quivers full of arrows, which, being their own familiar weapons, inspire them with no dread.

But Pounder one day suddenly gave us more help in the way of tools than any one could, short of an iron-monger: for, being sent forth on a Friday morning to help Ned Hilton bring in some cray-fish and oysters from the other side the island (the rain having then somewhat slackened), he brought, besides, one or two pieces of a very hard stone, transparent like glass, and splitting off to a sharp edge; such (I believe) as learned people call quartz, and simple folks call glimmer. He had found these in a crack or vein, between two rocks, down which ran a little rapid stream, that had loosened these pieces from the rocks; and he said there was a good quantity more of the same to be found in that spot. By this time we were better skilled in binding our stone hammers, or axe-heads, into the bamboo-handles, whereby we got on the faster at our work. At last we had cut away the rock so much, we left nothing standing on either side the kitchen but two pillars of a biggish thickness: and the place itself was an irregular oval of about fifteen feet across, the longest way; by twelve, the shortest. We would not then stay to shape it more to our fancy, nor to carve out a seat, or transom, round the walls, as was afterwards done; our next concern being to pierce a vent, or chimney, up through the solid rock, over that part where we designed to make our fire, slanting to westward of the ridge of our look-out.

This was the hardest task, by far, we had on hands; nor do I think, except for the lucky discovery of the glimmer-stones (that cut sharper and easier than others), we had ever accomplished it. But, by help of a determined will, and often changing the workmen, we overcame all obstacles: so, hauling up two young cocoa-palms into the cave, we made them into a rude ladder; lacing them across with those same tough tendrils we had made our rope of, which the men called supple-jack. Thus we made a something between a ladder and the shrouds of a ship, and by help of it we mounted to the rocky roof of our kitchen, and began to pierce it at a slant; so, hewing on with perseverance, we made us an opening about three feet across, for convenience of working: and by degrees cut our way upward into rude steps that supported one man at a time; but, from the cramped position he was forced to maintain, and heat of the place, no one could work at this more than a quarter of an hour at one spell; and we were stiff and weary too, when we came down.

After a full week's work at the chimney alone, one morning, when Tom Harvey had taken his turn at the work, as he was boring upward with the gun-barrel (for that we did first, to pioneer, and then cut away the sides with the glimmer), all at once he thrust the barrel forward freely to his arm's length; at the same moment some fresh wet earth fell into his eyes and mouth, and the cool

air blew down upon his face.  Harvey was blinded and
half choked ; down he came, floundering among us in the
kitchen, as we hewed at the pillars : nor could he answer
our questions but by sputtering with his mouth full of
earth.  But Hilton, going to the hole, shouted out, the
thing was done ! and, sure enough, when we ran to look,
we saw the light of day, like a pale star, at the top.

The rest was easy ; for Harvey having left his tool
sticking out at the top, when he was thus saluted by
mother Earth to his discomfiture, we had but to send one
of our party on to the promontory, and enlarge our
chimney-pot from above.  But we charged him ('t was
Pounder that went) only to make it wide enough to allow
vent for the smoke, and be careful to build it round with
bushes and sticks laid across ; as well to conceal it from
human eyes, as to prevent any wild animals paying us the
unwelcome honour of a visit down the chimney.

---

## CHAPTER L.

### ROCK ARCHITECTURE.

THEY who were not up the chimney at this trouble-
some work, had other employments ; this being one
among the things we had learned on the island, that man
is destined to labour, even in solitude and amid plenty, if
he would keep mind or body in health.  So, importing
another cargo of glimmer, with some fresh bamboos, into
our cave, we fell to making a good stock of mining instruments.  This done, then, we marked out the entrances to
several other rooms leading off from our main cave, and
hewed them out, as we had hewn the kitchen.

To go to work on a regular plan, we made a list of the
rooms we designed to have, which stood thus :

A *chapel*, to serve for our morning and night prayers,
and for our private devotions.  For we had begun the
habit of praying by ourselves a little, ere now ; and some·

# GROUND PLAN OF THE CAVE.

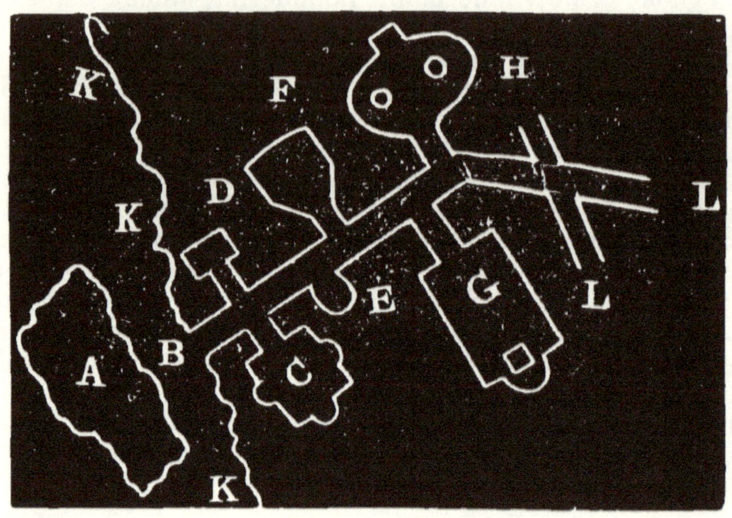

A. Hanging rock concealing the entrance.
B. Entrance; the serpent's hole enlarged.
C. Store-room, with lockers pierced in the walls.
D. Small room for gunpowder.
E. Well, supplied by a drip from above.
F. Work-room, and sleeping place.
G. Chapel with altar in the alcove.
H. Kitchen, with pillars and chimney: also used for the Indians' sleeping-place.
K, K, K. Face of cliff.
L, L. Further passages into the rock, afterward abandoned.

CHAP. L, p. 198.

times I would come on a sudden in our woods and walks upon one of our comrades on his knees, and I would strike into another path to avoid disturbing him; this sort of thing grew up, as 't were, by itself, and was getting quite common, no one noticing it as strange. This little chapel, too, was to be for our instruction on Sundays; for Don Manuel preached to us now every Sunday, and some other days, too; holy days, as he said, called so for one reason or another, which he told us as they come round. Lastly, on these days and Sundays our chapel served another chief purpose, as I will tell.

Then, we needed a *store-room*, as well for our dried meats as to lay up fruits and vegetables: we determined to make it with niches in the wall, like cup-boards without doors, all round to keep the stores apart from one another: besides, we thought to dig a kind of shallow well, or vault, in the floor of this store-room, at the further end, and cover it with palm and other leaves, to keep such stores as would spoil unless they were kept cool, as cocoa-nut milk, and such like. For all which reasons, we meant to have this room as far as could be contrived from the kitchen fire.

Item, one recess apart in the driest and safest corner of the cave, to stow away securely our small stock of powder: 't was but a mere handful, indeed, yet might prove the safety of us all in case of attack, or be our destruction if we were heedless enough to let any spark get to it.

Besides, we needed a work-room, for such employments as would litter or lumber our great cave (so we called it), too much to carry on there. 'T would be, indeed, a luxury more than necessity to us: nevertheless, as it was to be bought by labour, and lawful to enjoy, we determined to have it, in its turn: though it came lower down on our list. Further, a sleeping-place or two for ourselves, and another for the Indians. At one time, we thought of contriving a kind of stable, or outhouses (if they can be called so, that were inside the rock), for our live stock, to protect them from wild creatures of their own kinds, or beasts of prey. But our other works in the cave took up such a time, we were forced to give over this last plan. Nor was it of so much importance as the rest, after all; for our peccaries throve well enough in the ring-fence above our heads, and were never molested, or nothing to speak of: though once or twice a sea-eagle made a swoop on our farm-yard, and carried off a young pig.

I say, a young one; for, what with two or three litters bred in the farm, and some beside, that we captured and brought in from time to time, we were soon very thriving farmers of live stock; in short, we had so many, we were rather concerned to thin them out, than add to them. And thenceforward we never shot down peccaries for our larder; for that were like carrying coals to Newcastle: but when we took our bows (and we took them every day again, when the rains were over) 't was more to keep our hands in practice, and to fetch in a dainty, in the shape of a wild turkey, or brace of parrots, or what not. And at last, we took to shooting fish, too, with some success.

But to return to the cave; I believe nine men (unless galley-slaves, or exiles in the Siberian mines) seldom worked harder underground than we did, all through the rainy season: for it must be observed, we were miners on our own account, and worked for no task-master; who, the moment his eye was off, had no more work done for him.*  Nor were we ever reduced to drive a bargain, or haggle about charging by the piece, or by the time.   All was straight before us, and all was our own; our hands strong. our hearts cheery; and being bound together by one common interest, each was forward to help the others, well knowing he would be helped in turn.  Don Manuel gave us the plan, indeed, for our caves; but was far from being like some who insist on doing good in their own way, or not at all.  He adopted on the spot some changes we wished made; and took his turn so cheerfully

* If Don Manuel had heard (as perhaps he did) this remark of Owen's, he would probably have reminded his friend, that we are bidden, in our service to our Divine Master, not to resemble those servants who are only faithful as long as they are under their employer's eye.  " Servants," says the Apostle, " be obedient to them that are your lords according to the flesh, with fear and trembling, in the simplicity of your hearts, as to Christ: *not serving to the eye*, as it were pleasing men, but as the servants of Christ, doing the will of God from the heart; with a good will serving, as to the Lord, and not to men."—*Ephes.*, vi. 6.  So also *Coloss.*, iii. 22, 24.  ED.

in hewing the other rooms, we were eager to help him with the chapel.

I will have done with all this, after a few words about that chapel of ours. 'T was coved, or vaulted over, as high as we could well reach, standing mostly on a log and some large stones. Having time on hands, we took a pride in smoothing the roof fair and even; as to the walls, we determined not only to smoothe them, but plaster them too, as we afterwards did with well-kneaded clay, tempered and stiffened with a gluey kind of sap that we found oozing out from some gum trees up and down the island. This with small holes drilled here and there in the walls, as a kind of hold-fasts, made the clay stick well enough, and we were not a little proud of our plastered chapel. But the chief of our care we spent on the altar end; for there we hollowed out an alcove in the rock, vaulting the roof of it in a half circle. In the midst of this, we left the altar standing, being a block of the native stone, which we shaped by Don Manuel's directions.

Then, nothing would content us, but we must paint this end, as well as plaster it: so, while the clay was still moist, we contrived some red colour from the juice of a wild berry; the Indians fetched these to us, when they understood what we would be at. They also brought in some earth of a brownish yellow, like ochre, and this gave us two colours; being lighter in the natural unburnt state, and turning to a tawney red when calcined in our wood fire. Some black loam, or peat, of decayed leaves or fibres, made up our list of colours: with these four, we set to work; first mixing them up with our gum, till they were near as stiff as japan painting on a screen or tea chest. Then we drew patterns within the alcove, on the yellow-white of our clay plastering; marking it all over with regular lines, now in one colour, now with another, and here and there with an imitation of trees, plants, and birds. 'T was all under our friend's guidance; for he showed himself no mean artist here; and he executed a tolerable painting of the Crucifixion, right over where the altar stood. At length, our rock chapel was a wonder for its decorations, and when lighted up with candles, 't was really a sight to look at.

This bird and tree-painting (except only grinding and

mixing the colours) we pursued mostly on Sundays, after our morning devotions, and before evening prayers, or just before or after the sermon: for all these things we had every Sunday, and two of them, *i.e.* prayers, twice, with no sermon, every day.  It surprised me that Don Manuel, who was so exact in many things where we had seen no harm, should even encourage us to do this on the Sabbath day; but he explained to us, 't was not *servile* work, which alone is forbidden to Christians on Sundays and other holy days: artist-paintings like these, especially when done only for pastime, not for gain, being a liberal occupation, and what rich men do (if they have skill in it) to entertain their minds, who would scorn to receive payment for it.  From this he took occasion to remark, how needful it was to have a surer guide on such points, what was right and what unlawful, than men's own wayward fancies; and he repeated what he said to me once before (and vexed me at the time) about our eating meat with the blood in it, simply because the Church said we might.

"We must honour," says he, "a man for following his conscience; unless 't is so plainly astray that he *ought* to see 't is misleading him.  All this great exactness about keeping the Sabbath comes from a good principle; but a good principle may run mad, as it has done in this point.  It aimed at keeping the commandment; so far well.  But the human mind, left to its own guidance, fails to see where the commandment begins and ends; what observance is retained, and what is rightly altered.  If you obey the commandment to the letter, you ought to keep Saturday holy, not Sunday at all.  Except for the Catholic Church, I say again, you commit a sin every Saturday of your lives, and deserve to be stoned, as the man was stoned in the wilderness, for gathering sticks on the Sabbath.*  The Church, by the authority she derives from her Lord, has changed the day itself, and the mode of its observance. Your teachers, dear friends, have kept the Christian day, but not with Christian observance.  In England, I am told, Sunday is a very gloomy affair, while other evils are rife, which are too lightly thought of.  And in your colony of new England, the special plantation of Puritan colonists,

* *Numbers*, xv. 32, 36.  **Ed.**

they seem to make it criminal for a citizen to smoke his pipe on a Sunday, or have a hot dinner, or take a quiet walk for recreation. Poor souls, poor souls!" continued he, with a look of pity: "and well for them, if that were all! But '*they that in vain observe vanities forsake their own mercy.*'"

## CHAPTER LI.

### WHAT WE OUGHT TO HAVE KNOWN BEFORE.

OUR evenings were spent, as they had been out of doors, round our fire: but not idle time, neither: we scarce knew what it was to sit with our hands before us, as some do who have what they call "time on their hands," and find it weigh heavy enough: we always worked at somewhat, by the light of our candle-nuts, or lamps of shark's oil, or tallow of the peccaries kept heated, and a cotton wick. For in these three ways we had contrived lamps, or candles, whichever you please: and having good store, both of these and dry wood for fuel, and no poor in our community, for whom we need spare, and deny ourselves, we kept up a rousing fire, with plenty of light; so that our cave, on winter nights, was a cheerful place.

If our hands were busy, so were our tongues: for whether we filed arrow-heads, or fitted them to bamboo shafts, new-strung our bows, or plaited cocoa-fibre, or spun off our cotton, or sharpened knives and hatchets of glimmer, yet talk we did, all the while, with that freedom that comes from confidence and brotherly charity.

Don Manuel took a chief part in this; and 't was not in the nature of man to be dull when he was by: at one time he would entertain us with stories of what had chanced to himself in Spain, or since he left it; at another, with some strange adventure he knew to have befallen others. Several evenings together, at our request, he related some passages of his own life: and did it in such a simple, unaffected way. we never tired of listening to him, and would sometimes ask him to go over again our favourite stories. 'T was plain, he had experienced many chances and dangers; and the men, who had encountered such themselves, from a restless spirit that made them scapegraces at home, or from necessity to earn their bread at sea, wondered at a man like this, a gentleman born (for so he could not but imply, though he never said it), a scholar, and one of studious habits and refined taste, braving the wildest adventures for the love of God and souls. All this was more than a sermon to us, though given under the guise of pastime: so that even now, having got so far in this poor record of our own adventures, methinks a life of Don Manuel had been of more interest to the reader, had I earlier attempted it.

Well, such discourse tended to good, whether by its own nature, or by the turn he gave it: so that, begin at what point you would, in most cases we found ourselves end with a talk about religion. And 't was Don Manuel's way so to order things, that what he said was suited both to the Indians and ourselves: or now a bit for us, then again something for them. Besides, we practised their language by this discourse, and they ours; our talk being made up of a jargon betwixt English and Toonati-nookish, half and half. Indeed, I found this mode of speaking so hard to shake off, after the years we spent at it, that when I came back to England (a thing I never thought to do at the time I write of), I was for ever coming out with Indian words unawares: so that my friends would jest with me, saying, I was but a half-reclaimed savage. In particular, that exclamation of theirs, *Oora, oora,* at anything that pleased them much, would stick by me; together with *tabanna,* to express, thank you: and *ebelo,* a word signifying dislike or pain of any sort. But all this is by the way.

We had begun in such ignorance of whatever religion we were thought to profess, as made a great part of Don Manuel's discourse to the savages useful to us also. At first, indeed, my in-bred dislike against priests and Popery, with all those old wives' fables I had been brought up in (though softened by my knowledge of the man), made me watch his discourse narrowly, to discover the point, as I supposed, where true Christianity ended, and papistry began.  For though I acknowledged in my heart, the priest was a good man indeed, and a model for any, yet (said .I to myself), the Hindoo faquirs also lead austere lives, and Quakers are harmless, charitable people : also, I knew an old man living near Caerphilly, that believed in no rising again after death ; leaving it in his will, he should be buried under a rose bush at the end of his garden, with his favourite dog and magpie ; yet gave away beef to the poor at Christmas, and put out to 'prentice no less than five orphan children, besides other good deeds.  Yet they were all wrong in their opinions, of a surety ; and so,.said I to myself, may our friend here be, too, with all his good Christian life.

However, one evening, when he was speaking on a point that gave rise to such thoughts in me, I ventured, with respect, to remind him we were protestants, after all ; on which, he turns round to me with surprise, and (speaking only in Spanish now, with some little Latin intermingled, that the Indians might not perceive there was a difference betwixt us) :

" Why, friend," says he, " do not you believe that, as well as I ? "

" You know," he added, in a more affectionate way, " how sorry I should be to give you pain : but let me say, plainly, no one who does not believe what I was saying, can be called "—And here he stopped, seeming not to know how to go on.

" A Catholic, I suppose ? " said I to him.

" Well," he answered, " let us leave it so, for a time."

" A Roman Catholic then ? " I pursued, for I wanted to see what he meant by this.

" That was-not what I had on the tip of my tongue," says he, smiling, " nor is there any such distinction to be made between the terms : for there is no Catholic who is not a Roman Catholic, just as there is no true circle that is not described round its centre.  But shall I offend you, my friend, or shall I pain you, if I say what I really was thinking?  Would it not be better to follow this out another time :—say, next time we walk together ? "

" Do not fear, Señor," I replied, " for you could not offend me, unless you become other than I have known you up to this.  I will only ask for the one word you did not say.

The man who does not believe the Virgin Mary is to be venerated as the Mother of God, is not—what is he not?"

"Did you never," he asked, looking at me kindly, " begin a sentence, and then wish you had not to finish it?"

" Sometimes," I said, waxing somewhat impatient (for we Welshmen are apt to get heated in our tempers when we are crossed), " that is not the question just now. Pray tell me, Sir; he is not—what?"

" Well, then," says he, speaking slow, in a thoughtful way, "it may be the defect of his bringing up, and the false tradition of his fathers; or there may be excuses found for him, some of which I can see, and others I cannot see; he may be better in practice than his opinions would lead to; he may be ready and disposed to receive the truth whenever 't is really put before him : all those are favourable points in such a man's case."

" Well, well; granted: but he is not—what, if you please, sir?"

" He cannot, then," says the priest, " in a true sense, be called a Christian; that is, a disciple of our Lord Jesus Christ."

He spoke it as if it gave him real pain to say the word; which I am sure it did.  But at the moment, I only considered the words themselves; and felt staggered, like one who has received a sudden blow.  Don Manuel saw this; and only added, as tenderly as a woman, like :

" Listen, now; let us see what our Indian friends have to say about it.  They have no early prejudices to overcome; having never heard of Christianity but through a Catholic priest; observe how these truths affect a simple mind, that lately was like a blank sheet of paper on the first ideas of the Christian faith : then weigh and balance, for yourself, what you have been taught against all this; and see if two and two do not make four."

So he took my hand with more than his wonted kindness : for we sat next one another at the fire, the other men and the Indians making up the circle. though they had understood scarce a word.  Then he turned again to John Pounder.

## CHAPTER LII.

### ANOTHER LEAF OUT OF THE CATECHISM.

YET it seemed to strike him, the rest might be tired of speaking on such grave things for that time. "So I put it to the vote," says he, cheerfully. "Would you like, friends, to strike into some other discourse, or shall I now continue? We have about a quarter of an hour, I suppose, before 't is time for night prayers, and then to rest, after a hard day's work."

"Sir," says Dick Prodgers, "I being the oldest here, leastways of us white men, and so, 't is likely, nigher to my dying hour, would prefer, if agreeable, to hear some more about this: for I remember," says the old tar, in a way that brought the very tears into Don Manuel's eyes, "being told, not long ago, the things we shall soon find ourselves in the midst of, being eternal, d' ye see, are of greatest account."

So said the other men, more or less; I mean, each in his way; and Ned Hilton, being half asleep, gave a sort of grunt, to vote with the rest.

"Well," Don Manuel continued: "I will go on awhile; and to-morrow we will go to something else I have in my mind."

"Now, my dear children," says he to the three Indians, "do you know your names? We are going to make you Christians, and give you Christian ones, in place of what you have been called by. Toefa-oloo (this was the old man), what does your name signify in Toonati-nooka?"

I must explain, in what I here put down, Don Manuel had by this become so good a scholar in their language, he understood most things they said, and spoke it passably well, as indeed he deserved to do; having taken all occasions to converse with these poor creatures, for their good.

*Toefa-oloo.* "Tadoone" (it means, in their language, *father*, for by this name the priest had signified to us he had rather be called; so that we dropped the Don pretty much from that time onward) — "Tadoone," says he, "Toefa-oloo all same as Big Monkey."

At this, the men set up a laugh, and the Indians joined in it; though I would be bound, 't was out of compliment to us only.

*Don M.* (smiling): "Well, we will find a better name for you soon. What did I tell you you would be, when the holy water of life was poured over you?"

*Toefa-oloo.* "Den I be Mark, Tadoone."

*Don M.* "Yes, that will be your name. And why shall I give you that name?"

*Toefa-oloo.* "'Cause of one great much holy man; he make strokes so, so (making with his hand as though he were writing), in great holy book."

*Don M.* "And what was the book about?"

*Toefa-oloo.* "He put down in book much what great, great, great holy God He say, He do, He *hooroo-hooroo*" (Mark could not express *suffer* in English, so he used here the word in his language).

*Don M.* "What did He *hooroo-hooroo?*"

*Toefa.* "Much great, much great: bad bad mans take, bind, beat, beat, den" (the rest he expressed in Toonati-nookish, not finding words for it in English, which made me sorry the others did not understand him, for they had taken no pains to learn any but the commonest Indian words); "bad men," he went on, "took Him to a mountain, laid two trees on the ground, one fastened across the other, laid Him on the trees, beat great nails, longer than shark's teeth, quite through His tender hands and feet, into the trees; then set up the biggest tree, and the smaller to it, and Him on, till He died from pain."

*Don M.* (still in English). "Yes, that was what He suffered, indeed, and much more. But why was it He suffered? Who was He, all the time?"

*Toefa.* (bowing his head). "Great, great, great much holy God."

*Don M.* "And what is His name?"

*Toefa.* (bowing again, with the sign of the cross on his forehead and breast). "Otooma-Tehe, Jesus Christus."

I must explain here that *Otooma-Tehe* was the word Toefa had coined (for he had to coin it) to express the Christian idea of God, in distinction from their word for

an idol, which was *henatanoo*. Now, Otooma-Tehe is made
up of the three words, *Oteo* (one), *Tooma* (lord or chief),
and *Elehe* (spirit); and the poor Indian was not a little
fond of his new word: as I could discover by his singing
it to himself in a low voice while he was at work, as
though he delighted to have found one true God in place
of the multitude of his false ones. But to return.

*Don M.* "Tell me now, could not Otooma-Tehe do all
things that He would?"

*Toefa.* "O yes, O yes! all, Tadoone."

*Don M.* "What, more than Paowanga? more than
Havaeoeekee?"

The poor old man looked up into the father's face, surprised, to discover what he meant by asking this. Bu
seeing the priest smiled, he laughed outright, clapping his
hands; then he spat twice into the fire, to express his
contempt for his former idols: each time he did so, he
said, "Udan, Paowanga he no good! Udan, Havaeoeekee
he no good."

On this, the other two Indians began to spit likewise
into the fire; crying at the top of their voices, "Eaha-
noué, he he he no good; Eaha-noué, he he he no good!"
till the cave rang again.

Our thoughtless Hilton, being waked by this out of his
sleep, and learning what was going on, burst into an up-
roarious laugh, and was joined in it by the rest: so, what
with their merriment, and what with the poor Indians
making their act of detesting their idols (which they did
again and again), there was noise enough. When it had
ceased a little, though every now and then one would
burst forth again, so greatly did this proceeding take the
men's fancies, Don Manuel went on quietly.

*Tadoone.* "True, my dear: our good Lord and God is
Almighty; He can do everything He wills to do. Then,
why did He let those bad men take, and put Him to pain
and death?"

*Toefa.* "Tadoone, He give His own life up to dat."

*Tadoone.* "And why?"

*Toefa.* "O, oh! give His self to make Toefa-oloo be
happy, happy; and Rer-mimebolamba happy, and Poula-
faihe happy, and Eaha-noue in Toonati-nooka happy, all
happy, much happy, for long time, long, O, long!"

*Tadoone.* " And White Sas happy too?"

Old Mark (so we mostly called him) seemed puzzled to know what to answer; looking upon us, after all, as superior creatures; and, I believe, something as we look on the angels, beings that have never been redeemed, because they have never fallen. On the other hand, he was quite sure, if the brown man was to be made happy, the white man was (somehow) to be happier. So he was there, as in a cleft stick, and knew not which side to take: but sat, shaking his head, looking first at one then at another of us.

" Well, old mess-mate," cried Harry Gill, at last, " do you not wish us to be happy too?"

" O, oh!" he answered: " me 'spose white Sas much happy, much; me 'spose, white Sas happy one place, brown mans happy one place;" he meant, each would be happy, but separate. " Brown here," says he, stretching out his left hand, " White here," and stretched out his right.

" No, my dear brother," cries the priest, and leaned forward to embrace him; " there is one heaven, as there is one *Otooma-Tehe:* and may we all be happy there together!"

Then the other Indians, too, began repeating, *Oora, oora!* nodding their heads again and again.

At this moment, I whispered to him, he had not made the Indian prove to me, none but a Catholic could be a true disciple.

" Aye, indeed," says he, thinking; then turned to Toefa-.oloo again.

*Don M.* " But tell me this; when did our Lord Jesus Christus speak to *moönaee-etoeea* (all mankind)?"

*Toefa.* " Otooma-Tehe first dead, dead; then—

*Don M.* " Stay awhile; how could He die, if He is God, and Almighty?"

*Toefa.* " Tadoone, you me tell, Otooma-Tehe He no die, no die: but etoee (that is their word for *man*), yes, he much die: Otooma-Tehe He make His own self be etooe, so He, etooe, all one: so He die."

*Don M.* " True; God became man, that He might die for us all; and He is both God and man in One Person. But how did Otooma-Tehe become man?"

*Toefa.* "O, Oh! Otooma-Tehe He make, He choose, one much, much holy young maiden (he expressed this partly in his own language), He make her love all what Otooma-Tehe He love; He place great much strong *matangeeva* (shield) over :" (I now see, though I did not understand him at the time, he meant to repeat something the father had taught him of the Blessed Virgin being preserved from all sin, and 'the fiery darts of the most wicked one') : " den He come, He make His own self be her child."

*Don M.* " And what is this maiden's name ? "

*Toefa.* (bowing again).  " Maria Deotokos." *

*Don M.* " Quite right; and that means, Mary the Mother of God.  Why do we call her that ? "

Old Mark did not seem to see what Tadoone could mean by the question: and looked up again in his face, surprised.

" You see," said the priest to me in Spanish, " the question in itself is such a simple one, he thinks there must be something more in my asking it than he sees ; and so he does not answer."

" Please to make him answer, though, sir," said I to him again, in the same language.

*Don M.* (in English).  " Well, Toefa, who is Maria the mother of ? "

*Toefa.* " Maria she O much mother Otooma-Tehe, oora, oora, Tadoone."

" There you have it, friend," says the priest again to me, in his Spanish, " what want you more?  Mary is the mother of our Lord.  He is One Person, God and man : all that takes place in His human nature, being one of His two natures, takes place in the Person of God ; she bears Him in her pure bosom, therefore she bears her God : *quem genuit, adoravit:* she is His mother, and so she is most truly the mother of God.  Not to believe this, would be disbelieving that He is in One Person God and man ; but that is the essence of the Christian faith : so, to deny that Mary is Mother of God, is to deny the Christian faith."

He saw me look unsatisfied still : " Well," says he, gaily, " I will put it to him more closely for a moment ;

* Properly, *Theotokos*, the title solemnly given to the Blessed Virgin at the Council of Ephesus, A.D. 431, against Nestorius, who asserted the existence of two distinct persons in our Lord.  ED.

and then, no more.   John Pounder and Samuel, go; light the candles in the chapel, we will come in a minute. Now, Toefa, listen.  (He here began to speak Indian again.) What is that you used to put over your face (you told me) when you went into battle, to make yourself look terrible to your enemies?"

*Toefa.* (answering in Indian).  "A mask of red bird's feathers, father."

*Don M.*   "It hid your face, and you were behind it?"

*Toefa.*   "Yes, indeed."

*Don M.*   "But 't was not yourself, all the while?"

*Toefa.* (laughing).  "Oh, no, no."

*Don M.*   "Attend, now.   Was it in *that* way that God became man?   Did he merely conceal himself behind the nature or appearance of man?"   .

*Toefa.*   "No, my father; you have taught me, He became really, truly man for us."

*Don M.*   "As truly man as you and I?"

*Toefa.*   "Yes, praise and thanks: but all holy, pure."

*Don M.*   "Was He less God than before, for doing so?"

*Toefa.*   "Perfect God, perfect man, in one Person."

*Don M.*   "Then, whom did the Blessed Mary bear?"

*Toefa.*   "Ah, father! are you punishing me for some fault? why, God, to be sure."

*Don M.*   "That will do.   Blow the horn, wake up the sleepers.   We are going to prayers."

So we went to our prayers: after which we heard (for the first time) the Indians singing in their part of the cave, by way of practice, a morning hymn which Tadoone had composed for them; for they were to sing it, it seems, the first thing next morning, which was a festival day.   It went to one of their wild Indian airs: and had a strange kind of pleasing solemn sound about it which took the men greatly; so that we soon caught it, and made it part of our morning devotions.   Thus it ran:

> Goole majeela a bo tahapai,
>   Kowya reea teëgaro chee;
> Taharo ēlan eroo mata hai,
>   Mâte ka waia tohooda tahe.
> Shaīngalā tiri laine moaffa,
>   *Jesus* aüne ta hā lenehoo;
> Teema Tadoon' Etehēti nar'affa,
>   Faida *Maria* pakulla ta moo.

The meaning of it is, in English :

On the tops of our cocoa palms when first a light shines,
  Let us arise to adore Him that sustained us (in life) ;
Most pure, most merciful, pleased with obedient children,
  Who on the two trees (*i.e* , the Cross) showed us His great love.
He, the Redeemer, speaking (pleading, appealing), claims our hearts ;
  His thrice-holy name is Jesus, born and dying :
Let us love Him, with the Father and Holy Spirit,
  Next to them also Mary our Mother.

----

## CHAPTER LIII.

### SPRING-TIDE LABOURS.

EMPLOYED in such ways as these, we got through the rainy season : indeed, the return of fair weather surprised us, so much had we to do inside the cave, and so used did we become to close quarters, with cheerful labour. At length we issued from our retreat on a fresh spring morning, as Noe and his family stepped out of their ark on to the green earth, bathed in the waters of the flood : we smelled the flowers and the trees, and plucked the fresh shoots and blossoms in our abundance, with the birds singing round on every side; and nature seemed to burst forth at once with the vigour of a tropical spring. "And if nature can give such a new sense of life and joy," says Tadoone, "by the mere return of spring to the land of our exile, strewing such flowers on our pilgrimage path, what will it be to range the Paradise of God with the Saints, where the pure, bright atmosphere is charity, when sorrow and sin shall have fled for ever ? "

Among the first things we had to do, was to look to our farm ; for the violent rains had damaged the fences, so that if we had not sent out the Indians from time to time to repair some gaps in them, our peccaries would doubtless have escaped to the woods. We now made our ring-fence stronger, by driving in stakes here and there, of a kind of supple osier, which quickly took root, and shot out a strong, tough branch or tendril: so that, in the four years and a-quarter we spent in that exile, by lacing and weaving them, in and in, every spring as they shot forth again, we formed a hedge that, for strength and thickness, would have puzzled a whole herd of peccaries to break through.

Next, we thickened the plantation I spoke of before, to conceal the approach to our cave; we made more winding passages, and more decoys, or wrong turns, that led each to its pit-fall, or else to a blind alley so narrow that the enemy, did he get in, would scarce have room to turn in it; but, pushing on deeper, would find himself trapped almost as they snare wild elephants in India. We contrived these with some skill, and we laid down a rule for ourselves, to work a certain while every day, which was four hours in the cool weather (more or less, for we tied not ourselves exactly to it), and in the heats from two to two and a-half, early and late. Such, I say, was our engineering craft in the contrivance of this maze, that we made the pit-falls be just in a point that was overlooked from a thicket right above the mouth of our cave: so that one or several of us, concealed in the thicket, could pour our arrows upon the enemy in his perplexity, remaining unseen all the while.

Later on in our exile (for I may as well finish about this, once for all), that is, the third rainy season we spent on the island, having then, as I shall presently relate, more hands sent to us, whom we neither invited nor expected, we made our cave still bigger: for then we hewed out two more sleeping places, besides cutting shelves and cupboards in several of the passages, up and down. At length, the whim seized us, we would make us another entrance to our cave altogether, to serve us for an approach from the western side, or (as the rabbit makes two holes to its burrow) give us an escape in case our citadel was stormed by the grand stair-case. We made a survey how the ground lay above, treading up and down the table-land over the cave, or from that to westward, to see where the rock dipped nighest the level of the cave, so to have least trouble in cutting the passage. At last we found the spot where (by our closest reckoning) we had best begin: then, dividing ourselves into gangs, as before (but now with more than double the number in each gang, as the reader will see in a while), we worked steadily for the best part of two weeks, I am sure; and got down a prodigious way into the rock: further than we thought we should have to go, till we began to fear we were out in our reckoning of the depth, or had cut at a wrong angle for the slope. All at once, we broke indeed into our cave; but, whereas we hoped to light on a passage we had partly worked beyond the kitchen,* we found, instead, we had broken through the roof of our chapel, by its western corner, furthest from the altar: and we knew at once where we had got to, by hearing the plaster fall inward on the floor. The thing being done, there was no help for it: we made us another ladder of trees, with rounds of wood bound tight with flax and supple-jack, to reach up from the chapel floor to our new passage, and so used it from time to time; chiefly to bring down such heavy weights as we could not well sling up by the other door.

To go back from this to our first rainy season: of all our manufactures, some fishing nets (we judged) would be most useful; as afterwards they proved to be. We set about them as soon as we had mined ourselves fairly into the rock; working at them at odd times in the day, and by our fire-light every evening. Here, too, the Indians surpassed us in their handy twisting of the cocoa and other fibres for the nets' meshes; so by degrees we left the work in their hands, particularly in old Mark's, who was less able for the hard work of hewing the rock. He told us, they were well used in Toonati-nooka to make a sort of draw-net, or seine; with these they took large quantities of fish in the gulfs and inlets of their island, mostly in the spring-tide of the year. Sometimes they would venture out into the deep sea, but then always went in armed canoes, to defend themselves from the fishers of Hai-vavaoo, who were for ever coming out against them in strong parties, to dispute the fishery; and would now and then run in like so many pirates, into the bays of Toonati, and, after a fierce struggle, carry off both nets and fish together.

* Probably at the point marked L in the margin of the ground-plan. ED.

It seemed, these fisheries were the cause, or pretence, of that war that was for ever being waged between the savages of the two islands : though Toefa-oloo told us, several treaties of peace had been made (within his own memory) between them, in the most solemn way they knew how.   Namely, they assemble (said he) the chiefs of both sides, and the priests of that side on whose shore the treaty is to be made : or they take the priests out in a canoe, if 't is made at sea.   Then invoking Paowanga, who is reckoned to be the god of war among them (but the men of Hai-vavaoo have another idol named Komo-arrao, corresponding to him, whom they invoke on their part), they cut the throat of an animal, mostly of a goat, and each party drinks a portion of the blood, with various other ceremonies.   Such a treaty they profess to hold very sacred, at least till interest or enmity concur to break it again.

---

## CHAPTER LIV.

### SEA AND LAND.

TO return to our own nets : we made them carefully, of twisted cocoa-nut fibres and our supple-jack, dried by the fire and beaten out like hemp, with thread also spun from the cocoa-plants, of which we found a plantation self-sown, as I have related ; we found more of them later, scattered here and there in the swampy parts of the island, towards the centre of it, or from that to s.w.   The Indians told us, in their country they made the nets stronger and more supple with hairs from their enemies' heads, whom they slew in battle, or took prisoners ; for they never spared those whom they took, but offered them all in sacrifice to Paowanga, first shaving off their hair, or pulling it away with the scalp, then dashing out their brains with a club.   The poor fellows hereupon offered to part with the very hair of their heads to make our fish-nets ; for they wear it long, never suffering knife or razor to touch it after they come of age, but twisting it up on the crown of the head with a bone pin.  However, we would not suffer them so to despoil themselves; only, hearing them speak of these pins, we asked what bones they were made of; and when Tadoone heard, they were the arm-bones of their enemies, he made them untwist these trophies from their heads, and buried them with his own hand in the wood near our cave, speaking much to Mark and the others about that savage custom of theirs, and how repugnant it was to the feeling we should have for the living and the dead.

I could see, they parted with their ornaments with a bad grace, and only because Tadoone asked it : for it seems in their country 't is reckoned a thing disgraceful for any one who has been in war, to be seen without an arm-bone twisted into his hair; that being a sign that he was a coward, and slew no enemies in battle.  I made up the loss to them, as well as I could, by dividing a kerchief of gaudy colours I wore round my neck, half to one, and half to the other: for as to young Samuel, he had never been in battle, so had no right to a bone.  But Mark and Pounder were much delighted with their new head-dress, and wore it till the sun and rain so bleached the colours, you could scarce distinguish them.

Before the rainy season was over we had made us three good fish-nets, of a fairish size : and when the spring had set in, we were visited, about shark's Cove and the neighbouring shores, by such shoals of fish, some of them old acquaintances (as herrings and mackrel), others of a strange kind, inhabitants of these seas, as put us beyond all fear of falling short of Fridays' fare.  We were forced to devise methods of smoking and curing on the beach, so great were the numbers we drew to shore with our long net, or seine, and another which we threw in the manner of a cast-net.  In this we succeeded passably well, after some failures: our Indians proving useful here too, by pointing out one or two kinds of fish that were poisonous, or, at the best, unwholesome.

At one time, we thought of making a weir, or preserve for our fish, as we had made a farm-yard for our four-footed stock on land; we might have done it well enough, by driving stakes across a part of our inlet, in Shark's

Cove, at low-water, keeping them high enough above high-water mark to hinder the fish floating back with the tide; and weaving bamboos or cordage in and out, to form a wattle under water, free enough for the tide to ebb through, but not the fish.   But we gave up that idea; partly because, with the fresh water conduit, and other works then engaging us, we had (as the saying is) " other fish to fry;" also because the abundance of these shoals supplied us for a long time together.   The smaller fry were followed into the cove by large fish that came to prey on them; as bonitos, manchorans, albicores, dog-fish, and a kind of dolphin, besides some of our old enemies, the sharks, such of them as were able to thread their way through the inlet in the reef.   We managed to spear several, or shoot them with arrows (all but the sharks, whose hide is too strong for such spears, and we would not waste powder on them): then, waiting till the tide ebbed, or throwing round them a coil of our native rope, we got them ashore for their oil and bones, as well as meat.

Others we pierced with arrows, but especially with spears, having a biggish piece of bark or light wood tied to them by a strong twine, to act as a buoy, and prevent the fish getting away: by all these arts we captured no less than nine or ten large fish that were tolerable eating, and might have had as many dozens for the taking, only we grew lazy by reason of abundance; besides we had no means to salt down such a quantity, nor cared to keep them dried and tough, as they would have been.

I have left out one employment in which Don Manuel especially engaged, and kept to himself; 't was not much in the way of labour, but more by its importance to us.   I mean, the sowing of our two or three chance grains of wheat in a little nook of earth lying open to the south, which Tadoone carefully dug, and manured with some of the refuse of our fish, together with leaves and burnt seaweed,   To speak exactly, there were but three grains in all; one that stuck in my knife, as I have said, and two more I found later in my pocket.   He claimed these as his portion of our goods; promising us in return, if all went well, he would give us a good quartern loaf in a couple of years' time, besides supplying himself with what he needed for the altar, if altar he ever came by.   We could not but smile at the promise of a loaf two years to come; but freely yielded up the grains to him: what he did with them was this:—

Having prepared the ground with care, then, making a little hole in the soil with a stick, he dropped one of the grains into it: then again, perhaps six inches from this, a second hole, and dropped another grain; and the third, at a like distance. This, he explained to us, he had read in some old Latin book of agriculture, was the surest way of having an abundant corn-crop; as well, because the grains, thus planted apart, do not lie in each other's way for drawing moisture and fatness from the soil, as because this careful mode of putting them into the ground saves the waste of grain that takes place in throwing them broadcast into furrows.

True enough, the experiment prospered in his hands: for the blade shot up, tall and strong, bearing such ears as I have seldom seen in wheat, before nor since. He chose out of these the largest grains, and the most likely-looking, for his next year's crop, and sowed them in the same manner, some inches apart from one another; by which means, his second harvest came up stronger, with a larger yield than the first, even. After that, indeed, as I shall show at another stroke of my pen, a wonderful turn of events made him a less regular farmer, and changed the whole current of our life in this exile.

## CHAPTER LV.

### PREPARING FOR A CHANGE.

BEING in no mind to trouble the reader with why and wherefore I determined finally to embrace the Catholic faith, I will say little more than this, (to vindicate myself and the friend that became the instrument to me of so great a good), I did nothing in haste, nor rashly. For, to make so vital a change without due reflection, said Don

Manuel, a change to be made once for all, and involving an eternity, would be wrong and perilous to the last degree; and, he added, 't were an insult to the majesty of truth not to give it calm and deep reflection. No man, said he, as gifted with the faculty of reason, would undertake a much less concern without pondering it as well in its motives as consequences; or he would have himself to thank for failure and disappointment.

I resolved, then, to try every step, and keep the lead-line going, as the master of a vessel is bound to do in an unknown sea: nor can I now be grateful enough for this, inasmuch as it made my way secure, and hath delivered me from all doubtfulness ever since.

The priest (undying thanks to him for it) put the matter before me in so plain a light as appealed to my reason, but demanded my faith beside. For he bade me remark, the very notion of religion was a message from God to man, revealing His nature and His will; that it must be received (being once made plain), not discussed, as being that whereof we are to be disciples, not judges nor critics. This revelation, he said, because 't is the message of the Infinite Being to us poor narrow souls, must contain mysterious truths, whose depths we cannot fathom, though we are made able to accept them by faith. That 't is enough for us, and ample, if we are assured (by any authority on earth that can show itself to be His appointment and creation), such and such articles of teaching are His message; then our duty is, cordially to believe them: to fail in which, is failing in the first duty of the creature, and so brings the unbeliever into a state of perdition.

God, he said, is, by His own perfection, the God of truth as well as of holiness; wherefore, He demands from us belief in His truth, and all of it, no less than obedience to every part of His holy law. That, if we must distinguish between these two (though, indeed, always to go together) there was a precedence and prior claim to be noted; that faith came before obedience, as its motive, for " without faith it is impossible to please God;" though obedience must follow faith, as its result, because " faith without works is dead."

Then he went on to show that Almighty God, who first proclaimed the truth of His gospel by many miracles, wrought by Himself and His apostles, was pleased, before He visibly left the earth, to set up in it a great standing sign or miracle, which He made perpetual, and promised should be so: and that sign was to be ever fresh and ever at hand, while most other miracles were shown but from time to time; and that sign was to be in every quarter of the world at once, while others were local and limited; and it was not only to stand for proof of the gospel, but to instruct and console them that believed already; to cleanse and restore them if they unhappily sinned; to strengthen and feed them while they were in grace; to keep them in union with God, and be the means of conducting them to heaven.

And this great sign, says he, is "the Church of the living God, the pillar and ground of the truth;" "a city set on a hill," visible to such as do not wilfully close their eyes against it; a "straight way," whereon the simplest, if only they follow it trustfully, cannot go wrong, nor stumble. He went on to say, that the true Church is known from all others that pretend to her title, by four great marks, that are recited as such even by many who do not belong to her, when they say their creed; that she is One, Holy, Catholic, Apostolic: that a plain observation of facts will show these four marks to belong to the Church in union with the see of St. Peter, and to her alone: that all this was matter of promise at the first, when our Lord said: "Thou art Peter, and on this rock (Peter) I will build my Church;" and has been fulfilled in the history of seventeen hundred years, and will be, to the end of time.

This being so plain, says he, every man is inexcusable who, having the truth sufficiently set before him, does not embrace it: to behave thus is a grave offence against God, who reveals His truth, commanding it to be received; and will be punished with an eternal doom: but they who accept it, obtain therewith abundant graces to their souls, through sacraments, the channels made by Himself, enabling them to obey the rest of the Divine will; whereby they can merit an increase of it, from degree to degree, till they gain everlasting glory.

This is the sum of our conversations together.

What chiefly surprised me in them all, was the stress

the priest laid on my making the utmost use of my *reason* in this inquiry, until I received the gift of faith. For I supposed, he would have required me to surrender my reason, and believe all I might be told, whether unreasonable or no : having a heap of things thrust down my throat, and bidden to swallow them without inquiry. Whereas, here was a priest, and (as I found by degrees) a monk too, bidding me inquire, reason, and test what he said, until grace was given me to believe. On my telling him my surprise to find this, he only smiled, and asked me, was it possible that faith and reason could be opposed? I answered, it seemed so, inasmuch as a vast number of men, who professed to go by reason, where thereby led away from faith. To which he said again, they neither knew what was meant by sound reason, nor by true faith. For, says he, as both come from God, who is "not the God of dissension," one of His gifts can never go against another.

"How is it, then, sir" (I urged) "so many things are taught in your Church, as miracles, transubstantiation, and the rest, which contradict the evidence of our senses?" "Contradict, my dear friend?" says he, looking pleasantly at me; "there can be no contradiction between two things, when one simply goes beyond the other." "Why, sir," said I again, "do you mean to tell me there is no contradiction in saying that bread and wine are so much more than bread and wine as the Catholic Church bids her members believe?" "Certainly," answers he very gravely, "it would be a contradiction to say anything is what it is not, or more than it is. But tell me : can the senses judge of anything that lies beyond themselves? Or can one sense judge of what is only subject to another sense? Did you ever hear the colour or see the smell of a flower?"

I could not but smile at his questions; which, when he saw: "Well," pursued he, "as to that great mystery you have touched on, your senses can be no judges of the change of substance into substance, because they can only report as to the outward *appearances,* which remain as they were before: you might just as well expect the sentinel who stands outside the king's palace to know what transactions are going on in the audience-chamber or cabinet, where the king himself is within, removed from sight. But observe; as the eye is created, to tell the soul many things great and glorious which the ear cannot perceive, so faith is given to tell the soul glorious mysteries which 'eye hath not seen, nor ear heard, neither hath it entered into the heart of man.'" So he went on.

---

## CHAPTER LVI.

### OTHER REASONS.

TWO chief reasons determined me beside: one was the consistent Christian example of this good friend, whose conduct I had hourly opportunities to mark, nor ever found a thing in it that did not tally with his teaching. It became impossible to me to think so true a disciple and good liver, one so cheerfully holy, humble, prayerful, self-denying, charitable, and the rest, practising virtue from day to day, could be in such error as my early prejudices declared him. The second reason was, I felt my soul to need such confession of sins as I knew to be practised in his Church.

Removed as we were from the world, spending much time alone, 't would not have been in mortal man to prevent his thoughts turning inward on himself, and backward on his life. Our consciences became first awakened, then tender: so that we recalled our past sins, which we had utterly forgotten, and gone on as unheeding as if we were guiltless of them; I say, recalling these, they appeared to us quite in another light than before, as heinous offences against the Divine law, though perchance not crimes in the eyes of our fellow-men. Strange, indeed, how old sins of many years past would start out before me from some hidden nook in my memory; so that, at last, numbering how oft I had sinned against my own conscience, dark as it was, and how little I had cultivated grace by prayer, to preserve me from my own bad self,

I began to see my life had been almost one continued sin.

I could not find comfort in this distress of mind from general promises of pardon made to man on his true repentance: feeling somewhat to be needed beside, to apply those generals to my particular case. I would fain hear a voice say to *myself*, "Neither do I condemn thee, go and sin no more." "Thy sins are forgiven thee; depart in peace." Propounding this to my friend, he then showed me, the God of mercy had vouchsafed to meet my need; founding a succession of priests for the express end (among others) of assuring His pardon to the penitent.

"But 't is impossible," says he, "without an evident miracle, the priest should be able to pronounce pardon where he knows not the offence, nor the dispositions of the offender. Nor can he apply the remedies best suited to each several case, nor give advice, to serve the soul of his penitent, unless the state of that soul, its deeds, habits, failings, weak points, temptations, and so forth, be submitted to him. The priest who hears a man's confession is a judge commissioned to that office by the Supreme Judge of all: now, when any one is brought before a judge, there is evidence produced and sifted, and the cause determined on it, lest the guilty escape, or the innocent be condemned. Again the priest is a physician for the soul; and what physician in his right senses ever prescribed for his patient without first hearing the symptoms of his disorder?"

So he went on, with much more of the same kind; which, if I could recall precisely, 't would be useful to set it down. But it persuaded me (after much reflection) to close with such a merciful offer. Therefore, about three weeks after he and I had talked this over, I first received from him a conditional baptism, on a supposition of my never having been baptized before: "for baptism with you," says he, "is given (I fear) with so little of the care that befits a sacrament needful to salvation, as to make it more than doubtful whether 't is given at all." Then, this being secured, I made to our charitable and patient Tadoone a full, exact confession of my life, so far as I could recall anything that looked like a sin. And it is not for me to set down on paper the peace that took possession of my heart when I knew myself reconciled to God whom my sins had offended. Nor can I describe how truly I purposed to serve him for the remainder of my days.

But what is good for one is good for another, in what concerns all: so the men, partly taking example by me, seeing 't was not so strange a thing to become a Catholic, after all; partly by the simple goodness of our poor Indians, whom Tadoone had made Catholics already; and partly also by the reasons he showed them for it, determined to do likewise. Not that all did it together but in the following order:

First (strange enough it seemed to me), came Richard Prodgers, and was made into a good Catholic, and a happy one, in less than a week after myself. Then Ned Hilton; and after him, Gill; whose parents, it seems, inherited the farm they occupied in Kent from the days of the Commonwealth, and traced up their ancestors to some of Cromwell's followers, whom he had enriched with that freehold: so that Harry, careless sailor as he was, derived a smack of the puritan, leastwise, in the respect of prejudice, and was hard to convince of the Catholic doctrine. However, he came in at last, though 't was a good month or so after Ned, and Ned was some short time after me. But Don Manuel was not the man to hurry any one; and never showed more patience than when he reasoned with Gill, and won him by slow degrees.

It may seem strange that Tom Harvey, who was the best conditioned of them all at first, was the very last to enter the Church: but such was the fact, let any one explain it as he may. I once asked Tadoone whether 't was a secret pride that still kept Tom from submitting: but he would not hear of such a reason, which (he said) had too little charity about it; that God's ways are not our ways, nor His times ours; that Harvey's turn would come yet:— and so it did.

# CHAPTER LVII.

### SPIRITUAL MASS.

A WHILE ago, I said our chapel served us for another end besides daily prayers and weekly sermons. It would be leaving my reader in the dark not to explain it; at least, if I should get any readers at all: though that is a thing I am growing doubtful of. For a friend of mine, a bookseller in Paternoster Row, on my carrying these papers to him, when I had written out about a third of my rough notes, discouraged me all he could from going on: telling me the public would never be caught with such chaff, nor take up with a dull matter of fact like this; I stood a better chance (said he), with some cut-throat tale, full of murder and gunpowder, hair-breadth 'scapes, or the burning of one or two people alive, or massacring an Indian village wholesale. But I told him I was as little fitted to be a romancer as a stage-player, or any other kind of mountebank: and if folks who read books were not content with what befel a plain man and his companions, in an out of the way place and a strange exile of more than four years they might e'en let it be, and no harm was done, except the printer's bills to be charged on my executors.

I might (no doubt) have touched up my story, or dashed in some strong colours, like scene-painters, who will daub for effect at a distance: but where then had been the sober truth of my narrative? Or, (had I the wit to do it, which happily I lack) I might have given a freer rein to my thoughts, in some such pieces as an acquaintance of mine was bringing out in London before I quitted England, who, after wasting his talents on such trifles, went over to Lisbon in shattered health, and has gone further even than Lisbon to give in an account of all his writings. But I, that can admire genius at a distance, would not change places in the next world, no, nor in this, with the man who ever wrote one deliberate word that might lead a fellow mortal to a sin, be it of thought only.

Here I am straying again from my own paddock through the first gap in the hedge : so I come back from the bookseller in Paternoster Row, to our chapel in Assumption Isle. I have all along forgotten to say, we called the place of our exile so, from the great festival that had just passed when we discovered it : and long after, we had our joke against old Prodgers, who had put aside any Christian name for it, preferring to call it *No Man's Land.*

Well, 't was *spiritual Mass* we used our little chapel for, every morning, as a thing of course. And Don Manuel explained what we were going to do, the first time he proposed it, much after this fashion :

"You remember, dear friends of mine," says he, "how you thought me mad, or next to it, for being so affected when we found a grain of wheat : and I told you, at the time, 't was because the sight of that little grain seemed to bring me one step nearer to my great desire, the celebrating of holy Mass. That desire we cannot carry out, from want of other things needed for it; but we may cherish it as a desire, and turn that desire into prayer. You know, even in man's dealings with his fellow-man, the will is often accepted for the deed. Many is the time we testify, that we *would* do an act of kindness or service, if we *could :* and our neighbour holds himself equally obliged to us, as if we had done it. Much more does the Searcher of hearts look into the hidden desires of our souls, and accepts or rejects us by what He sees there. Even as to baptism, a sacrament necessary for any one to be saved, the earnest *desire* of it is accepted, where the sacrament is impossible. So, as I cannot have the comfort of celebrating Mass, we will do all we can in the way of desire, and may hope for many blessings in answer."

He went on to speak of some revelation granted to a Saint (I cannot recall the name), that her spiritual communions were to her sacramental communions as silver to gold; and exhorted us to assist at our spiritual Mass with such fervour as to supply (to our best) for the want of the divine reality.

"Holy Mass," says he, "is celebrated by the priest, and attended by the faithful, for several ends, as :

"To adore Almighty God for what He is in Himself, all His own infinite perfections, joining with the blessed

angels round His Throne, who are ever crying aloud to
Him, ' Holy, Holy, Holy !'  And, if we consider that He
is the One infinite and supreme, 't will appear our first
duty to accompany the adorable Sacrifice of Himself,
which He hath ordained, by such an act of devout
homage.

" To give Him praise and thanks for all His blessings
to us, for body and soul, which are numberless ; also, for
His benefits to others, especially those who will not praise
or thank Him for themselves.  Also, under this head of
praise, to adore Him for the graces He has bestowed on
His saints, from the creation to the present hour ; and to
congratulate the blessed Saints themselves on all they
have received.

" To commemorate the sufferings and death of our Lord
Jesus Christ, whereof Mass is so lively a representation,
as well as a continuance and daily application of the same
Sacrifice.

" To avert His anger from ourselves and all other sinners, by a humble acknowledgment of our offences, and
deep unworthiness.

" To beseech Him to pour upon ourselves, and all for
whom we are bound to pray, all the blessings needful for
us : this large intention including both supplication and
intercession ; as to ourselves, it includes all we can need,
for body and soul, for time and eternity : as to others, it
embraces Catholics on earth and in purgatory, as well as
heretics, sinners, sufferers, the heathen, in a word, all
God's rational creatures who were not in heaven nor in
hell : prayer for the first being needless, and for the latter,
of no avail."

Methinks I have now given as large an account as need
be (perhaps too lengthy) of that spell of twenty months,
or thereabout, of our life on the island, while we lived by
ourselves, without the increase to our society which I am
going to record.  Our farm-yard throve, and our crops
flourished well enough during this time ; but afterwards,
the great heat of our second summer, that burned like a
fierce oven, scorched up some of our young plantains and
bananas, so that they withered and came to nought.
'T was, indeed, through our unskilfulness in the choice of

a place for them ; the spot being too exposed to the sun
for tender plants : but we remedied this the following
season, choosing a small savannah, partly shaded by the
same ridge of sandy cliff that ran up into the bluff, or
headland, where we dug our cave; partly by a grove of
cocoa-palms on the other side. This lay a quarter of a
mile from the sun-burnt spot where we failed before, and
was washed by the stream that came from Riverhead, so
that we could water our new nursery-ground by hand.

As for our peccaries, a kind of murrain seized on them,
so that we lost half our stock within ten days, and the
rest were saved chiefly by the care of Ned Hilton, whose
father, it seems, was a small farmer in the county of Hun-
tingdon, where Ned had become learned in pigs. But
Don Manuel's wheat crop seemed to have some blessing
showered on it from the first ; or else from his choosing a
spot sheltered and moistened by a little ledge of rock from
the great heats, it throve better than our essays in farm-
ing. I am ready to think, 't was both of those causes
together : for on one hand, he was a kind of man that undertook nothing, but first he looked far onward, and
weighed all he was to do ; on the other, I am sure he
sowed this crop in tears of deep desire, and trusted to reap
it in spiritual joy.

As to that other crop of his, I mean our souls, that he
had been the means of saving, 't is not for me to turn
trumpeter to our little troop ; only I will say, if our regular habit of confessing may be taken as a sign, we scarce
ever missed going to Tadoone once in the week ; generally
on Fridays, to honour the Sacred Passion we had formerly
thought on so little, and done so much to dishonour. The
effect of this was clearly seen in the men's temper and
dispositions : as for myself, I say little, only I ought to
have advanced more in goodness, as my sense of it was
perhaps clearer. But amongst us now, such outbreaks of
passion as the men had used to give way to, came to be a
something unheard of : and, just as the last and most unlikely in a race will sometimes get ahead of the rest, so
the greatest change seemed to be wrought in old Dick
Prodgers. He had been 'fining down by degrees, after
our first week on the island : but when he had made his
confession, and been baptized under condition, he did in-

deed seem to put on the new man, and surprised us by his meekness and quiet spirit of prayer.  I may say much the same of the rest, some more, some less.

All this made us desire greatly to assist at Mass, and more particularly, to receive the Holy Communion, in the nature and effects of which Don Manuel instructed us. He bade us pray that our "hunger and thirst after justice" might be increased yet more, and then satisfied : and he exhorted us to make our spiritual communions with such fervour as might in some degree supply for our great want in not being able to receive the Most Holy.  We learned from him to join our intentions with those of every priest offering Mass, and all the faithful attending it, on what spot soever of earth assembled.

Thus time slipped by, leaving us content in spite of our cruel banishment ; and in many ways we might be called happy ; lords of all we saw round us, our dominions only bounded by the ocean, at peace among ourselves, and little fearing enemies from without, though prepared to receive them.  All this, I say, till a strange thing befell us on the seventeenth of April, the year of Redemption, 1741.

---

## CHAPTER LVIII.

### THE SPANISH ARMADA.

OF a sudden, on the day I have just named, we were startled by the firing of a gun out at sea ; the sound seemed to come to us from s.s.w., or thereaway : but so dull and faint, we hardly thought it a gun, till we heard the second ; and listening with eager ears, taken aback by the surprise, within a few minutes there came a third report.  Then we knew it for a vessel firing guns of distress ; but what help to bring her we saw not, only we thought to inform her crew, there were some at hand, though not able, yet willing, to help them.  So we clambered to the top of our rock, and thence to *Look-out Point,*

"When she neared, which was very slowly, we saw clearly enough what made her so short of sail: for her main-mast was gone by the board; also her foremast had but a mean kind of jury top-mast rigged, and the mizen (for she was a three master, though seemingly not a first-rate) was reduced to a stump, and carried a mere rag of a sail."—CHAP. LVIII, p. 231.

in great agitation of spirits : we had, by this, well-nigh
resigned ourselves to live and die on the island ; and so
sudden a prospect of some European ship brought a conflict of emotions to us, part of hope, part of apprehension.
For we knew not if we were about to encounter friends
or foes ; nor of what nation she might prove, nor how
disposed toward us. One thing we determined on ; to
reconnoitre with prudence before we made any sign in
return for their guns.

My perspective glass served us well here ; by which I
made out the hull of a large vessel, some three leagues
away in the wind's eye : she seemed to carry little sail,
which surprised us, till the tide, or current, favoured her
helm, and brought her in nearer ; for 't was plain she saw
our island, and was making for it. But when she neared,
which was very slowly, we saw clearly enough what made
her so short of sail : for her main-mast was gone by the
board ; also her foremast had but a mean kind of jury top-
mast rigged, and the mizen (for she was a three-master,
though seemingly not a first-rate) was reduced to a stump,
and carried a mere rag of a sail. Also, by her hull being
so low down in the water, as well as the slowness of her
sailing (though she was well in the current which, I have
said, set in towards the island from south by south-west) ;
from all these signs we plainly made out, she was water-
logged to that degree, she could scarce hope to reach land
at last.

This was confirmed when we saw her boats lowered,
and the crew stowing themselves into them : they had
three, a long boat, pinnace, and shallop, but 't was some
time before they put off from the ship : for what cause we
could not at first discover, but judged they were landing
provisions, or perhaps merchandise ; for they lowered into
the boats what seemed (at that distance) to be eight or
niue large bales, or packages, and laid them lengthways.
But as they drew nearer, we made out these to be sick
men in their hammocks, lying in the bottom of the boats,
and so much in the way of the oarsmen, as added to their
difficulties very much.

Indeed, the whole look of this crew, when we could distinguish their features, was as if a hospital had shipped
itself on board of a ship ; for a more meagre, starved-look-

ing set I never set eyes on : and they had scarce strength left among them to pull-in the boats towards land.  So that 't was chiefly through favour of the current (which ran swifter when it came to near Cape Look-out, and turned with an eddy, or in-draught, into Shark Cove), chiefly by this they managed to make any way at all; for they had no more to do, but by their oars and helm to keep the boats' heads fair with the stream, and catch what little wind was abaft.

This stream, though, took a swift turn when it came within a quarter of a mile of the point (our cape, I mean); and shot up to N.N.E., so bearing them towards the cove : when they found this, fearing, 't is likely, they might be carried off land again, not liking to trust the stream, or else wearied with rowing, they made efforts to shoot out of the ripple of the current into smooth water, under lee of the shore, and so land in another little cove, that was almost land-locked, N.E. of Cape Look-out.  Though the stream carried them some way beyond that point, they got out of the strength of it; and doubling back, rowed in, but feebly enough, till they lay on their oars within arrow-shot of the shore, debating how to proceed.

Now was our time : for we did not mean them to come nearer without holding them to parley ; the more so, as we now saw they had arms with them.  So, retreating from our ambush, we came back to our castle with all speed, then went down by our grand stair-case, the rope, and made our way straight towards the cove.  Then, still ambushed in the trees, we sent Don Manuel forward as our spokesman, or ambassador, with full powers to treat with them.  We crept as near as we could, without showing ourselves, to witness what passed, and support him on the instant, in case of need : for we had brought all our weapons with us, and mustered all our troops.

The priest went forward, till he came near to the water's edge ; then stood still, and waved his hand, as about to speak.  But it would have touched any heart to witness the joy of the poor famished creatures when they saw the form of a civilized man approach near to them.  Some of the crew stood up in the boats, waving their hats ; some clapped their hands ; others fell on their knees, raising their clasped hands to heaven ; all cried out, some one thing, some another, with such confused sounds of prayer, and surprise, and joy, we could not make out what language 't was they spoke in. But Don Manuel, having a quicker ear for his native tongue, knew it to be Spanish.

One would have thought this was like to give him great satisfaction; but he told us afterwards, the doubt came at once into his mind, they might be a crew of buccaneers,* and their ship a pirate vessel, fitted out for such, or run away with in some mutiny. 'T is true, their action of rendering thanks to God seemed to stamp them as honest men; though I have heard that the very buccaneers, with a kind of impious piety strange to think on, would invoke the divine protection on their marauding expeditions, and render solemn thanks on every success.

Being still doubtful of these new acquaintances, Don Manuel calls out to them in his own language, bidding them come in no nearer, but tell him truly what nation they were of, and whether honest men. On which they all cried, as with one voice, *Españoles, Españoles!* and asked him, was he indeed a Catholic priest? He, on his part, assented; then they protested vehemently, they were good Catholics too, and subjects of his most Catholic majesty (so, it seems, the king of Spain is always entitled); and that 't was but three short days since they committed to the deep their chaplain and confessor, who died on board of famine, or fever, or both, like the rest of the crew, except only themselves.

On this, he asked them, would they solemnly swear, as good Catholics, to submit themselves to the authorities on the island? Would they engage to lay aside their arms, or deliver them into safe keeping, during their stay? And, if they were compelled to stay indeed (as the condition of the ship rendered likely), would they enter into such fair conditions as should be laid down for them by those who

---

* This seems a strange inaccuracy, as the buccaneers, strictly so-called, were scarcely heard of after the taking of Carthagena, some forty years before this date. Moreover, as that association of pirates was chiefly composed of French and English adventurers, whose operations were directed against the Spanish colonies, they would scarcely have spoken Spanish on a sudden emotion, in preference to their native tongue. Perhaps the word *buccaneer* is here used for a pirate in general; or it may be a mistake of Owen's for *privateer.* ED.

16

had possession of the place?   To all this, with one voice, the poor men professed they were ready to swear on the spot.   Then Don Manuel opened his breviary and held it up before them, pointing, as he explained to them, to the words of the holy gospel in it, and bade them swear to every tittle of what he had said.

They rose up, or all that were able to stand, uncovered their heads, and with a grave and reverent demeanour, stretched forth their hands towards the book he held up to them.   Even the sick men in the hammocks, when they heard what was going forward, did what they could to raise their hands with the rest.   Having all sworn to observe these articles, Don Manuel then pledged his word as a priest, on behalf of himself and his friends, who, he told them, had possession of the place, they should meet all fair and honourable usage, and be received on their parole of good conduct, as well as have their sick tended with care.   "But first," says he, "for a pledge you mean as you say, deliver up to me the flints out of your mus-kets."   On which they set to work without a question, and hammered out all the flints from their pieces, and also from the pistols, of which each man had two or three. They wrapped these in a parcel of sail cloth, and held them up to him, in token they were now unarmed; for indeed, all they had left to them were a few boat-hooks, and two or three hatchets, with their cutlasses, and these too they delivered up on landing.

---

## CHAPTER LIX.

### HARBOUR AND HOSPITAL.

WHEN we had thus drawn (as the old fable says) the lion's teeth and claws, Don Manuel went on : "I will now show you, friends," says he, "we had the power to enforce submission, had we chosen to use it;" with that, he looks back to us in the wood, and waves his hand.

Out we marched at the signal (for so we had already
agreed), with our guns shouldered, our bows, and quivers
filled with arrows, at our backs; those that had no guns,
with bows and bamboo spears; ranging ourselves in a
half-moon along the strand of the cove, four of us on either
side of our ambassador. What with our wild shaggy looks,
dressed as we were, or disguised, in our untanned hog-
skins and palm-leaf helmets or hats, with formidable broad
swords and wooden clubs set with sharks' teeth, untrimmed
hair and beards, thus fully armed, and attended by our
Indians as wild as ourselves; notwithstanding the fewness
of our number, these poor fellows in the boats, reduced to
the last stage of weakness, were struck with amazement
on so sudden a spectacle. But Don Manuel assured them
by words and signs, telling them, the bargain was struck;
if they would be true to their parts, so would we to ours:
and to this he pledged again his word as a priest.

It being thus settled, we made them motions of friendship; and I, the only one except our priest that spoke
their language (or anything to signify), called out to them,
we would truly befriend them in their need, if their conduct justified it; and bade them pull in-shore. This they
did at once; when the boat grounded, the poor fellows
made hard shift to get out of her, feebly and slow; and
't was with still more pains they got the sick on shore.
Harry Gill and I stood to our arms; Pounder, with Samuel,
kept their bows ready: as to the rest, they went cheerfully to help at the landing, and piled their arms under
cover of our guns.

The first thing we insisted on was, that all the crews'
weapons, whether muskets, pistols, cutlasses, hatchets,
even to the boat-hooks, should be handed to us out of the
boats; which was done accordingly, before a man of them
put his foot on dry ground. For, though we would not
mistrust nor judge them hardly, we did not forget, the
better part of valour is discretion: let them be as weak as
they might singly, yet they so greatly outnumbered us,
as might tempt them, at some favourable moment, to over-
power us also. Being now quite unarmed, against a set
of men armed to the very teeth (for we put the flints into
their guns and pistols again, and stuck their hatchets and
cutlasses into our belts, as hostages for their conduct), it

would have been stark madness in them to move a finger against us.  But I was surprised from the first, to see the unshaken trust these poor men showed in our honesty ; till a thought told me, they took our character on the word of the priest, who (they knew) would not deceive them.  On our part, we were slower to be convinced of theirs ; and stood jealously on our guard, till all suspicion of them wore off by degrees.

The next thing was to land the sick men that lay in the boats; who were nine in all, and some of them so far gone as to be more dead than alive.  One, indeed, seemed so spent, we thought he would yield up the ghost before we could have him ashore : and Don Manuel, who had waded into the water to visit them (not waiting for the boats to be thrust nigher the beach), finding this poor man in such extremity, called to Samuel to run for a shaddock, to refresh him withal.  I could see, from his sitting on the boat's thwart by the hammock where the poor fellow lay, and putting his ear close to him, he had begun to hear the dying man's confession.  Soon the young Indian came running back with a fresh fruit or two, a bag of our bread, and a crock of water.  He plunged into the sea to get at the boat, and between them they tried to make the Spaniard swallow a bit, though never so small ; but 't was all too late.  What with scurvy and famine, and pining every way, he was now too far gone on his last journey, and could hardly swallow some drops of the water only.  In short, after a few faint whispers with the priest, he died under his hands, blessing the divine mercies with his last breath (so we learnt afterwards from the others that lay round) for sending to him the comforts of his religion in his dying hour, beyond all human hope.

So, leaving the dead man for awhile, to wait on the extreme needs of the living, we handed the hammocks out carefully, one by one, and laid these suffering creatures in a row, eight of them, under the shade of some cocoa palms, a stone's cast from the beach.  Several of the number seemed as near death's door as the one that was gone already : the priest and I attended them as best we might, each in our way ; though my choicest remedies were only cocoa-nut milk, with sliced shaddock and yams, yet we brought them round enough for Don Manuel to be left alone with them for their confessions; and, to be short, the second of them died within two hours after his landing, and the third that same night. As for the rest, those other two of the five worst, recovered; one wholly, and lived to be a serviceable member of our little government; the other lived for some time after, and went off in a dropsy. The four who were not so far spent with weakness at the first, got round quicker, one after the other, when they began to taste our fresh meat and vegetables; but by nothing more than by the cocoa-nut milk, of which we gave them three or four large draughts daily.

To return to their first landing: we found, besides these nine in the hammocks, there were thirty-two able-bodied seamen, for we counted them as they sat, or lay for very weakness, on the shore. To call them able-bodied, must be understood by comparison; they were just able, indeed, to lay their hand on an oar; but I doubt whether their whole force united could have given a turn to the capstan, or pulled-in a cable; and 't is not to be doubted, had their voyage lasted a few days longer, or had they met rough weather on nearing our island, not one of them would have landed alive. They were reduced to that extremity, two or three swooned outright, and lay for dead: I remarked many of them weep like very children, whether in thankfulness for escaping with their lives, or from a degree of weakness that is so strange a thing to any man reduced to it on a sudden from the vigour of health; while others dropped on their knees, and begged us, *per l'amor di Dios*, to give them some food.

Indeed, we should have thought of this ere now; but we were distracted by all we had to attend to: what with mounting guard over the living, tending the sick and dying, helping the weakest to land, and keeping the boats in-shore. But by this, I had gone through the wards of my hospital, and done what I could for my patients; so, leaving Don Manuel engaged in his proper work for their benefit, I came forward to the crew, rifle on shoulder, and the rest of us behind me, fully armed.

"My friends, and gentlemen," said I, in my best Spanish, which would not carry me very far in the dialogue: "you shall have food, without doubt, for you are our guests, and we bid you welcome. But," I went on, "we must understand one another from the first: we keep your arms safe for you, till we are better acquainted; and you make no attempt to move from the place we mark out for you to stay in. Otherwise, gentlemen," for I had learned that much of courtesy from our Spanish friend, "otherwise"— and here I tapped my rifle with my forefinger, nodding my head to make them know my resolution.

Comprehend they did, without doubt; and made signs of assent to all this. But one who seemed in authority (we found later he was fourth lieutenant, the only officer who had lived through the starvation, and taken command on the death of the others) came a little before the rest, and answered me in the purest Spanish: "Your gentleness,"* says he, "may rest assured, we will be faithful to the word we have sworn to our countryman, the priest yonder. We are men of honour," laying his hand on his breast, "and subjects of his most Catholic majesty: you are our benefactors; we are bound to you in honour and gratitude, both. 'T is true, *Señores Ingleses*, our countries are now at war with one another; but we trust you will not prosecute that war in such remote regions as these. 'T is a quarrel that is none of ours, and surely we may well let it lie. You have taken us at disadvantage, in the weak state we are in: but, as on our part we have pledged to you our sacred word, we trust to find men of honour and *caballeros* in return. We have delivered up to you our arms, and claim your hospitality, and the safety of our lives, liberty, with the vessel and cargo, or whatever we can save from her."

This was the substance of his speech; but he delivered it with such a straightforward, manly grace as took our fancies greatly, and secured my trust in him from that time onward. Parts of it, though I did not well understand; above all, where he spoke of our two countries being at war with each other. When we were last in port, 't is true, what with our ships pushing their contraband trade in Campeachy Bay, and other points of the Mexican coast;

* Owen is here translating literally the Spanish expression of courtesy, *Usted*, which is said to be a contraction of the words, *Vuestra Mercid;* your mercifulness, or your gentleness, in the same sense in which we use the word, *gentleman*, and the Greeks, ἐπιεικής. **Ed.**

with the reprisals of the Spanish guarda-costas, there were causes of rupture enough between the governments of Spain and England.  Yet, it appeared, we had put to sea a little before the news could reach us, that Admiral Vernon had sailed with a fleet against the Spanish West Indies, and open war had been declared.  This, together with events following, as the bombarding of Carthagena, the taking of Porto Bello, and the expedition of Commodore Anson (in which, it came out that our friends were nearly interested), we learned from the lieutenant more at leisure.

———

## CHAPTER LX.

### A TREATY MADE AND RATIFIED.

DON MANUEL had now joined us, and took a chief part in the conference with his Spanish countrymen.  To be brief, we drew up certain articles for both sides to abide by : indeed, the dictating of terms was clearly on our side, by force of arms.  And they were as follows :

1. Neither party to regard the other in the light of enemies ; but both to act as though war had not been proclaimed between our several nations.

2. A line to be drawn, to portion off for the Spaniards a part of the island, enough to dwell in for the present ; with permission to cut down wood to make themselves habitations, and for firing.

3. Water, if not readily found within their allotment, to be supplied by us, and brought to the spot, free of charge.

4. We engaged to supply them also in fish and flesh, together with bread, vegetable, and fruit, at a moderate charge : the said charge not to be made in money, which had no value here, but in tools, or other useful articles, if they could rescue any such from the wreck : otherwise on credit, under note of hand from the lieutenant to the governor or commander of some of the Spanish colonies.

5. Two persons named on their side, three on ours, and they alone, to have the privilege of passing the boundary line.

6. Any other but these two of theirs, caught on our side of the line, to suffer the penalties of such as transgress martial law, at our pleasure.

7. The wreck itself to remain Spanish property : we engaging to help to our utmost to bring it in-shore, or land such valuables from it as could be saved.  In doing which things alone, the boundary line of separation did not hold good, and might be broken.

8. In consideration of these good services, and in the event (which seemed unlikely enough) of their getting her off, or being rescued by some of their countrymen, we should be allowed a reasonable choice of any of the vessel's goods for our own use.

9. Should the wreck be refitted, or any Spanish vessel or other vessel friendly to Spain touch at the island, we were to have a free passage to any port she might afterwards touch at, at our choice.

10. Likewise, should any British vessel, or one from our colonies, touch at the place, the Spaniards to be allowed a passage on board of her at a fair average rate of passage-money, to any port that lay on their voyage, or which they might be driven into..

11. In the meantime, their fire-arms, weapons, and powder, whether now landed, or still in the wreck, to remain in our safe keeping, till we decided otherwise ; their supplies being secured to them, as above.

12. All fair and friendly treatment to be assured to either party at the hands of any force on the opposite side, should they heave in sight.

These articles being concluded, and solemnly ratified on both sides by oath, we proceeded at once to supply the poor famished men with food ; though for the present we did not eat with them (according to articles 2, 5, and 6 of our agreement), we took care they should want for nothing we could furnish.  Therefore we sent the Indians in all haste to our store-house, to fetch what might be at hand ; as, smoked peccary and cod-fish, with the cakes of yam and bread-fruits, made into a pulp, then strained and baked, such as we had learned by this time to make into palatable and wholesome loaves enough. But anything, no matter how coarse and ordinary, was a dainty at that moment to men who had been for weeks and months on short commons, as these our guests had been : and latterly almost without food at all. Our care was less to supply them with victuals enough (of which was no lack), but to hinder their making too free use of it. On my representing this to the lieutenant, and the danger of sickness, and death itself, to men who should indulge to their hearts' content after so long a fast, he entered at once into my views. Accordingly, we established a strict discipline among the crew in the order of getting their messes, and the quantity served to them.

The sick came first; for, where the disease was little else but scurvy and famine, or the exhaustion after fever, then Dr. Diet (as Tom Harvey said) was the best doctor to call in. Accordingly, we divided the food into small portions, giving them more of bread than flesh-meat, and this moistened with water into a panada, or bread-sop. It seemed a cruel thing, to deny so many famishing wretches as now came crowding towards us : but 't was done out of sheer kindness, to prevent the ill effects of giving them much at once. As they observed the conditions laid down, and would not, even pressed with hunger as they were, overstep the boundary line we had by this time drawn between us, we passed down on our side the line, and fed them in order. We kept our three Indians running at their full speed up to our castle, and back to us, bringing more meat and bread, till we had given the hungry Spaniards as much as I judged well for the time. But, as we promised them another meal soon, though many longing eyes from their meagre faces were cast at the remaining food, they were fain to submit; and first with a thanksgiving to God, then to us, retired a little from the boundary. Some lay down for very weariness, more of them sat silent; some talking together in broken sentences, some with us across the line; and a few retired with themselves to converse with God, and going upon their knees, continued their thanksgiving more at large. I am now sure, from what I knew of them on better acquaintance, there would have been more outward acts of devotion among them, but for the weariness that oppressed their famished bodies and weighed down their souls.

The lieutenant (or captain, as we must call him—for death, that took others from over his head, promoted him to command this handful remaining of a large crew, and the wreck of a large vessel),—this officer, I say, seemed most attentive to do all that lay in his power for the comfort of his men. He neglected his own needs, or took a morsel only now and again, till he had given what help he could in ranging them to receive their rations of food, and aiding the sick; who, to be sure, were more easily fed in due order, being unable to stir from their hammocks.

When the lieutenant had seen to this, and swallowed a few morsels (so much as we judged safe to allow him, which he ate ravenously, like his men), his next care was to try and save the ship, which we expected to go down every moment, so water-logged was she. The tide had shifted her in nearer, and saved her from being carried off by the current I spoke of; in which case she had beyond a doubt been lost to us, and carried away to the east of our island, into open sea, or else wrecked on the reefs, and broken up. Our only hope for her was, she might drift into shoal water; this she seemed likely to do, as we all stood watching her from the cove where these Spaniards had landed at the first. But it seems, the leak had gained too fast on her for this: being now deserted by her crew, who had made still some feeble efforts at the pumps, all the while they remained on board.

'T was by a Providence the tide was now at its rise, not at ebb; though the weather was so calm, with just a light breeze stirring, yet there was a sort of spring-tide on, and the water higher than common; for, had it been neap-tide, we had either lost her altogether, or at the least, all would have been spoiled in the water. For, as we debated with the lieutenant, whether we had now strength to man the boats, to board her, and contrive to pass a hawser round the foremast and so haul her in-shore, we found to our great concern she was beginning to settle down, and sink on her larboard quarter.

Now there was no help for it, but to wait on, and see

the end; for 't would be madness, indeed, to venture on board a sinking ship. But the lieutenant was in extreme grief at the .sight, being in charge of the vessel; having also (as we afterwards learned) a considerable interest in some of her stores. He gave utterance to this by passionate exclamations, walking up and down the beach, and throwing his hands abroad; till we reasoned with him, begging him to be calm, and take the dispositions of Providence like a man and a Christian. This, indeed, he did, after a while; but at first, passion had its way with him.

## CHAPTER LXI.

### THE LIEUTENANT'S STORY.

WE rejoiced to see after that one great heel she gave to larboard, she settled down no lower for the time; however, when nearly another half hour was gone by, her larboard bows dipped too, nigh upon a level with the quarter, and so she remained fast, never stirring after at all. We thought it might have happened thus, owing to the position of the leak; next day, however, showed us our mistake here. But now, we began to entertain great hopes of recovering at least a good part of the cargo, if not getting off the ship herself, when we had lightened her: besides, we hoped to be able to do somewhat towards stopping the leak, and to make her seaworthy again. In short, wild schemes came into our heads fast, at the sight of this vessel lying so close to us; we began to reason (in whispers among ourselves) as one good turn deserved another, and we had done the crew this great service, to give them hospitality in their famished condition, and save their very lives, 't was the least they could do in turn, to refit the ship with us, and take us on board on equal terms, and land us where we might choose.

Don Manuel not being with us (for he was busied with

his sick men), we kept this to ourselves for the time.   But of all persons, he that desponded most was the poor lieutenant; for knowing the condition of his ship, he assured us, her timbers were so strained, and the entire hull so rotten, he verily believed she never would float again.

By this time, night being upon us, we blew a loud concert on our horns, to give notice, 't was time for all to retire to quarters.   We furnished our guests with good store of fuel, whereof they made a cheerful fire; then *toeing a line* (as they say at sea) we handed them across the boundary a hot mess of stewed pork and potatoes, which the Indians had prepared for them, in more plenty and comfort than their former meal.   When they had finished this (and 't was soon done, with hungry men as they were still, both then and for several days after) we assembled all together, each party on their own side, while Don Manuel said night prayers for us: we said them to-night before our own supper, to let our weary guests have their rest without delay; and Tadoone said them in English first, then turned them into Spanish that all might have a share.

'T was a sight to make any one feel, who owned a heart, when these poor men, so lately rescued from death, knelt there by the fire-light, in the close neighbourhood of their dead and dying comrades, and made their thanksgiving aloud after the good priest.   A brief prayer he made, but a hearty; then gave them his blessing, and dismissed them to rest.   But we invited the lieutenant to be our guest at supper; leaving Pounder with his bow and arrows as a sentinel, or picket, half way between the camps.   After our meal, we begged for some account of the ship's adventures; which the Spanish officer gave us, almost word for word as I here set it down.

" 'T is no news to you, Señores," began the lieutenant, addressing us in Spanish as we sat round our fire, " that the name of our ill-fated vessel is the *Hermiona*, of Valencia; for you have seen that name painted on her boats, as you will see it again when you are so good as to help us in boarding the wreck.   Then, too, you will see her fifty-four guns, with whatever equipments may remain; but alas! of the crew, five hundred strong, besides our complement of soldiers, you may behold all that survive in the few starved wretches whom, under divine Providence," he

crossed himself devoutly, "you have saved from destruction." With that, the poor man paused a little, being
overcome by his feelings, and not well able to proceed.

After a while, having received from us all tokens of
sympathy, he recovered himself, and went on :

"We formed part," says he, " of a squadron of six vessels fitted out by his most Catholic majesty, to watch the
motions and cross the designs of an English admiral (Don
Georgio Anson by name) who had sailed, on the first breaking out of the war between his country and ours, with a
counter-squadron of five men-of-war, a sloop, and two victualling ships, to attack our colonies in Manilla. Upon
the first news of this expedition being afloat, we were
ordered to put to sea; which we did in such haste, as
caused the greater part of our disasters after. For we had
not with us, on leaving the Spanish coast, more than four
months' provision at the utmost, and even that, reckoned at
short allowance only; so that our best chance was to get
round Cape Horn before the English admiral could arrive
thither, and victual our ships at leisure, either at Juan
Fernandez or some point on the western coast of South
America. But first, we made an attempt to procure us
some provisions at Buenos Ayres, where we reckoned on a
supply ; and so steered for the Rio de la Plata from the leeward of the Madeiras, leaving our station near that island
early in the November of last year.*

Whilst we were lying off Madeira, to westward of the
island, in the latter end of the previous month (October),
we received intelligence from some trusty friends we had
there, (but most secretly, without knowledge of the governor) that a squadron of ships had arrived in Madeira Road,
that is, to the east, or windward, supposed to be the equipment under Commodore Anson, against which we were
sent out. But as several weighty reasons made us prefer
to encounter him in the South Seas, rather than near home,
we determined to leave him a clear passage, instead of
standing out to meet him on that side of the island. So,
after sending in the *patache* that waited on us, to reconnoitre every day close in-land, and having occupied that
station but a short week in all, we made sail, as I have

* That is, the year 1740. ED.

said, for the Rio de la Plata, in the very beginning of November; and, steering direct, arrived there early in January of this year.

"I now see our great error, as, doubtless, does our gallant admiral, Don José Pizarro, if he be still in life (if not, may God receive his soul; for a brave seaman he was, and careful of his men), our error, I repeat, in not rounding the island, to give battle to the commodore where he lay: in which case, we had either (through our superior force, for we numbered more guns and greater weight of metal), captured or dispersed his squadron; or at the least, disabled and delayed this expedition against our colonies: besides causing him much loss of provision-stores.  For we knew he had victualled and watered at the island of Madeira; so he would have been forced to throw over board great quantities of what he had just taken, to clear his ships for the chance of an engagement: and whether victor or no, would have thereby suffered both loss and delay.

"However, our course was now for Rio, to outmatch him in sailing, and get first round the Horn; to which end, parting company with two ships bound for the West Indies, we staid not till we dropped anchor in the bay of Maldonado, at the mouth of Rio itself.  But, before we could receive our stores from Buenos Ayres, another sure but secret intelligence reached us, our enemy was now at Santa Catarina, preparing to put to sea again with the utmost expedition.  Thus we found ourselves in the hard choice of going without the provisions we so greatly needed, with imminent risk of falling short indeed; or being beaten in our race across the ocean, to find the English squadron in the South Seas before us.

"We chose the first evil, as the least; yet it turned out to be the greater, as you, Señores, are now witnesses.  So, having stayed seventeen days only at Maldonado, thus narrowly missing all our provisions, which came down into the bay from Buenos Ayres within a day or two after we sailed, we now got under weigh, and put to sea before the enemy: but so close to him in point of time and nearness of sailing, that one of his ships (as we always believed, though from the distance we could only conjecture, for our admiral had given orders to the squadron to sail wide), mistaking our vessels for her own consorts, got within gun-shot of our admiral's ship, the *Asia;* and we, who watched the affair from our tops with our perspective glasses, had great hopes she would have been made a prize of.   But she discovered her error so as to put about, barely in time, and so got clear away."

"When we sailed from Maldonada," he went on, "'t was the third week of this present year: our voyage, too, was the longest and most perilous the greater part of our crew had yet made; and we dreaded the very name of Cape Horn, so formidable for the storms encountered in doubling it.   Our men became very discontented: for the weather had been brewing up for gales, which came on us; till, with every attempt to keep discipline aboard, signs of mutiny began to show among the crew: which increased so much, we had to clap half a dozen of the ringleaders in irons.  At length we were forced to double the sentries of marines, and keep a score of men under hatches, lest they might spread the mutiny.

"Matters were kept quiet for a time by an order from the admiral, that our seamen were to have part of their pay advanced to them in *specie,* that is, a portion assigned to each man, of the goods for barter and traffic we had brought with us from Spain: that they might dispose of them in the South Seas, and so be in the way of making their fortunes.   For instances were currently reported, both at home and in the fleet, of some who had brought back from our colonies a wealth in the precious metals, and gems of much value, in barter for mere trumpery wares in calicoes, or inferior silks, such as a Valencia tradesman's wife would not wear on a holiday: or even what was less than these, as beads, nails, knives, bits of looking-glass, old iron hoops, glass, or glittering baubles of any kind. The hope of such a gainful traffic buoyed our men up above their present miseries: for we Spaniards have always been seeking an *El Dorado* land of untold wealth, somewhere in the wide western sea; and there was not a common seaman, nor down to the cook's boy, who did not picture to himself his return home, with a triumph like Columbus, a wonder of riches and glory.  This, with a strict watchfulness, and some examples made of the most disorderly by our captain, kept down the mutinous spirit that was rising to a head.

"The time was near the end of February; by this, we had run down the coast of South America, and, by our reckoning, were in more than fifty-five degrees of south latitude, to give us a fair sweep to double the Cape: which we prepared to do, by standing to windward, in the very last night of that month.  But (whether 't was by the uncertain currents, both of wind and sea, that conflict with each other round that great promontory, or by what other cause we never discovered), certain it is, our ship, with two more of the squadron, the *Guipuscoa*, and the *Esperanza*, lost all sight of the admiral and the rest.  We were now greatly at the mercy of the current; making much leeway eastward, or by that to south-east, do all we could by luffing up into the wind's-eye: at length, after beating about within sight of the Falkland Islands for several days, our ship, together with the *Esperanza*, was able to pass the straits between *Tierra del Fuego* and *Staaten Island* on the sixth of March; but had here the discomfort of losing sight of the *Guipuscoa*, which we saw no more, nor know to this day, whether she has gone down, or doubled the Horn."

## CHAPTER LXII.

### THE SAME CONTINUED.

"NEXT day," continued the Spaniard, "though I fear to weary you, gentlemen, by prolonging the story of our misfortunes, we were encountered by a furious tempest from the north-west, or thereaway; for 't was difficult to account with any exactness for the wind's quarter, where all was a jumble of tempest, head-winds, and conflicting currents.  All I know is, we found it vain to contend with the fury of the elements; had we attempted to do more than put our helm about, and scud before the wind, I verily believe we had all ere now been food for fishes. Nor can I say whether our plight was worse than what befell the rest of the squadron, of whom we scarce caught a glimpse now and then, nor any at all, after the second day of this furious tempest. Once or twice, when lifted from the trough of the sea on the back of a rolling mountain of water, we thought we could catch sight of one of the squadron, running for it, close reefed, or partly dismasted, out to the south-by-east. This we thought to be the consort that had stayed longest by us, the *Esperanza*, of fifty guns, with four hundred and fifty men aboard, not counting her portion of an old regiment of foot, many of them broken down and invalided, but now carried out to strengthen our garrisons on the coast of Chili. Alas! where are all those brave souls now? have they found a grave beneath the waters, or are they cast away like ourselves, their unhappy companions?" And here the poor man stopped again a little, and wept outright.

We were urgent with him to take some rest, and let the remainder of his sorrowful story stand over till the morrow; but it seemed a relief to his pent up feelings to give us the tale of his misfortunes at once; so, after a little remonstrating, we let him go on.

"These, one would think, Señores," says he, " were calamities enough; but greater were in store for us, as your gentlenesses shall hear. The evening of that same second day, while we were doing our best to guide the ship, but with ill success, and drove helplessly before the wind, came a huge roller, a monster of a wave, that threatened to swallow us at a mouthful; struck us with full force amidships; and, but the *Hermiona* is a well-timbered sea boat (indeed, she is, or was, alas! a charming sailer on a light wind), it had then and there made an end of us. But it gave us a shrewd wrench, and one we never got over: the good ship staggered and trembled like a live thing under the heavy blow; and when we righted again (all but three poor fellows that were washed overboard into eternity), we found to our grief, almost to our despair, the binnacle,* with compass and all, had been

---

* The box which contains the compass for steering a ship. ED.

washed into the sea.  We were so ill-provided with the most necessary things for our expedition, owing to the haste of our sailing from Spain, you would scarce believe, Señores, this was the only compass we had on board : nor can I cease to wonder now at our improvidence ; but so it was, as we know to our cost.

"Being thus left forlorn on the open sea, and by the blackness of a continued tempest shut out from all observation of the stars, we let ourselves drive whithersoever the elements would take the vessel.  We thought it as likely we might be steering away from some friendly haven as making for it ; and we used the helm from that time, only to steady the ship : commending ourselves fervently to the good Providence of God to take us into harbour by His own secret guidance, whose ' way is in the sea, and His paths in many waters.'  To this we were tenderly exhorted by our good chaplain, Don Diego Rodez—"

"Diego Rodez !" exclaimed Don Manuel, not able to contain his astonishment and sorrow, "was Diego, then, with you in yonder vessel ? "

"Aye, truly, father," says the lieutenant, surprised ; "he was our chaplain, and sailed with us from Valencia, sharing all our hardships ; and continued ever to be the main-stay and comfort of the crew, till he was stricken down with fever : then edified us all by his holy death."

"Ah, Diego, Diego ! " cried the priest, in the first burst of his sorrow : "my early companion and friend !  Ah, thou saintly one, whose example I ought to have followed more faithfully ! and thou art gone—gone hence before me :"—he could say no more ; but sat with his face buried in his hands.

We were all silent for a while ; till Don Manuel, still covering his face, said, in a broken voice, in Latin, and I repeated in English : " May the souls of the faithful, through the mercy of God, rest in peace ! "  All answered, Amen ; after which the lieutenant went on to Don Manuel and me, in a lower tone.  As to the rest, they did not understand much of his Spanish, and one after another soon dropped off to sleep around the fire.

" Well, Sirs," says he, " we found the same sea that had washed away our binnacle, had sprung our main-mast to that degree, that not only was it useless to carry sail, but we feared, at every lurch the ship gave, the top-hamper would bring the mast down, and kill some of our men on deck. We were therefore compelled to cut it away by the board, though 't was like signing our death-warrants to do so : and, before we had got half through it, the ship gave another great heel, and saved us all trouble, throwing the mast sheer over her starboard quarter. We cut ourselves free from the tackle, and sailed on as we could; but our steerage was so damaged by the huge waves that had taken us abaft, the ship would scarce answer her helm : two days after, with the continual rolling, our mizen shared the fate of the main-mast, only that it did not go quite by the board. The *Hermiona* was now little more than a log on the water; all we could do was, to keep her head pretty fair with any ocean stream we might meet, and redouble our prayers.

" So far for our sailing disasters ; but the worst remains to be told. Our scanty provisions had fallen so frightfully short, that nothing but death by starvation stared us in the face. It was afflicting to the utmost to see brave men, who had set forth from their native country full of hope and vigour, now doomed to die on the wide sea, like so many caged birds, or mice, a death so horrible, and by inches. I believe, never did an impatient sufferer, groaning under some lingering disease, call more fervently on death to release him, than our poor fellows yearned and prayed for the English squadron to heave in sight, that they might at least die at their guns, for their king and country. But all to no avail !

" We had now been reduced to half our daily allowance; then this again was made less, till we came down to nigh a quarter ; then to the quarter itself. We now began to lose our men very fast ; a fever broke out with the famine, or following on it : and we had to throw many overboard every day. Still, the provisions declined almost in the same degree ; so that the number of starving mouths on board made us scarcely feel the relief afforded by those who had ceased to eat. At this period of our sufferings, we took to anything that offered, no matter how distasteful : the rats in the ship became valuable prizes, and were disposed of by any who was lucky enough to catch one, as his hunger or avarice dictated. I have known a rat to fetch four or five dollars; and when they had all disappeared, more than double that price would have been given for them. Some of the men stole the ship's lanthorns, cut the horn of them into strips, and kept themselves alive by chewing it in secret. Any old piece of untanned leather was most greedily seized; the soldiers esteemed it an advantage to have their gloves to eat; and seal-skin shoes were quarrelled and fought for: then later on, tanned or untanned, all came to us alike.

"At length—I tremble to think of it—one dreadful alternative began to force itself on our thoughts. No one spoke of it at first; then, by degrees, it began to be whispered about, but 't was never known who first gave utterance to it—that, if this extremity continued, rather than that all should perish, one, or some, must be sacrificed"—

Here he stopped again, overcome: we shuddered with horror, too, to think what he meant, and that 't was possible for Christian men, reduced to such straits of hunger, to turn cannibals, and devour one another. "And how were you saved from this horrible thing?" asked Don Manuel, at length: "for saved from it you were, I trust in God!"

"By him who is gone to his reward," answered the lieutenant, crossing himself again: "our good chaplain, I mean. When the gunner came to him, lying as he was, exhausted with famine and sickness, and whispered to him, such things were beginning to be breathed among us, he dragged himself up the companion-ladder, more dead than alive, and stood suddenly on deck. We shrank away from him, so death-like he looked; some of us doubted whether it were not his ghost: but gathering the last of his strength, he exhorted us so pathetically, for the love of God, and by faith in His providence, to abstain from this hideous resource, that we all went down upon our knees on the deck around him, kissing the hem of his garment, and swore a solemn oath, we would hold out three full days longer. It was the last service he rendered to his Lord; for he swooned, and lay for dead, almost before the words were out of our lips; in truth, he died that night. But, though we were reduced to the extremity of tearing up rotten planks from the deck, and gnawing the softer parts of the wood. yet we kept our word with him, though with great difficulty ; and before the three days were quite out, we discovered your island from the foretop, and fired our guns, which (I doubt not) you heard.  You know the rest, Señores : and to you, after God, be the thanks of the perishing given."

Having thus ended his narrative, the poor man feebly knelt to Don Manuel, to ask his blessing ; then saluted us with all the courtesy of his nation, though by this he could scarce speak for weariness, and retired to his side of the boundary, to forget his sorrows in sleep.

## CHAPTER LXIII.

### LAWFUL WRECKING

AT day break, next morning, the horns summoned us to spring up, and begin an important day for us all. First came morning prayer and spiritual mass, which we never omitted , and here I cannot pass by the astonishment and joy of the poor Spaniards, on finding we were Catholics like themselves.  They had taken it for granted that, being Englishmen, we must needs also be heretics ; and were slow at first to believe but there was some delusion here.  But when they were convinced of the truth, I could plainly see they not only were satisfied about ourselves, but regarded Don Manuel with yet more reverence, as having been the instrument to us of such a favour

Our next concern was to snatch a hasty breakfast, which was made as plentiful as time permitted, having hard work to do after it.  Pounder and the lieutenant, meantime, went down to the cove to look after the wreck : when they came back, each reported, in his own fashion, she had not sunk lower, but on the contrary, seemed to have been pushed by the advance of the tide further up on the reef, whereon she had grounded.  This, we made out, was the reason why she heeled so much to larboard; namely, her starboard bow had been shoved by the tide upon one of those coral reefs that made up our defences and the peril of our visitors; whereby the ship's balance was overset.

We ran down to the cove, eager to save what could still be got from the wreck: we found, as the lieutenant said, she had changed her place indeed, but whether better or worse for our purpose was hard to determine. For the whole of her forecastle and greater part of her starboard bow appeared now high and dry; but then, to balance that, her larboard quarter was deeper in the water, and half the quarter-deck was drowned. So we had little hope of being able to save her more valuable cargo; nor, what was of much more value to us, her store of powder, that lay too deep in the hold; nor whatever specie she might carry. But that last, the Spaniard assured us, was little enough, and only what would settle the ship's dues for provisions in port: for they rather had hoped to carry back silver to Old Spain than were equipped to carry out any; and partly were designed to relieve the galleon that sailed every year from Valparaiso, from making her voyage that year; which, by reason of the war that had broken out, and Commodore Anson's expedition, would have been hazardous, as it proved to be.

However, by dint of hard labour, with breaking up a part of the main-deck (though the greater part lay a foot or two under water) with help of crow-bars, and other tools we rummaged out on board, we made our way down to the officers' berths; but found little to repay our labour, except some clothes and fine linen, that were welcome enough to us. There was, indeed, some small store of money, too, and other valuables; but these were so little to our purpose, we had almost pitched them into the sea, for sheer vexation at finding nothing beside. 'T was with great difficulty we got at an arm-chest; when we had found it, there was no getting it up whole, for the weight, and depth of water; for half our work was to dive, or scramble rather, under the water, with a rope tied round us, to haul us up, if there was danger of our being smothered. But, not being used to diving, we could not stay under for more than three or four minutes at most; 't was blind work, too, after all, to feel about for such heavy things in the dark, and dangerous to venture more than a few steps from the hole in the deck by which we entered. So, after some hours' labour, each relieving the other, we got little enough for our pains, though Gill stayed under so long at one time, trying at the arm-chest, to break it open, that when he came up, the blood gushed from his nose and ears, and 't was some little time before he got his breath again.

Our Indians did us the best service here; for it seems, in Toonati-nooka they are all expert divers, and trained to it from their very infancy, going down several fathoms deep after pearl-oysters and other shell-fish, or coral for their ornaments; and even the children take to the water almost before they can run alone. Pounder and Samuel were delighted to render us this good turn: while we re-lieved them in mounting guard (for we harboured no unkind suspicions of our new friends, yet would not lay ourselves open to be taken at unawares), they kept plunging in, turn-and-turn-about, and stayed under an amazing time indeed. At last, between them the arm-chest was broken into; and they came up in triumph, bringing now a musket, now a cutlass, or brace of pistols, now some heads of boarding-pikes: in short, during two or three days (for I must go on faster in my account) working at this only, we got out no less than twenty-nine muskets, with seventeen large pistols, of the kind they call a *petronel*, or horse-pistol, besides six of a smaller sort: and we even made contrivance to unship and get into the boat a small brass mortar or short carronade, mounted on a swivel, such as would do wholesale execution if it were crammed with bullets, or even with nails, odds and ends of iron, nay, with stones and pebbles from the beach, provided we found powder to charge it with.

Of powder, we only found three large horns in the officers' cabins; one of these was touched by the water, so that great part was useless and spoiled. But we brought it all ashore; and later, by drying the damaged powder in the sun, we made it serve passably well, as also the rest of the wetted powder we got up afterwards from the powder-room in casks; only, it would miss fire by times, and we were never sure of it. But we had learned, by this time, not to rely on our guns at all; so, husbanding all our powder to garrison our fortress, we laid it up in the dry magazine in our rock, to serve us in any bout we might yet have with savages, or other encounters.

I may as well mention here, we began to make bows and arrows for our Spanish friends, too, and taught them how to use them: we went on with our regular practice from day to day; at least, after we had got everything from the wreck we could lay hands on. So that we might be reckoned well found in weapons of offence: having now powder enough, bad and good, for a great explosion, if not a great use; besides such a skill in archery that we thought it no rare feat to pick off a small bird from the top of the highest cocoa-palm in the island. Our Indians had made themselves javelins as well as bows out of the bamboo canes, and shod and pointed them with shark's teeth or glimmer: also, they hollowed out other bamboos, smoothing the inside with great care; then fitted a light arrow into them, and blew it forth with their breath with great force and an amazing good aim to a distance. So that, altogether, we were now a formidable body of archers, six-and-forty strong; and with our castle and powder-magazine, might have given battle or stood a siege against more than twice our number.

## CHAPTER LXIV.

### RUMOURS AND SECRETS.

OUR island now witnessed a new life, and at first a strange one; for if our being left here was beyond all expectation, six poor forlorn men, to shift for ourselves; 't was yet more so to find our colony increased by this second unlooked-for adventure. But truth, I have heard said, is stranger than fiction; and certain it is, should any one take into his head to invent such a tale, on the side of the Spaniards or our own, and put it on paper, he would be set down as a romancer, unworthy of belief.

When I returned to England, indeed, some years after (for I may as well outrun my story here), the war being then over, the commodore * raised to be a lord, and endowed with great wealth—all which he well deserved, not more for bravery and signal services, than for humane and honourable conduct through the war—I heard, among other rumours which I knew to be false, that the *Hermiona* was thought to have foundered at sea, when the Spanish fleet was driven back from Cape Horn by that tempest the lieutenant told us of.

Nay, this was even believed in Spain, as I learned from a merchant of that nation whom I met at a coffee-house in London, not so very long since.

His story ran as follows: That, with all the efforts of Pizarro, the Spanish admiral, and the commanders of the several vessels under him, to prosecute the enterprise that squadron had set forth upon, finding the tempest too much for them, in the disabled condition of their ships and crews (the one shattered and dismasted, growing leakier every day; the other worn out with fever, scurvy, and famine alike, dispirited with adverse fortune, not to speak of the exhausting labour of still working the ships' pumps in that state of weakness), they had all been forced to run for it before the wind;

That nothing was then left to them but to bear away for the Rio de la Plata, which place the admiral, in his own ship (the *Asia*), succeeded in making, but not till near the middle of May in that year;

That two other ships of the squadron, first the *Esperanza*,

---

* Anson, who returned to England with his only remaining ship, the *Centurion*, after the capture of a rich Spanish galleon, and nearly four years after he had set sail from Spithead, in command of five ships and a sloop. He came back with the twofold glory of as much naval success as the vexatious delays of the government permitted him to reap, and of being ranked among the circumnavigators of the globe: arriving at Spithead in June, 1744. His great success off Cape Finisterre afterwards crowned his reputation as a brave and skilful commander. He was thereupon created baron Soberton and, having risen, through every successive rank in the service, to be admiral and commander-in-chief of his majesty's fleet, died in 1762. ED.

of fifty guns, with four hundred and fifty men (or what remained of them), then the *San Estevan* of forty guns, that had taken from Spain a crew of three hundred and fifty, followed the *Asia*, and made Rio a few days after the admiral;

That the *Guipuscoa*, the largest ship of the squadron, a seventy-four, carrying an equal complement of men with the admiral's, that is to say, seven hundred strong, grounded and sank somewhere off the Brazils; but her crew, I mean the poor remnant that famine had not devoured, nor fever wasted, saved their lives in the boats, and some found their way back to Spain, others settled in the Spanish plantations;

That the *Hermiona* had without any doubt foundered at sea, since none of her crew were heard of after.

As to these items, with other details of the straits the five ships' companies were reduced to for want of provisions, and the horrors of famine aboard ship (all which agreed very well with the Spanish lieutenant's narrative), I could well believe each and every one, except the last article. Indeed, as to the rest, with this included, I had read it before in the narrative of Lord Anson's voyage, by his chaplain, printed for John and Paul Knapton in Ludgate Street.

If the reader should ask, why I have kept this so close, without giving (for I never have given) the least hint of it, whether to the Spanish or English governments, nor even in conversation with my friends, I would beg him to consider the circumstances under which these men, being at war with my own country, were cast on that island of which I might be reckoned (in some sort) viceroy, or governor: how we were all there together, in a corner of the world; how men, in circumstances so strange, in the utmost distress, needing each other's aid for very life, almost cease to belong to this or that nation, and merge into the great family of mankind. Let him reflect how barbarous and inhuman a thing it were in me, on touching my native shores, to turn informer on the whereabouts of brave men who had been the sport of such disasters; that, war or no war, they were my brothers in misfortune, fellow-colonists in the island while they stayed there, or colonists on their own account, if they returned; that, whether on our island, or in Toonati-nooka (if they ever reached that place), they had the same right to *liberty:* –but while I revise these sheets, three years after they were written, and arrive at that word *liberty*, I feel with sorrow, these are not days in which freedom from injustice is the portion of a seaman,* of whatever merit.

I have decided it, then, in my mind, that not they only, but their descendants for two, aye, and for three generations (in case they have settled in that country, without going back to Spain) shall remain undisturbed from any quarter, so far as I can provide for it; unless the restless spirit of discovery and enterprise now awakened among us, shall produce another South Sea Bubble, or another voyage round the globe. My friend, the Honble. John Byron† is about the most likely man I know of, to ferret out these my other friends in their retreat, should he hoist his flag again for those parts where he hath already suffered so great hardship. And the knowledge of there being such active spirits among us, together with other motives it were tedious to trouble the reader with, have determined me to leave these sheets in trust with a dis-

---

* This allusion seems to point clearly to the death, in 1757, of the unfortunate Admiral Byng, who was shot in that year for an alleged neglect of duty, but apparently to save the credit of an unpopular and incapable ministry. Owen Evans expresses, in his more homely way, very much the sentiment recorded in the Admiral's epitaph, placed by his family over his remains : " To the perpetual disgrace of public justice, the Honourable John Byng, Vice-Admiral of the Blue, fell a martyr to political persecution, on March the 14th, in the year 1757, when bravery and loyalty were insufficient securities for the life and honour of a naval officer."

The reader will observe, that reckoning three years after fifteen from Owen's misfortune in 1739, brings us precisely to 1757. ED.

† Commodore Byron, second son to William, fourth Lord Byron, and grandfather to the too celebrated poet, was born at Newstead in 1723, and went as midshipman in one of Anson's ships (the *Wager*), in 1740. This vessel was wrecked on the coast of Patagonia; whence, after enduring extreme hardships, he reached Chiloe, was made prisoner by the Spaniards, taken to St. Jago in Chili, and did not return to England for more than five years after his departure, *i.e.*, from 1740 to 1746. Eighteen years after this, again, he took command of an expedition of discovery to the South Seas; and having gone round the world, returned in safety two years afterwards. He commanded on the West Indian Station during the American war, and died in 1768. ED.

creet friend of mine, and with his son and grandson after him, their hereditaments and assigns; not to see the light till one hundred years, or thereabout, shall have come and gone, after I have passed out of this life into the world to come; when, sweet Jesu, receive my soul! Amen.

----

## CHAPTER LXV.

### THE BEST DISCOVERY OF ALL.

ASSURED of the honest purpose of these new-comers, we began discreetly to trust them: and we repealed those strict laws we had made on their arrival, forming thenceforth but one commonwealth, and having interests and property in common. "We will have nothing more to do," says Don Manuel, "with those cold words, *mine* and *thine*;" and he went on to say, in the first days of Christianity, the multitude of the believers threw all into a common stock, none saying that aught of the things which he possessed was his own. ".But what shall be done," I asked, "if any prove himself a worthless member of the community, and begin to disturb or injure the rest?" "Let him who discovers it take that man aside," answered the priest, "and reason with him in meekness and charity." "Well but," I went on (he and I were talking alone at this time), "and if he persist?" "Then let two or three of the elder and more moderate enforce on him what the first has said." "And if he be obstinate after that?" "Then bring him to me," says he, smiling; "and I will persuade him by those higher motives he possesses in virtue of being a Catholic." "And lastly, Tadoone, if he remain deaf, even to you?" "Then we will banish him," he answered, in a decided way, "to the further side of the island, till solitude or hunger bring him back to his senses and to us."

This being understood, we pursued our lives all together: and making no distinction of race, language, or date of coming, admitted the Spaniards to share our crops, farm, larder, cave, and all the natural advantages or contrivances of our banishment. They, for their part, shared with us the stores we got from the wreck day by day; always with a proviso, we would account for the value of these, or at least give in an estimate of our use and consumption of them, to any authorities of our several countries, should a kind Providence one day take us off this place of exile.

Having arranged matters thus, as the only thing to be done under the circumstances we were thrown in, we made it a part of our daily life to go off to the wreck, and fetch away all we could lay hands on. We were well content to find her settle down no further in the water: indeed, upon the coral reef she had struck on, that was out of the question; thus we were encouraged to wait for some low water, at the neap tide, when, the sea being calm, we might come at the stores that lay below our usual diving. Meantime, we got out of her whatever we could reach, by breaking up the upper deck with our crowbars, and diving to the orlop deck: though we found that dangerous, by reason of the entanglements of the place itself, and the broken bulk-heads and woodwork floating to and fro.

Indeed, one of our Spaniards, José Martinez by name, had a narrow escape with his life; being jammed under water by a beam of wood, so heavy he could not free himself. Only by the strength and courage of Tom Harvey he was saved at all; being quite senseless when Tom brought him up with infinite difficulty, and himself almost spent. As to poor José, we could not bring him round for some time, with rubbing, clapping the palms of his hands, blowing into his nostrils with tobacco smoke, and what not: I truly believe, had there been a swell on, though never so little, they had been both lost without remedy. But José never forgot the gratitude he owed his preserver: so a close friendship sprung up between these two, and they made a compact together, they would specially serve and befriend one another on all occasions. When this came to Tadoone's ears, he was not so well pleased at it; and sending for the men, he reminded them they were already under such a compact, not to each other alone, but to all the rest, and need not make it afresh as between particular persons. For being men, says he, and being Christians besides, we are bound to help, aye, and love one another. As men, we owe our fellow-men an obligation of mutual aid and good will: and as Catholic Christians, we are bound up together in the mystical body of our Lord, and so are " members one of another." I can have nothing (he added) to say against a true friendship between any two, that is based on their having a like character and tastes, or being companions in misfortune or success; so that general charity suffereth not thereby. And thus ended his little discourse to José and Tom.

'T were tedious to give a list of all we got from the wreck, by dint of hard working; every day saw our stores increase in things very useful to us in our condition. We carried away all that was portable, and made attempts at many things that were not: in particular, we became rich in damaged powder, and old iron, hoops, bars, nails, and clamps; some of them served our needs in the shape we got them in, others we contrived to forge into rude spades, chisels, arrow-heads, and what not, by heating them in the hottest wood fire we could make, then hammering them into shape between two stones. 'T is true, we were young in the smith's craft, as in many other trades: but necessity is the mother of invention; and, as we had only ourselves to please, we managed well enough. Also, the planks and beams we got from the ship, that came away by degrees as the irons were loosened, proved handy to us, chiefly for putting up divisions in our cave, and for firewood.

By these tools, besides, we so enlarged our cave itself, as made it more like a catacomb, with passages running one into the other at an angle: and, growing bolder from our increased numbers, with no sign of savages coming to molest us, we concluded to make an entrance from below as well as above. So, going to work within our entrenchments, we hewed a low arch into the base of our cliff, till we were seven or eight feet in: then cutting upwards, made a sloping passage with steps notched in the rock, and aimed (as near as we could guess) at the centre of our cave above. We were not so far out in our reckoning, neither; for when we had worked for the best part of a week, we found ourselves coming up through the rocky floor of that short passage that led out of our main passage into the kitchen. This, to be sure, was an awkward place enough to find ourselves planted in, with our new stair-case : but the thing, being done, was not to be undone; the best remedy we could devise was to cut us out another passage round about, avoiding the hole we had made in the floor : then we blocked the former entrance to the kitchen with some trunks of trees, laid lengthways, one over the other; and so used our new stair-case with much satisfaction.

To come back to the wreck; one of our greatest prizes was the finding of the chaplain's vestments and chalice (Don Diego Rodez, I mean, that had died on board). The Spaniards told us they were surely to be found somewhere; and we lit on them at last, stowed away in a chest with a few things, almost worthless, that had belonged to the poor good priest, and made up the whole of his worldly wealth. As. a very old cassock, pair of shoes much worn, a shirt or two, none of the best, a crucifix and small case of relics, his missal and breviary, two little books of devout prayers and meditations, a larger volume, which Tadoone said was a treatise on theology, and some Latin papers, with the seal of the bishop of Valencia. They were much spoiled by the salt water, and the leaves of the book so glued together, we made sure no man would ever read them again. But Don Manuel, to whom (I could see) these books were a great prize, by patient drying of them in the sun, so far restored them, that a good part of their contents became readable again : and he took much delight in making out these parts, giving us little choice bits of spiritual maxims and words of comfort, proper to our condition.

The priest's vestments had suffered from the sea-water as much, almost, as the books : yet by dint of care they came out pretty well at last. As for the little altar stone and linens to suit it, they were no ways damaged. With these, and the sacred vessels (with a case of pure Spanish wine that we found in the captain's cabin), and a pound or two of virgin wax to make tapers of, we had every prospect of having that Holy Sacrifice among us, that we had learned so much to desire, and were hoping to profit by.

In brief, Don Manuel, with much joy, applied himself to the bags (our Indians had woven them of plantain leaves), wherein he kept his store of wheaten corn, in hopes of such an occasion: grinding out a portion between two flat stones, he kneaded up the paste, and made, with much ado, some thin sheets of unleavened bread, whereof (after baking) he cut out round wafers, half as large again as a rix-dollar. Having made a couple of dozen of these, he laid them up in a dry shelf, or cupboard, in our cave: then announced to us, all things were ready to celebrate holy Mass the morning after.

This was joyful news to us, you may believe: our spiritual mass and communions having prepared us, by a degree of longing, to welcome this chiefest of blessings whenever it should come indeed. We spent the afternoon in getting ready for the happiest day of our lives, all of us going to make our confession: which occupied no long time, inasmuch as we (most of us) did that every week, and lived at peace with our neighbours, except a little breeze (or so) now and again; and were happily removed out of the way of temptation.

Next morning came, and with it came the blessing of holy Mass and Communion. I am a bad one to describe such things as these; so I must leave to my reader to suppose what we felt as we knelt round the altar which Tadoone had arranged in a little arbour we had built for our summer chapel, or part woven and part built, lacing the sides in and out with tendrils of osiers and supple-jack.

One of our Spaniards, Bartolomé Ramirez, served the priest's Mass, having been used to do so (he told us) in the Church of the Augustinians at Valencia; so, all went on orderly and devoutly: nor were we distracted by the newness of it, having had every part, and every ceremony, explained to us by our good Tadoone. But as I recall that morning to my thoughts, my eyes fill with tears I am not ashamed of: only, I had sooner drop my pen, and go on my knees, than write any more about it.

# CHAPTER LXVI.

### SIGNS OF ANOTHER MOVE.

ONE thing only seemed now to disturb our tranquil way of life; that was, the disturbance we soon began to notice in our friend and guide. Strange it was, that he that had upheld us often in wayward desponding moods, and disgust at our lot, now seemed to be unhinged by some troublous thoughts of his own. He said nothing on the matter, but kept it to himself, whatsoever it might be; trying to seem as cheerful as was his wont. Only, I noticed him to be now more retired by himself: not, as before, when he was engaged at his devotions only, but at odd times too, unless he could help us by labour, of which he was never shy, or advice on any point we needed. I came on him once and again, seated with his head on his hand, gazing out on the sea to that quarter whence the canoe had been driven by the hurricane, some two years before. When he observed me, he would rise, and pass it off with a remark on the weather or such common things; but I could see, he was thinking on something further off.

What opinion the others had on all this, I know not; for I would not share my thoughts with any upon it. They looked at him, 't is true, with some uneasiness; for he had become no small part of our well-being, and the idea of his being taken from us by death, or in any other way, was such as we could not endure: so much had his gentle manners and example softened down those rude natures to the temper of good Christians. But no one spoke about this change in him, except in whispers one to the other: I, for my part, was at no loss for a shrewd guess what it meant. I had not forgotten the night when his words showed that he was dreaming about Toonati-nooka, and converting the savages there; I made no doubt, 't was on that project his mind was fixed, and that he never would be content nor happy again, till he had contrived to go over, and visit that island.

One afternoon, that I found him in this musing way, I made free to approach him on the subject: I told him, in a half-jesting tone, methought I could read a little, too, in the book he was studying. He looked at me, as somewhat surprised, not seeing my drift; for he knew not I had discovered his thoughts. Then, presuming on our friendship, I went on in the like strain: I told him, I could put the title of the book in one word. He then asked me to give him the word. "Nay, father," said I, "what is the book you have nearest to your heart?" On this, he pulls out his constant companion, his prayer-book, from the bosom of his worn cassock, and shows it me, with a smile. "You see, friend Owen, there are two words on the title; read them—*Breviarium Romanum:* so you are out in your guess." "Well," I pursued, "may I put my question another way?" "Any way you wish," says he. "What is the book, then," I asked, "that is nearest to your heart, and furthest from your eyes? What is it you think on daily, and gaze after, and the name of which is oft on your lips in your prayers? Describe it to me by the name of a place." "Truly, my dear child," says he, "as you are turned catechist on a sudden, I hope, perhaps, 't is heaven."—"But short of heaven?"—"Why, short of heaven, I desire to find myself safe in purgatory."—"But short of purgatory," I insisted, "though a longer word, if not two?" "Ah," says he, smiling still, but shaking his head now: "yes, you have read my thoughts truly, and my book, I see: 't is, indeed, Toonati-nooka!"

With that, rising, he stretches forth his hand towards the sea, that divided him from the object of his yearning; and says to me with the tears in his eyes: "See, my son; below that horizon are multitudes of precious souls, bought, equally with you and me, at the price of the same Divine Blood," and he lifted his hat with great reverence. "Ah, how greatly they were beloved by that Heart that agonized for us all on the cross: yet how far are they from Him! how far from the knowledge of Him, or power to love Him!"

He stopped a little, overcome by what he felt: then laid his hand on my arm, and said: "Remember out of what depth of hideous wicked heathenism our three Indians

weie plucked : well, even in those dark depths are count-
less souls now lying there!" he repeated, thrusting his
arm again over the sea ; " there. there!"

"I see them," he went on, " as clearly as with these
bodily eyes; shedding one another's blood, dancing round
monstrous idols, sacrificing their prisoners, nay, their very
children, to demons, dropping, two, three, ten at a time,
dropping into *Hell:*" his voice sunk to a whisper, and he
covered his eyes.

Soon he raised his looks and hands to heaven, and
said in a pleading voice, *Regina Apostolorum, ora pro
illis!* "

His lips moved still in prayer, his hands clasped, the
very sweat standing on his brow for the extremity of his
anguish.

After a while, he returned, as it were, to himself, and
looked round.  Observing me again, as I stood staring on
him, doubtful what to say or do, he addressed me nearly
in his usual manner.

"My dear child," says he, as he calmed down again,
"you have never seen this before: that is because I have
withdrawn myself, that none should observe it.  You know
now what it is that possesses my whole soul.  'T is my
vision by day, and dream by night.  A voice is sounding
in mine ears: it says, 'Come over to Toonati-nooka, and
help us.'*  Do not think," he went on, smiling at me, for
I stared upon him all the while, at a loss what to think;
" do not suppose I am beside myself.  I never was more
in my right wits; and that you shall see when we return
to the rest.  I shall be calmer now, for having told you
what is in my heart : henceforward, we can discuss it together, and see what is to be done."

" And you would leave us !" cried I, transported beyond
myself with grief at the thought: "O father, just when
we are learning, through you, to love God;  when you
have brought us some steps forward on the good way, you
will leave the plants you have planted and watered ! leave
the sheep you have brought into the fold ! "

* See *Acts*, xvi. 9, to which apparently the priest refers.  He
might also have had in his mind " the voices of the Irish," which Saint
Patrick heard by some supernatural communication, urging him to
come and teach them the truth.  ED.

" You may well believe," answered he, struggling with himself, " I should not leave you all without much pain; but there is one great sentence, the constant motto and motive of a great Saint, which expresses the rule we should follow in all matters."

" And what is that? " asked I, fearing, I hardly knew what.

" ALL TO THE GREATER GLORY OF GOD," said he. Then he added, with vigour; " Why should we not all go together?  Or, if that would overload the boats, shall we draw lots to see who goes and who stays on the first voyage of discovery; and they who go, promise to bring back the boats within a reasonable time ? "

In short, soon after we came again to the rest, the priest proposed to them, that a certain number, with himself, should take two of the boats, and set forth on a voyage of discovery to Toonati-nooka.  It might, he said, have several advantages; for savages, living in the state our Indians had described to us, would be likely to welcome civilized white men, with whom they were not at war, nor had any cause of quarrel, and who could teach them the useful arts of life.  Should they find the country enriched with veins of silver or gold (as was more than likely), then, he said, they might receive a benefit no less than confer one : only, in that case, he insisted that they must deal fairly with the inhabitants; not exact from them more than was just, nor attempt by crooked means to get the upper hand, like some discoverers who have blackened the Christian name by their cruelties to the heathen to whom they went.  For himself, he had one purpose in going ; and 't would be his care to choose among them those who were not likely to thwart it : he professed, he gave them all credit for upright intentions, but even among the good, some might be bettermost, etc.

After this address, for which he assembled us all before night prayers that evening, Don Manuel said he would wish none to give an answer till our devotions were concluded the following morning, that we might both pray on it, and sleep on it; inasmuch as " he who goeth slowly, goeth securely."  Accordingly, the men, whispering together by their watch-fire, came to different conclusions, according to their several temperaments, or experience in chances and hardships. Some were for going, to seek fresh adventures; others would sooner stay quiet where they found themselves: but these were chiefly the veterans, who were so beaten with the storms of life, they had learned to set a value on repose. Nor, indeed, could I blame them; seeing that (to human reckoning) 't was a wild-goose chase that was now preparing. The priest had his own motives, we all knew, and went simply to save souls; as for the rest, what they went for, but a spirit of roving adventure, remained locked in their own bosoms; so, whether 't were folly or wisdom, I pretended not to judge.

But the end of it was, next morning, fourteen of the ship's company, with two of our Englishmen, that is, Gill and Hilton, volunteered to go.

---

## CHAPTER LXVII.

### PREPARATIONS THERETO.

WE spent many days in making provision for their departure. First, we gave them the long boat and shallop to carry them: or I should rather say, we lent these to the expedition; for in truth they belonged still to the wreck, and so to the Spanish government, by the articles of our treaty. However, Don Manuel, who I am sure was something more in consideration, or office, than he seemed, told us we need be under no concern on that score; that should any of our party arrive in Europe, or another Spanish ship touch here, we had but to mention the name by which we knew him, and that he was our fellow passenger in the *Enterprise* for part of the passage, and we should find it all right.

This being arranged, he would only take ten of those who had volunteered, putting back four, though gently, on the score of their weaker health: "for we shall have to rough it," says he, "on the open sea, with chances of weather, and even if we arrive, it may be in sorry plight."

He added, that in case of their provisions running short, 't was a main matter to have as few mouths to feed on the great wide ocean, as might be.  Above all, he bade us remember, there were three amongst us who had best right of all to take their choice, whether they would go or stay: namely, the Indians, to whom the opportunity was now given, to get back to their own native land.  So, turning to them, he put the choice before them, one by one, beginning with the old man, Poula-faihe.

'T was a touching thing to behold the struggles in these poor Indians, when they heard Tadoone was going to seek the home whence they came.  On the one hand, they had become truly attached to us, and were the most faithful, simple creatures I ever knew of; with no thought but to please us, to whom they owed their lives, and the priest, to whom they owed their faith.  On the other hand, the ties of blood were strong: we had never asked them questions about Toonati-nooka without seeing how they clung to the memory of those they had left there, and the hope of seeing them again.

Pounder, as it appeared, had been left friendless in this world: his father, elder brother, two uncles, and a cousin, had all been killed in a battle with the warriors of another tribe, and indeed another island or country, who came, he told us, in eight war canoes, about twenty-seven moons (so he reckoned) before he was thrown on our island. These savages made a descent on that part of the coast where John Pounder (who was then Rer-mimebolamba) lived with his family and near neighbours in a small village: here, paddling quietly along that coast, in a dark night, they surprised the inhabitants in their sleep.  But I must not run from one story into another; only to say, the warriors of the village, taken thus at unawares, made a fruitless resistance, though a desperate one: the greater part of them were killed outright, some few (when they saw all was lost) escaped into the woods, carrying off some of their children, with their wives; and so, striking up by difficult paths known to themselves, got so far into the country, the conquerors durst not follow them.  But these were a few out of the number; our friend John being one, though with a lance-wound in his neck, of which he showed us the deep scar.

The greater part of the men were killed, (you might say) over and over again, being savagely mangled as they lay, and the women and children carried off as slaves. Only Rere-mime's wife (as the poor fellow told us, the tears standing in his eyes) refusing to leave her hut, clung so fast round the pole of it, they could not get her away: so dragging her by the hair of her head, but to no purpose, at last, they pierced her with their spears. This was John Pounder's history in brief; which explained why he was most willing of the three to stay with us, and finally chose it.

As for the other two Indians, 't was both a happiness to themselves to go, and a benefit to the expedition: for they would serve as interpreters, not for the language alone, whereof Tadoone also had made himself master, but for manners and customs, to report what would make him acceptable in his mission, or might arm their countrymen's minds against him. All three, with the rest, began with equal zeal to help in the preparations: which were chiefly, laying in a stock of such dried provisions as we could store the boats with, as well as refitting the boats themselves, with sail, oars, and rudder.

All this took some time; for though we were now reinforced with hands enough, we had no carpenter: the carpenter on board the Spanish ship, and the carpenter's mate, having died early in their distresses. Had they been saved alive, I think we had made an attempt to build a large boat out of the fragments of the wreck, all rotten though she was, and fit out an expedition of our whole colony; so greatly did it go against us to part company with any of our comrades. Besides this, we had a curiosity to see the country they were going to: of which old Mark and the rest gave us great accounts in many ways. However, 't was no use to talk or wish, for the boats would not hold more than the number told off for them; at least to be safe for a boat voyage on the open sea.

For victualling the expedition, 't was clear no provisions were to be looked for from the wreck, in which was not one crumb of biscuit to be found, nor a morsel of pork, nor anything else in the way of food. But we got on shore a small mill-stone set with a rude handle; though clumsily enough, yet it would work : and we made it do service to grind our corn, and bruise a quantity of yams and bread-fruit to a pulp.  We mixed this with our wheat-flour, and kneaded it up well, worked it pretty dry, then rolled it out in sheets, cut them into lengths, baked them by a slow fire, and presented the expedition with a store of wholesome, well tasted biscuit, such as many a ship's company would be glad enough to come by on a voyage. Besides, we smoked and salted a quantity of our native pork, together with some wild geese and other large sea-birds; we stowed all this in three barrels, of those the *Hermiona* had carried her salted stores in, and got two into the large boat, and one into the small ; also, four tubs of fresh water, caulked and secured.  I gave them my fishing lines, doubling them for the deep-sea fishery ; to-gether with the rod, which I judged might be useful when they landed, though not at sea.  It ended by our giving them one of our best fishing nets besides ; for thus we put them beyond any chance of falling short of provender.

Next came the ordnance department, to furnish them with weapons : and here, knowing how great advantage the use of gunpowder gives to the civilized man over the strongest savage, we resolved to be liberal in our grants to them.  Indeed, 't was only bestowing on them what was already (in one sense) their own.  So we rolled down to the boats one barrel of gunpowder, whole and un-touched, besides more than half of another, which the water had got at, and spoiled, as we thought at the time : but by spreading it on a sail-cloth to the sun, then rubbing it betwixt our fingers, we found, by several trials in our muskets, the grain was quite dried, and took fire nearly as well as what was untouched by the sea.  For fire-arms, we gave them a musket a-piece, with two or three to spare : two pistols and a cutlass to each man ; nine pikes (what with our own bamboos, and some that were saved from the ship), and four boarding-axes to serve as wood-hatchets as well as weapons.

Their greatest want now was a compass ; but we saw no way to supply them, there being none known of on board, after the accident of the ship's compass being washed away.  At last, by great good luck, or a providence rather, we discovered a small pocket-compass at the bottom of a case of instruments, such as burning-glasses, and one or two implements of surgery and optics, that had belonged to one Don Garcia Nunez, doctor of medicine and man of science, to whom the Spanish Government had given a passage, for the sake of some observations he was to make on his way to Santiago; but he took to his berth and died, while the *Hermiona* was beating through the Straits Le Maire. This whole case of instruments we put on board for them; all but a scalpel or so, and some lint and bandages, which I kept back to serve our own needs.

In a word, we gave them whatever might turn to use, whether to defend themselves from savages, or cultivate their friendship, and astonish them with the manufactures and inventions of Europe. Each man, too, had a double set of clothing complete, to fence him from the cold; moreover, as we found means to get at some of the officers' chests, we rigged five or six of them out in uniform laced coats, and all the bravery we could invent, of hats and feathers, sword knots, buttons, and brocade: knowing such things to impress ignorant minds with the importance of the wearers.

---

# CHAPTER LXVIII.

### DEPARTURE.

NO small loss was it to the expedition, that we could not come at some of the bales stowed away in the *Hermiona's* hold; for she carried (as the lieutenant had told us) some Spanish fabrics, and English stuffs besides, for barter with the Indians of Chili, or other parts of the South American coast. Some few of these, 't is true, we managed to get up, by dint of hard diving; but in general they were so carefully stowed, and so deep in the hold, they were beyond our utmost efforts. What we got were only some inferior stuffs, as we should reckon them in

Europe; though, to be sure, they were prizes to us in our need: we looked on ourselves as very self-denying, to yield up the bales to be stowed in the boats for barter with the savages.

Indeed, we still had the ship with us, as a mine from which to draw more of that kind of wealth after the expedition was gone. But what was more to the purpose, we set about to provide their ammunition; though here we had difficulty enough, the magazine and powder-room both lying so deep under water (being in the hold itself) as made us all but hopeless to secure them any powder. At last, by much toil, taking turn and turn about with the Spaniards in diving (wherein some of them were expert), we secured, as I partly said before, two barrels and five bags of powder, but all spoiled (so we thought) by the sea; or wetted at least. But by spreading it out in the sun, as thin as we could spread it on a sail-cloth, with turning and sifting it several times in the day, then bruising or grinding it with much caution, in the small hand-mill we found on board, we contrived to save more of it than we thought at first.* Only, we were careful to grind it by very little at a time, lest any should take fire in the mill, and blow us to atoms: but the parcels were so small, though they took fire once or twice, 't was like a flash in the pan, and did us no harm. And thus we were able to save at least four-fifths of serviceable powder out of all we got from the wreck. As to what lay deeper in the hold, we gave up all hope of coming at that; nor in truth did we much need it.

Everything was now got ready for their departure: and, since 't was determined on, and the weather favouring, with a fair breeze from w.n.w. (such as we made out by the Indians, and our own observations, would be almost abaft for their voyage), no reason appeared why they should not cast off the rope, and get out to sea. Yet we kept them, and they lingered a whole day after this, under one pretence or other; now adding some stores, now

---

* There is some repetition here, as well as a discrepancy with what was said about the gunpowder towards the end of the last chapter. But the former may be accounted for by the great importance of this article to Owen and his companions; the latter, by the general carelessness of his writing.—ED.

stowing them neater in the boats, freshening the water and vegetables, caulking also the boats themselves (though quite sea-worthy) : in short, anything to persuade our own minds and theirs, they were not delaying without reason. For in this peaceful exile of ours, sweetened by religion and our kind, cheerful Tadoone, we had come to have no other thought, and scarce another wish than to lay our bones together in the island when our time should come.

But Don Manuel's zeal, with all his patience, would bear no delay beyond that one day, nor scarcely that : so the next morning early, having said the last Mass he ever said (to our knowledge) on Assumption Isle, and strengthened us all by Holy Communion (part of our two days' preparation having been spent by our small community going to confession for this purpose), we made him a farewell feast by way of breakfast : which had been a dismal meal enough, but that he strove to cheer us.

"I am not going to preach to you, my dearest children," says he, "for the time is now come to act : we must fall back on all those lessons of resignation and courage we have striven to learn and practise here together. Have we not proved to ourselves, in many ways, the only blessed thing is, to do the will of God, and resign ourselves to what He appoints or permits ? Now, there is no question, that Holy Will is taking us away for a time, and bidding you remain. What will come of it, is more than I can see; but 'we walk by faith, not by sight.' As we are bidden to pray, each day, for our daily bread, so it is always enough, on our pilgrimage, to see *the one next step.* This I now see, thanks to His providence, that makes it possible. Did I not fully hope to come back to you within a short time, I would not leave you at all : we would stay, or go together. But go you cannot; nor would you all be willing. Go I must, for I never cease to hear myself called. What remains, then, but that we should go, and you should stay, as they who are seeking the happiness of doing the will of our great and good Master?" "I am no prophet," he presently added (smiling through his tears, for he was much overcome), "yet something tells me, though I know not how, you will not be left long without a priest and without a Sacrifice."

We listened to him, wild-looking and grisly savages as we had grown in outward appearance, with the tears running down our rough cheeks and beards. 'T was of no use to restrain, or attempt to hide them; we were subdued to the tenderest grief at thus losing our spiritual father, and our brethren besides. When he had finished speaking, Tadoone rose up; we crowded round him, some on our knees, and caught hold on his garments, his hands; we kissed his very hat and breviary in the passionateness of our grief. He embraced us all with that fatherly tenderness he had ever shown us; then pointing to the sun, reminded us 't was full time to be on board. He gave us his last blessing with a voice choked by emotion; and without another word, gently freed himself from us all, and led the way down to the boats.

The rest of the men tore themselves away from their brethren, as best they might, Indian from Indian, Spaniard from Spaniard, with great signs of feeling at the separation. As for Hilton and Gill, they were moved, too, but in a soberer way, after the manner of our nation, that doth not (it may be) feel the less deeply because 't is slower to manifest it. In fine, they now jumped into the boats briskly, to get rid of sad thoughts; then hoisting sails, they began to sing the Litany our good priest had taught us, and steered out into the offing. For though, as belonging to different nations, and those at war with one another, they could not sing any such national sea-song as most seafaring countries possess of their own (since what was loyal in one part might be construed into an offence to the other), yet, being Catholics together, they could freely use what belonged to them in common, as members of the great family of the Church, and spoke of the interests of eternity.

We, who remained, kneeled on the shore till they had pulled so far away (the wind also setting off shore) as that all sound of their voices was lost to us; then we stood up, straining our eyes to catch the latest glimpse of them. One of the last things we saw was, Don Manuel stood up in the stern of the long-boat, and stretched forth his arms towards heaven, to invoke upon us a farewell blessing. At this, we dropped on our knees again, and wept like children, to think he was gone for a time long and uncertain, leaving us orphans behind him.   So, when the boats looked like mere specks on the sea, and then disappeared altogether, for the wind continued fair, and afterwards blew a breeze, we left the shore in much sorrow, and loitered about the rest of that day, not settling to any-thing.   We ate a cheerless supper; then I said night prayers (for I acted from that time as a sort of lay chap-lain), and we went to rest early, to sleep away as much of our grief as we might.

'T was a strange thing indeed for us to wake next morn-ing, and find no Tadoone, no meditation, nor Mass.   But, such being our condition for many a long day after, I need not dwell on what we became used to by degrees: only to record, that all things went on with us, orderly enough; though we felt dull in our spirits, and could not be recon-ciled to our great loss.   Neither did our tempers improve under the change; and Dick Prodgers, though he never returned to be what he was before the Faith was given him, yet now and then showed (as I may say most of us did, some more, some less) how weak a poor creature is man, when he is not supported above himself by sacra-mental grace.   This, indeed, Tadoone had warned us of, beseeching us with tears, to keep ourselves in the good dispositions he left us in.   Nor, truly, was it the disposi-tion that failed us, so much as the execution of what we had resolved on; for the " spirit was willing, but the flesh was weak."

We came round again soon, after these little outbreaks, which never grew to any real breach of the peace: only they gave us discomfort, making us out of sorts with our-selves, even while we forgave one another.   So that, with all our outward security and prosperous condition, we would often range up and down the shore, and like very children, stretch our arms over the sea, and yearn for Tadoone to come back to us again.

## CHAPTER LXIX.

### THE ERUPTION.

HOWEVER, these moods were broken in upon, and our life on the island took a new direction (or was cut short, rather), by something of the most unlooked-for kind, that chanced within ten days after.  I say, unlooked-for; for though we might reasonably expect savages, or even another ship to touch at our prison-house and take us off again, or pirates to attack us, we never forecast the strange event I am now to relate.

The mountain that lay to northward of our cave (though I knew it to have been once on a time burning, indeed we always called it the volcano), had looked to us as still and motionless as any other part of the place.  If ever I thought on the scene of devastation it had been formerly, 't was us we think of ancient history, the wars of Cæsar, or the Danes.  I little thought, the same convulsions were to spring out from it anew in our times; still less could I prophesy what good that same thing would minister to us.

This is putting (as they say) the cart before the horse; and, to begin this part of my narrative, I must record that, for some days, the air had felt sultry beyond ordinary, and the water in the spring that supplied our conduit from Riverhead had grown less and less.  We knew not why; for 't was the first time this had happened during our exile; winter and summer, it was always flowing. Besides, the water that now came up was not only scant, but troubled, and had a bad sulphurous taste and smell, that made it unpalatable, and (we thought) unwholesome. At last, one day it ceased altogether: we took this for a stoppage in the pipe; but, going to the spring to discover the cause, we found it as dry as the very mountain itself.

This disturbed us much, not only for the want of water (though that was a want indeed), but from apprehension of what it might portend; for I had read, and one of the

Spaniards confirmed it from his experience of the South American mountains, that before such volcanoes as we know of break into an eruption, the wells in the district are used to run dry. I suppose, by some alteration in the earth's veins, the water finds its way downward in place of upward, and, turning to hot vapour, adds to the force of the volcano; or, by the increased heat of the mountain when 't is about to discharge its fiery streams, the neighbour springs become sucked and dried up, as water is, if poured into the heated grate of a chimney.

Anyhow (for I write of it more coolly than I witnessed it then), our mountain began to groan in a way most dreadful to hearken to; rumbling beneath us, much as I have known a heavily loaded waggon to shake the houses on either side of a narrow street. For the very earth shook, as we thought; notwithstanding we were fain to persuade ourselves 't was only our fears suggested it. The air, too, turned to an oppressive, louring heat, that well nigh took away our breathing; and all was so heavy and so still, the very birds seemed to feel it as we did; for though at first they flew round and round, screaming and bewildered, yet soon they betook them to the trees, and there perched in silence, as not knowing what was to come. We noticed some animals, too, roaming about in a restless way, and heard them cry out, each after its fashion, as if in distress and fear.

For ourselves, we stood all together on the open shore, clear of rocks and trees, to give our lives the best chance, if indeed this should prove an earthquake, as we foreboded. We knew not what else to do at the moment, to save ourselves; fearing to go to our cave, or storehouse, lest we might be smothered by the roof falling in: fearing also to make for the boat, which lay tossing at her moorings; for by this time the sea had risen, with a strange, irregular tide, as though it were convulsed or heaved up from beneath: and we expected every moment to see our boat stove on the rocks. We stood, in such an agony of doubt and apprehension, as, I think, oppresses most men, when they can do nothing towards their own deliverance, but must wait and look on a great danger, and let it take its course, even if that be over their mangled bodies.

I say, we stood thus; but I should add that first one,

then another, dropped on their knees, and began to pray fervently to heaven for help.   At last, there was not one that joined not in this act; though there was, indeed, no unity in the words of our prayer, for some prayed one thing, some another: here one would make an act of hearty contrition, and cry out to heaven for a priest; there, another would resign himself into the hands of God, to live or die : on this side was a man who vowed what he would do, did he but escape with life: on that side was his comrade, struck dumb, and able to do nothing but quake for fear.

But there was unity enough in the intention, for we all prayed with our hearts for deliverance out of this great danger, so sudden and awful.   For my part, though I write calmly of it now, looking back on it through years of other adventures I afterwards went through, I bring to mind (as if it were yesterday) the overmastering sense that seized on me of the awfulness of God's judgments when His hand launches the arrows of vengeance, or when He speaks in the thunders of His majesty; also, the comfort it was then to me, though trembling as a sinner before Him, to reflect, I had used the grace given me to repent, while there was time.   For now, while we all seemed on the brink of such a grave, had the great work of salvation been to commence, I had been tempted or driven to despair.   But I recalled my past confessions : I besought mercy for any hidden things that might be un-confessed, because, after all search, unremembered; I renewed my contrition; I thanked my God for His graces bestowed on me, resigned my life and my soul into His fatherly hands, then did my best to awaken such thoughts and pour this comfort into the souls of my comrades like-wise.

While we did what we could for ourselves and one another, on a sudden, there came the most fearful trembling and upheaving of the ground beneath us, that ever (I be-lieve) was experienced by mortal man.   It seemed as if the whole island were being wrenched from its base, and some power below were going to fling it on one side.   All that part of the coast rocked to and fro; the sea at the same time ran high, and boiled over, like a cauldron, washing up so near us, as made it seem an even chance whether we were to be swallowed by earth or ocean. We reeled and staggered, like so many drunken men, catching hold on each other for support : but this had not lasted as long as I have taken to describe it, when a more violent heave flung us on our faces, with a strange, whirling motion that partly spun us round : so that, old seamen as most of us were, used to short, chopping seas and counter-currents, it made us feel as sea-sick as a landsman in his first gale of wind.

Before we recovered our legs (which we scarce attempted, for not knowing whither to flee, we thought it best to lie there) we heard the crashing of the rocks about our cave, by which we judged the cave itself to have fallen in : as afterwards indeed we found. At the same time, some large pieces of rock that were loosened from the top of our cliff, came rolling towards us, threatening to crush us at every bound. But even this was not so great a danger as the noisome sulphurous vapour that rose out of a deep cleft in the ground, not many yards from where we lay, confused and giddy; it volleyed forth upon us, like the smoke from the broadside of a ship when all her guns are discharged at once, but with so insupportable a stench of brimstone as had taken away our very lives, had we remained there a moment longer. I called on my companions, half stifled as I was, to rise and run for their lives : indeed, our only chance was to rise to our full height, and let this heavy, creeping vapour spread out along the ground, while we ran before it. But some of our number were, by this time, so stunned and amazed by all these new and awful things coming upon us in a heap, we had much ado to pull them up and put them in motion. What with the fumes of this vapour mounting to their brain, stupifying them, or whether the fear alone had quelled their animal spirits, some of them begged us to let them lie there, and die in peace. And as for one of the men, named Ruy Perez, he was so far gone in this fatal drowsiness, I thought we should never have gotten him up, nor yet brought him round.

19

# CHAPTER LXX.

### DEATH IN MORE SHAPES THAN ONE.

WE made the best of our way out of this rolling vapour, till at last we got clear of it, on to a little jutting promontory that made us safe from the lash of the sea; for it boiled with exceeding violence, though there was next to no wind stirring. When we all got safe on to this point, we seemed to have been conducted hither by some purpose of Providence, to make us beholders of the most awful, stupendous sight the eye of man could well behold, short of the last Judgment. There came another rumbling from beneath, but not so directly under our feet as the first, with the sound like the falling of one heavy bar of metal on another; and this sound came repeated four or five times. Then, on a sudden, an explosion like the roar of artillery (only far louder, and enough to crack the drums of our ears, as seamen have been deafened in a battle) came from the mountain itself, and the whole island seemed to tremble again: even the point of land whereon we were, rocked and heaved, till we thought it would have fallen into the sea, with us upon it. I could not have counted ten after this explosion, when a pillar of smoke rose up direct from a great cleft riven in the side of the mountain, nearer the top than base, and towered into the air, more like a tall palm tree* than anything else I can liken it to. It was followed by a shower of red-hot stones that went up like so many rockets, the smaller ones in great

---

* A curious coincidence of expression with the younger Pliny's account of the eruption of Vesuvius which overwhelmed Herculaneum and Pompeii, A.D. 79. "On the 23rd of August," he says, writing to Tacitus, "about one in the afternoon, my mother desired him" (the elder Pliny, who was commanding the fleet at Misenum, in the bay of Naples), "to observe a cloud which appeared of a very unusual size and shape. He immediately arose, and went out upon an eminence, from which he might more distinctly view this very uncommon appearance. At that distance, it was not discernible from what mountain this cloud issued; but it was afterwards found to as-

Chap. LXX, p. 282.

numbers, shooting into the pillar of smoke, then falling far into the sea, as well as nearer; the larger went a little way into the air, then fell, and rolled down the mountain, chiefly towards where we stood.

Ours was now a post of no little danger: and, besides the stones falling all round, there rained down upon us such a fine sand, or ashes, out of the cloud (which was, indeed, composed of it) as nearly took away our breath again, together with the suffocating heat of the air itself. But what was our grief, when the great mass of these stones fell (though they were shot out afterwards, too, from time to time), to see one of the poor Spaniards, Gutierre Vasquez by name, stricken down at our side, by a stone that took him on the head, so that he never spoke after; and another, Melchor Baeza, an oldish marine, hit so sharply with a stone that rebounded from the rock he stood on, as toppled him into the deep sea beneath our feet, and strangled him in the water, though the force of the blow alone was enough to dispatch him.

At another time, we should have mourned at leisure for these untimely deaths among our comrades; but at that very hour, the same fate seemed hanging momently over our own heads; and 't was strange how much a matter of course the death of others appeared to us, when we might any instant expect our own. By this, we were wrapped round in the dark, sulphurous cloud, so thick and intolerable with the smell and taste of brimstone, we had all been smothered on the spot had we not crammed our hats or neckerchiefs into our faces to escape its deadly choak. All at once, out of this darkness there flashed a brilliant light: then (the mountain all the while thundering and groaning like a live creature in direful pain) a sheet of liquid rock, or lava, appeared mounting over the brim of

cend from Mount Vesuvius. I cannot give you a more exact description of its figure, than by resembling it to that of a pine-tree; for it shot up a great height in the form of a trunk, which extended itself at the top into a sort of branches; occasioned, I imagine, either by a sudden gust of air that impelled it, the force of which decreased as it advanced upwards; or the cloud itself being pressed back again by its own weight, expanded in this manner. It appeared sometimes bright, and sometimes dark, and spotted, as it was more or less impregnated with earth and cinders."—*Plin. Epist. lib.* vi. 16.  ED.

the crater, like glue or pitch boiling over; and began to descend in a broad fiery stream to where we stood.  In its course, it swallowed up or mounted over every obstacle: it swelled over the rocks, and poured down them again; set the groves and bushes that lay on our path in a blaze; and, what with the roar of the conflagration, the crackling and hissing of this flood of fire the groans and thunders of the mountain beyond, and the howling of the wind and sea, that had now both risen high, I could almost think the last Day itself had truly come.

We stood rooted to the spot, without power to fly, as if spell-bound by the terror of this awful scene: till (too late) we found we were encompassed, part by the fire, that ran swiftly among the dry trees and underwood, part by the advance of this molten flood of lava, that came on at such a pace as an active man could hardly walk, and spread itself out broader, as it reached the level space between mountain and sea.  It were madness now to attempt to flee either way; for northward of our rock was the red-hot lava, much like a sea of iron running fresh out of a furnace, bearing on its surface biggish stones and pieces of rock, well nigh as red-hot as itself: and if we turned our eyes to south, we were met by the sight of a thick belt of wood, all a-blaze, whereinto had we rushed, we had been as so many suicides leaping on their funeral pile.

Which way could we now turn to escape so frightful a death?  Two choices were before us: the rock or the sea. Should we stay through the frying heat, or swim for it? As I proposed the question to my remaining comrades (poor Melchor and Gutierre being gone already), on looking down into the water beneath our feet, we found a ready answer to the question, that filled us with horror, and drove us all but to despair.  For though the sea (as I have said) was now risen, and began to boil up from below, we could plainly discover the fins of two or three large sharks (the reef being more open hereabout, easier to steer through) plying up and down.

These monsters were drawn hither (no doubt) by the blaze, and seemed to enjoy the warmth of the sea: but they kept eyeing us all the while, too, as if they saw a double advantage in keeping so near; and we could not doubt they had already made a half supper on our companion, Baeza. 'T was plain, from that moment, our only chance was to keep on the rock, and endure the suffocating heat as best we might. This now waxed so intense, as I doubt if any iron-forger was ever called on to face a much greater; and for us, who were unused to anything of the kind, it seemed out of the question to stand it out longer, but we must brave the sharks, and cast us down, from sheer necessity of cooling our over-scorched selves, into the sea. By this time 't was night; and, had we been at a safe distance, nothing could have been now grander than to witness this great spectacle; for the light from the mountain shot far up into the darkness overhead; the wreaths of red smoke curling along the sky to leeward, with large stones ever and again shot out, like hot shells out of a battery of bombs: and fresh lava, at a white heat (so it seemed to us) pouring out still from the lip of that rent in the mountain, and all the trees of the island so far as the eye could reach, in one great blaze. It is not for my pen to describe it; nor do I see how any one can imagine it that hath not seen the like. However, at that time, though the majesty and terror of the sight struck into our hearts, we were taken up only by the thought, how we could live through such a furnace as was raging round us.

At length two of our number, Domingo Gonzalez and Fadrique Correa by name, poor fellows! both having been used to the Barbadoes trade, and to see how the negroes there will encounter the sharks that infest their coast, with only a knife, to plunge into the fish when he turns on his side to seize them; they determined on making a like trial of their skill. Do what we could to persuade them how mad was their adventure, they were not to be turned from it. No man, they said, could die more than once; and for their part, they had rather run the chance of being strangled in the water, or drowned outright, than wait to be smothered by the intolerable heat and noisome vapours where we were. Then I bade them remember, no man had a right to throw away his life, which was not his own property to dispose of, but a mere loan, or talent, lent him for an appointed time; and this, I saw, had some effect on them, as Catholics, who had a clear view of an hereafter: till they answered me again, they believed it to be the best chance for them after all : that if they could run the blockade, and clear these fish, or encounter them with advantage (for they had their seaman's clasp-knives strung round their necks), then were they in better case than we who stayed on the rock : and more to the same purpose.

Seeing them not to be turned from this mad scheme, it only remained to pray for their safety, in which I bade the rest unite with me ; and the two poor men joined in it themselves with great fervour.  Then, making over their brows and hearts, the sign of the cross, and commending themselves to God, calling also on the Blessed Virgin and St. Iago of Compostella, they drew their knives, and plunged feet foremost into the sea, crossing their feet to cleave the water better, and rise again upright.  But alas ! we saw too clearly, the moment after, what was the sad fate they had courted.  For no sooner did we hear the splash of their fall, than we also saw these monstrous sharks plunge after them, and they never rose to the surface again : no, not so much as a limb, nor a shred of their garments, but all became the instant prey of those voracious bloodhounds.  The sea, too, was boiling so wildly, I question if some under-current would not have carried the poor fellows away, or rolled them over and so 'drowned them, had no sharks been on the look out for them at all.

This dreadful end of our rash comrades filled us with horror ; and would have done so the more, but for our own fate before our eyes, which seemed to come nigher at every step, in the shape of fire.  For all this while, the mountain continued to groan and bellow like some enraged wild beast, and poured out lava, fresh and fresh, so that now it ran down the sides swifter than before.  Only, we were comforted to see, this time it took a course more to the due south ; if I may call that comfort which threatened to destroy all our plantations that might have escaped hitherto, as well as block up the entrance to our cave itself.  But the peril we were in so swallowed up all other thoughts, we had no leisure now to care for our possessions, except only our dear lives.  A moment after, came a second shock of earthquake, under our very feet, so that the point of cliff whereon we stood, rocked again, and heaved beneath us to and fro.  I thought we should have been all thrown into the sea together; for several of us lost our footing, and we had to pluck one man back from falling straight over the edge.

But see, how the mercy of God ordereth events powerfully and sweetly; how all things work together for good in the ways of His providence!  For this new danger, which did us no harm beyond the fright of it, was the means of delivering us from the fiery flood that advanced upon us with open jaws, to swallow us.  When our rock ceased to tremble, looking forth again as well as we might, through the heavy sulphur smoke, we saw the earthquake had made a great opening, or dyke, between us and the stream of lava; and in a few minutes more, we heard it pouring heavily over the brink, down to the gulph in the earth below.  At the same time the breeze freshening, blew away partly this cloud of hot vapour that wrapped us round, and gave us a clear glimpse out to sea.

Never may I forget (like an unthankful wretch, as I should be) what I felt when Prodgers, shading his eyes with his hand, cried out, "Sail ho! to windward:" and all of us, eagerly turning our eyes thereaway, saw the red light of the volcano reflected on the sails of a ship!

# CHAPTER LXXI.

### OUR DELIVERANCE.

SHE was steering right in for the island, and soon hove-to, seeming afraid to venture in nearer.  We doubted not but they who commanded her were using their perspectives to view the eruption of our mountain.  The hope of our near deliverance now animating us, we all rose to our full height, and waving our arms abroad, joined in one shout, as long and loud as we could make it.  We learned from them afterwards, that being to windward they did not hear our shouting at all: but saw ourselves, which was more to the purpose; for our forms were clearly traced to them against the light of the fire. They lowered their long-boat at once, and the crew pulled cheerily towards us: their steerage being marked out for them by the glow from the mountain and the burning woods; though they, and we who waited for them with the utmost impatience, narrowly escaped death from the hot stones that volleyed forth at times from the crater. Indeed, one or two on both sides were hit, though not seriously, at least not to kill: at length they came up with us, and lying-to under lee of our rock of refuge, they threw up a rope to us. By help of this, we lowered ourselves one by one into the boat; and in good time truly, for the heat was become so intolerable now, I question if any of us had lived another half hour. We went to work carefully; for a slip might have handed us over to the tender mercies of our friends the sharks, who were prowling about, up and down, expecting another morsel from among us.

Our men, twenty-nine in number, got down safely into the boat: I was the last; for having (from one cause or other) some authority among them, I thought it behoved me to be last, as the captain always is, on leaving a wreck. I did my best to secure the rope round a point of the rock, and weighted it with stones: notwithstanding it loosened as I went down, and I got a shrewd tumble on the boat's thwarts, that had like to have broke my neck, and did cripple me for a week after; though 't was happy I fell into the boat, not among the sharks into the sea.

We got safe on board ship, though I had to be hauled up the side in a whip, being not able to stir hand nor foot. She proved to be the *Glorieux*, of thirty-six guns, commanded by Captain Dumoutier, chartered from Brest, cruising in these latitudes with sealed orders, and not friendly to our flag. But, on the relation of our calamitous history, the captain, with the spirit of a brave, generous man, waived all distinction of nation or flag, and took us on board in quality of passengers, to be set ashore at any point most convenient to us to make our way homewards. "To-morrow," says this gallant seaman to us, "we will speak, Messieurs, of your future plans: to-night, do me the honour to be my guests." So after a hearty and hospitable supper, which the fatigues and great harass of the day made needful to us, through exhaustion of the animal spirits, we turned into our hammocks with thankful hearts and short prayers. Meanwhile, the captain put the helm about, and stood off to a safe distance from the island, the wind now setting fresher in-shore.

We were up again at day-break, to watch the progress made in this destruction of our island; for such, indeed, it proved, and nothing less, as regards the E. and s. sides of it. The lava had flowed on, while we slept, as some of the crew told us; for, beside the watch, nearly all the ship's company had staid out of their hammocks, best part of the night, watching that great spectacle. As for ourselves, we were so clean exhausted with all we had gone through, I believe we could have slept through a salvo of artillery, or a general engagement. And truly, the noise from the mountain, at times, was not much less than that.

But in the morning light, 't was a desolate spectacle indeed: for the conflagration of our woods, having well nigh burnt itself out, presented such a view of bare and blackened trunks of trees, or stumps, with rocks split by the violent heat; our stream, too, either dried up, or forced from its bed through some of the great rents or cracks in the ground, sending out its hot vapours, together with the sulphur, as it boiled below: altogether (I say) the prospect was in miniature what I suppose the great globe itself will present when " the heavens shall pass away with a great noise, and the elements shall melt with fervent heat, and the earth, and the works on it, shall be burnt up."

Here we saw an end to all our labours for four years past, at a stroke: not that we considered it much at the time, but were occupied wholly by the great deliverance granted to us, against hope, both from the fiery mountain, and the banishment we had spent on our island. On this part of our adventure the French captain, when he heard our story from me (in my bad Spanish, for he spoke Spanish himself passably well), wished us heartily joy of our liberation; only, he said, he must perforce carry us partly on his own course, which was to Tobago: but promised he would set us ashore, under a flag of truce, at any English plantation in the West Indies, which the chance of war enabled him to touch at. But first he asked us, from our knowledge of the island, the likeliest place to find fresh water for his ship : on our telling him of that stream to westward where we had first so unhappily landed, he wore the ship round, and gave the island a wide berth, for fear of the reefs we told him of : then, sending a man to the mast-head to help our piloting, the sea being very clear, it could plainly be seen from that height how the reefs ran under water. Thus in four tacks, and no more, we came in the afternoon off the mouth of that self-same channel into which the traitor Hopkins had sent the long boat with us, the victims of his treachery. When I remarked this to the captain (for we easily made out the opening in the rocks, by help of our perspectives), he made us his compliments again, on the mercies that had shielded us then from a violent death, and preserved us ever since. This was said too, more in particular, by the chaplain he had on board ; being a French priest and a seminarist, of whom I might have much to say, but that these up-and-down memoirs of mine have spun out too long a yarn already. In fine, the priest was a good man, and a kind one ; though, to be sure, we never quite felt towards him as to our father that brought us into the fold, 't was a comfort to find ourselves again within the ministries of the Church ; and we experienced, from this very change of hands, the Catholic is always at home, when he can have the privileges of that universal family he belongs to.

It seems, this Captain Dumoutier was known as a good Christian man, as he was also a first-rate seaman ; having some influence with the government of his country, he had asked for a chaplain to sail with him on his voyage, when some of his cloth were likelier to petition against anything so irksome to a wilful sinner as the presence of a priest : whence it came to pass, we had the blessing of Mass on board when the weather was fair ; nay (the priest being a good sailor, as well as a good priest), having a bit of a sea on did not hinder his being lashed to a bulk-head in the captain's cabin, to kneel and stand at a small altar there : so, like some of the early martyrs, he cele-

brated the Holy Sacrifice in bonds. Nor can I forget the
first time I attended Mass on board the *Glorieux*, how
that prophecy, or hope, of Don Manuel came into my
mind, we should not be long without a priest and without
a Sacrifice.

When we doubled the point that shut in Shark's Cove
to the south, and came within sight of the Spanish wreck,
we found that by some upheaving of the reef from below,
the wreck had been thrown almost high and dry, and
almost her own length (so we judged) nigher to land.
Though this delayed us not on the watering expedition
(two of the ship's boats being sent forward with the water-
casks), yet the captain judged it worth while to board her,
and overhaul her stores. We could now indeed, get down
below the orlop-deck without hindrance, and so into the
hold, with some little pumping of the bilge-water; but we
found little that was worth the carrying away. 'T is true,
she had more stuffs and merchandize on board than was
usual for a ship of war, as the Spanish lieutenant had explained, together with the reason why. But then, having
been hastily packed, the bales of this merchandize of stuffs
had loosened, so that the water had got at and spoiled a
great part : and, though we got them out of the hold, we
found them so rotten that they came in shreds when we
handled them never so lightly. The same account is to
be given of the iron-ware and knick-knacks on board for
barter with the Americans ; for they were eaten with rust
to that degree, we flung the greater part of them into the
sea again. However, we saved some that had lain deeper,
or been packed tighter ; and we got out five or six bales
in fairly good condition. These the captain took on board,
as payment for the good turn he was doing us ; for though
the brave man himself would gladly have done that, and
more, without fee or reward (being the kind of frank,
open-hearted creature who I had been foolishly taught
could not be found in that nation, and more like a British
tar than a *Mounseer*, as Harvey said), yet he had others
to consider beside himself : and in brief, we begged him to
do it.

But, to make a long story short, as 't is time, and to
wind up my whole yarn, the captain, who was not the
man to burn daylight, sent his boats in at once, and Poun-

der with them, to show the way : then, having completed
his watering from what remained of that former abundant
stream (for the greater part had been dried up by the volcano, or found some other channel amid the earthquake),
and shipping on board what cocoa-nuts and other fruits
were at hand, together with a good supply of our cray-
fish, he stood off on his former course, making for the Car-
ribean Islands ; so that at sunset, on that eleventh day of
November, 1743, we took our last look of Assumption Isle
from the main-yards of the *Glorieux* ; first, we gave three
cheers that we were well away, then we said a thanks·
giving with the good chaplain, for our merciful deliverance
from a hope'ess exile.

But truly, whether we improved our condition by thus
going back into a world of danger, is more than I can pronounce on a review of our strange adventures ; or whether,
in the light of eternity, it had not proved best for us to
live and die in that secure retirement.  However, matters
being so ordered, that our priest was taken from us first,
and (with him) our best comfort, we had no fancy, any of
us, to stay there lonely and deserted.  I truly believe, had
not this ship, the harbinger of a kind Providence, touched
at the place, we had found no other resource than looking
out and praying for Don Manuel's return.

As to him, whether he did return, and the men with
him, must now (I suppose) remain hid from us till the day
when all things are made known.  Sure I am, if ever he
came back, it was for our sakes alone : wherefore I the
rather hope that success in his mission detained him ;
though I well believe, no success, not even the conversion
of all Toonati-nooka, could make him false to his promise,
or careless of us, his children in the faith.  He would have
come, or leastways sent, to see after us and fetch us off.
And sometimes in my dreams, even now, after so many
years, I seem to see a war-canoe of Toonati-nooka, manned
by Christians whom Tadoone has made so, steering in for
Shark's Cove, and the crew roving up and down the island
in search of us.  And there is Tadoone himself, grown
gray-headed with labour and care, but with his kind smile
and quiet ways, leading them to the ruins of our cave, and
Riverhead, and the parts of the island where they would
be likeliest to find us, and sorrowing to see no trace of us

anywhere; no, not so much as a grave to mark our bones. But that is a dream only; and I will end by another word on what did indeed befal us after.

---

## CHAPTER LXXII.

### WHAT HAPPENED TO US ALL AFTER.

OLD Dick Prodgers heads the list: his sea-going days being now well-nigh over, and he stiffening with age, having learned also to love quiet, and (as he said) to make up his soul, he no sooner landed at Tobago than he declined further adventures, and got employed about the port. From this he picked a comfortable living enough; and I have little doubt but he lived and died there, as good a Catholic as he had been on our island. Nor did his religion stand in his way in a colony like that, among men of all nations, as it would have done nearer home; as I afterwards found to my cost. So, beyond being now and then called a turn-coat by some ignorant fellow, who knew not which side his own coat was turned, nor if he wore any habit of religion on him at all, I believe Dick Prodgers slipped through the remainder of his life easily, and hath found (I trust) a better one beyond.

Tom Harvey, the only other of our original English crew that we carried away with us, staid not long in those parts; but making his way back to England, was taken by a press-gang for his Majesty's service. as empowered by the Seaman's Bill to authorize impressment, which passed the very year after we were left on the island. So Tom was carried on board the *Pembroke*, of sixty guns, where he served for some time, with a good character. At length, the ship being one of the fleet under Admiral Boscawen, in his expedition to the East Indies, was (rather better than five years back from the day I now write,*

---

* The *Pembroke* foundered, as Owen here states, on the 13th of April, 1749; so that his casual notice of the vessel may be taken as another evidence of his having written his adventures in 1754. ED.

and nearly twice that space of time after the day when Hopkins marooned us on the desolate island) overtaken by a dreadful tempest at Calderoon point, in the road of Fort St. David's : when, out of nigh three hundred and fifty brave men she had on board, only twelve persons were saved from the wreck. I grieve to record it, poor Tom was not among those fortunate few ; as I found too surely, seeing the list with my own eyes at the Admiralty, some time after that terrible disaster, when I had returned to England.

As to the Spaniards, most of them landed at Tobago, and thence, I believe, found their way to other ports of the Spanish West India plantations : but five remained in the ship then, and after I left her, entering themselves on the ship's books for regular service. Indeed, during their exile, they may be said to have belonged to no nation ; and when our little republic was broken up, 't was natural they should take so fair an offer as this good captain made them. The five were named Pedro Dolea, Christoval Ramirez, Rodrigo Melandez, Fadrique Santaens, and Estevan Guaxardo. I heard after, in a roundabout way, and without certainty, that Estevan and Rodrigo (unless it was some chance namesakes of theirs), when the *Glorieux* was paid off at Brest, volunteered into the *Elizabeth*, a French ship of sixty-six guns, bound for the Scottish coast, to convey thither the prince whom some folks called the Pretender, and others the Chevalier. But, being encountered by the *Lion* man of war, the ship was handled so severely as to be forced back into Brest, with considerable loss : and among the killed and wounded were our two poor comrades ; that is, Estevan killed, and Rodrigo wounded severely.

To go from grave to gayer, Rer-mimebolamba had the most laughable escape from slavery you ever knew. For, on our touching at Guadaloupe (whither we went from Tobago with a flowing sheet and a spanking breeze), when the French officers boarded us, to overhaul our papers, and give us a clean bill of health from the yellow fever, that was raging in some of the adjacent islands, what should they do, but seize on our poor Pounder for a runaway negro slave ! Do all I could to claim him for a British subject, they would not hear of it, and bade me remember (with insolence enough) the freedom that had been guaranteed to Tom Harvey and myself by the French captain, ought to suffice us. Plainly intimating, that (had they got their way) the *parole* which this good captain had given us, that our liberty should not be molested, had gone for nothing.

However, as to Pounder, in the teeth of our remonstrating, and that of the captain beside, who threatened them with I know not what, on his return to France, the end was, our poor Indian was marched off between two files of soldiers to the house of the governor, a chief planter in the colony, who was for claiming him at once as a slave. This was a man consequential to a degree, yet so ignorant as not to see the differences of skin and feature that mark off the African black from the Indian of Toonati-nooka, which are clear enough to any observer. And this my candid reader will allow, if he looks on the portrait of poor Pounder that was taken of him two years after, or more, in Nova Scotia; which I have left in my will to be copied and prefixed to these adventures of mine: nay, even more so than are there portrayed. But 't was of no purpose to insist on this to the governor; and things were going hard with Rer-mime, till at last I bethought me of an experiment in the way of language to decide the question. Calling into the room a negro who had bought his freedom, and then lived on the island as a sort of overseer, or slave-driver, I got the captain to prevail on the governor to have this man put on his oath to tell " the truth, the whole truth, and nothing but the truth." And that much, with some ado, the governor consented to at last.

This old negro was one, most of whose life had been spent in slavery; he was brought away from his native coast, near Sierra Leone, when he was not yet sixteen years of age: but he had kept the perfect use of his mother-tongue, by conversing with his fellow-slaves, together with a smattering of bad French he had learned on the island. When he was had into court, I confronted him with Pounder; then, in the presence of some of the chief men of the island, for learning and understanding (who chanced to be in town for a kind of assize then being held, and were drawn to the court-house by the novelty of this proceeding). I asked him on a sudden to repeat to me the Ten Commandments in his native tongue: begging the audience to give close attention. This he did, glibly enough; for I must say, the negroes of those French islands are well taught in their religion, when the priests are not thwarted in their efforts by some selfish, grasping planter, more intent on scraping money than on the welfare of his slaves. While the old man was speaking, I took down on a paper some sentences he uttered; then, asking the court to take notice that Pounder was ignorant of the French tongue, and knew not what the other had been required to repeat, I bade the Indian repeat the Commandments in the language of Toonati. This he did at once, and without a fault, thanks to Don Manuel's careful teaching: and their two languages were hereby shown to be so unlike each other, that the court went no further, but quashed proceedings, and decreed the Indian to be given back to us out of hand. Several members of it expressed themselves to me in a way I will not repeat, on what they pleased to term my ingenuity in manifesting the truth before them all. They insisted, moreover, on giving us an entertainment before we tripped our anchor; at which sentiments were uttered, full of friendliness toward us. Tom Harvey made them a speech, of which they understood not a word; as he, for his part, could make out none of their *lingo:* and I followed in his wake, with not much better success. But our good-will was accepted instead of language; so that at parting they declared, we were such good fellows, 't was a thousand pities we were not born Frenchmen.

From this point I met with some other adventures; none of them (I think) worth troubling the reader with, nor any that surpassed the common run of sea-faring haps and mishaps. I was shipwrecked, 't is true, some eighteen months after, in the *Racehorse* packet, that went to pieces on the rocks in the Bay of Fundy; when all hands, except eighteen seamen and three passengers, were lost. Pounder had the good fortune to be saved with me and the rest in the long boat, and we made our way, after some hardships, to Halifax. Here I set up in my profession, and had some practice for five or six years, with John Pounder as half companion, half servant; and a faithful fellow and good

Christian he proved. After that, my sight, that had been threatening me, so far failed as to disqualify me for practice; so, gathering up what little I had contrived to save, I bade farewell at once to my profession and to foreign parts; but not before I had married in Halifax a French wife, of my own age and station, whose family came from Montmagny, nigh to Quebec: a good Catholic she was and is, and keeps me up to my religion.

After various chances in London, where my religion stood in my way at every turn, and kept me low in the world, at length, through the kindness of Captain Byron, who was above narrow prejudice, though he had no taste for my creed, I was appointed deputy harbour-master in the place from which I now write: viz., Great Yarmouth, in Norfolk, under a worthy man, Mr. Thomas Williamson, well known to the elder brethren of the Trinity House, who carries an honourable wound (indeed, 't is the loss of three fingers, beside a severe splinter-scar) from the action under the gallant Anson off Cape Finisterre.

And here I bring to a close this record of some years of a life, that hath nothing in it so remarkable as a course of providences exerted for one most unworthy, who can but make some efforts to be not wholly unthankful.

---

### NOTE.

It may appear strange that the irregular and confused account, now presented to the reader, should have remained unwritten till eleven years had elapsed from Evans' leaving the island. But a parallel case is furnished by Commodore Byron, referred to at p. 259, whose account of his early sufferings on the coast of Chili in 1740, were "written by himself, and now first published," in 1768. In his preface he says: "As the greatest pain I feel in committing the following sheets to the press, arises from an apprehension that many of my readers will accuse me of egotism, I will not incur that charge in my preface, by detaining them with the reasons which have induced me, at this time, to yield to the desire of my friends. It is equally indifferent to the public to be told how it happened, that nothing should have got the better of my indolence and reluctance to comply with the same requests, for the space of twenty years." ED.

# SUPPLEMENT.

---

VERSION OF A LATIN MS.

## PICKED UP AT SEA,

*BY H.M.S. RAMILLIES.*

COMMANDER GEORGE DUTTON.

MAY 14TH, 1773, IN W. LONG. 43°; S. LAT. 24° 5′

PRECEDED BY

CAPTAIN DUTTON'S REPORT TO THE

ADMIRALTY.

**H.M.S.** *Ramillies*, off Spithead,

June 8th, 1773.


TO

# THE RIGHT HONOURABLE THE EARL OF SANDWICH,

FIRST LORD OF HIS MOST GRACIOUS MAJESTY'S ADMIRALTY.

K.G., P.C., ETC., ETC.

MY LORD,

I have the honour of forwarding to your Lordship, together with the *Ramillies'* log, the accompanying *manuscript*, picked up (as your Lordship will observe by the entry in the log itself), the 14th ult., on our homeward voyage. It is curious, both from the materials that compose it (being written on the leaves of the palmetto, or some other broad-leaved tree), and from the manner in which we found it secured. It was attached to an unpainted buoy of light wood, rudely shaped by a hatchet or some other iron instrument; but the whole thing was so covered (at least the under part) with barnacles and other shell-fish, and so eaten with sea-worms throughout, that it had evidently been a considerable time in the water. I should say, from my experience of the condition of old ships, that not a vessel in his Majesty's service (and I have been in some dangerous ones) would be allowed afloat after so long an immersion, without careening.

This buoy was furnished with a kind of outriggers, made of rude boards of the same sort of wood, ingeniously attached to it by cords of twisted, or rather plaited, cocoa-fibres, much decayed by the water; though they appeared to have been steeped in oil to prevent it. On the top was a small flag staff, still carrying, pinned into it by wooden pegs, a shred of some woollen stuff, almost gone, which we judged to have been once a seaman's jacket, fastened there in order to make the buoy more visible at sea.

Observing the buoy, I slackened sail, and sent a boat to bring it on board. When we hoisted it on deck, we found attached to it a case or covering of laths, neatly spliced, somewhat in the form of a small keg, bound tightly with the same kind of fibre, and payed* all over with a coating of Indian gum, which lay on it, in some places, three-quarters of an inch thick. So careful had the writer, or his friends, been to preserve the MS. from injury. Not-withstanding, in one place the gum, or Indian rubber, had slightly given, perhaps from the case getting foul of the buoy in some shifting of the currents, floating exposed, and cracking in the sun. From this, as your Lordship will perceive, the writing on a few of the outer leaves has been somewhat damaged. I forward it, however, in the condition in which we found it on opening the case. This case itself, together with the buoy and its appurtenances, I intend to have the honour of presenting to the Admiralty Museum, or to the collection belonging to the Royal Society, or that of Sir Hans Sloane, at your Lordship's discretion; as a specimen of work which I take to be that of savages, assisted by some one more acquainted with the arts of civilization.

* A seaman's expression, meaning to daub or anoint the surface of any body, in order to preserve it from the injuries of the water and weather, etc.

As to the contents of the leaves, having forgotten whatever little acquaintance I once had with the language they are written in, and our chaplain having been set ashore at Falmouth, besides that they are written close, in a foreign hand, and the ink (of whatever sort originally) now extremely faded by time, I think it best to forward them to your Lordship without further comment. When they were picked up, we were at least twenty leagues from any land laid down on the ship's charts; whatever colony or mission of discovery they refer to, was perhaps ten times the distance from us at that moment; and must have prospered or decayed beyond need or possibility of help, when the papers were committed to chance of winds and waves. All this considered, I stood on my course, without any vain attempt to trace the fate of the writer.

As soon as some remaining duties permit, I shall come from Portsmouth within the next two days, and present myself to your Lordship and the Board of Admiralty: awaiting which honour

I am, my Lord,

Your Lordship's most faithful,

obedient servant,

GEORGE DUTTON,

Commander.

P.S.—Mr. Symes, your Lordship's cousin, desires me to add his respectful duty. I shall have the pleasure to report well of his conduct in detail, together with that of my other officers: but I cannot forbear particular mention of Lieut. Pilkington, of whose deserts and claims on your Lordship's favour for promotion, I shall take occasion to speak more at large.—G.D.

# DON MANUEL'S NARRATIVE.

HERE followeth the true relation of me, Manuel of the Seven Dolours, ex-provincial, concerning the state of thirteen companions, with myself, on an unknown island, being, so well as we can guess somewhere to the south of . . . . . . . . .*

I beseech you, brother, whosoever you be, who by the Divine permission may find these writings, to transmit the same, or a copy of them, so soon as it shall be possible for you, to my most Reverend Lord and Father in God, Don Pedro Velasquez, bishop of B . . . . . .* or to my Very Reverend and beloved Father, the provincial for the time being, of the Order of . . . . . . or, at the least, to deliver them to the Bishop or Governor of any city in old Spain, or in the Spanish colonies, whereat ye shall touch : and may the merciful Lord therefore reward you.

These are to make known, to the glory of God, and to obtain help for the strengthening of this mission, that we have been one year and seven months in this heathen and savage place, without prospect of being visited or relieved by any European ship. Hither we came, impelled by the desire of announcing to the Indians the truths of eternal life : and came by a series of wonderful providences, marked by the hand of God; having been first deserted on one island (sufficiently distant from this) by men that seem made the instruments in His hand who brings good from evil in His own time and way, first of saving a perishing crew on that place, subjects of his Catholic majesty ; and now, which is the greater work, of bringing the gospel to a populous heathen land.

* It is of course, impossible to supply for these blanks in the MS. with any approach to certainty, or even probability, and the reader may feel indebted to the painstaking labour of a gentleman in the MS. department of the British Museum, for deciphering the early and more damaged portion. *B* probably stands for Barcelona. ED.

We were received at first with some mistrust, because of our landing with arms in our hands; yet, to have gone thither defenceless would have been throwing needlessly our lives away. The inhabitants crowded down upon the shore, filled with wonder, rather than animated by enmity or fear. They had never before seen the white faces of the children of Europe. But, as we had brought with us two of their own nation, thrown by Providence on the island whence we came, and by grace converted and baptized, our communication with them was soon established. For the moment, we arranged a barter with them for food, by means of some trifles we had brought with us; mere nails and bits of glass, or scraps of iron, which to them were worth hogs, goats, vegetables, fruits, fresh water in gourds, and any other production of their country.

Two swift messengers started up into the interior to announce our arrival to their king, or cacique,* who lives in the chief village in the island, half a day's journey up the country: meantime, they assigned to us for a temporary abode a narrow strip of land on the shore, almost surrounded by water. Though they erected a strong and high palisade of pointed stakes across the neck of this land to prevent our passing beyond it, and also made us promise that we would not use our boats (of which we had two) to pass to any other point of their country; yet, they showed great friendliness; and crowds were constantly coming and going with insatiable curiosity to look at us, and speak with us through the bars of the palisade. It was chiefly with our two Indians and myself that they conversed; for I had gained (through these two) a sufficient knowledge of their language to speak it with ease. They had numberless questions to ask about our nation, king, laws, customs, religion, wars, dress, barter, productions, down to the most minute details of our lives: and they would scarcely allow us time to sleep, nor me, unworthy priest, leisure to read my breviary, so eager were they, day and night, to listen to everything we could tell them.

* Don Manuel is probably incorrect in giving to the King of Toonati-nooka a name which he must have borrowed from his knowledge of the native chiefs of Chili, Peru, and the other Spanish settlements of South America. ED.

I was glad to be able thus to commence my mission among them ; and I announced to them, with caution and not *ex professo*, some of the first truths of religion, the unity of God, the punishments of sin, etc.  But the work became so fatiguing (the crowds increasing continually, as the report of our arrival flew abroad), I was truly glad when a cry arose, from those who were furthest from the palisade, " *Tooma, tooma !* " which is their word for king, or principal lord ; by which I concluded the king himself had come down to see us.

He came, surrounded by his guards, who could scarcely keep off the crowds, even by beating them severely with the staves of their spears.  All those who could approach him performed the usual ceremony in token of submission, which is, licking the king's feet.  He bade the two Indians and myself come forth to him, to the other side the palisade.  This we were not prepared for, being quite uncertain of his relation towards us : at first I designed to make the king and his chief men (for he was surrounded by many whom it was easy to remark as persons in authority), take an oath, in the solemn manner of their country, that our persons should be safe among them.  On second thoughts, however, I remembered that such oath was likely to consist in some idolatrous rite, and the invocation of one of the many demons worshipped among them ; and I resolved rather to trust myself in the merciful hands of God than countenance such an act.

I answered, however, with an air of authority, that we were messengers from a great king, who had sent us hither on a negociation of the utmost importance to Toonatinooka ; that my King had done me the honour to admit me near His person, and had laid on me an office that usually kept me employed about His throne ; that we came as ambassadors, not as supplicants, and for the benefit of himself and his people, not for any necessity or advantage of our own.  I went on to say, though we were few in number, compared to those who surrounded us, yet the weapons in our hands (for each of our men carried two muskets, and had three or four pistols in his belt) were of so tremendous a kind as made us capable of slaying numbers, if we were so disposed, though we came on an embassy of peace.  Therefore, if we were to treat, it must be on equal terms: that I, as ambassador, would present myself before the king, if his guards (all but two only), would lay aside their spears for the present, and the rest of his subjects keep to a distance of three spears' lengths around us: also, if two hostages of their chief men, unarmed, would pass inside the palisade, for every one of us who went beyond it.

These terms, together with the tone I assumed, astonished the king; and he called his chiefs around him to deliberate on what I had said. After a while, he sent to us one of the oldest among them, a sensible man, who told me these were new and unheard-of things for a stranger to propose; that our coming was unlooked for, and our appearance unusual: in a word, that the king desired some proof of the power we brought with us, such as should not harm his people, whilst they convinced himself and his chiefs.

Upon this, I turned to one of my companions, who was reckoned the best marksman among us; and, pointing to a sea-eagle wheeling above us at no great height, I bade him take steady aim, and shoot in the name of God and Saint James. May our good Lord forgive me if I was guilty of any presumption in this; but I trusted, not alone to my faith and poor prayer, but to the man's known skill with his weapon. Also, I was sure that, did he hit or did he miss, the effect on the savages would only differ in degree, and that the dreadful noise and sudden surprise of the explosion would not fail to impress them with reverence for us, and dread of our weapons.

As I supposed, so it turned out. No sooner had the sailor discharged his piece, than such a yell arose from the multitude, as if an earthquake or other terrific thing had happened. The greater part of them fell to the earth, hiding their faces; some ran like scared creatures into the woods: others called on their gods to save them. But what was their astonishment when the eagle, transfixed with the ball, fluttered down, and fell dead in the very midst of the assembly. From that time we had no need to assert our equality with them; for they acknowledged us at once as superior beings. So great was their dread of us now, it was not easy to find, among all their bravest warriors, six who would come within the palisade as hostages.  We on our part, made all signs of friend-ship; and told them, this dreadful thunder and lightning (so they called our weapon) was only used against our enemies; that we had it so completely under our control, it would only explode when we pleased : and we solemnly assured them, by the great King who sent us, if they attempted not to harm us, it should never explode against them.

On this, they took heart again, and six chiefs (who were afterwards rewarded by the king with a string of shells a-piece for this act of daring) came in among our men, while our two Indians and myself were received outside by the king, his guards having laid aside their arms as I had required.

His first demand was, to see one of these wonderful weapons nearer; but that it should not make the noise, nor shoot forth the fire, again.  I called back to the man who fired, to pass his musket to me through the palisade; and holding it, I addressed the king, telling him, he should judge by what I was now about to do, whether I had spoken truly that these weapons would fire or not, as we willed. I made him remark, I was going to do what the man had done before: pledging my truth as an ambassador, it should make no more noise than the king himself would, by snapping his fingers.  There was to be no fire, I said, but one spark only : and if it thundered forth as before, or anything like it, he might disbelieve my message, and send us away as impostors.

––––––––––

THE king and all the assembly were half afraid of the thing being done over again; but I solemnly assured them, I would rest the whole credit of my mission on the result : then, amid a breathless silence in the vast con-course, I pointed the gun upward, as though I took aim at some other bird, and so pulled the trigger.  When the king heard the snap, and saw the spark from the flint, and nothing further, he threw his arms into the air, and shouted out, that we were, since we had absolute control over these dreadful creatures, rather gods than men. Then, in spite of our agreement, his chiefs pressed round us, and, do what I would to prevent it, they all licked my feet, after the custom of the country. I seized the opportunity to proclaim the true God, asking the king to judge if we, who were but the poor servants of Him in whose name we came, could do such mighty wonders, what must be His own power and majesty! And thus we already disposed both him and his nation to receive the faith.

Then he asked me, on what terms was he to treat with this great King? What did he require? I answered, my King required nothing but what was to make the king of Toonati-nooka and his subjects happy: that for this very purpose had I been sent; that my King, being more powerful than all others, and more abounding in possession of wealth and happiness, needed nothing as being necessary to Him: being as good and merciful as He was rich and powerful. His delight was to make all other kings and their subjects happy: and again, being as wise as He was powerful, rich, and happy in Himself, He sent His ambassadors into every quarter of the earth, to proclaim the laws and ordinances by which alone men could be happy while they lived, and happy after they were dead. Lastly, I repeated, it was for this and no other object that I was come and had brought hither my companions.

I told him I sought not the gold or wealth of his kingdom; that my King willed that he should still occupy his throne and be obeyed by his subjects; that the best security for his person and kingdom would be, to submit himself, and cause them also to submit, to my King's wise and benevolent laws, which teach men to be obedient to lawful authority, and not do only what they must needs, but what is right because it is right. Other things of the like kind I added; and though he seemed incapable of understanding what I said about right and justice, yet, seeing him listen attentively, I resolved not to lose the occasion.

The king pondered greatly on what I said, and sat silent for some space; then, calling to him the grave, venerable chiefs who were his counsellors, he deliberated with them: and they declared it was good, though new.

This they repeated several times, as though surprised at
its being new and unheard-of, yet approving it as
good. And I heard them repeating this often to themselves, to one another, and to the king : *new, but good ;
new, but good.*

Then the king went on to ask me many questions about
the laws and ordinances I had come to proclaim ; and
whether any of them would be against the laws established
in his kingdom by those who had been before him. This
question, as being difficult to answer, I evaded for the
time : for the Gospel of our Lord Jesus Christ must needs
be in opposition to the idolatrous and wicked customs of
the heathen ; as said the apostle : " What fellowship hath
light with darkness ? And what concord hath Christ with
Belial ? Or what part hath the faithful with the unbeliever ? " Therefore I answered him, that as yet I was
not so well acquainted with the customs of his kingdom,
and could not speak as to particulars ; but sure I was, the
laws of a king so wise, so just, so benevolent as mine
needs be the best and happiest possible ; and that, did it
chance any of those in Toonati-nooka differed from them,
it would be for his happiness to conform to my King's laws
without delay.

He seemed to think this was reasonable, as did his counsellors too : they sat silent again, pondering on all I had
advanced ; now one, now another, nodding with his head,
and saying *it was good.* At length the king rose up, and
taking off his head-dress of feathers, placed it on me, as a
mark of special favour and inviolable hospitality. He also
chewed one half of a betel-nut, and invited me to chew
the other. Then he bade me to a feast, which had been
preparing under a grove of trees, while we were in conference. He promised at the same time, to send abundance of provisions to our men, which he amply fulfilled :
and allowed me to send back the younger of my two Indians to the enclosure, to serve as interpreter, and carry
messages to and fro.

Our feast was as ceremonious as a state banquet ever
was ; indeed, many ceremonies were especially observed
in my honour, and I was glad to find, they were not
accompanied by any superstitious observances, which I

could not have joined in.  But before it concluded, there came in a number of slave dancers, to dance before the king and his guests, whose performance was heathenish to a degree, and wounding to Christian eyes.  On this, I told the king, my Master forbade His servants to be present at such exhibitions ; and begged him to let the dancers retire.  He answered, laughing : "O honourable ambassador ! what matters it for the time, inasmuch as your king sees you not ? "

To which I replied by asking him respectfully, would he consider any of his subjects faithful, who only obeyed his laws while his eye was upon them ?  He considered awhile, then said, with a frowning countenance : "No, indeed; if I knew of any one transgressing my laws at a distance, I would send to him this my servant."  On which, he beckoned the public executioner (who always attends him), a tall, athletic man of ferocious aspect, with a large sword, made of a wood almost as hard as iron, and quite as heavy. "This is the messenger," says he, "I send to all my subjects who forget their duty.  Tell me, O slave," he continued, addressing the executioner, "how many notches hast thou on thy sword ?" "O king," answered he, "they are six, fifty, and two hundred" (so they always reckon backwards in this country).  "Good !" cries the king, laughing ; then turned to me and explained, the custom was for the executioner to make a notch on his weapon for every malefactor's head he cut off.  " And thy father before thee," continued the king ; " how many notches did he make in his time ?"  "O king !" answered the executioner, "my father had two swords, given him by the king your father ; and they were so full of notches, there was not room to make one notch more."

"You see, now, O ambassador," says the king to me, " we know how to punish those who transgress our laws." "And my Master, O King," answered I, "has not one ambassador only, nor one executioner, nor one army, but more than I can count, all ranged round His throne.  The swords of His executioners are of fire, and pestilence, famine, and death.  One of them, once sent out by my King, slew seventy thousand men in three days: another went forth alone against the King's enemies, and in one night slew five thousand, and eighty thousand, and an hundred thousand."*

On this, the king's nephew, who had just come in from a hunting party, and had heard nothing of what had passed before, burst out laughing, and showed signs of incredulity as to what I asserted. But the king reproved him with an angry countenance, and related to him at large the firing of the gun; asking him, if such were the dreadful creatures carried by an embassy of peace, what might not be expected of the war implements and executioners' swords of so great a King?"

"But I do not understand, O ambassador," continued he, "how your king secures your obedience to His laws when you are out of His sight? My subjects" (he went on whispering in my ear) "observe my laws carefully, because they know I have spies in every part of my kingdom who would report their disobedience. But if I sent them on a distant embassy, like yours, I believe they would think little of disobeying every law my forefathers enacted."

To which I answered, though my King was indeed out of my sight, yet I was not out of His; that His eyes pierced into every place; that He had servants and messengers innumerable, who could fly with the speed of light to give in to Him their account of all that passed over the whole earth; yet that He needed them not, though He was pleased frequently to employ their services, which they rendered most willingly, with a great love of their King: finally, that (by some of His courtiers) He kept a great book, in which were written down all the actions of every one of His subjects, even to the meanest and poorest person, even the smallest action, or the least ' whisper of a word; and according to these entries in the book, the King rewarded or punished His subjects without fail, sooner or later, as His wisdom decreed.

On this he pondered a little at the first; then laughed and said, it must needs be a large book, indeed, and a

* The reference here is evidently to the three days' pestilence recorded in II. *Kings,* xxiv. 18, and to the destruction of the host of Sennacherib, IV. *Kings,* xix. 35. It would appear to be the idiom in Toonati-nooka, as among the ancient Greeks, in stating a high number, to proceed from the lesser numerals to the greater. **Ed.**

great deal of trouble to keep it: and asked how many scribes were employed on this, and what kind of writing they used. To this I returned an evasive answer, not wishing to give him more to think of at that time; and turning the discourse, I said to the king, though he had been pleased to comply with my request, and send away his dancers, yet my King did by no means forbid any amusement that was harmless; and if he would condescend to witness a war dance of my countrymen (so I called their exercising with their weapons), he would see how regularly they could perform it.

The king seemed highly delighted with this proposal; only he made me promise, these javelins of lightning (so he called our guns) should not be shot forth again without his express permission. I did this; and moreover, on my sacred character as ambassador to the Great King, the men were to return to their palisade when the dance was over, at least for that night, until the king had determined how he would receive us into the country.

---

THIS being concluded, I called out to the men in Spanish, that eight of them (five of whom had been marines in our wrecked ship, and the other three veteran invalided troops of the line) should march out in order, shouldering their arms, and should give a great example of discipline. Accordingly, they came forth with fixed bayonets, marching in step, and filing in front of the king, suddenly wheeled round, and presented themselves in a line before him, grounding their arms, which made a great clash on the ground. But this startled both him and his chiefs, who expected nothing less than that all the muskets would explode together. He rose up in consternation, throwing a thick shield of bull's hide before him, and crouching down behind it: several of his chiefs betrayed their fear by running behind the trees, and of the multitude, a great number fell on their faces again, and set up loud cries. On this, I came before him again, smiling, and with outstretched hands asked him whether he had forgotten that I had pledged my word, the javelins should not explode? This brought him and the chiefs to them-

21

selves again; some of them seemed rather ashamed of the fear they had shown; and the king told me he wished the war-dance to proceed.

On which, strictly charging the men not so much as to level their guns in any direction where spectators were assembled (who, indeed, surrounded us on all sides), I bade them go through some of their common exercises. They did so with great precision, under the command of one of the veterans, who was a serjeant, and had seen much service. The exercise, or war dance, so delighted the king, that before it was half concluded, he leaped from the ground where he was seated, laughed, shouted, clapped his hands; then, calling for his spear and shield, rushed with a wild yell into the midst, with violent gesticulations; brandishing his weapons. He then began to shout a tremendous war-song at the top of his voice. This example so excited his chiefs to warlike fury, that they followed him to the very letter. They seized their spears, and formed a circle round him, joining him in the war-song; moving round at first more slowly, then quicker and quicker, as the excitement or passion of battle increased: at times they struck their spears into the earth as though they were slaying an enemy; and the song became louder continually, till they seemed to lose all command of themselves, and rushed round and round, their eyes inflamed and countenances distorted with phrensy, shrieking out their battle-cry like so many furies.

The converted Indians now drew near to me, and said with alarm, that we were in much danger from them; that when this excitement seized them, they became unable to distinguish friends from foes; and, moreover, when the king thus joined in a war-dance with his chiefs, it seldom ended without their striking their lances through several of the spectators. On this news, I drew our men together in line, bidding them present their bayonets in self-defence towards these furious savages, in case they showed any further sign of hostilities: then with my two Indians, I commenced, at the full pitch of our united voices, a simple hymn which I had composed for them in their native language. At the first strains, I could perceive the fury of those war-dancers somewhat abate; and we had not sung half a dozen lines, before they subsided into something of their former tranquillity. We continued steadily looking on them with unmoved countenances; and before the hymn ended, they stood listening, having cast aside their weapons, fixed with curiosity, and a kind of rude reverence, or fear.

We finished our hymn as we walked back quietly to the place where the king had now re-seated himself; and by this, all danger and disturbance had ceased. He expressed his approval, nodding his head several times; then asked us, what was the meaning of what we had sung. Was it a war song, or a lament over those who had fallen, or a song to one of the gods of our country, or the history of some famous warrior? To this, I answered, it was one of our modes of addressing my King. Were those words, then, asked he, addressed to the King who sent you? I signified, yes. But, pursued the king, we never sing any song of so solemn a nature, unless to lament over the dead, or to address our gods. " Stand forth, Ta-kaeeuga," continued he, turning to his chief bard, or priest, " and sing us my ancestor's song to Havaoeekee."

On this, I could scarcely restrain my converted Indians from giving expression to their disgust at hearing the name of the idol they had once worshipped. I, for my part, was equally determined the idolatrous hymn should not be sung in our presence; therefore, turning to the king with a resolute countenance, I told him, my King was much more powerful than Havaoeekee, or any of the gods of the island: that to sing a hymn in his praise, while we were by, would be reckoned an insult to my King, of which I felt sure the king of Toonati-nooka would not be guilty, were it only out of hospitality, but which my King could punish on the spot, if it were persisted in: and a good deal more to the same purpose. He listened with the greatest wonder and astonishment, as did also his chiefs. When I had done speaking, he conferred some time with them, then beckoned me again to come to him alone, where he was seated. Here he caused a mat of honour to be spread for me beside his own: a distinction to which none of his chiefs pretended, and generally reserved for his nephew alone, who was to succeed him in the kingdom. Then, taking my hand, and looking me very seriously in the face: " Tell me, O ambassador of the great King!" says he; "is your King truly, truly, greater than Havaoeekee; greater than Paowanga; greater than all the rest we worship?"

"O king!" answered I, "it is true indeed; as true as that you have honoured me, His ambassador and servant, and placed me by your side. Let us only rest to-night after our weary voyage; to-morrow, if you have courage, I will show you a proof of the power of my King."

He laughed at the idea of his not having courage, or not so much courage as I, who was a man of peace; till, his eye resting again on our muskets, he checked himself, remembering the fears he had felt at them before.

By this time, the evening began to close in; but as there was light enough still for a farewell shot, I thought it best to wind up all I had said, by repeating this proof of our powers. I therefore reminded him, we had faithfully kept to our promise of not exploding the fire-javelins hitherto; but asked him, would he now desire to see how much stronger they were than any lance or bow in his country? I promised that, to prove this, they should only explode once, as before.

He hesitated awhile at this proposal; then consulted again with his chiefs, amongst whom also there was a difference of opinion. Some appeared to think once was quite enough for such an experiment; but others had arrived on the spot since our conference began, and were eager to witness what they had heard so much talk of; till the rest, I suppose, were ashamed to show how great was their dread. At length, the king gave a sort of unwilling consent: on which, I asked for the strongest shield among his warriors to be brought before me. It was of hard wood, clumsily fashioned into a rude board of some thickness, which was strengthened with a double covering of untanned goat's hide. This was indeed the king's own second shield, borne after him in battle by his shield-bearer, in case of the first being pierced or broken. I caused the shield to be placed upright, supported by two spears, at about half musket shot from where we sat. Then, calling aloud, I said, "O warriors of Toonati-nooka! strong are your arms; swift and sharp are your spears! Do your worst on yonder shield; then stand aside, to see what the servants of my King can do!"

At the king's command, three of the strongest chiefs now stepped out; and, after choosing their sharpest-pointed javelins, one after another hurled them against the shield. It was considered much above the average, in the way of darting, that their weapons should, at that distance, pierce through the two goat's hides, and remain quivering in the wood of the shield. When they had each delivered their spears, with the utmost force, the king turned to me with an air of triumph, asking me what more I could do. I answered him, "O king! this is indeed well done; and I believe the arm of the strongest man could hardly do more. But my King has allowed us to possess weapons that put the weak on a level with the strong. To prove this, I will call on one of our warriors who was nearly dying a short time since, and has not yet recovered his strength:" and here I beckoned to one of the veteran invalids, whose pale, sickly looks confirmed what I had said of him. He was a very steady shot, however; and I committed the proof to him with confidence.

When he stood forth, the musket in his hands, there was the greatest consternation among those who had heard the last gun fired, and the greatest curiosity among those who had not. I think, by this time all the population of that part of the country must have been assembled on the spot. There could not have been less than fifteen thousand men immediately about us; and the rising ground was covered with women and children. It was a sea of dark faces and eager eyes, all fixed upon our marksman. Indeed, when I considered the importance of the stake on which I had now set everything, I almost wished I had not risked it. I betook myself inwardly to prayer, that all might go well.

We made the king understand, a lane or avenue must be cleared behind the shield, to avoid all danger to his people: to which he showed himself very indifferent, in comparison with his curiosity. So dense was the crowd, it was with difficulty, and not without many blows, this was effected. When all was ready, I again commended the matter to God, and bade the soldier fire.

The report of his gun produced even greater effects than the former. There rose a shriek from the multitude, and from the hill, such as I never heard before, nor ever wish to hear again. The whole assembly fell upon their faces thinking they were wounded by the flash; and only by degrees, first one and then another rose again, feeling their heads and arms to see whether they were whole. Then the chiefs ran to the shield; and were astonished to find the two bullets (for the piece was double-loaded) had gone through hides, wood, and all, and lay on the ground beyond. These they brought to the king, together with the shield itself.

But when he had seen with his own eyes the passage cut by the bullet, and examined the ball itself, he was the more confirmed in his belief, that it was the veritable thunder we carried in our guns. For it seems that meteor-stones had been known to fall into Toonati-nooka, in the midst of great thunder-storms: and he was fully persuaded, the bullets (which were beaten out of shape in their passage through the shield) were some such stones, only under our command, to launch or keep back as we pleased. This circumstance crowned our reputation; the king ordered a robe of honour (a red and yellow cloak of birch-bark and bird's feathers) to be brought, and thrown over my shoulders: also, he rewarded the marksman with a string of berries which he took from his neck, and two hogs; which were sent to the palisade.

---

WE were now surrounded by the chiefs, who said a great many things in our honour. But I bade them only pay honour to the King who had sent me; that we were but His servants, and all the power we possessed came from Him; that He had commanded me to show other wonders beside these, and to tell all the people of Toonati-nooka some very good news, which we reserved ti'l the following day: but that now we craved leave to r' ire.

They crowded so closely round us, showing such anxiety to ask a multitude of questions, that we had great difficulty in making our way back to the boats. Our men, however, needed rest: therefore, after taking our leave of the king (who would scarcely let us go), we were making our way back, when the chief bard, whose office was to chronicle the valiant deeds of the king and his warriors, stepped before me and chanted, to a kind of rude lute with five strings, the following verses :

> " Great is the King who sent His ambassador,
> Bearing in canes the thunder and lightning !
> Strong are the warriors of Toonati-nooka,
> Stronger the pale men beyond the salt water."

This song was taken up by the multitude and the chiefs ; nay, the king himself did not think it beneath his dignity to join in it : and it swelled into a deafening shout, as they formed a procession to accompany us to the palisade. Indeed, every one was now anxious we should come from this separation, and be with them : but I foresaw, it would be quieter and more secure for us to stay there, at least for the time. So they accompanied us to our quarters ; then, with many greetings, we dismissed the six chiefs who had been kept as hostages : they were wild to know all that had taken place. The multitude remained a great part of the night outside the palisade, lighting up large fires, aud chanting the same song, and others which they made in our praise : so that it was difficult to get any rest for the noise.

At day-break the next morning, the king sent (in respectful terms) to beg we would come to him. As I was engaged in reciting my breviary, I sent back word, that I was then employed in the service of my King, but would come to him as soon as possible. Meanwhile, the crowd collected in such numbers outside, and kept up such a continual talking with our two Indians, as greatly disturbed me, and them also. At length, seeing no other help for it, I called them, with the other men, to morning prayers, telling the savages we were going to speak to our King, and they must remain silent. So, indeed, they did, with the utmost respect, not once interrupting us. When this was finished, I opened my breviary again, and bade the Indians precede me, singing one of the hymns I had composed for them in their own language. So we all walked out very slowly, while I managed to recite my office. The multitude crowded round us, leaving us just room to walk ; and they supposed this was some solemn procession we were engaged in. Nor did they offer to

disturb us; but now and then they would break out, singing the verse their bard had made the night before : some
who were nearest, and could catch the words that our two
Indians sang, joined in them as well as they could : whence
it came to pass, that they pronounced the sweet names
of *Jesus* and *Mary* before they knew the meaning of the
words.

We found the king surrounded by his priests, preparing
to offer a sacrifice to the idol of the place, Paowanga.  He
greeted me joyfully, yet with great respect, and threw
another string of berries round my neck, inviting me to
take part with him in the ceremony.  But I answered, I
was then engaged in communicating with my King, who
was much greater than Paowanga, as I had told him last
night.  On this, the priests became very angry; and,
pointing to where the idol stood, asked me, was my King
more powerful than this great god of Toonati-nooka?  I
looked, and saw at a little distance, a monstrous and
hideous idol, rudely carved out of the stump of a large
tree.  This idol was of a terrible countenance, having an
enormous mouth armed with shark's teeth : into which, it
seems, the poor deluded people used to put their offerings,
such as hogs, goats, etc. (for the idol's mouth would easily
contain one of those animals), together with yams, potatoes, bread-fruit, or whatever offering they brought.  Sometimes, I believe, they did the same with human sacrifices.
They supposed that Paowanga devoured all these things;
but the priests, who had their dwelling in a sort of college
behind a palisade close to the image, had contrived a trap-
door in the back of his head, and came to take out by night
what the poor worshippers had put in by day ; and so lived
very comfortably, in great indolence.

Part of this I had learned through our Indians ; but the
particular fraud of the trap-door was discovered after
what I am going to relate.  For the present I answered
the priests (who had already, as I could see, become our
enemies), that, if the king permitted, when I had done
speaking to my King, we would see which was greatest,
my King, or Paowanga.  Then I walked quietly on, reading my book, my two Indians with me, still singing their
hymns.  As to the people, they seemed divided, whether
they should follow us, or attend the sacrifice : but by far

the greater part came with us, and I believe Paowanga never had so thin an attendance ; for this was a solemn sacrifice, which took place " twice every moon," as they expressed it.

I went some little distance, out of sight : but could not get beyond the sound of their heathenish shoutings round the idol, nor the noise of the great instruments like drums, they beat in his honour, and which I afterwards found to be made of the skins of their enemies slain or taken in battle.

I knelt down, and prayed for some time with all the fervour I could command, that our good Lord would inspire me with wisdom and courage for what was to follow. I also asked the two Indians, in a whisper, whether they were prepared to share the danger I resolved to incur for the glory of God, to open the eyes of those idolaters at one bold stroke.

They answered me, that they were prepared : for they were, in truth, so deeply imbued with our holy faith, I believe they would have felt no greater joy than to embrace martyrdom on the spot. Seeing the danger was so near, they asked for a little time for their confessions, which allowed me to finish great part of my office. After this, I heard them, first the elder, then the younger ; motioning the savages to keep a little distance. They looked on with a respectful silence, as on something mysterious, which they understood not.

When this was concluded, returning as leisurely as we came, we found the heathen sacrifice just over, and all around the king, waiting for us.

" Now, O king," said I, " if you will permit me to return to my companions, I will fetch a proof that Paowanga is no god at all : and if I fail to prove it," added I, turning to the priests, " I will give you leave to put me straight into his mouth." At this, the king laughed greatly ; but I noticed the idolatrous priests to look at me, full of malice, and whisper to one another. " Go," then said the king, " O ambassador ! but how long will you be away ? " " Before the sun," said I, " has travelled over the little space between yonder tree-tops, I will come again."

On this, I took one of the two Indians with me ; but the other was kept back by the king, who wished to entertain

himself by asking him a thousand questions about us and
our ways and customs. When I got to the boats, I asked
the gunner's mate of the wrecked vessel (who was one of
our party) to make me up quickly a strong packet of
powder, containing about three-quarters of a pound, with
a slow burning match, a few inches in length. While he
was doing this, I selected from a case of philosophical instruments which we had saved from the wreck, a strong
burning-glass, or magnifier; for I had already formed my
plan. When the packet of gunpowder was ready, I went
back with it in my hand, and arrived within the time I had
promised.

Presenting myself before the king, I spoke as follows:
"O king!" I said, "when two chiefs contend in battle,
or wrestle in a trial of strength, if one is able to lift the
other off his feet, and throw him to the ground, is he not
the strongest?" "Yes, indeed," cried out the king and
the chiefs; and all the multitude repeated it after them.
"But," I continued, "if the chief sends one of his mere servants, with no weapon in his hand; and the servant is
able to throw down that other; what will you say of the
strength of the chief who sent him?" "O, O, O," cried
they all, in great surprise; and listened for what I should
say next. "Now tell me," I went on, "is Paowanga a
mighty god?" "Oh, mighty, mighty!" cried out all the
priests in chorus; and the king, with some of his chiefs,
said it too; but, I perceived, not with so much vigour:
for they had begun to disbelieve in him since they had
spoken with me. "But how can you show me," said I,
"he is so mighty?" "Oh," said one of the principal
among the priests, pointing to the idol, "see how much
he can eat!" In truth, one of the hind legs of a goat was
even then sticking out of the huge mouth; the rest having
disappeared into the cavity of the trunk. And, it seems,
among these savages, it is reckoned one of the great
qualities of a chief to be able to devour enormous quantities of food.

"Well," said I, laughing, "I am going to give him something to eat, too; and if it does not prove too much for
him, I shall think him very strong indeed."

So saying, I moved towards the idol with my packet of
gunpowder.

Here the priests, suspecting some harm to their favourite, began to urge the king not to allow me to proceed. But he, with his chiefs, overcome by curiosity, seemed anxious for nothing but to see the end. I promised, on my part, having once put something into Paowanga's mouth for him to eat, I would not approach him again. " I have no wish," said I, " to be near him, since he is an enemy and rival to my King." They scarce knew how to interpret all this; but there was the greatest silence and wonder among chiefs and people alike: except only the priests, who kept murmuring and scowling at me.

I walked up to the idol, inwardly praying to God to direct me; then mounting the rude blocks, piled up like so many steps, by which worshippers came to make their offering to his mouth, I cried aloud, so that all might hear: " O Paowanga! it is not to honour or praise you, not to do you homage, that I now put this into your mouth: but, on the contrary, to show this king and all his people, that my King who has sent me hither is alone to be honoured or worshipped as God." With that, I thrust the gunpowder into the idol's mouth, taking care to expose the slow match to the sun: then, swiftly pulling out my burning-glass, I brought the sun's rays to bear on the end of the match, which instantly lighted. Then I put the glass again into my pocket, came down the steps, and walked quietly back to the king.

---

ALL the people were standing at a respectful distance from the idol, and I was not much afraid of their being hurt by the explosion. Notwithstanding, I begged the king to command them to remove farther off, which he did, and they reluctantly obeyed. I motioned with my hand, that no one should stir; but there was no need to command silence; all being in anxious expectation of something, they knew not what. Their eyes went continually back and forward, first to the idol, then to me; and I could see, they began to feel some contempt for him, for his not having avenged, by some great judgment, the public affront I had offered him.

But in two or three minutes, the match having now burnt to the powder, all on a sudden, there came a more terrific explosion than any thunder-clap they had heard in their lives before.  The image was rent from the top to the bottom; his monstrous head cleft in twain, the shark's teeth scattered into the air: and the whole trunk, loosened from the earth, tottered for a moment, then fell forward on its face, down the steps.  It is impossible to describe the astonishment, the dread, that seized on the whole assembly.  They fell down, as before, stopping their eyes and ears; no one ventured to breathe or look up: until I ran and stood forth in the midst, having taken the king's spear into my hand.  "So falls Paowanga," I cried with a loud voice: " he falls by the hand of the meanest servant of the great King! So, soon or late, must fall every enemy of my King and my Lord."  With that, I struck the spear deep into the prostrate trunk.

The people all answered with a shout, again and again repeated, in honour of my King above all other kings, and of my God above all gods.  Then they commenced yelling forth frantically the verse they had learned; and the sound, from so many thousands of throats, was like the roar of a cataract, and was taken up from the hills by the shriller voices of the women and children;

> " Great is the King, who sent His ambassador,
>     Bearing in canes the thunder and lightning: "

only now, they altered the third line, to suit the occasion, and sang,

> " Strong was our god Paowanga but yesterday:
>     Stronger the pale man beyond the salt water."

As to Paowanga's priests, they knew not which way to turn, and would fain have made their escape; but the people hemmed and pressed them in.  They were afraid for their lives, and began to supplicate for mercy: on all sides they were met by indignation and contempt.  All at once, the king was seized with a fury of hatred against his former instructors: he caught up his second spear, and shouting out the battle cry of his nation, hurled it amongst them, and struck down one of the highest in rank, who died almost instantly from the wound.  This was the signal for the chiefs and the people, who rushed upon

them, and commenced an instant massacre.  I was horror-
struck at the sight, and flew after the king, entreating,
imploring, in the name of my King, who desired not (I
exclaimed) the death of His enem: es, but that they should
turn to be His friends.

It was all in vain ; the movement had been too sudden,
and my voice was drowned in the uproar of shrieks and
yells that rose from the midst of the massacre.  I could
save the lives only of three, by staying the arms of the
chiefs as they were hurling their spears ; and succeeded at
last in making my voice heard.  But, to my grief, when
the tumult subsided, there were no less than nineteen dead
bodies lying on the ground.

Richly as these idolatrous priests had deserved their
death, for the impositions they had practised on the people, I was afflicted beyond measure at their tragical end ;
having promised myself (it may be, presumptuously) the
consolation of presenting to my Lord this whole people,
converted to Him without the shedding of one drop of
blood.  I cast myself on my knees beside the mangled
corpses, endeavouring to staunch their wounds, or to find
so much as a token of life among them.  Some, it is true,
yet breathed ; but one after another they died under my
hands, so sure and forcibly had the spears been hurled.

It was a fresh cause of astonishment to the king, to see
me thus engaged : he could not forbear to ask me the
reason of it.  "Have I not said, O king !" I replied, " that
my king is all goodness and love?  He has no enemies,
but those who make themselves so ; and even those He
wins back by His patience and benefits."

" Then why," answered the king, "did he not try and
win back Paowanga ? "

" I will tell you, O king !" said I, amid tears and sighs,
" when my mind is more calm : at present I grieve for
those unhappy souls, who have been sent out of the world,
enemies of my king."

But it was time to follow up the advantage God had
given us.  Wherefore, placing the few priests who remained alive, together with the families of them all, in
charge of the elder of my two Indians, I solemnly appealed
to my King (raising my hand to heaven) to witness, that
they were thenceforward under His own protection, and

no man's hand must be raised against them.  This I said
in the presence of the king and his chiefs, with a resolute
countenance, by which they seemed in a manner over-
awed, and at length promised it should be so.  I then led
him to the idol, on which the multitude were by this time
heaping all kind of insults, hacking and hewing it to
pieces.  I showed the king the trap-door that was made in
the back of Paowanga's neck, by which the offerings
placed in his mouth, were appropriated to the use of the
priests and their families.  This roused his indignation
again, and that of the people ; forasmuch as these ministers of an idolatrous worship were supported, besides, by
a liberal contribution made throughout the district every
new moon.  But I reminded him of his promise ; sooner
than a hair of their heads was touched, I demanded from
him that the priests and their families should be given to
my King, as His servants.  This he readily granted ; and
from that time I was looked on as their special protector ;
the people (for my sake) being so afraid of injuring them,
they would not even go near them : though it was plain
they still regarded them with much hatred and contempt.

It needed now but a short time to cleave the idol in
pieces, and set him on fire.  While this was preparing,
the king desired to see my breviary, in which he had seen
me read from time to time ; and asked me whether it was
my *oloeeo*.  This is a word whereby they express a sort of
charm, or amulet, in which they believe another of their
false gods, named Havaeoeekee, resides.*  I had heard of
these amulets before, from our Indians ; and this appeared
a favourable occasion of finishing the work we had begun.

"No, O king !" answered I ; "this is no *oloeeo* ; nor does
my King permit His servants to keep, or to believe in, any
such thing.  Oloeeo, and Havaeoeekee, who (you say)
lives in it, are *watee, watee* (naught, naught), even as Paowanga."

On this, the king and his chiefs all cried out again.
Perhaps it was destroying their Gods a little faster
for them then prudence might warrant ; yet I seemed
to myself only to employ the occasion that now presented.

* See above, p. 143.  ED.

"How?" said the king at length, "do you tell us, O wonderful man! that Havaeoeekee is no more than Paowanga, whom you have destroyed?"

"I will leave you to judge, O king," answered I. "If Paowanga were indeed a God, would he not have avenged on me the insult I offered him?"

"True," cried the king, and his chiefs assented; "we expected every minute to see you struck dead for that."

"And what do you think of Paowanga now?" I asked smiling.

Upon which, the king and all around him made a gesture of the utmost contempt.

"Well," I continued, "Havaeoeekee will do me no more harm than the other : and, if you will collect for me all the *oloeeos* you can find, I will burn them in the same fire with Paowanga."

"O! O!" cried they, aloud; for it seems they were in greater dread of these charms than of the idol itself. Nevertheless, as I persisted in it, and assured them, if there were any vengeance, it would fall on me alone, the king gave the word, and six or seven of these amulets called *oloeeos* were collected from the neighbouring huts. Then, seeing that the people had by this time made a mighty heap of fuel, and placed on it the prostrate stump, and all other pieces of the idol they could gather after the explosion, I stood in the midst, my two hands full of *oloeeos*, and cried aloud :

"O Havaeoeekee! if indeed thou art a demon inhabiting these things, and not a vain imagination of this deluded people, then thou knowest, O foul spirit, thou hast no power against my King : of which I now give proof, by burning thy house over thy head!" On which, I cast the *oloeeos* on the top of the pile, and bade the by-standers set fire to it. Then, while it blazed up, fanned by the wind into a mighty conflagration, the two Indians and I took up our hymn again and sang it slowly, till the multitude caught it from us ; and there arose from that vast assembly the words of a Christian hymn of praise to God, in regular cadence, louder than the roaring of the fire.

When the blaze died down (and the whole thing was over in a short time, the people fanning the fire continually with mats, fly-fans, or anything they could lay hold on), the multitude rushed over the embers, treading them out and stamping them into dust with their feet; as though they could not show contempt enough for the idol by which (and his ministers) they had been so long deluded.

---

TO celebrate this great event, the king now proclaimed a festival to be held by all his subjects; of whom the numbers that flocked around us were ever increasing. Presents from these poor simple savages were offered to us without measure; so that, had our purpose been to enrich ourselves, we should have been able to do so on the spot. For they laid at my feet many silver ornaments, and even some of gold, very rudely fashioned; whereby I knew they had in their mountains some veins, at least, of these precious metals, were they but skilled in working them. But I put these presents all aside, remembering that the Apostle was able to say to his converts, as a model for all pastors: *Argentum et aurum, aut vestem nullius concupivi, sicut ipsi scitis:** and I explained to them, the purpose for which my King had sent me was to do good to them, not to grow rich upon them. I do believe this answer surprised them almost as much as the blowing up of Paowanga himself: they had been so used to the extortion and tyranny of their petty chiefs, even up to the king, that anything like disinterested charity came to them as a novelty and a wonder. I seized the occasion to preach to them something (in a guarded way) of the power and attributes, especially the gratuitous love, of the One True God; to which they listened with eager ears, especially those of the poorer sort. Truly, the gospel has ever been the emancipator of the oppressed.

However, I did not feel justified in withholding from the brave seamen who had come to share my perils, any advantage they might derive from the good-will of the Toonati-nookans. I no sooner made this known, than the natives pressed upon them the acceptance of those presents I had refused. But, consulting for their interest, and

* "I have not coveted any man's silver, gold, or apparel, as you yourselves know."—*Acts*, xx. 33. ED.

wishing to obtain for them something more permanent than the heap of presents that lay before us, I conferred with them apart to know what were their views regarding their future lot.  For myself, I said, I was bound by engagement to return, after a certain time, to the island whence we had come; nor could I think (apart from my promise) of remaining absent from our friends there, more than from eight to ten months, at most.  I declared, however great this work of converting the heathen might prove (as it promised fair, hitherto), I must not abandon those children of the faith whom our Heavenly Father had thrown by such a providence within reach of the Sacraments.  What I chiefly hoped (I said), was to be able to establish some regular communication between that island and Toonati-ngoka; and so either fetch off our friends thence, if they were disposed to come and join us, or send some of our savages thither (after making good Christians of them) to help to plant and settle the place as a colony. In that case, having two flocks in different islands, I should think time and labour well spent in making passages in the long-boat, from one to the other, to attend to their spiritual needs so long as God might spare me.

They deliberated not long upon this; but all with one voice exclaimed, they desired nothing better than to stay on this island, where they had plenty for their needs, and the goodwill of the inhabitants; to say nothing of the consolations of their religion, which they possessed so long as I remained with them.  To all these reasons I assented, only bidding them remark, they were now doubly bound to show a good Christian example to the savages among whom they were; that all eyes would be on them, from day to day, and every action scanned: and I implored them, for the love of all they held sacred, not (like too many who call themselves Christians) to throw any scandal in the way of the heathen, and so hinder their conversion to the faith.  This they seriously promised, one and all: and to prove their sincerity, they bound themselves on the spot to approach the sacrament of penance once in the fortnight.  Indeed, I am thankful to record, the greater part of them exceeded this measure; and not more than two fell off from it, whose retributive and miserable end (if time permit), I shall have to speak of in sor-

22

row: if not in this writing, yet to those who may come hither in my life-time.  For it affords a striking example of the just judgment of God on such as sin against light, and with scandal.

Having their determination made known to me, I came back from where we had spoken together, to the king and his chiefs (who, I found, were called *tayakee*, a word signifying at once a brave warrior and a man of rank), and then the feast proceeded: but to my great satisfaction, I had not to petition the king this time to send away his dancers.  He had given express orders they should not appear, since it displeased the white ambassador (so he called me): though I learned afterwards, it was an invariable custom for the king to be thus entertained at his banquets.  He made me sit next to him, and on his left hand; which with them is the place of honour, because it gives more facility to the entertainer, whether king or chief, to put morsels of food with his own hand into the mouth of his guest.  This was a distinction with which I would gladly have dispensed, had it been possible; since the royal hands might have been much improved by some ablution.  His nephew, who usually occupied the left hand, being his heir and successor in the kingdom, was for this time placed on the right.  His discontent at what he considered a slight put on him by his uncle, began even then to work in his jealous mind, and soon caused us troubles which, even as I write, seem likely instruments of the enemy of souls against the reaping in of the abundant harvest we might else have hoped for.

The king, both then and afterwards, plied me with numberless questions about my country, my King, the number of His subjects, where He chiefly resided, what was the form of His palace, how far was his capital from Toonatinooka, how he should send an embassy to return the favour my King had conferred upon him by sending us hither, and more enquiries than I can here put down.

I now found it necessary to answer him, that the great King by whose will I had come, was indeed the King of kings and Lord of lords; that His dwelling was in heaven, and His dominion over heaven, earth, and all things: that under Him, and only by His permission other kings reigned, but quite in a different way; some over islands, some over continents: that they were mere men, like the king of Toonati himself, and me, but with a lawful authority which their subjects must obey, so long as they commanded nothing against the Great King in heaven.

Here he interrupted me, asking me with great eagerness, whether I was indeed only a man like himself? I answered him, I was so in truth, and nothing more; born like himself, and, like himself, soon to die. "But where," said he, "will you go, O white prince, when you die?" To this I replied, if I was found faithful to my King when the great book was opened of which I had told him, I should be taken up into the palace of my King, and be with him for ever. "Oh," said he again, "Oh! you are faithful, faithful! you will go to Him, be sure you will go." "Nay," said I, "my King reads all the thoughts of my heart, always, and He sees many faults which no man can see. I cannot be sure of going to Him; for He has lent me many things to use for Him, and will reckon with me for them all."

He asked me, "What things?" then, pointing to the guns, which were piled up together, with one of the mariners mounting guard, to prevent the savages from touching them: "Were those dreadful lightning tubes," he asked, "the things my King had lent me?" To this I answered, by reminding him, I had said there were many kings reigning on earth, men like ourselves; that one of them, the king of Spain, was my earthly master, and the lightning-tubes belonged to him. "Then," asked he, "which king sent you here to us, the king of Spain, or the great King above?" I replied, that being in attendance on the great King, I had received no direct orders from the king of Spain on this subject; that I was bound to obey the latter in all things lawful and temporal, but the great King at all times, in all things and places. This I tried to make as plain to him as I could; but it was difficult to put such things in a language ill-fitted to express them: nor did he seem to apprehend my meaning clearly. But one thing, I could see, gave him satisfaction; for he perceived we had come on no mission from the king of Spain to disturb his temporal authority, nor sought to dethrone him, nor lower him in the eyes of his subjects.

The king then returned to his questions, and asked, if

the guns belonged to the king of Spain, and we were his subjects, but not sent by him, how did we become possessed of them?  Had we taken them from the king without his leave?  In reply, I gave a brief account of my being first left, with a few others, on the island from which we came; then of a Spanish wreck that was drifted in thither; all which is too long to detail here, and belongs not to the purpose of my writing.  Then he asked again, how long ago had the great King bidden me to come?  I told him, for some time I had been having it made known to me, more and more; but had not at first been able to leave others to whom my King had sent me.  On this he asked, with what voice the great King spoke to His servants to make known His commands?  I endeavoured to explain something about the revelation made by God to His creatures, first through His prophets, then through His Church; distinguishing it from the interior inspirations whereby He speaks to our individual hearts.  I told him, it was in this latter way that I knew my King's will in this case, being out of reach of those who could tell it me by an exterior voice, and with authority from Himself.

"Ah, then," said he, " you have priests among you also, as we have?"  I replied, that I myself was a priest of this great God; that others, again, were over me, and nearer to my King: and I was bound to consult them when it was possible, and take my commands from them in all things that concerned my duty.  "But, O white prince!" pursued he, bowing towards me, "if even you are an inferior priest, what greater powers have they who are nearer the King?  Have they more lightning-tubes (so he continued to call our guns) at their command than you have?"  I could not forbear smiling at the idea of Church authority being measured by an armament of musketry; I answered, *that* was not the kind of power I meant; that these lightning-tubes were the property of the kings of the earth, and were employed by them in their wars, one against the other, even as he employed javelins and clubs against the king of Hai-vavaoo.

He then asked, what the superior priests could do, that I could not?  This made me enter briefly upon the distinction of orders in the Church, the powers of the episcopacy, the succession of priests maintained by the Sacrament of Order, the supremacy of one Bishop of bishops in the centre of Christendom, and similar topics. I scarcely touched, however, on the sacraments at all; fearing to open at once to him the mystery of the Incarnation, with its stupendous consequences: and I resolved to keep this for a later conference. It was difficult to evade his questions, so prompt and eager were they. His *tayakees*, or chiefs, sat round us, drinking in every word with the most fixed attention: and at times, when any point of the discourse pleased them, saying *Oora, oora!* or else they turned to one another to express their surprise and satisfaction in a low tone.

----

IN short, I felt the providence of God had (so far) placed the conversion of these precious souls in my hands, all unworthy as I was of such a favour: and I lifted my heart sincerely to Him, to beseech that no sin of mine, nor want of prudence in speech or act, might mar the working out of this great purpose. But for the present, I intimated to the king, with much respect, we had spoken enough. He seemed disappointed; but I had resolved rather to give him something to think over, than to weary him with too much at once.

Turning to another subject, he asked how long we purposed to stay with him; saying he should esteem it a happiness to himself and his kingdom, to keep us so long as we chose to remain. To which I answered, for my own part, I had come to deliver to him the message of my King, and had no wish but to remain as long as the object of my embassy required; that when I departed, it would only be for a time, to confer with some I had left behind on the island I had spoken of; that, with the king's leave, I would give them the choice, to remain in that place, or come back with me, and settle in Toonati-nooka. Or, if he preferred, I would carry over with me some of his subjects to colonise that small island, and so ply backwards and forwards, extending his dominions there, while I proclaimed my King's message here. This was the substance of my discourse, to which all listened eagerly; and the *tayakees* began to whisper to one another, but so rapidly, and in such a low tone, I could not catch their meaning.

All that I said appeared to please the king; who at once offered my followers as much land a-piece as one of their rude ploughs, drawn by two men (for they have neither oxen nor horses in the island) could mark out within the space of an hour. But, thanking him for the offer, I preferred for them, and for myself, a visit to his capital, and a journey through the island: after which, I said, we would determine whether to disperse ourselves through his dominions, or locate our party in one spot, and form a colony of white men. He agreed readily to give us our choice; and so the affair ended for that time.

The king soon after signified his intention of carrying us with him to his capital the following day, at daybreak. To this I agreed, only stipulating for an hour's delay that I might offer a solemn sacrifice to my King. He seemed delighted at this proposal, and said, the best of the hogs and goats in that part of the island should be at my service. But I smiled, and told him my King was not pleased with such offerings as these; He had prepared a Victim, the only one worthy of being offered to Himself: and had committed this sacred function to my hands. On his inquiring, with great eagerness, what this victim was, I excused myself for the time from further explanation; I said during my residence with him I should have much to say on this subject; but even thus, I could scarce free myself from his urgent curiosity.

I had brought with me all things needful for celebrating the holy Sacrifice; and I determined to offer it on the very spot whence we had thrown down Paowanga: making the steps that once led to that hideous idol's devouring mouth, become the steps of a true Christian altar. Accordingly, no sooner did I see the first dawn of light, than I prepared and blessed a quantity of holy water, wherewith I sprinkled the whole place round about; the steps also themselves, and some blocks of trees the natives brought at my request, which I disposed as a rude altar, and laid on them the small altar stone I had brought, and some clean linen cloths.

The heathens, all this while, stood round us in vast multitudes, and breathless silence, watching everything I did. When they saw the devotion with which my companions received the aspersion of holy water, they came pressing round by one impulse, and begged for their share. I imparted it to them willingly, hoping it might be a prelude to their future baptism. But I soon had reason to repent of my rashness; for the crowds who were behind, eager to receive the aspersion, pressed so much on the front rank, as to throw them into confusion; and, forcing them in upon me and my companions, we were all but suffocated by the mere pressure of the crowd. I cried out to them, in their own language, to keep some order; happily my voice reached one or two of the chiefs, who came running to the spot with their spears, and laying about them vigorously with the butt-ends, preserved our lives; or I truly believe we should have been trodden underfoot by the unreasoning zeal of these poor savages. This made me feel yet more, how large a field was opened to me for missionary labour, if only I could occupy it. Yet, while I was thankful for being sent to so promising a harvest, I could not but deplore finding myself alone, where ten times the number would hardly suffice for the work before me. But His strength is perfected in weakness; nor ever is His hand more visible, than where no human forces appear to account for a great result.

Putting such thoughts aside, except to direct my intention in offering the holy Sacrifice, I now prepared to say the first mass that was said in Toonati-nooka since the world began. I had brought with me, I say, all things needful; having received them as by the ministry of the winds and waves, when a Spanish wreck drifted upon the island whence I came. All being ready, with a great illumination of candle-nuts on the altar, beside my waxen tapers, I vested, with the usual prayers. I could not repress an abundance of tears at the thought of that solemn moment, the sanctification of another spot on God's earth to His true worship and by His sacramental presence. Then, standing on the altar steps, I turned to the many thousands watching me with eager eyes; and raising my voice, spoke to them much in this way:

"O men of Toonati-nooka!" I exclaimed, "many new and wonderful things have you seen since we came among you; and we have given you tokens of the powers we bring with us, for your good, not your destruction. But what I am now to do is far more wonderful than anything I have hitherto done in this island! Though you will see nothing, and hear nothing, yet I pledge my truth as an ambassador of the great King " (here I lifted my hand to heaven), " that He is Himself about to come down, and be present among you, enthroned on this altar."

When I had said that, the multitude was thrown into great agitation; and began to cry out, as with one voice, beseeching me that the great King might not come so near to them: for they made sure they should be con-sumed by fire, or struck dead with the thunder, at the awful presence of my King. The king of Toonati-nooka himself, with his chiefs, showed signs of much uneasiness at hearing what was to take place: he sent one of his principal chiefs to me, where I stood, beseeching me to intercede with my King, not to come personally among them: that he would send Him any tribute from the island, and acknowledge himself and all the inhabitants as His vassals, if only He would spare them that dread visit. But in order to quiet their fears, I continued, with a smiling countenance:

" Do not imagine, O king and people of Toonati, the great King is coming to you in any way but extreme kindness and condescension. No; He is so filled with good-will to you all, and so greatly wishes to manifest it, and to benefit you, that while He comes because He loves you, He comes concealed, lest He terrify you. You could not, it is true, endure the unveiled majesty of His pre-sence; for He is ten thousand times brighter and more glorious than this sun now rising over the mountains. His voice causes the great powers of His court to tremble, while they bow before Him. His frown is unendurable in terror. But now, even as a prince may walk among his subjects under disguise, in poor raiment, so the great King is coming down among you; yet you will not see Him, you will not hear Him. I, His ambassador, promise you this. You will hear nothing even so loud as my voice is at this moment that I address you. He is coming by reason of His love for you, to teach you to be happy in loving Him. I only ask you to believe me, that He will be in the midst of you unseen. When you hear this little shell sound (here I showed them a small bell we had made for Mass out of a sea-shell), then throw yourselves on your knees; pray the great King to make you able to know Him and to love Him. I too, will ask of Him the same favour for you all."

This discourse struck them with the greatest astonishment. Of course, they could not comprehend my meaning, nor so much as guess at it: but they were over-awed, and in suspense, at what was to take place. Having thus prepared them, I proceeded with holy Mass, my companions kneeling round, and the younger of the two Indians (for this, I thought, would impress them more) serving at the adorable Sacrifice. The most profound silence reigned through the vast multitude, though it was the silence of intense expectation, not the reverence of faith. At length, when young Samuel sounded the little shell, I heard a rush behind me, and around me, of thousands falling on their knees at the same moment. It was like the sound of a mighty cataract; it almost overcame me with emotion, but served to direct my intention more earnestly for the conversion of these poor heathens, for whom I was offering the Spotless Lamb to the Eternal Father. Through the remainder of the holy Sacrifice there was no sound, nor interruption from them: they remained kneeling, and looked on with the same intense curiosity, till they saw it was over, and I began to take off my vestments again. Then the king approached me, and bade me to the morning meal: but I excused myself, till I had spoken a little farther to my king; so he left me for a while.

----

WHEN I joined the king at table shortly after, he plied me with questions as to what I had just been doing. I answered with much reserve; telling him, these things were not yet lawful for me to speak to him about: that he could not know what they meant till the holy water of life had been poured over him. They were (I said) such hidden mysteries as he could not so much as conceive of: but they formed the highest mode of communication with my King, one that He had especially appointed. and by means of which He became most truly present to His subjects.

I could see that he wondered the more at my speaking so : but, turning the conversation, I asked him, to what part of his dominions he was now to carry us. He answered, that all the island was open to us, to visit or settle in as we chose ; but said, he wished first to take us to his capital, and show us to the queen, as well as to his mother and the rest of the royal family : also, that many things had come into his mind in which he was sure I could improve the condition of the island : a favour he begged me earnestly to grant. I answered, all the servants of my King were bound to assist those who were in want, either by imparting knowledge, or in any other needful way of help. It was true (I said) that in our own country we had a better method of building than was shown in the rude huts around us ; also, of cultivating the ground, so far as I observed. In this latter respect, however, my King had been very good to him and his subjects ; giving them a favourable climate and a fertile soil, that needed little care, and produced of itself the fruits and vegetables they needed. I then described to him a winter in Europe ; having in the course of my life been both in the Netherlands and in Poland, I told him, I had seen the ground, the hills, the rivers, and the very roofs of the houses, all muffled in a covering of white, colder than the coldest rivers in Toonati-nooka, and that lay in some places several feet thick, for weeks, nay, months, together. The rivers and lakes, I said, became as hard as a stone, and so smooth, that the inhabitants fastened pieces of iron or bone to their feet, by means of which they ran for miles upon the surface of the water, much faster and easier than they could run on the ground, more like to birds flying through the air : and even little children could become skilful in this.

Nothing could exceed the surprise with which I was listened to by the whole assembly. They interrupted me several times, and shouted with wonder, after their manner ; then, imitating the actions of skating and sliding, as I described them, they besought me to give them this power, or obtain it for them. The king urgently asked the same : adding a request that (if it were possible) he and some of his chief warriors might be furnished with eagle's wings, that they might soar above the men of Hai-vavaoo in battle, and pounce down on their villages. To all this I replied, that my King gave different gifts and powers to His servants, as it pleased Him in His great wisdom: Toonati-nooka had been placed by Him sc near the sun which He made to warm the earth, that this white covering would never come on the ground, nor the water harden. But if he could not hope to see that won derful sight, I assured him, he and his people were preserved from much suffering which the men of those countries had to endure; then I told him, the cold there was sometimes so great as caused the fingers and toes, nay, the very noses of the inhabitants to drop off, and even took away their lives, by casting them into a deep sleep. Then I described the sagacity of the dogs of Mount Saint Bernard, in finding travellers over that mountain, who were perishing in the snow; but first (I found) I had to give some description of a dog, of which they have no notion, there being none in the whole island, nor in Hai-vavaoo.

To his second request I made answer, that my King (whom I now began to call by the name which came nearest to express the True God, *Utumatahee**) had not granted wings to human creatures; though He had count- less servants and messengers who could fly with the speed of light: that for us, here below, there was a hope held out of one day being as swift and glorious as they; but this great privilege was to be gained by obedience to the King until the moment of our death. "But will you, O white ambassador," asked the King, "one day shine as bright as the sun above us?" I answered that he himself, with every one of his subjects, if they would acknowledge my King for the true God, and have the water of life poured over them in His name, and if they thenceforward lived according to His laws, might attain even to such a glory as this.

* The reader will observe, on referring to Owen Evans' narra- tive, a slight discrepancy in names, as given here by Don Manuel; though not more, perhaps, than may be accounted for by the differ- ence of the same foreign word when pronounced by two persons, espe- cially when their own native languages also differ from each other. ED.

All I here said was something quite new to them : for
it seems, their highest notion of future happiness was, to
be transported after death to a large island beyond the
setting sun, where the good (that is, the brave, for courage
was their chief standard of goodness) would spend an existence between hunting immortal buffaloes and other wild
animals, and intervals of a drunken sort of repose.  To
secure their friends' enjoyment of this heathenish heaven,
they had a custom of burying with them two javelins, as
well as their bow and arrows, and a drinking cup of cocoa-
nut shell, the best they could procure ; this, they imagined,
would be filled with some intoxicating beverage, better
than the best palm wine : one draught of which would
make them forget all the sorrows and pains of this life,
and the agony of death itself.

Coming back to the other point on which I thought to
improve the condition of the men of Toonati-nooka, I mean
their buildings, I explained to the king how we built stone
houses in Europe ; that we joined the stones by a cement,
or mortar, made of burnt lime and sand, and roofed them
with a kind of flat stone, more durable than leaves : how
many rooms we made in them, how high we raised them,
how strong they were to resist winds and weather, etc.
He listened with the greatest interest, then asked me to
t ll him truly, how high were our highest houses.  I feared
to compromise my character for truth, even when I was
answering him most truly.  But knowing that simplicity
is the truest wisdom, I measured with my eye some tall
cocoa-palms that grew near the scene of our banquet, then
recalled to my mind the tower of the cathedral of Seville ;
and I answered the king, we did not reckon a building
extraordinary high that was three times the height of
those palm-trees.  This caused another shout of wonder ;
till I showed them in miniature our mode of building ;
piling up some small stones, while I bade them remark
how to make the stones rest one on the other, like a pyramid, or strengthen each other like an arch.  But this instruction came to little in the end : for I learned that the
island was subject to shocks of earthquake ; though not
very frequent nor (in general) so violent as in other
volcanic countries, yet enough to make them prefer light
huts of reeds or slight timber, one story in height.

Everything being now ready for our departure to the interior, I bade my companions draw together in marching order, and keep in strict discipline : for we were surrounded by such crowds as might (with all their dread of our guns) have overwhelmed or trodden us down at any moment.  But the king commanded his own body-guard to keep close to us, and keep off the multitude : so that my men suffered little inconvenience.  For myself, the king insisted on my being carried in a covered litter or palanquin, next to his own, and with precedence over his own nephew.  Urge what I might, he would not be overruled in this : at length, after several denials, I was forced to yield, though I not only disliked the honour, but foresaw how it would embitter the mind of this savage (whose name was Toöhaeca) still more against us.

Before leaving the boats, I placed one of our men in each, with the young Indian to serve as interpreter : and not satisfied with this, I begged the king to command his subjects to leave them untouched.  He did this, sternly enough ; and besides, he proposed to me to declare the men, the boats, and all the stores they contained, *emoé*,* or holy, and not to be touched by any one for two moons, on pain of death.  But, in spite of the advantage to be secured from this proposal, I could not bring myself to accept it ; feeling it was probably an observance in some way connected with their idolatry.  I therefore preferred to trust to our good God for the safety of the men and boats ; and I charged them to stand off shore and keep on their guard, never sleeping all at one time, day or night. I promised that, if things turned out well with me, I would come or send for them within four days ; and I left five muskets and two brace of pistols among them, strictly charging them not to fire for mere amusement, but endeavour in every way to keep the natives friendly, at the same time keeping them at a safe distance.

I then left them, with my blessing ; and returning to the king and those around him, found everything ready for our departure.  The king had only waited for me ; and

* Something, it may be supposed, like the mysterious *taboo* existing in the islands of Polynesia, which appears to be some religious restriction affecting persons, places, and even things ; but the nature of which has not been fully ascertained. ED.

immediately stepped into his palanquin, which was lying on the ground, inviting me, by waving his hand, to do the same with mine. Then Toöhaeca, the nephew, likewise entered his palanquin, with a scowl of rage at my precedence, which the king still insisted on. These palanquins are made of a frame-work of light bamboo, very easy and springy, lined with soft grass or moss; they are borne on the shoulders of four men a-piece, who, in consideration of such service, have many privileges, and are exempted even from war, except in case of invasion. They carried us swiftly, at a round trot; and the swinging of the palanquin was so easy, that after the excitement and fatigue I had gone through, it lulled me into a deep sleep, so that I lost the opportunity of observing much of the country we passed through, on our way to the capital.

---

THIS capital, indeed, when at length we reached it, was a wretched collection of bamboo huts, built without order or plan. Each hut was little more than a number of bamboo poles, stuck into the ground in a rude circle, made to meet at the top, and bound loosely together with the tough tendrils of a creeping plant, leaving a vent for the smoke of the cooking fire to escape. The huts of the *tayakees*, or chiefs, it is true, were built with somewhat more care, and were larger than those of the common sort; but even these were ill-built, comfortless places. All the skill of the natives seemed to have been spent on the royal hut, which occupied the north side of a square, or cleared space, measuring about fifty yards * every way. This hut, or series of huts, differed from the rest in having upright posts of larger trees driven into the ground for the walls or supports. They were woven in and out with oziers and young bamboos, laid horizontally, and the interstices stuffed with moss, bark of trees, and long grass from the savannahs. The roof was formed of bamboo poles placed slopingly on the uprights, to shoot off the wet in the rainy season; it was thatched with the leaves

* Six hundred palms. ED.

of the cocoa-palm, and another large and tough leaf from some tree which I had never before seen.

Around the king's own hut, just under the eaves, I observed a horrid barbarous ornament indeed; being a row of human heads, some of them dried in the sun, till the skin looked like tanned leather; some wasted away, till little more than the skull-bones remained. Four other heads were stuck on poles before the entrance, two on either side: besides these, I saw a number of the larger human bones grouped in fanciful patterns over the door and by the door-posts. I afterwards learned that the heads under the house-eaves had been those of some of the bravest of the king's enemies, either killed in battle, or reserved (according to their dreadful custom) to be sacrificed and eaten on their return home after a victory; but the heads on poles were those of noted rebels, who had attempted to usurp the kingdom, once in the reign of the king's father, Matai-tehepe, and still further back, in that of his great-uncle, Eyca-Sousaeoo.

By this time, our palanquin had been set down before the entrance; and the king, observing my eyes fixed on those hideous proofs of their barbarous customs, exclaimed several times, in great delight, " Hai-vavaoo !" to make me know these trophies had come from that hostile island; at the same time brandishing his spear. But, seeing from my looks what I thought of the whole scene, he took my hand, in order to divert my attention, and led me into the hut.

Here we found the queen, surrounded by her attendants, prepared to receive and welcome us: for the news of our arrival, and of all the wonders we had worked at the sea-coast, had come before us on a thousand tongues. It was all I could do to prevent the queen from falling at my feet, by telling her I was nothing in myself but a poor mortal, like those who surrounded me : that I claimed all honours for my King, none for myself; and that the truest way to pay Him the reverence due to Him, was to listen to His message.

She answered with much humility, that, by all accounts, I had given proofs enough of my embassy from a great King; that, in spite of my disclaimers, every one in Too-nati-nooka, from .the king downwards, felt prepared to

acknowledge us as a race of demi-gods, rather than men;
that, for her part, she was only desirous to learn what was
the will of that mighty King from whom I came, to fulfil
it in all things not contrary to the customs of her nation
and the will of her royal husband: with much more to the
same effect.

All this was delivered with a natural and simple grace,
that augured well for her candour and good dispositions
to receive the truth. The king also showed his approval:
then, thinking I must be weary, he led me into a separate
hut that had been prepared for me; and, telling me a feast
would be held in an hour's time to celebrate my coming
to his capital, advised me to sleep till then. I inquired
after my companions, and what preparations had been
made for them. He assured me they had been well taken
care of; that some of the principal people in Ehoto-böe,
his capital, had vied with each other for the privilege of
entertaining them; and that most of them were lodged in
the chiefs' huts: all which I found to be true. However,
I felt anxious to warn the men again, and put them on
their guard as to their behaviour with the savages; so,
begging the king for some escort who would show me
their lodging, he gave me one of the chiefs who always
attended him, and a youth of the blood-royal (though not
in direct line of succession) to go with me.

We made the round of the principal huts in the place,
where I found the men treated with great honour and distinction, after the rude fashion of their entertainers. But,
as they had made little or no progress in the language of
Toonati-nooka, their conversation was carried on chiefly
by signs, with a few words of each language, which had
been picked up by either party, and were now repeated
amid shouts of merriment by these new allies. I warned
my companions one by one, how necessary it was to remain at peace with the natives, giving no cause of offence,
but keeping on the watch, especially with regard to our
guns, in which lay our superiority against their over-
whelming numbers. But they assured me, the natives
had still so great a dread of these weapons, they had
shown uneasiness till they had been safely put away:
accordingly, they showed me their guns, which every man
had put in the corner of the hut, keeping still his pistols

in his belt. As the natives had never seen any of the
pistols fired, they had more curiosity about them than
dread; and even when their use was explained to them,
seemed rather amused at them than otherwise. They
supposed them to be worn for ornament, and called them
by a phrase which may be translated, *pigmy thunder-cases.*

This duty performed, I returned to my hut, still accompanied by my two guides, who seemed to think it a part
of the obedience they owed to the king to keep close to
me. Indeed, they helped me in ways I could have dispensed with; for, on our walk, did we but come to a broken
path, a little brook, or any impediment which in their eyes
justified the proceeding, they fairly lifted me in their arms,
and carried me over.

By this time the feast was prepared; we were summoned
to it by three stout trumpeters, who blew such a blast on
hollow goats' horns as rather sounded like a charge to
battle. The banquet was as abundant as goats' flesh, sea
and other birds, and the vegetables of the island, could
make it: but I observed that no kind of corn was produced, though the natives made a sort of bread, or thin
cake, as a great delicacy, from the roots of a certain tree,
grated, dried, and baked. I was pleased to think I should
be the instrument of giving them so great a blessing as
that of wheaten corn, of which I had brought a bag with
me. This I explained to the king, who seemed impatient,
from my description, to possess so great a treasure; and
said, they need no longer make their bread out of a poisonous root,* but from the white man's *wholesome grass,*
this being the only word in their language by which I
could express *corn.* He asked me various questions about
our mode of growing, grinding, and the other arts of the
farmer and the baker; but nothing astonished him so
much as the description I gave of ship-biscuit, and the
method employed in our dock-yards, of rolling it out and
cutting it up.

Neither the queen nor her attendants took any part in
this banquet, it being against the laws of their forefathers

---

* Probably the *manioc,* from which the cassava bread of the West
Indies is baked, after carefully grating the root and pressing it with
heavy weights, to extract the poisonous juice. ED.

23

for the women to eat with the men.   Indeed, in this, as in
all other heathen countries, these poor creatures seemed
to be looked on as inferior beings, and were condemned to
hoe in the fields, bear heavy burdens, and in a word, to
slave throughout the day, almost as if they were captives
taken in war; while their lords and masters took their
ease in smoking and conversing, when they were not
absent at war or in the chase.   The king asked me how
all this was arranged with us; but I answered him with
caution, fearing to make him despise our holy religion by
telling him anything so strange as that the Gospel had
raised, to a spiritual equality with men, those whom heathenism oppressed and degraded. .

The feast was scarcely over, when we saw two men
running with the utmost swiftness from the direction of
the coast whence we had journeyed.  No sooner were they
perceived, than the whole assembly cried out, something
must be amiss; and my mind instantly misgave me about
the boats, and the men I had left in them.  Some of the
*tayakees* darted off at full speed to meet these messengers,
and learn their tidings: they, however persisted in coming
on to the king, though so much exhausted by running,
that when they reached the mat where he was seated,
they fell down before him panting, and were unable to
utter a word.  But by degrees, in broken sentences they
made it known, our men had been surprised in the boats
by some of the natives, and been deprived of their arms;
and that the boats themselves had been dragged ashore,
broken up, and burnt.

Instantly the king broke into the most terrific rage I
ever beheld in mortal man.  Forgetting his late contempt
for his idols, he called for the vengeance of Paowanga,
Havaeoeekee, and the rest on these violators of our rights;
assured me they should be torn limb from limb, and roasted
piecemeal: then, turning to his executioner, bade him depart at once for the coast village, and bring him the heads
of all who had been concerned in this, with those of their
wives and children.  At the same time he beckoned out
two or three chiefs to go and assist to carry out this decree
of blood.

BUT I threw myself before them, entreating. them to pause; then appealed to the king, that as the offence was committed against me, so I might judge the case myself, with the prisoners brought safely before me. It was with much difficulty I prevailed in this; so greatly was his rage excited against the criminals in this lawless deed. He felt, indeed, his authority over his subjects, and his honour towards myself, equally touched by what had been done.

At length, when I represented that my King was always angered when vengeance took the place of justice in the hands of human kings, and when they made the innocent suffer for the guilty, he gave way, and signified that I should have my will. It was now arranged that the young Indian should go with three chiefs, bearing the king's *wand of peace* (which, truly, was sent by him much less often than the sword of execution), in token that no blood was to be shed on the spot. They took with them some forty or fifty armed men; and were to arrest all against whom there was probable evidence that they were parties to this outrage; but none others: they were to bring these to us, bound, without torture or ill-usage. Least of all were they to harm the families or relations of the accused. All this charge I delivered to my young Indian: whose discreet behaviour on receiving it, together with the mildness of the injunction, produced a great effect on the bystanders. Their sense of justice (so far as they had it) taught them to compare this line of conduct with the outbursts of ferocious vengeance they had been so long used to. All agreed, it must be something very happy to live under the laws of that great King I served, and whose service I desired to teach them. Thus all tended to good under the Hand of Providence: this very event, disastrous in itself, became a vehicle for the gospel.

I was now surrounded by eager crowds, listening to all I had to say about the justice which man owed to his brother man, and the charity which linked each true Christian soul to his fellow Christian. Then I went on to speak of the unity and perfection of God; that there could be no more than One; that idolatry was invented by a bad spirit, the enemy of mankind, to lead men away from God, and make them miserable with himself here, and after death, etc. When I had wound them up to a great pitch by saying this, I started up on a sudden, crying out: "Down with all idols! There is no God but One!" The whole multitude caught up the cry: and pulling me by the skirts of my cassock towards a huge idol near the king's palace, besought me to *put thunder into his mouth*, as I had done to Paowanga.

But this time, I resolved it should be their own act and deed. So I reasoned with them, saying, my king would be more pleased with them for using their own hands than mine to destroy His enemies: that I had blown up Paowanga and burnt the *oloeeos*, while they still believed in them; but now, they having confessed my King for the true God, I gladly committed the work to them. To this they assented with much joy, and I gained time to recite my office while the work of destruction went on. So many were the hands employed, and so great the zeal, that before the sun went down, almost all the *oloeeos* in Ehotoböe (except a few remaining in the houses of some obstinate old idolaters, whom I had to protect from the public indignation) were consumed in one blazing pile, together with the fragments of the three great idols worshipped in the capital, viz., Tamâta-Sollû,* who in their system represents the sun, Chondadûeea, or the moon, and our former acquaintance, Paowanga, who was, indeed, before these two eventful days, the established idol of all Toonatinooka. In short, I had to interfere several times to settle disputes among these poor savages, who in their newborn zeal were anxious to have each his morsel or chip of the idol to carry to the flames.

On a review of all this, I could not but wonder at the rapid progress of Truth in the minds of these idolaters, who now first heard it. Yet, knowing the subtlety of the enemy of mankind, and taking into account the inconstancy of most savage dispositions, I prepared myself for any check or reverse that might occur. Seldom has the

* Here again, on a comparison with Evans' narrative, will be found that degree of discrepancy between two Indian words, which would result from their being caught by the ears, and repeated by the lips, of Europeans belonging to different nations. ED.

Gospel been sown, but in the blood of those who carried forth the precious seed.  On this reflection, I offered my life anew to my Lord; beseeching him that, whether by my labour or suffering, or both, His truth might be sown abundantly in the hearts of those around me; and that in the end "coming I might come with joy, bearing my sheaves."

But the thing which above all afflicted me was, that this great task of converting a large island to the faith, was committed to one feeble pair of hands; seeing it might well exercise the zeal of a whole college of priests and catechists.  I also ardently longed for the presence and gentle human:sing influence of some consecrated sisters of religion, to speak to the poor heathen women, who were sunk in a state of darkness and degradation equal to that of their savage lords.  I could do no better than send up sighs from my inmost heart to heaven, that our merciful Lord would deign to fit me to gather in some handfuls of this wide harvest.

The last thing we did that evening was, to build up an altar for my Mass of the morrow; for I had brought all requisites with me from the sea-coast, and thus the most precious of our possessions had been saved from the pillage.  I nò sooner made known my wishes to prepare this altar, than the crowds around me began to supplicate for a share in the work.  They urged with the simple earnestness of children, that as they had a hand in destroying the idols, I should allow them to take part in erecting an altar to my King.  As the confusion caused by so many would have hindered instead of helping the work, I selected twelve strong men who stood nearest to me, and eight others by lot; directing them how to proceed, and to bring large stones to the centre of the space cleared for the royal palace, or hut: arranging these stones in a square form, and to a convenient height.

While I was thus employed, raising my eyes, I beheld the enemies' skulls that decorated the palace-door and eaves, grinning on me hideously; and I observed also the bones and other trophies of war.  These, I determined, should be removed before the sacrifice of the Spotless Lamb was celebrated in that place.  At the same time, knowing that I was now about to lay the axe to the very

root (or one great root) of the poison-tree of their heathenism, and was likely to offend their warlike pride, I resolved to proceed with caution.  Wherefore, going to the
king (who had bidden his attendants admit me at all times
to his hut), I represented, that among the titles my King
most delighted in was, Prince of Peace; that war, indeed,
might be undertaken on a just cause, but then must be
conducted with as much mercy as the success of it made
possible; that to insult a vanquished foe by hanging up
his mortal remains was a thing contrary to the spirit of
my King, and to right reason.  This was the way I put
it; since to speak to savages of the duty of avoiding barbarous and savage acts, would be a foreign language to
them indeed.  There was a difference, I acknowledged,
between the case of enemies and malefactors; by which I
excused his keeping in some places the heads of those
traitors on poles, to warn others against following their
evil deeds.   But I pleaded, that as I was about to offer a
solemn sacrifice to the King of Peace, all such mementos
of crime and blood should be removed from this particular spot: otherwise, said I, myself will remove, and complete this holy solemnity in some place apart.

On this, the king cried out, he desired above all things
the same sacrifice he had seen performed in the coast-
village, Maheine-taho, should be repeated in the court before his own dwelling; and though, he acknowledged, I
had asked a hard thing, and what was unheard of before,
seeing these trophies were reckoned so many proofs of the
valour of himself and his *tayalcees*, yet, sooner than appear
to slight my King's will, he would order them to be removed.  This was accordingly done, much to the wonder
of the multitude, who could not comprehend the reason of
it, and for the first time showed some symptoms of murmuring.  However, the skulls, poles and all, were taken
into the king's hut, and set up over the place where he
was used to dine, and also to receive audiences and ad-
minister justice: at least such justice as was known in
Toonati-nooka; of which I was soon to have a specimen.
As to the other heads, bones, scalps, and the rest of those
barbarous trophies, I persuaded him at length, though
with much difficulty, to let them all be buried in one pit
beyond the precincts of the court-yard.

I promised, on my part, if he would consent to this, I would write an inscription over the spot, both in his native language and my own, setting forth the valour and triumph of Paramarama and his brave *tayakees*. This idea pleased them all; and the king himself became so impatient to have it done at once, that he seemed to have forgotten what he was so eager about a few moments before, the sacrifice to my King. I was content, however, with directing the pit to be dug under a spreading tree, with a soft white wood, like a plane-tree, into which I cut the inscription next day, according to my promise. Having had the bones deposited in it, I now went on with preparations for holy Mass; which were continued until the sun set, and the sudden darkness of the tropics came on us.

---

NEXT morning, early, we were awakened by confused outcries, partly of angry shouts, partly of supplication and wailing. These made me know that the chiefs and warriors had returned with their prisoners from Maheine-taho. Indeed, it appeared in their zeal to bring them before us, they had hurried them on through the night; so that the poor wretches were half dead with fatigue as well as terror; covered with mud, from being dragged through swampy ways; and bleeding from the cuts and wounds they had received from rocks and the prickly shrubs of the island. On questioning Samuel, the young Indian Christian, he assured me he had done all in his power to prevent this rough treatment being used; but he found, the utmost his *wand of peace* would do was, to preserve their lives: had it not been for that, the natives would have brought back, not the offenders themselves, but their heads only.

I now requested of the king, as I was to judge the accused, so I might dispose of them before the trial; which I proposed should take place after the sacrifice I was about to offer. He readily consented to this; supposing I meant to keep them without food, blindfolded, and close pinioned, according to their custom. But he was much surprised when I gave directions to have them taken into my own hut, and tended by the Christian Indians, who fed them and washed their wounds. All this was above his comprehension; but I could see by their looks that many among the multitude approved of it, though they dared not say so. It gave me an opportunity of repeating, that my King loved both justice and mercy; and I said, it was neither merciful nor just to treat men before their trial as though they had been found guilty. I was on the point of saying, that my King had once come down on earth, and when there, had washed the feet of his own followers; but I forbore, feeling it was only by degrees that anything so supernatural as the sacred mysteries of the Incarnation could be imparted to these barbarous minds.

" But," said the king, turning to me, " how will you perform the trial, since you have burnt all the *oloeeos?* " I ought to have said, that among the superstitious uses those objects were put to, they were usually brought forth, with solemn incantations and many ceremonies, and used in some way to decide all accusations and disputes; being first smeared with blood drawn from the arms of both the contending parties. But in offences committed (or supposed to be so) against the king himself, I found he was in the habit of simply sending his executioner to bring him the head of the accused person, without further inquiry by *oloeeo* or any other mode.

For the present, I only smiled at his question, and told Para-marama he should see something of the way in which we administered justice in my country. Then, finding from the Indians that the accused had eaten, and were refreshed, I placed a guard at the door of the hut in which they were kept, and forbade, on pain of my severe displeasure, that any one should enter. This had its effect; and I proceeded to vest for Mass.

This time, I had no need to exhort the multitude to silence and reverence: for those who had come with us from Maheine-taho (or had run on before us), had already, as I afterwards found, translated to the people of Ehoto-boë, nearly word for word, the short address I had made before celebrating holy Mass there. The same intense curiosity now prevailed, mingled with awe: and I observed that the queen and her attendants were kneeling within the door of the royal hut. I thought it well, how-

ever, to give the multitude an exhortation, as I had done
at the coast-village : and this time I drew somewhat nearer
to the great mystery of the Incarnation ; telling them, my
good Lord and King was so filled with love for all mankind,
that He had come to visit them, and still remained on
earth among them, in a way of His own appointment.  I
enlarged on those words, *deliciæ meæ esse cum filiis hominum :* * I promised that hereafter I would explain to them
the great way He had taken to dwell among men for
thirty-three years.  That, I said, was a long, long time
ago, before the reign of Matai-tehepe, before Eyca-sousaao,
before the kings their predecessors, for thousands upon
thousands of moons.

When I mentioned so long a time back, as they were
little used to any long reckoning of time, what I said to
them struck them with wonder : they broke into murmurs
of surprise, saying, " *Too-pooe, too-pooe !* " which means,
*strange*, or, *wonderful*.  I resumed my discourse, saying,
they must not be surprised at this ; for I had much greater
wonders to tell them as to the length of time (they had no
word in their language, till I afterwards made one, to express *eternity*) that my King had reigned.  But, to come
back (I said) to His more especial dwelling among them,
when the thirty-three years had expired, the period He
had determined to remain, and when He was to go up to
His Throne in heaven, He decreed another wonderful
method by which He should still be with His subjects
below.

" So " (continued I) " the great King is upon earth by
one method, and in heaven by another.  Besides, His
power is so great, that He can be in many places on earth
at one and the same time : and, in truth, He is so.  Fur-
thermore, there are places which He comes thus to visit,
from time to time, as He is now coming (for the first time
in this particular way) to Ehoto-boë.  You cannot understand these things, O men of Toonati-nooka ! but they are
true, and most true.  Believe me when I tell you ; for
this is part of the message of the great King to you, and
for your good."  Then I added much the same exhortation
as at Maheine-taho ; beseeching them to make an act of

* " My delights are to be with the sons of men."—*Prov.*, viii. 31. ED.

belief in the Presence of the great King, and to adore Him on the altar when they heard the little shell sound. I bade them ask Him, as a great gift, to make them able to believe in His Presence, and do His will.

Then I proceeded with holy Mass. As regards the behaviour of the vast multitudes now collected on the spot (and I believe we had there the great majority of the inhabitants of this island), it was a repetition of what had taken place the day before on the coast, only on a larger scale. A more strange and solemn spectacle, I think, was seldom witnessed since the days of the Apostles, than this crowd of simple savages, thirsting for the waters of life, prepared to believe, and only waiting to be instructed. Thus, for the second time within two days, the Adorable Victim offered Himself by my unworthy hands for their salvation.

While I made my act of thanksgiving after Mass, my companions who had been left in the boats, arrived; having travelled hither more at leisure than the accused men had been dragged along. The new comers shared in all the honours of the feast that was now prepared for myself and the rest: the king showing no small anxiety to wipe from our remembrance the insult offered to us at Maheine-taho.

·The banquet over, I proceeded at once to the trial. For this, I told the king that, as I was not come to deprive him of his lawful authority, I requested him to preside over the whole proceeding, and to confirm the judgment I should pronounce. He consented to this: only, as such a ceremony was totally new to him, he stipulated that he should be called on to do no more than sit upon a seat elevated above mine, while I conducted the trial. I was therefore placed on a mat, on the king's left, but raised enough to enable the crowd to see and hear me; while the king sat on a rude throne of logs, four or five feet higher. When the accused Indians (who were but eleven in all, some of the rest having escaped up the country) were brought before us, I perceived, from their looks of terror, they expected nothing but instant death, or perhaps lingering tortures.

I therefore spoke to them mildly; saying, the crime they were charged with was (no doubt) a grave one: that all nations held the ambassador from a great king to be a kind of sacred person, and this they knew, from the respect wherewith the envoys between Toonati and Hai-vavaoo were treated on both sides. But I assured them, not only should they have a patient hearing, but the evidence brought against them should be carefully sifted, and every doubtful point allowed in their favour. Whatever could be urged as a fair or pardonable motive for their act, should be taken in the best sense, and weigh on their side. In short, I tried my best to state, in this savage place, the principles of equity that guide (or ought to guide) our Christian courts of justice in Europe. It was plain to see, all this was new to them; once or twice, the king and his *tayakees* showed signs of displeasure and impatience at what they heard. But the poor oppressed people drank in all I said with eager ears; and as far as they dared in the presence of those who had acted so differently to them, testified their assent and joy.

After this (having taken care that the witnesses should be kept separate, without opportunity of conferring together), I entered upon the trial, by summoning them, one after another, to give evidence. The rest, meanwhile, were placed under guard, by my orders, out of ear-shot: and each witness, after saying what he had to say, and being cross-examined by the accused (in which they exhibited great shrewdness and ingenuity), was marched off under custody of one of the king's guards, to a rising ground beyond, where he could not hear what was going on. This I provided, in case they might be summoned back on some point of evidence: but it was the least popular part of my proceedings; both witnesses and guards being so intensely curious to hear everything of this new process, that the utmost vigilance was needed to prevent their stealing back to the spot. At last, I put them all in charge of my old convert Indian, and gave him six of the men with their muskets to over-awe them, and keep them aloof.

***

IT needed no small patience to thread the maze of such counter-evidence, mutual accusations, noise, rage, wailing, entreaties, protestations, denials, as now arose. The accused being eleven in number, and the witnesses, altogether, as many as thirty-six, the process was long and intricate. But I soon found, many of these pretended witnesses had seen nothing; so that their evidence was worthless. They had trumped up a story in concert, which broke down at every turn. This they had done, partly from motives of private revenge towards certain of the accused, partly to curry favour with the king and myself: thinking we should be pleased with the punishment of some, at least, guilty or not, to satisfy us for the outrage committed.

I thought it well to make an example of these false witnesses; so, after three cases of such deliberate lying had been proved. I interrupted the trial to give them a summary punishment.

First, I explained to the by-standers, and the offenders themselves, how heinous a crime they had been guilty of. I told them, though they did not as yet know all the laws of my King, they had a law written in their own hearts, bidding them act justly and speak truth. This law, I said, bound at all times, and even in trivial things; how much more, then, when the life of a fellow-creature was at stake? What crime could well be more hateful, than to swear away another man's life by a false oath? Proceeding in this way, I then said, it was a very lenient sentence I was about to inflict, that each false witness should receive a dozen strokes with a bamboo cane, one half on the soles of his feet, the other half on his shoulders.

The multitude greatly applauded this sentence, which was executed without delay; and the cries of the sufferers formed a sort of proclamation, more relished perhaps by the people than by the king and his *tayakees*, that upright justice was thenceforward to be the rule in Toonati-nooka.

Having cleared away this mass of false evidence, I found there was only proof remaining against five or six, at the most, as being implicated in the attack on the boats: and, though many appeared to have been more or less abettors or sympathizers, I kept strictly to such evidence as went against the actual transgressors. These few, moreover, were proved to be among the men of Ehoto-boë who had been most forward to welcome us on our arrival. They had expressed themselves delighted at our coming, and had persuaded some of their kinsmen and others, not so well disposed, to treat us with hospitality. Several witnesses also appeared to speak for their general character. On the whole, it became evident that the attack had been made in no hostile spirit, but was dictated by an irresistible desire to keep us amongst them, and prevent all chance of our sailing from Toonati-nooka again.

This was confirmed by evidence of our two white men, and the Indian, left in the boats. They declared, the attacking party, though resolute for the destruction of the boats, had treated themselves with as much gentleness as they could, under the circumstances. They had, indeed, disarmed our men by force, coming on them suddenly while they were overcome by sleep in the heat of the day. And so far, our men frankly acknowledged the fault was in great measure their own: for, had they observed my strict charge, and kept one always on the watch, this great disaster, which has perhaps determined our fate for the rest of our days, never had happened. But, beyond securing the boats, to destroy them, the Indians gave our men, and their own countryman, all possible good usage: even carrying them ashore on their backs, so that not a thread of their clothes was wetted. They also entreated them, on their knees, not to be offended at what they had done: they assured the two Europeans (through the Indian interpreter) it had been only to secure the happiness of having the " white lords " reside among them, for the good of themselves, their families, and the whole island and nation. Finally, they had besought them to intercede with the king, and myself, to screen them from the punishment which they reasonably feared was hanging over their heads.

All this considered, I felt bound to make every distinction between the degree of fault on the part of the aggressors, and the amount of misfortune we suffered thereby. True, this destruction of the boats has probably made our leaving Toonati-nooka for ever hopeless, by leaving us no independence of action. For I scarcely think we shall be able to persuade the king to grant us a war canoe to return to Assumption Isle, whence we came. And, the more valuable and important we become to him, as I trust we may, by the conversion of himself and his subjects to faith and civilisation, the less likely will he be to part with us. Yet, on the other hand, this very obstacle may turn to a benefit, if it settles the minds of our white men to become colonists in the place: and for myself, it has solved (in a way I little thought of) a painful doubt that vexed me : being under promise to return to my little flock in Assumption Isle, yet seeing so wide a field of labour for souls opening on me here.

The end of the trials was, the culprits were let off with a slight punishment; much slighter than that inflicted on the false witnesses : and this difference made between the two classes of offenders was another instruction to the minds of the savages, on the nature of truth, of justice, and the rights of man.

I have little more to add, but that since our first landing, the grace of God and the power of the evil one have been contending for the possession of these poor heathens' souls. They listen to me, indeed, with great eagerness, and acknowledge the goodness of my Master's laws. They are most grateful, too, for my interference with the king and his *tayakees* on their behalf, and for the temporal improvements I have effected, and the arts of life I have taught them. On the other hand, the power of corruption is strong: they shrink from the holiness of the Christian laws; and I foresee, one great obstacle to its being received will be the absolute necessity of their renouncing some of their heathenish customs and polygamy.

The enmity of Töohaeca, the king's nephew, is likely to prove another source of trouble to us, or even danger. I am credibly told, he has vowed vengeance against us ; and though hated by most for his cruel and overbearing disposition, he has a party of *tayakees* with him : men of like mind, who have taken him for their leader. They would side with him more openly, were it not for their dread of the king, who favours us in so signal a way. How long that favour may last, or how soon the enemy of souls may succeed in troubling our peace, is known to God alone. Upon His loving providence we repose securely. And, with a prayer that the wild elements may be overruled to waft this my narrative to hands capable of sending us help, I commit it to the waves, on this, the thirteenth anniversary of my religious profession, and of our residence in Toonati the seventh month of the second year.

THE END.